BUSINESS DECISION MAKING WITH 1-2-3®

MARK S. ALBION

EDWARD J. HOFF

Graduate School of Business Administration
Harvard University

BUSINESS DECISION MAKING WITH 1-2-3®

Prentice Hall, Englewood Cliffs, New Jersey 07632

Library of Congress Cataloging-in-Publication Data

ALBION, MARK S., 1951-
  Business decision making with 1-2-3 / Mark S. Albion, Edward J.
Hoff.

    p.   cm.
  Includes index.
  ISBN 0-13-094194-8
    1. Lotus 1-2-3 (Computer program)   2. Business-Data processing.
  3. Management—Data processing.   4. Decision-making—Data
  processing.   I. Hoff, Edward J.   II. Title.   III. Title: Business
  decision making with one-two-three.
  HF5548.4.L67A42 1988
  658.4'03'0285536—dc19   88-2394
                                                              CIP

Editorial/production supervision and
  interior design: *Pamela Wilder*
Cover design: *George Cornell*
Manufacturing buyer: *Margaret Rizzi*

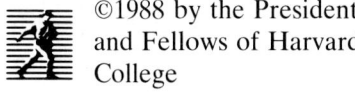
Printed in the United States of America
10   9   8   7   6   5   4

ISBN 0-13-094194-8
ISBN 0-13-094186-7{MAIL ORDER}
ISBN 0-13-094178-6{TRADE}

Prentice-Hall International (UK) Limited, *London*
Prentice-Hall of Australia Pty. Limited, *Sydney*
Prentice-Hall Canada Inc., *Toronto*
Prentice-Hall Hispanoamericana, S.A., *Mexico*
Prentice-Hall of India Private Limited, *New Delhi*
Prentice-Hall of Japan, Inc., *Tokyo*
Prentice-Hall of Southeast Asia Pte. Ltd., *Singapore*
Editora Prentice-Hall do Brasil, Ltda., *Rio de Janeiro*

To JOHANNA

Who is the Joy in my life
And the Sun of my spirit

To KATHLEEN

Who believed in this project
And believes in me. With Love

Contents

Preface

Business Decision Making with 1-2-3 has been developed over the past four years at the Harvard Business School. Earlier versions of this computer training program have been used to introduce Harvard's first-year MBAs to Lotus 1-2-3 and to the personal computer. The materials have also been used in certain Harvard Business School executive education programs.

This latest version of the program is designed for individual as well as classroom use. It has been tested internationally with managers from a wide range of industries. Most had little or no experience with Lotus 1-2-3. Some were interested in learning to use 1-2-3 themselves; some wanted to improve their ability to manage others who would use spreadsheet analysis at their company.

The program teaches not only the mechanics of how to use 1-2-3 but also emphasizes how a manager can make effective use of it. Our belief is that the personal computer is useful for repetitive calculations, but even more useful as an analytical tool that greatly enhances managerial decision making.

The case study approach is used to analyze a marketing budgeting decision at Helene Curtis, Inc., for a $100 million brand of shampoo, Suave. Lotus 1-2-3 is used to analyze the market, the potential effectiveness of advertising, and the marketing and financial implications of proposed budgets. At all times the case study follows the logical order of how a management team approached an actual business decision.

The program is designed to be self-teaching and self-paced. It is organized to allow different users to tailor the materials to their own personal needs. Functions and commands are learned through step-by-step instructions—by using 1-2-3 and "seeing" it work, rather than by reading a manual.

The program begins at a level that assumes no personal computer or 1-2-3 experience. The essentials of 1-2-3 are learned first; practice is provided to reinforce those skills. That foundation is used to learn more advanced aspects of 1-2-3.

The program begins with an Introduction that provides the new user with a brief, friendly explanation of personal computer hardware and software, DOS, and the fundamentals of 1-2-3. A mistake-proof tutorial diskette is included. The Computer Case Series follows, with a Guide and Directory to the case series and its computer instructions. The case series is divided into 18 lessons. The data for each lesson are contained in a separate file on the enclosed Suave Data Diskette. Each lesson can be completed separately.

Many of the essentials of 1-2-3 are taught in the first lesson. The remaining lessons provide practice in database management and teach more advanced functions, commands, and uses of 1-2-3 for spreadsheet analysis and graphics. A Harvard Business School case, the Suave Budgeting Case, completes the case series and explores in greater depth the management issues raised.

The program concludes with some supplementary materials concerning personal computers in business, advertising budgeting, and the educational philosophy of the program. The Index of 1-2-3 functions and commands allows the book to serve as a reference tool at any time.

ACKNOWLEDGMENTS

We are indebted to many colleagues who made this project possible.

Professor John McArthur, Dean of the Faculty of the Harvard Business School, has provided the vision and leadership to ensure that our students acquire the skills necessary to be successful, modern-day managers. His decision to introduce personal computers into the MBA curriculum led to the development of this type of material.

Professor Warren McFarlan, Chairperson of the Required Course Subcommittee, was in charge of the introduction of the personal computer into the MBA curriculum. He set the standards and parameters for this material and provided the resources for its development. Without his stewardship, the computer training program would never have been refined to its current state.

Professor Benson Shapiro, Director of Research, had the direct responsibility to supervise the development of this material in 1984. His guidance nurtured the initial creative process. We deeply appreciate his willingness to take a chance by entrusting this new type of material to two young colleagues.

Professor Thomas Bonoma, Chairperson of the MBA program, has overseen the implementation and evolution of the computer training program since 1985. His keen insights have led to significant improvements in the organization and presentation of the material to our students.

Many others have been involved in the extensive implementation efforts at the Harvard Business School. Most notably, Professors Thomas Kosnik and Patrick Kaufmann have supervised the program and provided invaluable feedback and reviews of earlier versions. They and other professors in the first-year marketing group have given substantial support and expert instruction in teaching the material since 1984. The continued support of Frayda Galvin, the Manager of Academic and Microcomputer Services, has also been crucial to implementing the computer training for 800 students each fall at Harvard.

The Division of Research has been instrumental in helping us to improve the material and have it published in its best form. In particular, Joanne Segal, Assistant Dean and Director of Administration for the Division of Research, and Caroline Michel, Project Director, have lent essential administrative support throughout the life of this project.

Helene Curtis, Inc., especially Gil Smith and Robert Thomas, provided the original data that made this project a reality. Wordsmith, Inc., particularly Fred Miller and Valerie Strange, delivered efficient word processing services for this final manuscript. And Jane Barrett expertly processed a camera-copy instructor's manual in record time under severe time pressure.

Finally, Daniel Cheng, Manager of the Harvard Business School Project at Data Resources, Inc., was fundamental to the development of the entire project. He performed all the required technical work and wrote much of the instructions in the earlier versions. He also provided careful, insightful reviews of our computer instructions and the case series in this book.

USING DIFFERENT HARDWARE

This section provides an update on technical issues concerning *Business Decision Making with 1-2-3*.

THE TUTORIAL DISKETTE

On certain personal computers, the tutorial diskette will not start until you put "drivers" on the diskette. This requires two extra steps (numbers 3 and 4 below) beyond those described on page 9:

1 Load DOS. Enter date and time. Get to an A> prompt.
2 Remove DOS from Drive A. Insert the tutorial diskette in Drive A.
3 At the A> prompt, type: **install** and press **[Enter]**. The Install program will ask you simply to select the display adapter card in your personal computer.
4 Select one of the five options and press **[Enter]**.
5 After installation, you will be returned to the A> prompt. Type **tutor** and press **[Enter]**. The tutorial will now start.

OS/2

The new operating system, OS/2, replaces DOS in IBM personal computers. This system has a "compatibility box" to run Lotus 1-2-3 and the enclosed diskettes. There should be no problems.

About the Authors

Mark S. Albion

Edward J. Hoff

Mark S. Albion has been an Assistant Professor of Business Administration, Harvard University, in the marketing area since 1982. He received his undergraduate degree in economics from Harvard University, as well as an A.M. and a Ph.D. through a joint program of the Graduate Schools of Business Administration and Arts and Sciences in Business Economics. His doctoral dissertation won an American Marketing Association national dissertation award.

Professor Albion has written two books on the economic effects of manufacturer's advertising on mass retailers and has appeared in various media, including *60 Minutes*, *Fortune*, and *The Wall Street Journal*, as both a columnist and expert. He has served on the board of directors of four companies and been active in a number of Executive Education Programs for manufacturers and retailers. He is currently developing an organization that customizes educational programs for Fortune 500 companies on the use of personal computers in general business management and most specifically, in marketing decision-making.

Edward J. Hoff has taught marketing at Harvard Business School, where he received his MBA degree and was named Baker Scholar. He has co-authored an article in the Harvard Business Review and has written several case studies dealing with marketing and competitive strategy. He is currently completing his Ph.D in Business Economics at Harvard University. He previously served as Cabinet Secretary for former Governor Byrne of New Jersey.

BUSINESS DECISION MAKING WITH 1-2-3®

CHAPTER 1

Introduction

GUIDE TO USING THE INTRODUCTION

This introductory section is intended primarily to help those readers who have never touched a personal computer or who have used a personal computer but never used Lotus 1-2-3. It can also serve as a helpful review or memory refresher even for those who have some experience with 1-2-3.

The section is divided into three parts:

1 A First Look at Personal Computers;
2 DOS: The Disk Operating System; and
3 A First Look at Lotus 1-2-3.

"A First Look at Personal Computers" provides a friendly explanation of PC hardware, disks, and software. If you have little or no experience with PCs, be sure to look at this part. The questions and answers purposely avoid technical terms or sophisticated explanations.

"DOS: The Disk Operating System" will help the new PC user learn how to use this essential software. You need to know how to use DOS before you can use Lotus 1-2-3. This part will tell you only what you need to know about DOS in order to use Lotus 1-2-3 and this book.

"A First Look at Lotus 1-2-3" will tell you how to use the specially designed tutorial diskette included in this book. If you have little or no experience with 1-2-3 (or wish to ensure that you understand the fundamental concepts of 1-2-3), be sure to use this brief, mistake-proof tutorial. You will also learn how to prepare brand new Lotus disks for use. If you need to install the drivers on your Lotus disks—or want to know what installing the drivers means—read this part.

If you have some experience with PCs or with 1-2-3, *you can either skim or skip entirely the familiar parts of this introduction, proceeding directly to the Guide to Using the Computer Case Series*. Each of the three parts is brief, so it should not take long to look through them, reading only the material of interest to you.

A FIRST LOOK AT PERSONAL COMPUTERS

A FIRST LOOK AT HARDWARE

What Is a Personal Computer?

A personal computer (or PC) is a device that allows you both to process and to store information—quickly, efficiently, and in enormous quantities. Personal computers were made possible by the dramatic miniaturization of key computer parts, particularly the computer *chips* that either process or store information. A PC allows an individual to have immediate access to the computer; larger computers are usually more difficult to access and often not readily available.

What Comprises a Personal Computer?

There are six key parts to a personal computer:

1 The *microprocessor*, the chip that actually processes the information;
2 The *memory*, the set of chips that stores information;
3 The *disk drives*, which retrieve information from a diskette or transfer information to a diskette;
4 The *display monitor*, the screen that shows your ongoing work;
5 The *display adapter card*, which translates information so that it can be shown on a specific kind of display monitor; and
6 The *keyboard*, for entering information or commands.

In addition, most PC users have a computer *printer* connected to the PC for printing the results of their work.

What Does the New User of a PC Need to Do?

If you are a new user of a PC, you need to:

1 Find out what kind of hardware you have. In particular, you should know:
   • The brand of PC you are using.
   • How much memory capacity your PC has. Memory capacity is measured in *thousand bytes*, such as 512K bytes. Memory capacity varies significantly on PCs and can be quite limited on some. Extra memory can be added.

- The type of monitor and display adapter card (i.e., IBM color graphics, Monochrome, Hercules, or Compaq) you have.
- Whether you are using a PC with a diskette system (one or two disk drives) or a PC with a hard-disk.
- What brand and type of printer you have.

2 Properly connect all the parts: the printer, monitor, and keyboard should all be connected to the PC.

3 Become familiar with the PC keyboard. Here are two suggestions:

   a Some PCs have *software tutorials* to help you become familiar with the PC. For example, IBM has an excellent tutorial entitled "Exploring the IBM PC." See the following sections on disks and software to help learn how to *load* these software tutorials.

   b Lotus Release 2.01 provides, in the package of accompanying materials, a set of pictures of the most popular keyboards. Those pictures will help you to identify certain keys that will be used later. If you are not familiar with your keyboard and have the Release 2.01 package, be sure to look at these materials.

A FIRST LOOK AT DISKS

If Personal Computers Have Disk Drives, Then What Are Disks?

Disks (or diskettes) are specially designed pieces of plastic that are used to store information. This information may be software programs, such as Lotus 1-2-3, which tell the computer what to do, or data, such as words or numbers.

Not all disks for PCs are the same. Some PC disks measure $5\frac{1}{4}$ by $5\frac{1}{4}$ inches; these are usually called *floppy diskettes*. Other disks measure $3\frac{1}{2}$ by $3\frac{1}{2}$ inches. Be sure you know what kind of disks your PC uses.

How Do We Use Disks?

We will insert disks into the PC's disk drives, either to put information into the PC or to save information on the disk itself. Be sure to follow these simple rules in using a diskette:

1 Treat a diskette carefully. Do not bend it—especially the $5\frac{1}{4}$ inch floppy diskettes.

2 Do not leave diskettes in hot places or near magnetic devices.

3 Make sure your diskettes are inserted properly. If they are not, your PC will tell you when you first try to use the diskette. The method for inserting a diskette into a disk drive depends on what type of PC you have. With some PCs (such as most IBM PCs) the diskette is inserted horizontally; with other PCs (such as Compaq PCs) the diskette is inserted vertically. Most diskettes come with some kind of label. To help you know if you are inserting the diskette correctly, when the diskette is inserted the label should be facing up in horizontal disk drives or to your left in vertical disk drives.

4 Blank diskettes need to be *formatted* before they can be used. The section on "The Basics of DOS" will help explain this step to you.

What Is a Hard Disk?

A *hard disk* is a set of memory chips that can increase the memory capacity of a PC manyfold. In fact, the storage capacity of a hard disk is usually measured in megabytes (1 million bytes). Many hard disks have 10-, 20-, or 30-megabyte capacity—an extraordinary amount of memory. If a PC has a hard disk, the PC user can usually store software (such as Lotus 1-2-3) permanently on the hard disk in the PC rather than on a separate diskette.

A FIRST LOOK AT SOFTWARE

What Is Software?

A software program is a set of instructions that tells the computer how to work. Different software programs tell the PC how to do different tasks. Usually, you will have to *load* the software program—that is, put the software in the PC memory cells—before you can use that program.

How Do You Load Software?

When you buy a software program, you buy a diskette that contains the software: a set of instructions that tells the computer how to perform certain tasks. To load the software, you insert the diskette into a disk drive and then complete some steps. (We cover these steps later.) The disk drive then *reads* the software program off the diskette and stores the software program in the *memory* of the PC.

If you are using a personal computer with a regular disk drive system (that is, without a hard disk), you will have to load the software from the diskette every time you want to use that software. If you are using a PC with a hard disk, you can load the software from the diskette just once and then keep it in storage permanently on the hard disk.

What Software Will We Use?

We will use the following software:

1 DOS, the Disk Operating System;
2 The Lotus 1-2-3 program; and
3 The Lotus PrintGraph program.

You should have a copy of each of these software programs. The instructions will explain how to load each of these software programs. We begin with a look at the DOS program, which is needed to run any IBM or IBM-compatible PC.

DOS: THE DISK OPERATING SYSTEM

THE BASICS OF DOS

This introduction to DOS is intentionally brief. Entire books have been written on DOS. However, this section and the next, "Using DOS to List and to Copy Files," should explain all that is necessary for you to start using Lotus 1-2-3. If you like, refer to your DOS manual for further information.

What Is DOS?

DOS stands for *Disk Operating System*. DOS is the software program that tells all IBM or IBM-compatible PCs the basics about how to work.

Why Do We Have to Use DOS with Lotus?

In most instances, DOS must be the *first* software program loaded any time we want to use the PC, no matter what other software we intend to use. After we load DOS, we can then load additional software, such as Lotus 1-2-3.

Loading DOS

To load DOS into a PC with a diskette system (not a hard disk), follow these steps:

    1 Insert the DOS disk into Drive A.
    2 *Boot* the personal computer. There are two ways to boot a computer:
      a Just turn it from off to on (often called a *cold boot*).
      b If the PC is already on, then press a set of keys all at once. For IBM PCs these three keys are **[Ctrl]**, **[Alt]**, and **[Del]** (often called a *warm boot*).

Once DOS is loaded into your PC, the PC will direct you to "Enter new date." If you enter the current date, then that date will be listed with any file you might later save. To enter a date such as June 8, 1988, type in:

6-08-1988

and then press **[Enter]**. If you wish, you can just press **[Enter]** and the "default" date of 1-01-1980 will be listed with any files you later save.

    The PC will then direct you to "Enter new time." DOS uses 24-hour notation, such as 18:00 for 6:00 P.M. Again, you can just press **[Enter]** and a default time (12:00 A.M.) will be listed. However, if you wish to enter the correct time, such as 3:30 P.M., type in:

15:30

and then press **[Enter]**. The A> prompt will then appear.

Note: **[Enter]** and **[Return]** are the same key.

The DOS A> Prompt

The A> prompt indicates that the personal computer is ready to accept a new command. There are many times that we will want to get an A> prompt.

When the A> prompt appears, we can perform several important commands, including:

- Format a diskette;
- Load additional software;
- List a directory of the files on a diskette;
- Copy a file from one diskette to another;
- Copy all the files from one diskette onto another diskette; and
- Make an exact copy of a diskette.

One or Two Disk Drives

The introduction assumes you have two disk drives, Drive A and Drive B. If your PC only has one disk drive (and no hard disk), think of your one disk drive, Drive A, as being both. You will then have *Diskettes* A and B to exchange in that one drive. DOS will direct you when to exchange Diskette B for A, and vice versa.

Follow the instructions, keeping in mind that if a command denotes Drive B, you will put the second diskette, Diskette B, in your one drive. You must switch diskettes in and out of the disk drive when DOS directs you.

Formatting a Diskette

Before a blank diskette can be used, the diskette *must be formatted* so that DOS can read it. You need to format a diskette only *once*, before using the diskette for the first time. If you are using a PC with two disk drives you can format a blank diskette by completing these steps:

1 Insert the DOS disk into Drive A.
2 Load DOS and wait for the A> prompt.
3 Insert the blank diskette into Drive B.
4 Type in   **format b:**   and press **[Enter]**.

(If you are using a PC with one disk drive, follow the same steps—except in Step 3, remove the DOS diskette and put the blank diskette in Drive A and in Step 4 type in **format a:** .) DOS will now format your blank diskette, so that the diskette is ready to use.

If you have already formatted a diskette, be aware that formatting it again will erase all the files on the diskette. So, if a diskette has been formatted once, do not format it again unless you intend to erase all the files on the diskette.

Note: DOS and 1-2-3 list the names of files using capital letters. However, to type in a file name or command, you can always use capital or lowercase letters.

Loading Additional Software

After DOS has been loaded, we can load additional software programs at the A> prompt. These software programs will then all work with DOS. To load new software, such as the Lotus program, complete these steps:

1 Get to an A> prompt.
2 Remove the DOS diskette from Drive A.
3 Insert into Drive A the disk containing the new software (for example, the Lotus System Disk).
4 Type in the name of the file containing the software and press **[Enter]**. For example, to load the Lotus Access System, type **lotus** and press **[Enter]**.

USING DOS TO LIST AND TO COPY FILES

Accessing a Directory

A diskette can contain *files* of either software programs or data. All information stored in a diskette must be contained in a file, and each file must have a name.

You may want to know what files are on a diskette. DOS will list the names of the files on any diskette. To list such a directory of files, complete these steps:

1 Get to an A> prompt.
2 To list the files on a diskette in Drive A, type **dir a**: and press **[Enter]**.
3 To list the files on a diskette in Drive B, type **dir b**: and press **[Enter]**.

Copying Files from One Diskette to Another

DOS allows us to:

- Copy single files from one diskette to another;
- Copy all the files from one diskette to another diskette; and
- Make an exact copy of a diskette.

Copying a Single File from One Diskette to Another

To copy a single file from one diskette to another (using a PC with two disk drives), follow these steps:

1 Get to an A> prompt.
2 Remove the DOS disk from Drive A. Into Drive A insert the *source* diskette that already contains the file.
3 Into Drive B insert the *target* diskette that will receive a copy of the file. (This target diskette, of course, should have already been formatted.)
4 Then type   **copy a:[File's name] b:**   and press **[Enter]**.

Later you will see that files usually contain *extensions* that explain what kind of file it is. For example, with the DOS file FORMAT.COM the extension .COM explains that this file named FORMAT is a <u>communications</u> file.

For example, if the name of the file is FORMAT.COM you should type **copy a:FORMAT.COM b:**   and then press **[Enter]**. Recall that you do not need to use capital letters, but you must type the extension .COM (or .com).

Copying All the Files on One Diskette to Another Diskette

DOS also gives us an easy command to copy all the files on one diskette to another diskette. The target diskette will then end up with any files it had already contained plus all the new files being copied onto it.

To complete this command, follow these steps:

1 Get to an A> prompt.
2 Remove the DOS disk from Drive A. Into Drive A insert the *source* diskette, and into Drive B insert the *target* diskette.
3 Then type in   **copy *.* b:**   and press **[Enter]**.

Making an Exact Copy of a Diskette

DOS also allows us to make an *exact* copy of one diskette onto another diskette. This command will copy all the files from the source diskette, but it also will erase any files that might have been on the target diskette. Therefore, be sure that you really do want to use this command (and not the copy *.* command) before proceeding. To make an exact copy of a diskette, complete these steps:

1 Get to an A> prompt.
2 Be sure DOS is in Drive A. Then type in   **diskcopy a: b:**   and press **[Enter]**.
3 DOS will direct you to "Insert source diskette into Drive A:" and "Insert target diskette in Drive B:." Do so, and then press any key to begin.

This process does not require the target diskette to be formatted already. If you place a blank, unformatted diskette in Drive B, DOS will format it for you and then copy all the files. However, it is still good practice to format all blank diskettes. This will also accelerate the *diskcopy* process for DOS.

This command is particularly useful for making copies of important diskettes. *Be sure always to make copies of any important diskettes.* Let's now take our first look at Lotus 1-2-3.

A FIRST LOOK AT LOTUS 1-2-3

USING THE TUTORIAL

You should find a diskette labeled "Tutorial" in the jacket of this book. This diskette contains a mistake-proof software program that:

1 Explains in a friendly manner the fundamental concepts behind Lotus 1-2-3;
2 Is mistake-proof because it will advance only when you press the correct key;
3 Provides actual experience in using Lotus 1-2-3; and
4 Can be completed in one-half hour or less.

For the new user, this tutorial explains the key ideas behind Lotus 1-2-3 and allows you to begin using Lotus 1-2-3 without worrying about making a mistake or losing your place. It will also help a new PC user become familiar with the keyboard. Feel comfortable taking extra time to think about the concepts and steps that are being explained.

For the more experienced user, this brief tutorial helps to refresh your memory about some of the fundamentals of Lotus 1-2-3. The simply explained conceptual framework may also help you to organize your own thinking about how Lotus 1-2-3 works.

It is easy to start the tutorial on most personal computers. Complete these steps:

1 Load DOS. Enter date and time. Get to an A> prompt.
2 Remove DOS from Drive A. Insert the tutorial diskette in Drive A. At the A> prompt, type: **tutor** and press **[Enter]**.

The tutorial will then direct you, step by step, what keys to press. It should help you both to understand what 1-2-3 is all about and to increase your confidence in your ability to learn how to use 1-2-3. Try it now before reading the remainder of the introductory material.

(On certain PCs, you may need to complete a few more steps to start the tutorial. *If the tutorial does not start*, refer to the section "Using Different Hardware" in the frontmatter.)

THE DIFFERENT RELEASES OF LOTUS 1-2-3

Once you have finished the tutorial, it is time to look at 1-2-3. Lotus 1-2-3 is the software program that the tutorial and lessons in this book are designed to teach. There have been three *releases* (versions) to date of Lotus 1-2-3: Release 1A, Release 2, and Release 2.01.

The instructions in this book are written for Release 2.01, the most recent release. *However, these instructions can be easily followed by users of Release 1A or Release 2.* [Many long-time users of Lotus 1-2-3 have decided not to change their software from Release 1A to Release 2.01 or from Release 2 to Release 2.01.] The instructions mark the relatively few places where the releases differ.

Readers who are using Release 1A and who do not expect to upgrade to Release 2.01 soon should just continue with the instructions. (Readers who are using software programs that work like Release 1A, such as TWIN, should also just continue with the instructions.) The section "Guide to Using the Computer Case Series" discusses some of the minor, specific ways in which Release 1A differs from Release 2.01.

We do suggest, however, that if you own Release 1A or Release 2 and you do expect to upgrade to Release 2.01, do so now. It will save you some effort in learning later how Release 2.01 differs from earlier releases.

Make sure that your Lotus disks are prepared for use. Then you will be ready to begin the Computer Case Series.

PREPARING YOUR LOTUS DISKS

Unfortunately, you cannot use the Lotus disks fresh out of the package, except in limited circumstances. In general, you must complete several steps to prepare your Lotus disks before you can use them. These steps are somewhat technical and complex. Rest assured that once these steps are completed, using 1-2-3 is more straightforward and intuitive.

Lotus provides a booklet entitled "Getting Started," which explains how to prepare the Lotus disks. Below is a summary of the steps to complete if you are using:

1 A personal computer with a diskette system (that is, no hard disk); and
2 Lotus Release 2.01.

If you are using a personal computer with a hard disk, refer to the instructions in the booklet "Getting Started." The following brief instructions will help you prepare your Lotus disks.

The Lotus Disks

There are six Lotus disks (if you are using $5\frac{1}{4}$-inch disk drives):

• System Disk;
• Backup System Disk;
• PrintGraph Disk;
• Utility Disk;
• "View of 1-2-3" Tutorial Disk; and
• Install Library Disk.

If you are using $3\frac{1}{2}$-inch disk drives, then there are five Lotus disks, because the PrintGraph program is included on the System Disk.

Put Write-Protect Tabs on All Lotus Disks

To protect your Lotus disks, just put write-protect tabs on all of them as soon as you open your package. This tab ensures that the information on the diskette can be used but not changed. For $5\frac{1}{4}$-inch disks, place a silver tab, provided with your Lotus disks, over the small indentation on the right side of each of the diskettes. For $3\frac{1}{2}$-inch disks, slide the small cover over the small hole on the back of each disk. Later, we will temporarily remove write-protect from the System and Backup System disks to make some alterations. It is a good practice, however, to have write-protect on all disks containing software, except for those few times when you specifically need to put new material on a software disk.

Make a Copy of the Lotus Disks (Except the System Disks)

The Lotus System Disk and the Backup System Disk are copy-protected. The Lotus Development Corporation does not permit these disks to be copied. That is why a Backup System Disk is provided in the Lotus 1-2-3 package.

However, Lotus does direct us to make a copy of the other four Lotus disks (three disks for $3\frac{1}{2}$-inch diskette PCs). Therefore, follow these steps:

1 Take four blank diskettes of your own. Use the **diskcopy** command of DOS to make a copy of each of these Lotus disks:
• PrintGraph disk;
• Utility disk;
• View of 1-2-3 disk; and
• Install Library disk.

(See the section on "Using DOS to List and to Copy Files" for how to use the **diskcopy** command. Note that you do not have to remove write-protect to copy *from* a disk.)

2 Use the diskette labels that Lotus provides with the 1-2-3 package to label each of the copies of the Lotus disks.

Copy the DOS File COMMAND.COM from the DOS Disk to the System and Backup System Disks

The DOS COMMAND.COM file is found on your DOS diskette. We need to copy this DOS file to the System and Backup System Disks.

1 Remove the write-protect from the Lotus System Disk. Insert the Disk in Drive B.
2 Place the DOS disk in Drive A. Turn on the PC. Enter date and time.
3 At the A> prompt, type   **copy a: COMMAND.COM b:**   and then press **[Enter]**.
4 When the A> prompt appears again, remove the System Disk from Drive B. Then remove write-protect from the Backup System Disk and insert that disk into Drive B.
5 Repeat Step 3.

Before Continuing, Store Five Lotus Disks

Before continuing on to the Install Program, complete these steps:

1 For now, replace write-protect on the *Backup* System Disk only.
2 Store the following five Lotus disks (four disks for 3½-inch diskette PCs) in a place protected from damage, extreme heat, or magnetic fields:
a Backup System Disk;
b Original PrintGraph Disk;
c Original Utility Disk;
d Original View of 1-2-3 Disk; and
e Original Install Library Disk.
In this way, you will have an entire set of Lotus disks safely protected and stored in their original condition (without the drivers installed).

Use the Install Program

The Install program allows you to put *drivers* on the Lotus disks. The drivers simply specify what kind of PC hardware you are using for the Lotus software, so that Lotus can work well with your hardware.

Release 2.01 has a friendly program to help install these drivers. You will use that program. First, be sure you know what kind of personal computer, printer, and monitor you are using. Then complete these steps:

1 Be sure the A> prompt is displayed on the screen.
2 Insert your copy of the Lotus Utility Disk in Drive A.
3 Type **install** and press **[Enter]**.

The Install program will take about 30 seconds to load. It will then give you very specific directions and ask you to answer specific questions about your hardware. Follow the program and answer the questions as directed. As part of the program, you will alternatively insert each of these Lotus disks into Drive A:

• System Disk;
• Copy of the Install Library Disk;
• Copy of the Utility Disk;
• Copy of the PrintGraph Disk; and
• Copy of the View 1-2-3 Disk.

There are two answers that you probably should choose during installation:

1 When the Main Menu appears, choose First-Time Installation. Then the program will guide you through the questions to answer.
2 When the program asks "Do you want to name your driver set?" choose No. Do not press the **[Escape]** key. Press the **[Return]** (same as **[Enter]**) key to use the driver name 123.SET. Otherwise, things get complicated.

When the program is finished, put write-protect on all five disks with which you were just working. These disks are now ready for use.

CHAPTER 2

Guide to Using the Computer Case Series

The Computer Case Series (Chapters 3–6) is the core of *Business Decision Making With 1-2-3*. The Computer Case Series:

1 Provides step-by-step instructions that allow the new user of Lotus 1-2-3 to build skills gradually before moving on to more advanced lessons;

2 Provides the flexibility for a reader with some experience in 1-2-3 to use the case series selectively and efficiently; and

3 Ensures that while learning *how* to use 1-2-3, the reader will see *why* a manager might use 1-2-3.

The Computer Case Series, therefore, can be used to fit your individual background and situation. A discussion on how to use the Computer Case Series depending on (1) your level of experience and (2) your professional needs follows in the next section.

The Basic Structure

The Computer Case Series describes an actual business situation in which managers must make a decision about an advertising budget. The managers were able to make extensive use of 1-2-3 in their analysis and decision making.

The case is divided into 18 lessons. These are arranged in a logical sequence of analysis that the managers themselves might actually follow. These 18 lessons, in turn, are grouped into 4 stages.

Each of the 18 lessons begins with an overview and proceeds with the relevant portion of the case describing how the managers would use 1-2-3 for that analysis. Computer Instructions immediately follow. Each lesson then concludes with a discussion of the management issues raised in that lesson.

The Suave Data Diskette

For each lesson you will use the Suave Data Diskette included in this book and a Lotus 1-2-3 System Disk. The Suave Data Diskette contains 18 files of information, corresponding to each of the 18 lessons. You will *retrieve* the appropriate file for each lesson.

  The Suave Data Diskette is permanently protected—you can neither erase the files on it nor put new files on it. However, this diskette could still get damaged by bending or heat. Therefore, make a backup copy of this diskette.

Your Data Diskette

The computer instructions will direct you to format a blank diskette to use as your data diskette. You will save the work that you complete on this data diskette. (To avoid confusion, do not save your work on your backup copy of the Suave Data Diskette.)

You Will Learn by Using 1-2-3 and "Seeing" It Work, Not by Reading a Manual

The Computer Case Series is designed to have you learn 1-2-3 by actually using it. Friendly, step-by-step instructions help you use 1-2-3 and see how it works. In this way, *Business Decision Making With 1-2-3* follows a very different approach from manual-type books.

Move at Your Own Pace

The Computer Case Series is also designed to allow you to complete the lessons at your own pace. Spend as much time as you like to read the instructions carefully and to let the lessons sink in. As your skills develop, you can complete the lessons more quickly. *Move at your own pace* is the golden rule of the program.

Guidance and Support

The computer instructions provide guidance and support in three ways:

1 Whenever you learn something new, the instructions will tell you step by step exactly what to do.
2 The instructions will frequently provide a picture of how the screen should appear on your monitor.
3 The completed worksheet for each lesson is provided right on your diskette for easy reference.

The Completed Worksheets

Here is a list of where the completed worksheets appear on the Suave Data Diskette. These cell references will become clearer when you begin the lessons.

Lessons	Cell Where Completed Worksheet Begins
1–6	A101
7–10	Q1
11–18	A101

Please review the completed worksheets any time you want in order to see how the worksheet should appear.

What to Do if You Make Mistakes or Need Help

First, if you make a major mistake in one of the early lessons and are confused, we suggest that you just remove your diskette, retrieve the file again from the *Suave Data Diskette*, and then start the lesson over.

If you need some help with a specific command or step, try using the Lotus *Help* system. No matter where you are in Lotus, if you press the **[F1]** function key, Lotus will provide a help screen. To return to the worksheet, just press **[Esc]**. Some users like this help system; others find it confusing.

Using the Directory of Computer Instructions and Management Issues

Immediately following this guide is a directory that lists the first time a Lotus 1-2-3 function or command is used in the Computer Case Series. The next section discusses how this directory can guide your use of the Computer Case Series.

Using This Book as a Reference

An index is provided at the back of the book. This alphabetical and cross-referenced index lists where all the Lotus 1-2-3 functions and commands are first introduced. This index will be a helpful reference when you use Lotus 1-2-3 on your own later: You can turn to the appropriate section quickly any time you want to refresh your memory about a 1-2-3 command or function.

HOW TO USE THE COMPUTER CASE SERIES DEPENDING ON DIFFERENT LEVELS OF EXPERIENCE WITH 1-2-3

The Computer Case Series is designed to offer significant flexibility so that the readers with different levels of experience can use the program efficiently to meet their individual needs.

For the Reader Just Beginning to Learn 1-2-3

Lesson 1 *by itself teaches almost all the essentials of Lotus* 1-2-3. The instructions guide you through every single step. You can move at your own pace in completing Lesson 1 and all subsequent lessons.

As the lessons progress, you will complete exercises to practice and reinforce what you have already learned. Eventually, you are directed to complete the exercises *on your own*, without the step-by-step guidance. In this way, you will achieve self-sufficiency in your use of Lotus 1-2-3. You can always check your work by referring to the pictures of computer screens in the instructions.

Also, new functions and commands are gradually introduced in the lessons. The Computer Case Series is designed so that you build on what you have learned. When new aspects of 1-2-3 are first explained, step-by-step instructions are always provided.

Lessons 9–13 in the Computer Case Series explain some of the more-advanced functions, commands, and uses of 1-2-3. The directory of computer instructions and management issues shows where these more advanced 1-2-3 capabilities are introduced. You can use the directory to decide whether you want to tackle these advanced lessons. If you have completed the previous lessons, however, you should have no trouble learning them.

For the Reader with Some Experience Using 1-2-3

The Computer Case Series permits you to decide how you want to approach each lesson—and every part of each lesson. For each part of a lesson or for an entire lesson, you have the flexibility to:

1 Follow the instructions and explanations thoroughly as you complete the exercise;
2 Complete the exercise on your own—only skimming any instructions and explanations; or
3 Skip the exercise completely, and just examine the completed worksheet as you think about the management questions.

To help you decide how you want to approach a lesson or exercise, use the directory of computer instructions and management issues as a guide to what aspects of 1-2-3 are taught in each lesson. You can also examine the section headings that are included throughout for a more-detailed look at what is covered in each lesson.

If you already know certain aspects of 1-2-3 but choose to follow the instructions thoroughly, you will probably find that you are able to complete the lesson quickly anyway. If you choose to complete the exercise on your own without following the instructions, check your work by referring either to the pictures of screens in the instructions or to the completed worksheet on the file. If you choose to skip an exercise altogether, remember that you should still take the time to understand the management implications of that exercise. Look at the completed worksheet in the file.

HOW TO USE THE COMPUTER CASE SERIES
DEPENDING ON DIFFERENT PROFESSIONAL NEEDS

As the use of personal computers increases in businesses and in schools, the needs of different people to understand PCs and Lotus 1-2-3 will depend partly upon their profession and position. Following is a discussion of how senior executives, managers, and students with different requirements might approach *Business Decision Making with 1-2-3*.

> **Requirement:** *To gain a solid working knowledge of how to use 1-2-3 and to understand what 1-2-3 can do to assist in business decision making*

Most students, many managers, and some senior executives may want to gain solid skills in using Lotus 1-2-3 as well as to experience how 1-2-3 can assist a manager in business decision making. If you wish to acquire strong proficiency in using Lotus 1-2-3, consider using the book in the following manner:

- Complete all the lessons thoroughly. As you acquire skill and experience, you will be able to complete the lessons more quickly. The additional practice in each lesson is the key to building speed and comfort.
- Be sure to examine the management issues while you complete the computer instructions. It is important to focus on *why* you are using 1-2-3 while you learn how to use it.

> **Requirement:** *Primarily to gain an understanding of what 1-2-3 can do to assist in business decision making and to acquire some knowledge of how to use it*

Senior executives and managers may primarily want to understand what 1-2-3 can do to assist a manager in making business decisions but not to become regular users of 1-2-3. These people are more interested in directing others to perform various analyses using personal computers (and 1-2-3) rather than using the computer themselves. Therefore, spending some time on a real example of how 1-2-3 can be used in market analyses or financial projections would be of some benefit. A ready and friendly reference of all the key elements of Lotus 1-2-3 might be useful to help gain a working knowledge of only the essential functions and commands of 1-2-3.

If you fit the preceding description, you should consider using this book in the following manner:

- Complete Lessons 1 and 2 to learn the essential functions and commands of 1-2-3.
- Examine the case for each of the 18 lessons and retrieve the file to see how the worksheet file fits the situation facing the decision makers in the case. Then examine the completed worksheet included in every file to see what Lotus 1-2-3 was able to do. (See the previous section for a listing of where the completed lessons are located on each file.)
- Decide whether you would like to complete a lesson to learn more fully how Lotus 1-2-3 was used to complete that worksheet file.

- Read the management discussion at the end of each lesson to see how 1-2-3 was used to address important management issues.
- Use the directory of computer instructions and management issues to help guide you on which lessons you want to read and complete thoroughly.
- Be sure to examine the discussion and instructions in Lessons 11 and 12 on how to list clearly the assumptions that underlie financial projections and how to organize a spreadsheet.

STARTING EACH LESSON: LOADING LOTUS 1-2-3

The beginning of each of the 18 lessons will direct you to do the following:

1 Load DOS. Enter date and time.
2 Load the Lotus Access System.
3 Load 1-2-3 software program.

For directions on how to load DOS and enter date and time, refer to the section "The Basics of DOS."

Loading Lotus

These directions apply to all releases of Lotus 1-2-3. After loading DOS, when you get to the A> prompt, remove the DOS disk from Drive A. Then insert the Lotus System Disk into Drive A.

At the A> prompt, type **lotus** and press **[Enter]**. This step loads the Lotus Access System.

When the Lotus Access System screen appears, press **[Enter]** to load the 1-2-3 program. (You will learn more about the Lotus Access System in Lesson 5, when you will use it to return to an A> prompt, and in Lesson 15, when you learn how to print graphs. For now, you just need to know that to gain access to the 1-2-3 program, press **[Enter]** when the Lotus Access System screen appears.) Once Lotus 1-2-3 has been loaded, you will then need to load a file from the Suave Data Diskette.

THE DIFFERENT RELEASES OF 1-2-3:
WHICH DISK DRIVE TO USE FOR DATA DISKETTES

At the beginning of each lesson, after you have loaded DOS, the Lotus Access System, and Lotus 1-2-3, the instructions will then direct you to load a particular worksheet file. The worksheet file for each of the 18 lessons contains the data you will use for that lesson. These 18 worksheet files are stored on the diskette (enclosed in this book) entitled Suave Data Diskette.

The instructions will direct you to insert the Suave Data Diskette into the appropriate disk drive. Which disk drive is appropriate depends on which Lotus 1-2-3 release you are using, whether you are using a PC with one or two disk drives (or a hard disk), and which method you prefer to use.

Release 2.01 or Release 2; Two Disk Drives

These releases always look for worksheet files in Drive A, unless you direct otherwise. So, there are two methods you can use:

1 After you have loaded Lotus 1-2-3, remove the Lotus System Disk from Drive A and then insert the Suave Data Diskette into Drive A. Then follow the computer instructions to choose the file you want.

2 When you insert the Lotus System Disk into Drive A, also insert the Suave Data Diskette into Drive B.

(The rest of this will become clearer when you begin Lesson 1.) After you use the **/File Retrieve** command, the following will appear: **Name of file to retrieve: A:\.** Press **[Esc]**; then type **b:** and press **[Enter]**. Then choose the file you want.

Release 1A; Two Disk Drives

Release 1A always looks for worksheet files in Drive B when there are two disk drives. So, when you insert the Lotus System Disk into Drive A, insert the Suave Data Diskette into Drive B. Then follow the computer instructions.

One Disk Drive

No matter which release you are using, after you have loaded Lotus 1-2-3, remove the Lotus System Disk from Drive A and then insert the Suave Data Diskette into Drive A. Then follow the computer instructions.

Hard Disk

A PC with a hard disk has one disk drive. If you wish to load Lotus 1-2-3 permanently into the hard disk, follow the instructions that accompany the Lotus manual. Otherwise, you can just load Lotus 1-2-3 each time you use it. In that case, follow the instructions for one disk drive. These instructions should be followed whenever you use any data diskette.

THE DIFFERENT RELEASES OF 1-2-3: FILE NAMES AND EXTENSIONS

Lotus 1-2-3 creates three types of files: worksheet files, graph (or picture) files, and print files. The Computer Case Series will introduce you to these different types of files. A file name in 1-2-3 cannot contain any spaces or more than eight characters.

For example, a file can be named LESSON1 or LESSON01, but not LESSON 1 (with a space in the name).

Lotus 1-2-3 always includes an abbreviation, or *extension*, after each file name to clarify whether it is a Worksheet (WK1 or WKS), a Graph (PIC), or a Print (PRN) file. Therefore, when you save a file, 1-2-3 will automatically append the appropriate extension to the file name. Release 2.01 and Release 2 will always show the file extension whenever it lists a file name. For example, the first worksheet file you use will be displayed as LESSON01.WKS. These extensions will help you remember with which type of file you are dealing.

Release 1A does not display the extension to the name of the file. Only if you use the DOS Directory command (DIR) will you see these extensions. In the Computer Case Series, the instructions will refer to files with the extensions. If you are using Release 1A, just ignore the extensions. All files saved using Release 1A can be retrieved and used in Release 2.01 (or Release 2). That makes it possible for people who upgraded to Release 2.01 to use files that they have created earlier with Release 1A. *However, files that are saved with Release 2.01 (or Release 2) cannot be retrieved easily with Release 1A. The compatibility runs easily only one way: going from 1A to 2.01.*

Worksheet files that are saved with Release 1A carry the extension WKS when they are then used with Release 2.01 or Release 2. All files on the Suave Data Diskette were saved with Release 1A so that they can be used with all three releases of 1-2-3. Worksheet files that are saved with Release 2.01 or Release 2 carry the extension WK1. These details will all become clearer as you use the Computer Case Series.

WHAT YOU NEED TO START: A CHECKLIST

Before beginning Lesson 1, be sure of the following:

1 You know what kind of hardware you are using.
2 You understand how to use DOS.
3 You complete the tutorial, if appropriate.
4 Your Lotus disks are prepared and ready to be used.
5 You have read the section on "How to Use the Computer Case Series" so that you know how to tailor the Computer Case Series to your individual needs.
6 You understand how to load Lotus 1-2-3 and which disk drive to use for the Suave Data Diskette.
7 You have located the Suave Data Diskette in this book and made a backup copy of it.
8 You have formatted a blank diskette to use as your data diskette.

Remember that Lesson 1 is by far the longest lesson for new users of Lotus 1-2-3. It teaches almost all the essentials of 1-2-3. So, feel comfortable taking your time with this first lesson. Experienced users can move through Lesson 1 more rapidly, reading the detailed explanations of the new commands only when necessary.

DIRECTORY OF COMPUTER INSTRUCTIONS
AND MANAGEMENT ISSUES

This directory lists the first time a specific function or command of Lotus 1-2-3 is explained in the computer instructions. A star (*) indicates the more advanced functions and commands. The directory also lists the management issues raised in each lesson.

Stage 1

Computer Instructions: The Essentials of Lotus 1-2-3

Management Issues: Market and Consumer Analysis

Lesson 1
New Computer Instructions

Computer Instructions: The Essentials of Lotus 1-2-3

Management Issues: Market and Consumer Analysis

Computer Instructions: The Essentials of Lotus 1-2-3

Management Issues: Market and Consumer Analysis

Stage 2

New Computer Instructions: Practice of the Essentials of 1-2-3

Management Issues: Advertising Effectiveness

New Computer Instructions: Practice of the Essentials of 1-2-3

Management Issues: Advertising Effectiveness

Stage 3

New Computer Instructions: Creating Spreadsheets and Data Tables

Management Issues: Financial Projections

New Computer Instructions: Creating Spreadsheets and Data Tables

Management Issues: Financial Projections

Stage 4

Computer Instructions: Creating Graphs

Management Instructions: Graphs for Communication and Analysis

---

Computer Instructions: Creating Graphs

Management Instructions: Graphs for Communication and Analysis

---

Computer Instructions: Creating Graphs

Management Instructions: Graphs for Communication and Analysis

---

INTRODUCTION TO THE CASE STUDY

This case study describes a decision facing the managers of a consumer packaged goods company and presents a logical order of analysis that the managers might follow to reach that decision.

Lotus 1-2-3 can significantly assist the managers in making this decision. It facilitates analytical calculations, financial projections, and graphical presentations of data. It should be recognized, however, that the use of Lotus 1-2-3 is only one part of the overall analytical process. It is a less significant analytical tool at certain times than at others. For example, some sections of the case study that address the consumer buying process lend themselves more to qualitative analysis.

The case study is divided into 18 individual lessons. These lessons cover four areas of management analysis: market and consumer research, advertising effectiveness, financial projections, and graphical presentation.

The case study concludes with an integrated Harvard Business School case called the *Suave Budgeting Case*. This case incorporates the marketing and financial analysis you will complete during the 18 lessons. In addition, it provides further information on the complexity of the business situation facing Helene Curtis. This capstone case will allow you to enhance your understanding of the marketing and financial factors that affect your decisions on the relevant management issues.

SETTING AN ADVERTISING BUDGET FOR SUAVE SHAMPOO

Gail Lanznar, director of market research in the Consumer Products Division of Helene Curtis Industries, Inc., arrived at her office particularly early that Monday morning. She knew that the primary task for the Suave management team during the coming month would be to develop the fiscal year (FY) 1985[1] advertising budget for Suave shampoo. The team included Lanznar, Brad Kirk, group brand manager for Suave (and related products), and Ellen Vallera, brand manager for Suave.

During the month, the team would focus their efforts on providing Bob Thomas, vice president of marketing, with the analysis necessary to arrive at a well-supported advertising plan for Suave shampoo. Market and consumer research, sales projections, and financial analysis would each comprise an important part of the presentation made to top management at the end of the month.

Lanznar's first task was to analyze the extensive data that Helene Curtis had collected on the shampoo market. She believed that, with thoughtful analysis, important conclusions could be reached on Suave's position in the market, on how consumers buy shampoo (and Suave, in particular), and on different ways to segment the market. These conclusions would help determine the value of advertising for Suave.

Lanznar realized that her analysis represented only the beginning of the work that the team would need to complete in formulating their presentation for corporate management. Once her market and consumer analysis was finished, she would send copies of the market-research report to Vallera, Kirk, and Thomas. Any comments from Kirk and Thomas would be duly noted.

After Vallera had studied the findings of the report, the two would meet to review Lanznar's results and conduct a preliminary economic evaluation of the effectiveness of advertising for Suave shampoo. This evaluation would serve as the analytical foundation for Vallera's principal task: constructing market projections to test the potential financial impact of different advertising budgets on Suave shampoo.

When the team had finished analyzing Vallera's report, they would convene to develop a presentation for top management. They planned to generate some graphics to help analyze the data and to communicate their findings.

The team had decided to organize their work into four distinct stages:

Stage 1 (Lessons 1–4) Lanznar develops a market and consumer research report.

Stage 2 (Lessons 5–8) Vallera and Lanznar conduct a preliminary economic evaluation of advertising.

Stage 3 (Lessons 9–13) Vallera constructs financial projections to test different advertising budgets for her financial report.

Stage 4 (Lessons 14–18) The team prepares a final presentation with graphics for top management.

Bob Thomas would make the final decision on the advertising budget for Suave shampoo. He would consider the implications of the presentation before arriving at any conclusions. Other factors would also be examined in making the final decision. (The Suave Budgeting Case covers these additional factors.)

---

[1] March 1, 1984–February 28, 1985.

CHAPTER 3

Stage 1: Market and Consumer Analysis

An analysis of the shampoo market raises certain fundamental management issues. You should consider the following questions as you complete your analysis:

- What does your analysis in Stage 1 tell you about the role of advertising in the marketing of shampoo?
- Do you think that advertising is relatively more or less important for the Suave brand than for other shampoo brands? Why?
- What consumer group(s) would you try to reach with advertising for Suave shampoo?

INTRODUCTION

Gail Lanznar had responsibility for the first stage of work that the Suave management team would complete. She needed to analyze an extensive set of data on the shampoo market.

Fortunately, Lanznar had a personal computer at home as well as in the office. She always kept extra copies of her Suave data diskette and continually updated it for use at home or in the office. She knew that, whereas her personal computer would facilitate quantitative analysis, insight would come from time spent thinking about the data.

She decided to organize her analysis into the following four sections:

1 Market Analysis: Brand Shares
2 Competitive Analysis: Pricing, Advertising, and Market Segmentation

3 Consumer Analysis: Demographic Characteristics
4 Consumer Analysis: Psychographic Characteristics

These data were contained in separate files on her Suave data diskette. To complete the necessary calculations in the first two sections, Lanznar used data on sales and advertising expenditures for certain brands of shampoo (Table 3.1),

TABLE 3.1   SHAMPOO SALES AND ADVERTISING EXPENDITURES, FY 1984
(IN MILLIONS)

Brand	Unit Sales	Retail Sales	Ounces Sold	Ad Dollars[a]
Suave	61.0	$ 104.4	1,161	$ 6.00
Agree	13.8	25.5	196	5.51
Flex	34.5	74.2	563	3.48
Head & Shoulders	55.1	105.5	637	16.82
Jhirmack	21.7	39.4	124	9.40
Pert	24.9	41.7	285	9.43
Prell	36.0	64.9	298	15.95
Silkience	13.8	30.1	198	5.22
Vidal Sassoon	18.0	51.0	133	13.49
Generic	11.7	15.1	182	—
Private Label	36.6	62.6	695	—
Others	202.9	545.1	4,088	32.20
Total	530.0	$1,159.5	8,560	$117.50

[a]Media expenditures only; production costs not included.
Source: Company records.

LESSON 1   MARKET ANALYSIS: BRAND SHARES

OVERVIEW

COMPUTER INSTRUCTIONS

In the first lesson, you are introduced to many of the functions, keystrokes, and commands of Lotus 1-2-3 that are essential to the use of this software in business management. You will complete three questions in this first lesson. You will receive specific step-by-step instructions for the first two questions and will then be directed to complete some parts of the third question "ON YOUR OWN." In this way the new user will build a strong understanding of the basic logic of Lotus 1-2-3. You should feel comfortable taking your time as you complete the first lesson.

It should be noted at the outset that Lessons 1 and 2 will provide you with a thorough familiarity of Lotus 1-2-3 essentials. To include explanations of the underlying logic of 1-2-3, these lessons are necessarily denser and more time consuming than those that follow. The conceptual foundation developed in these two lessons, however, will prove invaluable to your future learning. Divide the lessons into smaller segments as you like and as your time permits.

MANAGEMENT ISSUES

Lesson 1 introduces the basic management concepts of a *brand* and of *market share*. Lotus 1-2-3 helps you calculate the market shares of the leading shampoo brands in units sold, retail revenues, and ounces sold.

MANAGEMENT DISCUSSION QUESTIONS

    1 What is a brand?
    2 Is the shampoo market dominated by any one brand, or concentrated among a few brands?

CASE

Lanznar used the data in Table 3.1 on unit sales, dollar (retail) sales, and ounces sold to answer these first three questions:

    1 What was the market share in unit sales (number of bottles sold) for each brand?
    2 What was the market share in dollar sales for each brand?
    3 What was the market share in ounces for each brand?

These calculations gave her an overview of the relative sales position of different brands of shampoo. Next, she wanted to use these data along with data on advertising expenditures to improve her understanding of the competitive situation.

COMPUTER INSTRUCTIONS

Before you begin this first lesson, once again please be sure you have completed the steps listed in the section "What You Need to Start: A Checklist." These steps will help you to become familiar with PC hardware, the DOS system, and the worksheet and the command system of Lotus 1-2-3. In particular, you should have available a blank, formatted diskette of your own. You will need this blank diskette to save your work.

Loading the Lotus 1-2-3 Software

Now that you have become (or already are) familiar with PC hardware and the use of diskettes, complete these steps:

  1 Load DOS. Enter date and time.
  2 Load the Lotus Access System.
  3 Load the 1-2-3 software program.

Please feel free to review the sections "The Basics of DOS" and "Starting Each Lesson: Loading Lotus 1-2-3" if you need to check on how to complete these necessary steps.

We can now load the data that we will use in Lesson 1.

Loading the Worksheet File for Lesson 1

The data that we will use in each of these 18 lessons are stored in the diskette (enclosed at the back of the book) entitled "Suave Data Diskette." Take this diskette from the back of the book and load it into the appropriate disk drive. (If necessary, review "The Different Releases of 1-2-3: Which Disk Drive to Use for Data Diskettes" for instructions on which disk drive is appropriate.)

Good. Now we're going to begin using Lotus 1-2-3. Just take your time in this lesson and follow carefully the step-by-step, keystroke-by-keystroke instructions. *This should be the most time-consuming lesson for the new user.* Remember, this first lesson contains *detailed* instructions and explanations for the new user.

If you do not need a certain explanation or set of instructions, feel free to skim them or skip them entirely.

Press the following keys:

Description	Keys to Press

Display the 1-2-3 command menus: **/**

(The first menu line displays menu choices, used to execute different commands. The second line offers a helpful explanation of the choice currently highlighted in the command menu. The /Worksheet command is currently highlighted on the first line. The second line shows the next set of commands under the /Worksheet command.)

Select the /File command using the arrow keys: **[right*4] [Enter]**

(Note that the explanations or commands in the second line change as we move to new menu choices.)
(Note: When we press [Enter], the menu that had been in the second line moves up to be displayed in the first line. A new menu is now displayed in the second line. We can also back up a step in our command choices at any time by pressing [Esc].)

Select the Retrieve command: **[Enter]**

(Note that the diskette light turns on momentarily as 1-2-3 "looks" to see which worksheets are present on the diskette. A list of available worksheets is now displayed.)
(The top of the screen will ask for the name of the worksheet to retrieve.)

Select the worksheet LESSON01.WKS, which contains the market data shown in Table 3.1 of the case: **[Enter]**

(1-2-3 proceeds to retrieve the worksheet from the diskette.)

The following screen should appear:

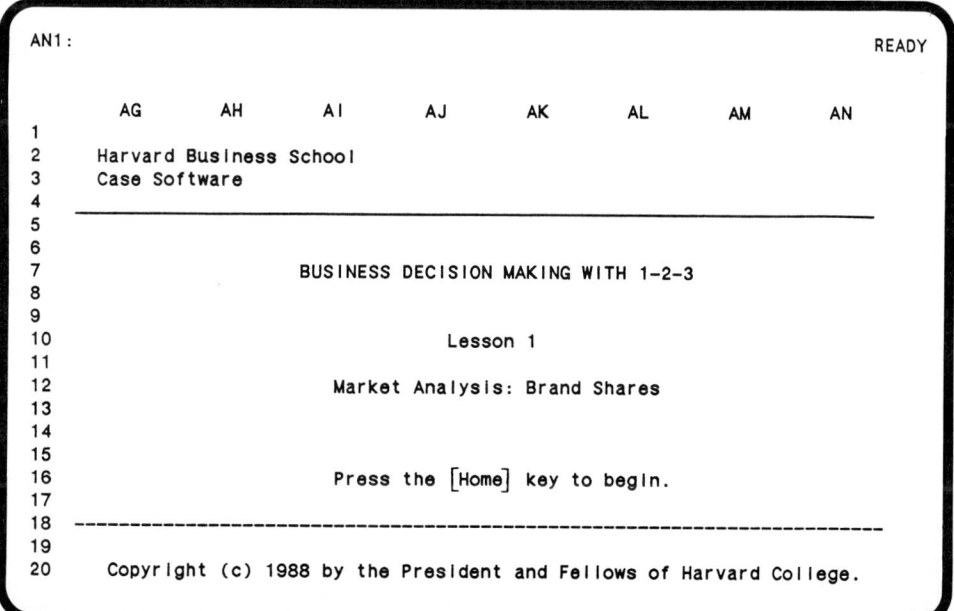

```
AN1:                                                               READY


           AG       AH       AI       AJ       AK       AL       AM       AN
  1
  2    Harvard Business School
  3    Case Software
  4    _____
  5
  6
  7                      BUSINESS DECISION MAKING WITH 1-2-3
  8
  9
 10                                    Lesson 1
 11
 12                         Market Analysis: Brand Shares
 13
 14
 15
 16                      Press the [Home] key to begin.
 17
 18    -------------------------------------------------------------------
 19
 20     Copyright (c) 1988 by the President and Fellows of Harvard College.
```

Press the [Home] key as instructed: **[Home]**

Good. Your screen should appear as follows:

```
A1:  ' LESSON 1                                                          READY


        A         B        C        D        E        F        G        H
1    LESSON 1                                 Table 3.1
2
3                        Unit     Unit    Retail   Dollar   Ounces     Ad
4                        Sales   Market    Sales   Market    Sold   Spending
5    Brand               (mm)    Share    ($mm)    Share    (mm)     ($mm)
6    ---------------   -------- -------- -------- -------- -------- --------
7    Suave              61.0             $104.4             1,161    $6.00
8    Agree              13.8              $25.5               196    $5.51
9    Flex               34.5              $74.2               563    $3.48
10   Head & Shoulders   55.1             $105.5               637   $16.82
11   Jhirmack           21.7              $39.4               124    $9.40
12   Pert               24.9              $41.7               285    $9.43
13   Prell              36.0              $64.9               298   $15.95
14   Silkience          13.8              $30.1               198    $5.22
15   Vidal Sassoon      18.0              $51.0               133   $13.49
16   Generic            11.7              $15.1               182     ---
17   Private Label      36.6              $62.6               695     ---
18   Others            202.9             $545.1             4,088   $32.20
19   ---------------   -------- -------- -------- -------- -------- --------
20   Total             530.0           $1,159.5             8,560  $117.50
```

Note: If you mistakenly choose the wrong command, you can return to the previous menu by pressing the **[Esc]** key. If needed, you can press the **[Esc]** key more than once. Also, you can get out of the command menu system altogether by pressing **[Esc]** enough times until the command menu is no longer displayed and the READY indicator has appeared in the upper right corner of the screen.

Note: You should use your own separate blank, formatted diskette to hold all the new files of data we will create. The Suave Data Diskette does not have enough room for both the files of Lessons 1–18 and your newly created files. Further, the Suave Data Diskette is protected (you can read data from the diskette, but you cannot input any data onto the diskette) to ensure that you always have one complete copy of the files for Lessons 1–18.

So, follow these simple steps:

1 Remove the Suave Data Diskette from the disk drive.
2 Place your own blank (formatted) diskette into that same disk drive.

Now we are ready to answer Question 1 by creating a formula for the unit market share.

QUESTION: **1** What was the market share in unit sales (number of bottles sold) for each brand? Rank in descending order; leave "Others" as the last number.

    Procedure: Divide the unit sales for each brand by the total (530.0). Put in percentage form. Sort.

SOLUTION: To answer this question we will:

1.1 Create a formula for unit market share;
1.2 Copy the formula for all brands;
1.3 Express the results in percentage form; and
1.4 Rank the brands (except "Others") in descending order according to unit market share.

    Note: The solutions to these first few questions will require a significant amount of time to complete for the new user. As you move on to the other questions, procedures similar to the ones learned in these questions will become more familiar and easier to perform. Our goal is to increase your knowledge of 1-2-3 gradually through repetition and reinforcement of previously acquired skills.

    Remember that each worksheet from the Suave Data Diskette includes the solutions, for your convenience. In Lesson 1, the solutions begin in row 101.

1.1 Creating a Formula for Unit Market Share

The formula for calculating "Unit Market Share" for each shampoo brand is:

$$\text{Unit Market Share} = \frac{\text{Brand Unit Sales}}{\text{Total Unit Sales}}$$

Let's enter a formula using "pointing" to calculate this value for Suave shampoo. We'll store the formula in the cell D7. Press the following keys:

Description	Keys to Press
Position the cell pointer to D7 where we'll store the formula:	**[right*3] [down*6]**
Signify that you will begin a formula:	**+**
Point to Suave unit sales in C7:	**[left]**
Confirm that C7 is the cell to use and indicate division:	**/**
Point to total unit sales in cell C19:	**[left] [down*13]**
Confirm and complete formula:	**[Enter]**

Good. The value 0.115094 has appeared in cell D7. This tells us that Suave shampoo has approximately 11.5% of the shampoo market as measured by unit sales. Although we could simply repeat this process 11 more times to calculate the unit market shares for the remaining brands, it would be much easier simply copy the formula we just entered.

Note: When we create a formula using Lotus 1-2-3, we will always signify that we are starting a formula by pressing the + key. Also, after we "point" to a cell by moving the cell pointer, we will both: (1) "confirm" that it is the cell we want, and (2) move on to the next step in the formula by simply pressing one of these keys: addition +, subtraction −, multiplication *, division /, parenthesis), comma (,), period (.), or formula completion [**Enter**].

Note: If you have made a mistake while creating the formula, pressing the [**Esc**] key allows you to back up a step. If needed, you can press the [**Esc**] key more than once. However, if you have "confirmed" the complete formula (by pressing the [**Enter**] key), you can go back to the cell and start over. 1-2-3 will automatically replace the old formula with the new one. (In Lesson 3, we will learn how to use the **/Range Erase** command to erase the contents of any cell.)

Let's now copy the formula for all brands using the 1-2-3 **/Copy** command.

1.2 Copying the Formula for All Brands

The 1-2-3 **/Copy** command permits you to copy the contents of one cell (or range of cells) to another cell (or range of cells). Let's copy the formula for unit market share in cell D7 to the cells D8 through D18. Press the following keys:

Description	*Keys to Press*
(Be sure the cell pointer is at cell D7. Use the arrow keys, if the cell pointer is not already at D7.)	
Display the 1-2-3 command menus:	/
Select the /Copy command using the arrow keys:	**[right*2] [Enter]**
(The top of the screen will ask for the cell range to copy FROM.)	
Confirm D7 as the cell to copy:	**[Enter]**
(The top of the screen will ask for the cell range to copy TO.)	
Position the cell pointer to the first cell to copy TO (D8):	**[down]**
Anchor D8 as the first cell:	.
Move the cell pointer to the last cell to copy TO (D18):	**[down*10]**
(Watch the cell pointer expand.)	
Confirm D18 as the last cell and perform the /Copy command:	**[Enter]**

   Observation: You should see ERR (for "Error") appear in cells D8 through D18. We'll explain this momentarily. Let's first review what just happened.

   Note: The **/Copy** command requires a "cell range" to copy FROM and a "cell range" to copy TO. A cell range is simply one or more adjacent cells which may be part of a row and/or column. In the example above, D7 was being copied to the cell range D8 through D18. We used the period (.) to "anchor" D8 as the first cell in the cell range and then used the remaining **[down]** keys to cover ("paint") the cells from D8 to D18. 1-2-3 displays cell ranges as the starting and ending cell references separated by two periods. Thus the cell range D8 to D18 is shown in the upper left-hand corner as D8...D18.

   Why didn't the unit market share values for each of the other brands calculate? Let's examine the formulas involved.

- Look at the formula in D7 displayed (in the top left corner):   +C7/C20
- Press the **[down]** key once to look at the formula in D8:   +C8/C21
- Press the **[down]** key once more to look at the formula in D9:   +C9/C22

   What happened? Intuitively, it would seem that a **/Copy** command should copy the formula +C7/C20 verbatim into the cells D8 through D18. Instead, the original formula has been adjusted somehow by 1-2-3. Let's pause to rethink our understanding of formulas.

   A formula is simply a mathematical relationship between cells. We specify which cells should be included in the formula by referring to their column letters and row numbers (often called cell references). When you specify a value cell (a cell that contains a value) to be used in a formula, 1-2-3 remembers only the relative distance of the value cell from the cell containing the formula.

   In our worksheet, the formula in D7 (+C7/C20) is conceptualized by 1-2-3 as follows:

   the formula for this cell (D7) is the value of the cell *one cell to the left* (C7) divided by the value of the cell *one cell to the left and 13 cells down* (C20).

When you copy a formula, the *relative* distances in formulas are preserved. Thus, when the formula in cell D7 was copied to D8, the cell references C7 and C20 were changed to C8 and C21, respectively. Let's interpret the formula for cell D8 (+C8/C21) just to check:

   the formula for this cell (D8) is the value of the cell *one cell to the left* (C8) divided by the value of the cell *one cell to the left and 13 cells down* (C21).

Notice that the same holds true for the formulas copied into cells D9 through D18.

Explaining the ERRs

Now that we understand how 1-2-3 copies formulas, we return to the issue at hand, calculating unit market shares. Why are there ERRs in the cells D8 through D18? Press the **[up]** key and look at the formula in D8. Note that although 1-2-3 copied the formula we specified in D7 correctly, the formula in D8 (+ C8/C21) doesn't make any sense since there is no entry in cell C21![1] What we really want for D8 is the formula + C8/C20.

In terms of what 1-2-3 needs to understand during a **/Copy** command, we need to tell 1-2-3 that the first cell reference (C7: unit sales by brand) is *relative* (adjusted when the formula is copied) but that the second cell reference (C20: total unit sales) is *absolute* (not adjusted when the formula is copied).

All the cell references you have entered so far have been "relative." Absolute cell references, as displayed in the upper left corner, look very similar to relative cell references except that the column letter and row number are prefaced by a dollar sign ($). In our situation, instead of using the relative cell reference for total unit sales (C20) we need to use the absolute cell reference, $C$20.

Let's recreate the formula for the unit market share of Suave in D7 using an absolute cell reference for total unit sales (C20) and then copy the formula again for the remaining brands. When we input the new formula, Lotus 1-2-3 will automatically erase the old formula. We'll use pointing to create the formula and the **[F4]** key (called the Absolute **[Abs]** key) to change a cell reference from relative to absolute.

Description	Keys to Press
(Be sure the cell pointer is at cell D7. Use the arrow keys, if the cell pointer is not already at D7.)	
Begin the formula:	**+**
Point to Suave unit sales in C7:	**[left]**
Confirm and indicate division:	**/**
Point to total unit sales in C20:	**[left] [down*13]**
(Get ready to watch the formula displayed in the top left corner change from + C7/C20 to + C7/$C$20.)	
Make this cell reference absolute:	**[F4]**
(This special "function" key is located on the left side of or on top of most IBM and IBM-compatible keyboards.)	
Confirm and complete the formula:	**[Enter]**

[1] As far as 1-2-3 is concerned, empty cells and cells that contain a label have the value zero. Thus, since division by zero is not mathematically possible, 1-2-3 reports the value of the formula + C7/C20 as ERR.

Observation: This is the first time we have used one of the special function keys, labeled F1 to F10. Lotus 1-2-3 has a specific use for each of these keys. We will use many of these function keys in the 18 lessons.

Note: The Lotus 1-2-3 package for 5¼-inch diskettes contains a guide that will help remind you how the function keys are used by Lotus 1-2-3. If you are using a PC with 5¼-inch diskettes, place the guide around the function keys on your PC if you have not done so already.

Let's see how using the **[Abs]** key has changed the formula in D7. The formula we have just entered in D7 (+C7/$C$20) says:

> the formula for this cell (D7) is the value of the cell *one cell to the left* (D7) divided by the value of the cell *C20*.

When this formula is copied, the first cell reference will change, but the second will always remain $C$20.

Now let's copy this formula for the other shampoo brands. Press the following keys:

Description	Keys to Press

(Be sure the cell pointer is at cell D7. Use the arrow keys, if the cell pointer is not already at D7.)

Display the 1-2-3 command menus:	/
Select the /Copy command using the arrow keys:	**[right*2] [Enter]**

(The top of the screen will ask for the cell range to copy FROM.)

Confirm D7 as the cell to copy:	**[Enter]**

(The top of the screen will ask for the cell range to copy TO.)

Position the cell pointer to the first cell to copy TO (D8):	**[down]**
Anchor D8 as the first cell:	.
Move the cell pointer to the last cell to copy TO (D18):	**[down*10]**

(Watch the cell pointer expand.)

Confirm D18 as the last cell and perform the /Copy command:	**[Enter]**

Finally! We now have the correct formulas for the unit market share of each brand. Use the **[up]** and **[down]** keys to examine the formulas you have just created to see that they are correct. Your worksheet should appear as follows:

```
D7:  +C7/$C$20                                                           READY


          A        B      C        D        E        F        G        H
 1   LESSON 1                              Table 3.1
 2
 3                            Unit     Unit     Retail   Dollar   Ounces   Ad
 4                            Sales    Market   Sales    Market   Sold     Spending
 5   Brand                    (mm)     Share    ($mm)    Share    (mm)     ($mm)
 6   ----------------  -------- -------- -------- -------- -------- --------
 7   Suave                    61.0 0.115094   $104.4             1,161    $6.00
 8   Agree                    13.8 0.026037    $25.5               196    $5.51
 9   Flex                     34.5 0.065094    $74.2               563    $3.48
10   Head & Shoulders         55.1 0.103962   $105.5               637   $16.82
11   Jhirmack                 21.7 0.040943    $39.4               124    $9.40
12   Pert                     24.9 0.046981    $41.7               285    $9.43
13   Prell                    36.0 0.067924    $64.9               298   $15.95
14   Silkience                13.8 0.026037    $30.1               198    $5.22
15   Vidal Sassoon            18.0 0.033962    $51.0               133   $13.49
16   Generic                  11.7 0.022075    $15.1               182    ---
17   Private Label            36.6 0.069056    $62.6               695    ---
18   Others                  202.9 0.382830   $545.1             4,088   $32.20
19   ----------------  -------- -------- -------- -------- -------- --------
20   Total                   530.0          $1,159.5             8,560  $117.50
```

Note: The "value" of a formula is independent of whether relative or absolute cell references are used in its creation. In our example above, *we could have entered the unit market share formula for each of the 12 brands one at a time without the need for absolute references.* Only when we tried to use the **/Copy** command did we need to tell 1-2-3 to treat some cell references differently from others.

Having created the formulas for unit market share, let's express these results in percentage form.

1.3 Expressing the Results in Percentage Form

Although 1-2-3 maintains a high degree of numerical precision when calculating formulas, we can request 1-2-3 to change the *appearance* of a cell's contents by altering its display format.

Our current task is to express the results of our unit market share calculations in percentage form. Fortunately, 1-2-3 has a Percent display format which we can use. Let's use the 1-2-3 **/Range Format** command to do this now. Press the following keys:

Description	Keys to Press

(Be sure the cell pointer is at D7. Use the arrow keys, if the cell pointer is not already at D7).

Display the 1-2-3 command menus:	**/**
Select the /Range command using the arrow keys:	**[right] [Enter]**

Description	Keys to Press
Select the Format command:	**[Enter]**
Select the Percent command:	**[right*6] [Enter]**
(The top of the screen will ask for the number of decimal places to display.) *(1-2-3 will display 2 decimal places unless we specify otherwise.)*	
Specify that we want only 1 decimal place:	**1 [Enter]**
(The top of the screen will ask for the cell range which will use this format.)	
Move the cell pointer to the last cell in the range, "covering" the unit market share formulas for all brands:	**[down*11]**
(In the /Range Format command, we do not need to "anchor" first before covering the range.)	
Confirm D18 as the last cell and perform the /Range Format command:	**[Enter]**

Good. You should now see the following:

```
D7: (P1) +C7/$C$20                                                        READY


       A        B        C        D        E        F        G        H
  1  LESSON 1                              Table 3.1
  2
  3                             Unit     Unit    Retail   Dollar   Ounces     Ad
  4                             Sales   Market    Sales   Market    Sold   Spending
  5  Brand                      (mm)    Share    ($mm)    Share     (mm)    ($mm)
  6  -----------------        -------- -------- -------- -------- -------- --------
  7  Suave                       61.0    11.5%  $104.4              1,161    $6.00
  8  Agree                       13.8     2.6%   $25.5                196    $5.51
  9  Flex                        34.5     6.5%   $74.2                563    $3.48
 10  Head & Shoulders            55.1    10.4%  $105.5                637   $16.82
 11  Jhirmack                    21.7     4.1%   $39.4                124    $9.40
 12  Pert                        24.9     4.7%   $41.7                285    $9.43
 13  Prell                       36.0     6.8%   $64.9                298   $15.95
 14  Silkience                   13.8     2.6%   $30.1                198    $5.22
 15  Vidal Sassoon               18.0     3.4%   $51.0                133   $13.49
 16  Generic                     11.7     2.2%   $15.1                182    ---
 17  Private Label               36.6     6.9%   $62.6                695    ---
 18  Others                     202.9    38.3%  $545.1              4,088   $32.20
 19  -----------------        -------- -------- -------- -------- -------- --------
 20  Total                      530.0          $1,159.5            8,560  $117.50
```

Observation: Note that only the *appearance* of cells D7 through D18 has changed. The numerical precision in each cell remains the same.

Also, look at the top corner of the screen. The symbol (P1) indicates that the cell is using the Percent display format with one decimal place. In the worksheet, these cells are displayed in "percentage form" (multiplied by 100 and followed by a percent sign). However, the "value" of cell D7 when used in other calculations is still 0.115094, not 11.5%.[2]

Note: You can always determine the "display format" of a particular cell by moving the cell pointer to the cell and examining its contents as displayed in the top left corner of the screen. The display format will be shown in parentheses ( ) as a letter code and a number. The letter code designates the kind of display format in use, while the number designates the number of decimal places to display.

Having expressed the unit market share values in percentage form, let's rank the brands in descending order.

1.4 Ranking the Brands in Descending Order According to Unit Market Share

1-2-3 has the ability to rearrange groups of cells into either ascending or descending order as part of its database management capabilities.

Look at your worksheet. We need to:

1 Identify which cells to rearrange;
2 Choose a "key" to sort on; and
3 Determine whether we are sorting in ascending or descending order.

To rank the brands, we will use the 1-2-3 **/Data Sort** command. Press the following keys:

Description	Keys to Press
Position the cell pointer to A1:	**[Home]**
(The [Home] key will normally return the cell pointer to A1, except in certain cases explained in later lessons.)	
Display the 1-2-3 command menus:	**/**
Select the /Data command using the arrow keys:	**[right*7] [Enter]**
Select the Sort command using the arrow keys:	**[right*2] [Enter]**
(We now need to ask 1-2-3 which cells we want rearranged.)	
Select the Data-Range menu choice:	**[Enter]**
(1-2-3 will ask us to enter the data range.)	
Move the cell pointer to the top left corner of the cells we wish to rearrange:	**[down*6]**
Anchor A7 as the beginning of our data range:	**.**
Specify the data range to include all brands except "Others" and to include all the data in the work-sheet:	**[down*10] [right*7]**
(The data range A7..H17 should be displayed in the upper left corner of the screen.)	
Confirm our selection for Data-Range:	**[Enter]**

---

[2]Of course, note that 11.5% is the same as 0.115, since the percent sign indicates that the value is to be divided by 100.

Description	Keys to Press

(Note: We needed to specify the data range to include all the data relevant to each brand. If we had not covered columns E, F, G, and H, these data would not be rearranged when columns A, B, C, and D are rearranged. If that happened, rearranged brand names in column A would then be lined up with the wrong data in columns E, F, G, and H.)

(We now need to tell 1-2-3 which column to use as the basis of the sort.)

Select the Primary-Key menu choice using the arrow
keys: **[right] [Enter]**

Move the cell pointer to the Unit Market Share column, whose values will be used to sort the brands: **[right*3]**

(We could use any cell in this column to indicate that this is the column we want.)

Confirm our selection of column D (Unit Market
Share) as our Primary-Key: **[Enter]**

(The top of the screen will ask for either A for sorting in ascending order or D for sorting in descending order.)

Select descending order (by pressing D and then [Enter]): **D [Enter]**

(We now need to tell 1-2-3 to sort the brands.)

Select the Go menu choice using the arrow keys: **[right*3] [Enter]**

Good. The shampoo brands in column A are now ranked in descending order according to unit market share. Your worksheet should now look like this:

```
A1: ' LESSON 1                                                       READY


        A        B        C        D        E        F        G        H
1    LESSON 1                              Table 3.1
2
3                              Unit     Unit    Retail   Dollar   Ounces    Ad
4                              Sales   Market    Sales   Market    Sold   Spending
5    Brand                     (mm)    Share    ($mm)    Share    (mm)    ($mm)
6    ----------------        -------- -------- -------- -------- -------- --------
7    Suave                     61.0    11.5%   $104.4             1,161    $6.00
8    Head & Shoulders          55.1    10.4%   $105.5               637   $16.82
9    Private Label             36.6     6.9%    $62.6               695     ---
10   Prell                     36.0     6.8%    $64.9               298   $15.95
11   Flex                      34.5     6.5%    $74.2               563    $3.48
12   Pert                      24.9     4.7%    $41.7               285    $9.43
13   Jhirmack                  21.7     4.1%    $39.4               124    $9.40
14   Vidal Sassoon             18.0     3.4%    $51.0               133   $13.49
15   Silkience                 13.8     2.6%    $30.1               198    $5.22
16   Agree                     13.8     2.6%    $25.5               196    $5.51
17   Generic                   11.7     2.2%    $15.1               182     ---
18   Others                   202.9    38.3%   $545.1             4,088   $32.20
19   ----------------        -------- -------- -------- -------- -------- --------
20   Total                    530.0           $1,159.5            8,560  $117.50
```

Observation: Notice that all data in columns C, D, E, F, G, and H (except "Others") have been rearranged. This is because we included all these cells (A7..H17) in our data range. As a result, the correct data for each brand are still lined up with that brand's name in column A.

Note: The **/Data Sort** command rearranges the *rows* of cells within the cell range specified by Data-Range. Note that the cells outside of the Data-Range (e.g., "Others") were not affected. We need to remember to include all appropriate columns in the data range, or else information will get misaligned as some columns are rearranged and others are not. The Primary-Key specifies the basis or "key" according to which the sort will be made (in this case according to the unit market share).

Reviewing What We've Learned So Far in Lesson 1

We've covered a lot of material in the first question of this lesson already!

- When you start 1-2-3, the worksheet is empty. We can use the 1-2-3 **/File Retrieve** command to load previously stored worksheets from the diskette into 1-2-3.
- Instead of entering the same formula over and over again, we can use the **/Copy** command to copy a formula from one cell to many cells. In doing so, we discover that relative cell references (e.g., C7) will change in the newly copied cells but that absolute cell references (e.g., $C$20) will not. When we enter a formula using pointing, we can make a cell reference "absolute" by pressing the **[F4] ([Abs])** key.
- The **[Esc]** key allows us to back up any number of steps both in selecting commands and in creating formulas. This key, therefore, is very helpful for correcting mistakes.
- We can change the appearance of any cell in the worksheet by using the **/Range Format** command. We used the Percent display format to display the calculated unit market shares in percentage form. The display format in effect for a given cell is displayed in the top left corner of the screen along with the cell's contents.
- We can rearrange a group of rows within a specified area into either ascending or descending order according to the values in a specified column using the **/Data Sort** command. The group of rows to sort is specified by Data-Range. We used this command to specify all the brands of shampoo except "Others." The column whose value is used to determine the ordering of the rows (the "key") and the order of the sort (ascending or descending) is specified by Primary-Key. We used this command to specify that the sort was to be based upon the values in column D, Unit Market Share, and that the sort was to be in descending order. Finally, the **Go** command was used to complete the sort.

Let's move on to Question 2. With the skills we have just acquired, using 1-2-3 to find the answers will be much easier.

QUESTION: **2** What was the market share in dollar sales for each brand? Sort in descending order, except "Others."

SOLUTION: To answer this question we will:

2.1 Create a formula for dollar market share;
2.2 Copy the formula for all brands;

2.3 Express the results in percentage form; and

2.4 Rank the brands (except "Others") in descending order according to dollar market share.

You have already learned all the skills you need to solve this question from the previous lesson. Let's use this question as a chance to practice these skills. We will still provide step-by-step instructions, but to avoid unnecessary repetition we will leave out many of the explanations provided earlier.

2.1 Creating a Formula for Dollar Market Share

The formula for calculating "Dollar Market Share" for each shampoo brand is:

$$\text{Dollar Market Share} = \frac{\text{Brand Dollar Sales}}{\text{Total Dollar Sales}}$$

Let's enter a formula using "pointing" to calculate this value for Suave shampoo. We'll store the formula in the cell F7. Press the following keys:

Description	Keys to Press
(We will now see how to use another of the function keys: the [F5] or "Go To" key. Follow these steps: (1) press [F5]; (2) type in F7 as either F7 or f7 [you do not need to use the shift key as you type in the letter F]; and (3) then press [Enter].)	
Position the cell pointer to F7:	**[F5] F7 [Enter]**
(We can normally use either the [F5] "Go To" key or the arrow keys to move the cell pointer to a new cell. However, in completing a formula or command, such as specifying a data range in the /Data Sort command, only the arrow keys can be used.)	
Begin the formula:	**+**
Point to Suave retail sales in E7:	**[left]**
Confirm and indicate division:	**/**
Point to total retail sales in E20:	**[left] [down*13]**
Make this cell reference absolute:	**[F4]**
(Do you remember why? If not, return to "Copying the Formula for All Brands" in Section 1.2.)	
Confirm and complete formula:	**[Enter]**

Good. The value 0.090038 has appeared in cell F7. This tells us that Suave shampoo has approximately 9.0% of the shampoo market as measured by retail dollar sales.

Now let's use the **/Copy** command to copy this formula for the remaining brands.

2.2 Copying the Formula for All Brands

Press the following keys:

Description	Keys to Press
(Be sure the cell pointer is at cell F7. Use the arrow keys, if needed.)	
Display the 1-2-3 command menus:	**/**
Select the /Copy command using the arrow keys:	**[right*2] [Enter]**
Confirm F7 as the cell to copy:	**[Enter]**
Position the cell pointer to the first cell to copy TO (F8):	**[down]**
Anchor F8 as the first cell:	**.**
Move the cell pointer to the last cell to copy TO (F18):	**[down*10]**
Confirm F18 as the last cell and perform the /Copy command:	**[Enter]**

Good. Your worksheet should appear as follows:

```
F7:  +E7/$E$20                                                             READY


          A        B        C        D        E        F        G        H
  1   LESSON 1                                Table 3.1
  2
  3                              Unit     Unit     Retail   Dollar   Ounces    Ad
  4                              Sales    Market   Sales    Market   Sold    Spending
  5   Brand                      (mm)     Share    ($mm)    Share    (mm)    ($mm)
  6   ------------------      --------  -------- -------- -------- -------- --------
  7   Suave                      61.0    11.5%   $104.4 0.090038   1,161    $6.00
  8   Head & Shoulders           55.1    10.4%   $105.5 0.090987     637   $16.82
  9   Private Label              36.6     6.9%    $62.6 0.053988     695     ---
 10   Prell                      36.0     6.8%    $64.9 0.055972     298   $15.95
 11   Flex                       34.5     6.5%    $74.2 0.063993     563    $3.48
 12   Pert                       24.9     4.7%    $41.7 0.035963     285    $9.43
 13   Jhirmack                   21.7     4.1%    $39.4 0.033980     124    $9.40
 14   Vidal Sassoon              18.0     3.4%    $51.0 0.043984     133   $13.49
 15   Silkience                  13.8     2.6%    $30.1 0.025959     198    $5.22
 16   Agree                      13.8     2.6%    $25.5 0.021992     196    $5.51
 17   Generic                    11.7     2.2%    $15.1 0.013022     182     ---
 18   Others                    202.9    38.3%   $545.1 0.470116   4,088   $32.20
 19   ------------------      --------  -------- -------- -------- -------- --------
 20   Total                     530.0           $1,159.5           8,560  $117.50
```

Now let's express the results in percentage form.

2.3 Expressing the Results in Percentage Form

To express the dollar market share values just calculated in percentage form, press the following keys:

Description	Keys to Press
(Be sure the cell pointer is at cell F7. Use the arrow keys, if needed.)	
Display the 1-2-3 command menus:	**/**
Select the /Range command using the arrow keys:	**[right] [Enter]**
Select the Format command:	**[Enter]**
Select the Percent command:	**[right*6] [Enter]**
Specify that we want only one decimal place:	**1 [Enter]**
Cover the dollar market share formulas for all brands:	**[down*11]**
Confirm F18 as the last cell and perform the /Range Format command:	**[Enter]**

Good. You should now see the following on your screen:

```
F7:  (P1) +E7/$E$20                                              READY


         A        B       C       D       E       F       G       H
 1    LESSON 1                             Table 3.1
 2
 3                            Unit    Unit   Retail  Dollar  Ounces    Ad
 4                            Sales  Market  Sales   Market  Sold   Spending
 5    Brand                   (mm)   Share   ($mm)   Share   (mm)    ($mm)
 6    -----------------    --------  ------ -------- ------- ------ --------
 7    Suave                   61.0   11.5%  $104.4    9.0%  1,161   $6.00
 8    Head & Shoulders        55.1   10.4%  $105.5    9.1%    637  $16.82
 9    Private Label           36.6    6.9%   $62.6    5.4%    695    ---
10    Prell                   36.0    6.8%   $64.9    5.6%    298  $15.95
11    Flex                    34.5    6.5%   $74.2    6.4%    563   $3.48
12    Pert                    24.9    4.7%   $41.7    3.6%    285   $9.43
13    Jhirmack                21.7    4.1%   $39.4    3.4%    124   $9.40
14    Vidal Sassoon           18.0    3.4%   $51.0    4.4%    133  $13.49
15    Silklence               13.8    2.6%   $30.1    2.6%    198   $5.22
16    Agree                   13.8    2.6%   $25.5    2.2%    196   $5.51
17    Generic                 11.7    2.2%   $15.1    1.3%    182    ---
18    Others                 202.9   38.3%  $545.1   47.0%  4,088  $32.20
19    -----------------    --------  ------ -------- ------- ------ --------
20    Total                  530.0          $1,159.5         8,560 $117.50
```

Remember that only the appearance of cells F7 through F18 has changed. The numerical precision in each cell remains the same.

Let's rank the brands in descending order.

2.4 Ranking the Brands in Descending Order According to Dollar Market Share

Look at your worksheet. We need to:

1 Identify which cells to rearrange;
2 Choose a "key" to sort on; and
3 Determine whether we are sorting in ascending or descending order.

To rank the brands, we will use the 1-2-3 **/Data Sort** command. Press the following keys:

Description	Keys to Press
Position the cell pointer to A1:	**[Home]**
Display the 1-2-3 command menus:	**/**
Select the /Data command using the arrow keys:	**[right*7] [Enter]**
Select the Sort command using the arrow keys:	**[right*2] [Enter]**
(We now need to tell 1-2-3 which cells we want rearranged.)	
Select the Data-Range menu choice:	**[Enter]**
(1-2-3 displays the setting of the last /Data Sort we performed! We can remove the last setting by pressing [Esc] or Reset, as we will learn in Lesson 3. Here, however, we do want to use that previous setting again.)	
Confirm the existing setting for Data-Range:	**[Enter]**
(Notice how easy 1-2-3 made that step by remembering the previous setting.) *(We now need to tell 1-2-3 which column to use as the basis of the sort.)*	
Select the Primary-Key menu choice using the arrow keys:	**[right] [Enter]**
(Note that 1-2-3 also remembered the setting of the last Primary sort key.)	
Move the cell pointer from the Unit Market Share column to the Dollar Market Share column, whose values will be used to sort the brands:	**[right*2]**
Confirm our selection of column F (Dollar Market Share) as our Primary-Key:	**[Enter]**
(1-2-3 will now direct us to choose ascending or descending order. Here again 1-2-3 displays our previous selection of descending order.)	
Confirm the existing selection for descending order:	**[Enter]**
Select the Go menu choice to perform the sort:	**[right*3] [Enter]**

Good. The shampoo brands in column A are now ranked in descending order according to dollar market share. Your worksheet should now look like:

```
A1:  ' LESSON 1                                                      READY


     A        B       C        D        E        F        G        H
 1   LESSON 1                          Table 3.1
 2
 3                           Unit     Unit    Retail   Dollar   Ounces     Ad
 4                           Sales   Market    Sales   Market    Sold   Spending
 5   Brand                   (mm)    Share    ($mm)    Share    (mm)     ($mm)
 6   ----------------       -------- -------- -------- -------- -------- --------
 7   Head & Shoulders         55.1    10.4%   $105.5    9.1%     637    $16.82
 8   Suave                    61.0    11.5%   $104.4    9.0%   1,161     $6.00
 9   Flex                     34.5     6.5%    $74.2    6.4%     563     $3.48
10   Prell                    36.0     6.8%    $64.9    5.6%     298    $15.95
11   Private Label            36.6     6.9%    $62.6    5.4%     695      ---
12   Vidal Sassoon            18.0     3.4%    $51.0    4.4%     133    $13.49
13   Pert                     24.9     4.7%    $41.7    3.6%     285     $9.43
14   Jhirmack                 21.7     4.1%    $39.4    3.4%     124     $9.40
15   Silkience                13.8     2.6%    $30.1    2.6%     198     $5.22
16   Agree                    13.8     2.6%    $25.5    2.2%     196     $5.51
17   Generic                  11.7     2.2%    $15.1    1.3%     182      ---
18   Others                  202.9    38.3%   $545.1   47.0%   4,088    $32.20
19   ----------------       -------- -------- -------- -------- -------- --------
20   Total                   530.0           $1,159.5           8,560   $117.50
```

Note: 1-2-3 will "remember" the previous settings for both the Data-Range and the Primary-Key. In this question, we used the same Data-Range and therefore only had to confirm the previous setting. In fact, since the Data-Range setting did not change, we could have skipped the step completely, although it is good practice to verify the range before proceeding. We did, however, change the Primary-Key and therefore had to move the cell pointer from column D to column F before confirming our choice. 1-2-3 also "remembers" the previous selection for sorting in descending order. Since we wished to sort in descending order again in this question, we only had to confirm our previous choice. In Lesson 3, we will see how we can clear all previous settings by pressing **/Data Sort Reset**.

Reviewing What We've Learned in Question 2

The purpose of this question was to practice what we learned in Question 1. Using only the **/Copy, /Range Format**, and **/Data Sort** commands, we have been able to rank the shampoo brands by dollar market share! We also learned that:

- Many 1-2-3 commands "remember" the last setting used. In **/Data Sort**, 1-2-3 remembers the previous Data-Range and Primary-Key settings used. Any setting which 1-2-3 remembers need not be typed again. However, it is good practice to examine and confirm the previous setting by selecting the menu choice and then just pressing **[Enter]**.
- 1-2-3 also remembers the previous selection for ascending or descending order.

For this command, we have to confirm the previous selection or change to the other selection and then confirm. This step cannot be skipped.

- The **[F5]** "Go To" key can be used instead of the arrow keys to move the cell pointer to a new cell. The key cannot be used, however, in a formula or in a command. Arrow keys, of course, can always be used.

Let's move on to Question 3.

QUESTION: 3   What was the share of ounce volume ("ounce market share") for each brand? Sort in descending order, except "Others." In addition, calculate the total share of ounce volume.

SOLUTION: To answer this question we will:

3.1 Insert a new column between columns G and H in which to place our formulas;
3.2 Create a formula for ounce market share;
3.3 Copy the formula for all brands;
3.4 Express the results in percentage form;
3.5 Rank the brands (except "Others") in descending order according to ounce market share;
3.6 Create a formula for total ounce market share; and
3.7 Express the total in percentage form.

In this question, you will learn a new skill: how to insert a column into a worksheet. You also will be given a chance to practice the skills you learned in the first two questions.

Beginning with this question, the instructions for some 1-2-3 commands and skills which you have already mastered (e.g., creating a formula through pointing, copying a formula, formatting a cell's results) will not be documented with as much detail as in previous lessons. These areas will be identified with the title **ON YOUR OWN** and will list both the general tasks that need to be performed and the specific steps that need to be completed. We will continue to use keystroke detail for introducing new commands. In this way, you can become confident in your ability to use 1-2-3 with less step-by-step guidance.

3.1 Inserting a New Column into a Worksheet

So far we've been storing formulas in columns which have been left blank for us. In this lesson, we will need to insert a column and title it before creating our formulas. Although we could use a blank column further to the right, let's place our results near the Ounces Sold column for clarity.

We can use the 1-2-3 **/Worksheet Insert Column** command to insert one or more columns into a worksheet. Let's insert a single column between columns G and H, where we'll store our formulas for share of ounce volume. Press the following keys:

Description	Keys to Press
Move the cell pointer to any cell in column H; let's use H1:	**[F5] H1 [Enter]**

(We moved the cell pointer to column H instead of column G because the /Worksheet Insert Column command inserts columns to the left of the column containing the cell pointer.)

Display the 1-2-3 command menus:	**/**
Select the /Worksheet command:	**[Enter]**
Select the Insert command:	**[right] [Enter]**
Select the Column menu choice:	**[Enter]**

(The top of the screen will ask you for the column insert range to place the new columns in. 1-2-3 assumes that the range starts and ends in the current column (H1..H1) unless you specify otherwise. The number of columns in the column insert range is the number of blank columns that will be inserted.)

| Confirm the insertion of a single column: | **[Enter]** |

What happened to the original column H, "Ad Spending"? Let's find out. Press the following key:

Description	Keys to Press
Move the cell pointer to any cell in column I, let's use I1:	**[right]**

(The column Ad Spending, formerly in column H, is now in column I!)

    Note: When you insert a column, 1-2-3 shifts the existing columns to the right. Thus, the cells which were formerly in column H are now in column I, the cells formerly in column I are now in column J, and so on. No cells are lost when performing a **/Worksheet Insert** command. *As a matter of fact, 1-2-3 even preserves the relationships in effect prior to the column insertion. Thus, if a formula referred to cell H1 prior to the column insertion, 1-2-3 would change the formula to refer to cell I1 after the column insertion.* This is even independent of whether the cell reference to H1 was relative or absolute. The point is that 1-2-3 ensures that formulas will calculate the same results before *and* after a column insertion.

    Note: When you moved the cell pointer to I1, column A (containing the shampoo brand names) no longer appeared on the screen. This is because the screen can only display a certain number of columns at a time. As you moved to the right, a column on the left was "scrolled" off the side. However, you'll notice that parts of the brand names are still visible in column B *even though the cells in column B are blank!* We'll address this problem in the next lesson.

Release 1A Users: When the column containing the labels (column A) is scrolled off the screen, all the labels in the column are no longer visible. The cells in column B will appear blank.

Good. Now we need to type in a title for the column. Press the following keys:

Description	Keys to Press
Position the cell pointer to cell H3, where we'll store the following words:	**[left] [down*2]**
Type in the label:	**^Ounce [Enter]**

(On most PC keyboards, the ^ symbol is located on the top of the [6] key. Press the [Shift] key to type the ^ symbol.)
(The ^ symbol, like the ' symbol, is used to tell 1-2-3 that the keys that follow are part of a 1-2-3 label. The difference between ^ and ' is that the former centers the label for display, whereas the latter left-justifies the label (starts the label from the left side of the column).)
(The ^ symbol does not appear in cell H3.)

Move the cell pointer to the next cell:	**[down]**
Type in the label:	**^Market [Enter]**
Move the cell pointer to the next cell:	**[down]**
Type in the label:	**^Share [Enter]**
Move the cell pointer to the next cell:	**[down]**
Type in 8 dashes:	**"-------- [Enter]**

(The " symbol, like ^ and ', tells 1-2-3 that the keys which follow are part of a 1-2-3 label. The " symbol is used to right-justify the label (ends on the right side of the column).)

Note: In addition to the ' symbol, we can use ^ and " to inform 1-2-3 that what follows is part of a label. These symbols are called *label-prefixes* and control how a label is displayed within a cell. If you do not specify a specific label-prefix, 1-2-3 will use left-justified.

The following chart highlights the differences between each label-prefix:

'Hi	^Hi	"Hi
Hi	Hi	Hi
Left-justified	Centered	Right-justified

Observation: For labels that are right-justified there is a one character space between the end of the label and the right side of the cell. This space is used for special symbols such as the "%" sign so that the cell can be formatted later.

Let's finish the column by adding an underline in cell H19.

Description	Keys to Press

Move the cell pointer to cell H19: **[F5] H19 [Enter]**

Display the 1-2-3 command menus: **/**

Select the /Copy command using the arrow keys: **[right*2] [Enter]**

(Instead of using the presumed cell range to copy FROM: H19..H19, let's specify our own.)

Press the [Esc] "Escape" key to "back up" a step: **[Esc]**

(Note: 1-2-3 assumes that the cell range to copy FROM always begins at the cell we were in, unless we specify otherwise by pressing [Esc] and then moving to the cell where we want the range to begin.)

Position the cell pointer to the cell to copy FROM
(H6): **[up*13]**

(Note: You cannot use the [F5] key here, in a command. Try it and your PC will beep.)

Confirm H6 as the cell to copy FROM: **[Enter]**

(Note that the cell pointer has returned to H19 so we need only to press [Enter] to confirm.)

Confirm H19 as the cell to copy TO and perform the
/Copy command: **[Enter]**

Good. Your worksheet should appear as follows:

```
H19:  "--------                                                    READY


        B        C        D        E        F        G        H        I
1                                  Table 3.1
2
3                Unit     Unit     Retail   Dollar   Ounces   Ounce    Ad
4                Sales    Market   Sales    Market   Sold     Market   Spending
5                (mm)     Share    ($mm)    Share    (mm)     Share    ($mm)
6       -------- -------- -------- -------- -------- -------- -------- --------
7                55.1     10.4%    $105.5   9.1%     637               $16.82
8                61.0     11.5%    $104.4   9.0%     1,161             $6.00
9                34.5     6.5%     $74.2    6.4%     563               $3.48
10               36.0     6.8%     $64.9    5.6%     298               $15.95
11               36.6     6.9%     $62.6    5.4%     695               ---
12               18.0     3.4%     $51.0    4.4%     133               $13.49
13               24.9     4.7%     $41.7    3.6%     285               $9.43
14               21.7     4.1%     $39.4    3.4%     124               $9.40
15               13.8     2.6%     $30.1    2.6%     198               $5.22
16               13.8     2.6%     $25.5    2.2%     196               $5.51
17               11.7     2.2%     $15.1    1.3%     182               ---
18               202.9    38.3%    $545.1   47.0%    4,088             $32.20
19      -------- -------- -------- -------- -------- -------- -------- --------
20               530.0             $1,159.5          8,560             $117.50
```

Note: When 1-2-3 asks for a cell range (for example with the **/Copy** command, or the **/Data Sort Data-Range** command) a presumed cell range might be displayed. We can tell 1-2-3 to back up a step by using the **[Esc]** key to change the cell range. This gives us the ability to reposition the cell pointer to another starting cell. In the example above, we changed the cell range from H19..H19 to H6..H6.

3.2 Creating a Formula for Ounce Market Share

The formula for calculating "Ounce Market Share" for each shampoo brand is:

$$\text{Ounce Market Share} = \frac{\text{Brand Ounces Sold}}{\text{Total Ounces Sold}}$$

This time, let's have you create the formula on your own. The required steps are almost identical to the ones you followed in Questions 1 and 2. Be sure to review the steps if you wish. We will put the formula in cell **H7**.

ON YOUR OWN: Press The **[Home]** key to return to **A1**, so we can see the brand names in column A. Use the arrow keys to move to **H7** where we will store the formula. Now, press the **+** key to begin the formula. Use the arrow keys to move left to cell **G7**. Press the **/** key to confirm and indicate division. Then, use the arrow keys to move to cell **G20**. Press the **[F4]** key to make this cell reference absolute. Press the **[Enter]** key to confirm and complete the formula.

Good. The value 0.074415 has appeared in cell **H7**. This tell us that Head & Shoulders shampoo has approximately 7.4% of the shampoo market as measured by ounce volume.

Now let's use the **/Copy** command to copy this formula for the remaining brands. Again, let's have you complete this step on your own. If necessary, review the step-by-step instructions in Questions 1 and 2.

3.3 Copying the Formula for All Brands

ON YOUR OWN: Be sure the cell pointer is in cell **H7**. Display the command menus by pressing the **/** key. Select the **/Copy** command. When asked by 1-2-3, confirm **H7** as the cell to **copy FROM** by pressing **[Enter]**. Then when asked by 1-2-3 for the range to **copy TO**, use the **[down]** key to move to **H8**. **Anchor H8** by pressing the **period (.)** key. Use the **[down]** key to move to **H18** covering all brands. Press **[Enter]** to confirm and complete the copying command.

Now let's express these results in percentage form. Again, you can complete this familiar step on your own.

3.4 Expressing the Results in Percentage Form

ON YOUR OWN: Be sure the cell pointer is in cell **H7**. Display the command menus by pressing the **/** key. Select the **/Range** command. Select the **Format** command. Select the **Percent** command. Specify one decimal place by pressing the **1** key and then **[Enter]**. Use the **[down]** key to move to **H18** and cover all brands. Press **[Enter]** to confirm **H18** and perform the formatting command.

Good. You should now see the following:

```
H7: (P1) +G7/$G$20                                                    READY

         A      B      C        D        E        F        G        H
  1   LESSON 1                            Table 3.1
  2
  3                          Unit     Unit     Retail   Dollar   Ounces   Ounce
  4                          Sales    Market   Sales    Market   Sold     Market
  5   Brand                  (mm)     Share    ($mm)    Share    (mm)     Share
  6   -----------------   -------- -------- -------- -------- -------- --------
  7   Head & Shoulders       55.1    10.4%   $105.5    9.1%     637      7.4%
  8   Suave                  61.0    11.5%   $104.4    9.0%   1,161     13.6%
  9   Flex                   34.5     6.5%    $74.2    6.4%     563      6.6%
 10   Prell                  36.0     6.8%    $64.9    5.6%     298      3.5%
 11   Private Label          36.6     6.9%    $62.6    5.4%     695      8.1%
 12   Vidal Sassoon          18.0     3.4%    $51.0    4.4%     133      1.6%
 13   Pert                   24.9     4.7%    $41.7    3.6%     285      3.3%
 14   Jhirmack               21.7     4.1%    $39.4    3.4%     124      1.4%
 15   Silkience              13.8     2.6%    $30.1    2.6%     198      2.3%
 16   Agree                  13.8     2.6%    $25.5    2.2%     196      2.3%
 17   Generic                11.7     2.2%    $15.1    1.3%     182      2.1%
 18   Others                202.9    38.3%   $545.1   47.0%   4,088     47.8%
 19   -----------------   -------- -------- -------- -------- -------- --------
 20   Total                 530.0           $1,159.5          8,560
```

Let's rank the brands in descending order. Once again, you can complete this task on your own.

3.5 Ranking the Brands in Descending Order According to Ounce Market Share

Look at your worksheet. You need to:

1 Identify which cells to rearrange;
2 Choose a "key" to sort on; and
3 Determine whether we are sorting in ascending or descending order.

To accomplish the ranking, you will use the 1-2-3 **/Data Sort** command.
ON YOUR OWN: Press the **[Home]** key to return to **A1**. Press the **/** key to display the command menus. Select the **/Data** command. Select the **Sort** command. Select the **Data-Range** menu choice. (Notice that 1-2-3 again remembered the setting of the last data range. 1-2-3 even adjusted automatically so that the range now includes Column I, since we inserted a new column.) Press **[Enter]** to confirm that you want this existing data range. Select the **Primary-Key** menu choice. (Again, 1-2-3 remembered the last primary key.) Use the **[right]** key to move to **Column H** for **Ounce Market Share.** Press the **[Enter]** key to confirm **Column H** as the column that will be used as the basis of our sort. Then press **[Enter]** again to confirm that you want descending order. Finally, select the **Go** command to complete the sort command.

Good. The shampoo brands in column A are now ranked in descending order according to ounce market share. Your worksheet should now look like:

```
A1:  ' LESSON 1                                                    READY


       A      B      C       D       E       F       G       H
 1   LESSON 1                            Table 3.1
 2
 3                        Unit    Unit    Retail  Dollar  Ounces  Ounce
 4                        Sales   Market  Sales   Market  Sold    Market
 5   Brand                (mm)    Share   ($mm)   Share   (mm)    Share
 6   ----------------     ------  ------  ------  ------  ------  ------
 7   Suave                61.0    11.5%   $104.4  9.0%    1,161   13.6%
 8   Private Label        36.6     6.9%   $62.6   5.4%      695    8.1%
 9   Head & Shoulders     55.1    10.4%   $105.5  9.1%      637    7.4%
10   Flex                 34.5     6.5%   $74.2   6.4%      563    6.6%
11   Prell                36.0     6.8%   $64.9   5.6%      298    3.5%
12   Pert                 24.9     4.7%   $41.7   3.6%      285    3.3%
13   Silkience            13.8     2.6%   $30.1   2.6%      198    2.3%
14   Agree                13.8     2.6%   $25.5   2.2%      196    2.3%
15   Generic              11.7     2.2%   $15.1   1.3%      182    2.1%
16   Vidal Sassoon        18.0     3.4%   $51.0   4.4%      133    1.6%
17   Jhirmack             21.7     4.1%   $39.4   3.4%      124    1.4%
18   Others              202.9    38.3%   $545.1  47.0%   4,088   47.8%
19   ----------------     ------  ------  ------  ------  ------  ------
20   Total               530.0            $1,159.5         8,560
```

3.6 Creating a Formula for the Total Ounce Market Share

The formula for calculating the total share of ounce volume is simply the sum of ounce market shares for all brands. Now we could create a formula which summed the share of ounce volume across each brand, but 1-2-3 provides an easier way, through the "@SUM" function. Press the following keys:

Description	Keys to Press
Position the cell pointer to H20, where we'll store the formula:	[F5] H20 [Enter]
Begin the formula:	+
Use the 1-2-3 @SUM function by typing in the following:	@SUM(
Point to Suave ounce market share in H7:	[PgUp] [down*6]
(Note: The [PgUp], [PgDn], [End], [Tab], and [Shift-Tab] keys can be used just like arrow keys, even in creating a formula.)	
Anchor H7 as the first cell in the cell range for the @SUM function:	.
Point to "Others" ounce market share in H18:	[End] [down] [up]
Complete the @SUM function:	)
Complete the formula:	[Enter]

Good. You should see the value 1 appear in cell H20.

Note: A "function" is a mathematical operation like $+$, $-$, $*$, and $/$, except that it can operate on cell ranges (one or more adjacent cells) as well as individual cells. In the example above, we used the "@SUM" function to compute the total over the cell range H7 through H18. We could have just entered the formula:

$$+H7+H8+H9+H10+H11+H12+H13+H14+H15+H16+H17+H18$$

to achieve the same effect, but using "@SUM" is easier.

Note: In general, you can use any of the cell pointer movement keys (**[up]**, **[left]**, **[right]**, **[PgUp]**, **[PgDn]**, **[Home]**, **[Tab]**, **[Shift-Tab]**, and **[End]** to move to cells at any time, even when you are creating formulas. You will find that these keys permit you to move over large distances more quickly.

The use of the **[End]** key deserves special attention. When used in conjunction with one of the arrow keys **[up]**, **[down]**, **[left]**, and **[right]**), 1-2-3 moves the cell pointer according to the following rules:

1 If the cell pointer is in a blank cell, it is moved to the first nonblank cell encountered in the direction specified by the arrow key.

2 If the cell pointer is in a nonblank cell, it is moved to the last adjacent nonblank cell in the direction specified by the arrow key.

Thus, in our example, we used **[End] [down]** to move the cell pointer from H7 (a nonblank cell) to H19 (the last nonblank cell before a blank cell: H20). You may use this combination to move the cell pointer quickly.

Having calculated the total ounce market share, let's express this result in percentage form. You can complete this step on your own.

3.7 Expressing the Total in Percentage Form

ON YOUR OWN: Be sure the cell pointer is in **H20**. Press **/** to display the command menus. Select the **/Range** command. Select the **Format** command. Select the **Percent** command. Press **1** and then **[Enter]** to specify one decimal place. Press **[Enter]** to confirm that **H20** is the only cell in the range we wish to format to complete the formatting command.

Good. The value 100.0% should have appeared in cell H20.

Observation: For practice, you can use the same procedures to express the Industry Total Unit Market Share in cell D20 and the Industry Total Dollar Market share in cell F20 (each 100.0%).

Reviewing What We've Learned in Question 3

The purpose of this lengthy question was to continue practicing what we learned in Question 1 and to learn the following new procedures:

• We can use the **/Worksheet Insert Column** command to insert one or more columns into a 1-2-3 worksheet. Columns are shifted to the right to make room for the newly inserted columns. Furthermore, 1-2-3 preserves the relationships which existed between cells before the column was inserted. In our situation, the Data-Range setting for the /**Data Sort** command was adjusted to include column I, Ad Spending, which had been previously stored in column H.

- The screen can only display a certain number of columns at a time. When you try to move beyond the edge of the screen, 1-2-3 adjusts the screen so that the new column becomes visible. However, the column on the other side of the screen is no longer in view.

- A "label-prefix" is used by 1-2-3 to denote that what follows is part of a label. The three label prefixes ', ^, and " denote left-justified, centered, and right-justified labels, respectively. When no label-prefix is specified, the label-prefix is assumed to be initially set for left-justified.

- Just as the **[Esc]** key allows us to back up a step when choosing a 1-2-3 command from the menu, it can also be used to back up a step when working within a 1-2-3 command. In this lesson, we learned how to back up within the /**Copy** command in order to respecify the range to copy FROM.

- In addition to the mathematical operators: +, −, *, and /, 1-2-3 provides "functions," which may be used in building formulas. Functions are identified by the @ symbol which precedes the function name. In this lesson, we learned about the @SUM function, which calculates the total of the values in the specified cell range. [1-2-3 also has a number of financial functions using the @ symbol. Interested users can learn easily how to use these on their own or see Lesson 12.]

- In addition to the arrow keys (**[up]**, **[down]**, **[left]**, and **[right]**), you may use the **[PgUp]**, **[PgDn]**, **[Tab]**, **[Shift-Tab]**, **[Home]**, and **[End]** keys for "pointing" at any time, even when creating a formula. In particular, the **[End]** key when used in conjunction with an arrow key may be used to move over large groups of cells quickly. From now on, feel comfortable using these keys whenever appropriate.

Let's now compare our results with the completed Lesson 1 beginning at cell A101. In so doing, we will learn another command often used by managers to move data around a worksheet.

Using the /Move Command

We can move our cell pointer to A101 quickly with the **[PgDn]** or **[F5]** keys. Use whichever one you like:

Description	Keys to Press
Move cell pointer to A101:	(Use the [PgDn] or [F5] keys.)

Look at column H. What happened to the data that was present there? Press the **[Tab]** key to see columns I and J. Remember when we used /**Worksheet Column Insert** to create an empty column for the Ounce Market Share formulas? When we did so, the new column was inserted for *all* rows in the 1-2-3 worksheet.

Let's move the data in columns I and J back to columns H and I. To accomplish this, we'll use the 1-2-3 /**Move** command. First, press the **[Shift-Tab]** key to return to the cell pointer to A101.

To move the data in columns I and J to H and I, respectively, press the following keys:

Description	Keys to Press
Position the cell pointer to I101:	**[right*8]**
Display the 1-2-3 command menus:	**/**
Select the /Move command using the arrow keys:	**[right*3] [Enter]**
Cover columns I and J (cells I101 to J120):	**[End] [down] [End] [down] [right]**
Confirm I101..J120 as the cells to move FROM:	**[Enter]**
(Note: We only need to specify the first cell of the upper-left-hand corner of the range to move TO.)	
Position the cell pointer to the first cell to move TO (H101):	**[left]**
Confirm H101 as the first cell and perform the /Move command:	**[Enter]**
Return cell pointer to A101:	**[Shift-Tab]**

Good. Your worksheet should look like this:

```
 A101:  ' LESSON 1C                                                    READY


        A        B       C        D        E        F        G        H
  101 LESSON 1C                           Table 3.1
  102
  103                            Unit     Unit    Retail   Dollar   Ounces   Ounce
  104                            Sales   Market   Sales    Market   Sold     Market
  105 Brand                      (mm)    Share    ($mm)    Share    (mm)     Share
  106 ----------------         -------- -------- -------- -------- -------- --------
  107 Suave                      61.0    11.5%   $104.4    9.0%    1,161    13.6%
  108 Private Label              36.6     6.9%    $62.6    5.4%      695     8.1%
  109 Head & Shoulders           55.1    10.4%   $105.5    9.1%      637     7.4%
  110 Flex                       34.5     6.5%    $74.2    6.4%      563     6.6%
  111 Prell                      36.0     6.8%    $64.9    5.6%      298     3.5%
  112 Pert                       24.9     4.7%    $41.7    3.6%      285     3.3%
  113 Silkience                  13.8     2.6%    $30.1    2.6%      198     2.3%
  114 Agree                      13.8     2.6%    $25.5    2.2%      196     2.3%
  115 Generic                    11.7     2.2%    $15.1    1.3%      182     2.1%
  116 Vidal Sassoon              18.0     3.4%    $51.0    4.4%      133     1.6%
  117 Jhirmack                   21.7     4.1%    $39.4    3.4%      124     1.4%
  118 Others                    202.9    38.3%   $545.1   47.0%    4,088    47.8%
  119 ----------------         -------- -------- -------- -------- -------- --------
  120 Total                     530.0   100.0%$1,159.5   100.0%    8,560   100.0%
```

Observation: The **/Move** command allows you to relocate a given range of cells from one location to another. Just as when we used the **/Worksheet Insert Column** command, 1-2-3 preserves the relationships between the cells *before* and *after* the command. Note that **/Move** is different from **/Copy** in that the former relocates existing cells, while the latter creates new cells.

Now let's learn how to print our results and save our worksheet.

Using The Print Screen [PrtSc] Key

We have two ways to point out the results of our worksheet:

1 We can easily print out exactly what we see on our screen (no more, no less) by using the Print Screen **[PrtSc]** key.
2 We can use the Lotus 1-2-3 **/Print** command to print a specific range of cells (which might be more or less than shown on any one screen).

Let's first see how the **[PrtSc]** key works. Be sure your printer is attached and ready to receive data from the computer ("online"). Press the following keys:

Description	Keys to Press

Be sure that the original screen from cells A1 to H20
   is showing: **[Home]**

> *(Note that on most personal computers, you will have to hold the [Shift] key down as you press the [PrtSc] key.)*

Press the [PrtSc] key: **[PrtSc]**

> *(Wait for the printer to stop printing.)*

You now have a printed copy of exactly what you see on the screen—including the cell reference in the upper left hand corner and the word "READY" in the upper right hand corner of the screen.

However, notice that we were not able to print the Ad Spending figures in Column I because they were not on the screen. Using the Lotus 1-2-3 **/Print** command, we can print ranges larger than an individual screen.

Note: You can print exactly what you see on the screen *at any time,* just by pressing **[PrtSc].** It is that easy. You just need to be sure that your printer is attached and online.

Now let's see how to use the **/Print** command.

Using the /Print Command to Print a Specific Cell Range

Press the following keys:

Description	Keys to Press
Display the 1-2-3 command menus:	**/**
Select the Print command:	**[right*5] [Enter]**
Select the Printer command:	**[Enter]**
Select the Range menu choice:	**[Enter]**

(The top of the screen will ask for the cell range to print. We want to print the entire table.)

Be sure the cell pointer is at cell A1 and anchor it at the top left corner of the cell range we wish to print: **[Home] .**

Cover our table using the [End] key, the arrow keys, and the [Tab] key: **[End] [down] [End] [down] [Tab]**

Make sure that "Enter Print range: Al..I20" is shown in the upper left corner. Confirm this range: **[Enter]**

(1-2-3 keeps track of the number of lines on each page, making sure that it does not print over the page creases. So we need to tell 1-2-3 that we are starting from the top of a new page. We will do so with the Align menu choice.)

Select the Align menu choice: **[right*5] [Enter]**

(Before you actually begin printing, make sure that your printer is:
    1 Connected to your computer;
    2 Turned on;
    3 "Online" (Ready indicator on); and
    4 Set so that the page crease is just above the printing head.)

Select the Go menu choice to commence: **[right] [Enter]**

(The printer will now print the cell range specified.)

Select the Page menu choice to advance the paper to the next page crease: **[left*4] [Enter]**

Select the Quit menu choice to return to the work-sheet: **[right*5] [Enter]**

Good. Your printer should have produced two pages that show all the results of your work in this lesson. The first page should show columns A through H and the second page should show columns I through P.

Note: Printing with 1-2-3 is easy. All we need to do is to specify a cell range and then say Go! So what was the use of Align all about? 1-2-3 keeps track of the number of lines printed and leaves the top 5 and bottom 5 lines blank to skip over the page creases. Of course, since 1-2-3 can't detect where the top of each page actually is, we need to Align where the paper physically is with 1-2-3's internal line counting. Before printing, it is good practice always to use Align and to make sure the paper is positioned so that the top of the page is just above the print head.

Saving Your Worksheet in a File on Diskette

Just as we used **/File Retrieve** in Question 1 to load the worksheet containing market data, we can use the 1-2-3 **/File Save** command to save our worksheet in a file on our own formatted diskette.

Be sure that you have replaced the Suave Data Diskette with *your own* formatted diskette. Then press the following keys:

Description	Keys to Press
Position the cell pointer to A1:	**[Home]**

(Note: When we retrieve a file, the worksheet will initially be displayed just as it was when the file was saved. So, it is good practice to return to Al just before you save a file, so the worksheet will be displayed at cell Al when you later retrieve it.)*

Display the 1-2-3 command menus:	**/**
Select the /File command:	**[right*4] [Enter]**
Select the Save menu choice:	**[right] [Enter]**

(The top of the screen will ask for a save file name and will list the presumed name: LESSON01.WK1, which will be used if you press [Enter]. Let's instead use the name LN01 for Lesson 1 completed.)

Enter the name LN01 and confirm:	**LN01 [Enter]**

(The diskette drive should turn on while your worksheet is being saved.)

Good! We have saved all our work!

Note: A file name in 1-2-3 cannot contain any space nor can it be more than 8 characters.

We can use the **/File List Worksheet** command to show the worksheets present on the diskette. Let's try it. Press the following keys:

Description	Keys to Press
Display the 1-2-3 command menus:	**/**
Select the /File command:	**[right*4] [Enter]**
Select the List command:	**[right*5] [Enter]**
Select the Worksheet menu choice:	**[Enter]**

(The screen will be cleared and a list of all 1-2-3 worksheets present on the diskette will be displayed. So far, you have placed only one file, LN01.WK1, on your own data diskette. You should see it listed.)

Press the [Enter] key to return to the worksheet:	**[Enter]**

Reviewing What We've Learned About Moving Data, Printing, and Saving Files

In this last part of Lesson 1, we introduced the **/Move** command, the **[PrtSc]** key, and the **/Print, /File Save, /File List** commands.

- The **/Move** command allows you to move data around the worksheet to present results more clearly. The **/Move** command preserves all existing relationships between cells when moving the data.
- The **[PrtSc]** key may be used at any time to print out exactly what appears on the screen. This service is provided by DOS.
- The **/Print** command may be used to print out a specific cell range in a 1-2-3 worksheet. The use of Align synchronizes 1-2-3's internal line counter with the actual physical position of the paper in the printer.
- The **/File Save** command may be used to save the current contents of the worksheet in a file on diskette. The **/File List Worksheet** command may be used to display the names of all the 1-2-3 worksheets on a given diskette.

Congratulations! You have now completed Lesson 1. You have learned many of the essential elements of Lotus 1-2-3 and many of the principal commands that are used in management analysis.

Every lesson from here on will be easier than Lesson 1. We will build on the basic understanding of Lotus 1-2-3 that we gained in Lesson 1 as we learn more about how to use 1-2-3 commands. In addition, we will gain valuable practice to make our use of Lotus 1-2-3 easier and quicker. Finally, and of utmost importance, we will see examples of many uses of Lotus 1-2-3 in business analysis.

MANAGEMENT DISCUSSION

1 What is a brand?

A brand is a name associated with a company's product that allows consumers to identify the product, just as a person's name identifies the person. The brand name may stand for certain characteristics consumers will expect from that product.

2 Is the shampoo market dominated by any one brand or concentrated among a few brands?

Suave is the leading shampoo brand in ounces and units sold; Head & Shoulders is the leading shampoo in dollars sold. It is hard to argue that either of these brands dominates the shampoo market, unlike Campbell's for soup or Heinz for ketchup. In fact, the market is not even highly concentrated among a few brands, as is the U.S. peanut butter market (Skippy, Jiff, and Peter Pan). The shampoo market is fragmented, which means competition is often fierce, many different strategies are pursued, and brands frequently enter or leave the industry.

> **LESSON 2   COMPETITIVE ANALYSIS: PRICING, ADVERTISING,
> AND MARKET SEGMENTATION**

OVERVIEW

COMPUTER INSTRUCTIONS

In Lesson 2, you will practice the essential functions, keystrokes, and commands that were introduced in Lesson 1. In addition, you will learn some new commands and techniques. In some places, Lesson 2 contains complete step-by-step instructions. In other places, Lesson 2 will ask you to complete familiar steps on your own.

Lesson 2 is relatively long. Take your time, take breaks whenever you like (just remember to save your work), and feel comfortable that the lessons to follow build on the concepts learned in these first two lessons.

MANAGEMENT ISSUES

Lesson 2 introduces several critical management concepts and issues: pricing policies, packaging, advertising policies, and market segmentation. The lesson provides a familiarity with these important concepts but is not designed to cover the management issues in depth.

MANAGEMENT DISCUSSION QUESTIONS

1 Why is the range for the retail price per unit narrower than the range for the retail price per ounce?
2 What does the advertising/sales (A/S) ratio tell you about the relative advertising policy for each brand?
3 What additional information is provided by a measure of a brand's share of industry advertising relative to its market share?
4 Why are some brands priced higher per ounce than others?
5 Why do some brands have higher A/S ratios than others?
6 Why do higher-priced brands tend to have higher A/S ratios?
7 What managerial implications can be drawn from a 3-by-3 matrix segmenting the shampoo market by price and the A/S ratio?

CASE

Lanznar thought that the data in Table 3.1 could offer further insight into the strategies and competitive positions of the brands she was analyzing. To understand the pricing, advertising, and positioning of the various brands of shampoo, she asked the following questions.

Pricing Policies for Brands of Shampoo

1 What were the average retail prices per unit for each brand and for the market?
2 What were the average retail prices per ounce for each brand and for the market?
3 What were the average package sizes (in ounces) for each brand and for the market?

Advertising Policies for Brands of Shampoo

4 What was the share of industry advertising spending for each brand?[3]
5 What were the advertising/sales (A/S) ratios for each brand and for the market?[4]
6 Develop an index (base: 100) for each brand that compares that brand's share of industry advertising spending with its market share in dollar sales.

Market Segmentation and Product Positioning

7 Divide the shampoo market into three segments based on price per ounce: low (less than 10¢), medium (10¢–20¢), high (more than 20¢). Which brands are in each segment, excluding "Others"?
8 What was the market share in unit sales of each of the three segments, excluding "Others"?
9 Divide the shampoo market into three segments by the A/S ratio: low (less than 7%), medium (7%–13%), high (more than 13%). Which brands are in each segment, excluding "Others"?
10 What was the market share in unit sales of each of the three segments, excluding "Others"?
11 Develop a 3-by-3 matrix for segmenting the shampoo market by price and the A/S ratio. Which brands are in each segment?

COMPUTER INSTRUCTIONS

Retrieving and Examining the Worksheet File for Lesson 2

To begin Lesson 2, we need to retrieve a new worksheet file from the Suave Data Diskette. First, follow these steps, if necessary:

1 Load DOS. Enter date and time.
2 Load the Lotus Access System.
3 Load the 1-2-3 software program.

---

[3] Some marketing executives referred to a brand's share of advertising spending as that brand's "share of voice."

[4] The advertising-to-sales ratios in this exercise are based on retail sales. Marketing executives often computed advertising-to-sales ratios on manufacturers' sales as well.

Insert the Suave Data Diskette into the appropriate disk drive. (Review the sections on "The Basics of DOS" and on "Starting Each Lesson: Loading Lotus 1-2-3" if you need assistance to complete these steps.)

Now, to retrieve the worksheet file we need, press the following keys:

Description	Keys to Press
Display the 1-2-3 command menus:	/
Select the /File command using the arrow keys:	[right*4] [Enter]
Select the Retrieve command using the arrow keys:	[Enter]
Select the file named LESSON02.WKS:	[right] [Enter]
Press the [Home] key as directed:	[Home]

The first screen appears just as we left it at the end of Lesson 1. Note that we have included the formulas for Total Unit Market Share and for Total Dollar Market Share.

Switch Diskettes: Since you have retrieved the file we need, switch the diskettes back again. Remove the Suave Data Diskette from the disk drive and replace it with your data diskette. This step will prepare you for saving your work on your own data diskette later in the lesson.

Now, let's look at the rest of the worksheet. Press the **[Tab]** key to see how we have labeled and arranged columns I through O to make the exercises in Lesson 2 clearer and easier.

Note that Ad Spending has been moved from column I to column L. Also, we have included labels for columns I, J, K, and M, N, O—where we will put the results of our calculations in Lesson 2. (The labels were not all centered with the ^ symbols, as in Lesson 1, for appearance's sake.) And do not forget to refer to the completed table beginning at row 101 whenever you like.

There are 11 questions in Lesson 2. The first 6 questions involve computations using Lotus 1-2-3. The last 5 questions will ask us to take these computations and to perform some quick but important exercises by hand. Take your time, but you should find that the lesson moves at a much faster pace than Lesson 1.

QUESTION: **1** What were the average retail prices per unit for each brand and for the market?

SOLUTION: To answer this question we will:

1.1 Freeze certain columns as "titles" to prevent them from "scrolling" off the left side of the screen;
1.2 Create a formula for average retail price per unit for each brand;
1.3 Copy the formula for all brands;
1.4 Create a formula for average retail price per unit for the market; and
1.5 Express the results in currency form.

1.1 Using 1-2-3's "Titles" Capability (Vertical)

In our last lesson we inserted a column between column G (Ounces Sold) and column H (Ad Spending). After the new column was inserted, we moved the cell pointer to column I to see what happened. In so doing, column A (containing the brand names) "scrolled" off the left side of the screen. In Lesson 2, we will use not only column I but also columns J through O. But in using these columns, how can we see the brand names in column A that correspond to the data in columns I through O? Although we could use the arrow keys (**[up]**, **[down]**, **[left]**, and **[right]**) to move the cell pointer back and forth, 1-2-3's "titles" capability provides a better alternative.

Let's use the 1-2-3 **/Worksheet Titles** command to "freeze" columns A and B. Press the following keys:

Description	Keys to Press
Let's start at cell A1:	**[Home]**
Position the cell pointer to any cell in column C.	
Let's use C1:	**[right*2]**
(We will "freeze" all columns to the left of this column as "titles.")	
Display the 1-2-3 command menus:	**/**
Select the /Worksheet command:	**[Enter]**
Select the Titles command using the arrow keys:	**[right*5] [Enter]**
Select the Vertical menu choice using the arrow keys:	**[right*2] [Enter]**

Good. Now let's move the cell pointer to the right toward column J and see what happens. Press the following keys:

Description	Keys to Press
Move to column I:	**[right*6]**
(Notice that columns A and B have not moved, but column C has disappeared!)	
Move to column J:	**[right]**
(Notice that columns A and B have not moved, but column D has disappeared!)	

Observation: The **/Worksheet Titles Vertical** command is used to freeze one or more adjacent columns so they do not scroll off the left edge of the screen when the cell pointer moves off the current viewing area (in our example, when we move the cell pointer to columns I and J). Instead, unfrozen columns are scrolled off the screen from left to right (columns C and D above). This feature lets you view both the columns of data that would not normally be on the first screen and the row labels entered on the left (such as shampoo brands) on the same screen. Using this command, we can see the brand names in column A while we are creating formulas in columns I and beyond!

Of course, once one or more columns are frozen as "titles," you can't move past them! Let's see if we can position the cell pointer to A1.

Description	Keys to Press
Press the [Home] key to try to move to A1:	**[Home]**
(Notice that the [Home] key now moves us to cell C1, the top left corner of the part of the worksheet that is not frozen.)	
Try to use the arrow keys to move to A1:	**[left*2]**
(Notice that the cell pointer is still in C1.)	

Observation: The beeps you heard were 1-2-3 telling you it could not complete your request. Once one or more columns have been frozen as "titles," they become part of the display and can no longer be directly accessed.

How do you remove titles? Use the 1-2-3 **/Worksheet Titles Clear** command to return all columns to normal. (Let's leave columns A and B frozen as titles for now.) Note that the analogous capability to freeze rows as "titles" (so that they do not scroll off the top edge of the screen) is available using the 1-2-3 **/Worksheet Titles Horizontal** command.

1.2 Creating a Formula for Average Retail Price per Unit

The formula for calculating "Average Retail Price per Unit" for each shampoo brand is:

$$\text{Average Retail Price per Unit} = \frac{\text{Retail Sales}}{\text{Unit Sales}}$$

Let's enter a formula to calculate this value for Suave shampoo. We'll store the formula in the cell I7. The formula is **I7 = E7/C7**.

Description	Keys to Press
Position the cell pointer to I7 where we'll store the formula:	**[F5] I7 [Enter]**

Note: What happened? The **[F5]** key, when used to move the cell pointer to a *cell not on the screen*, automatically puts that new cell address in the upper-left-hand corner (next to the "frozen" columns). This may not always be desirable.

Description	Keys to Press
Return to C1 by pressing [Home]:	**[Home]**
Starting from C1, position the cell pointer to I7, where we'll store the formula:	**[right*6] [down*6]**
(Note that column C has "scrolled" off the left side of the screen but that columns A and B remain!)	
Begin the formula:	**+**
Point to Suave retail sales in E7:	**[left*4]**
Confirm and indicate division:	**/**
Point to Suave unit sales in C7:	**[left*6]**
Confirm and complete formula:	**[Enter]**

Good. The value 1.711475 has appeared in cell I7. This tells us that the average retail price per unit for Suave shampoo is approximately $1.71.

Notice that we did not use the **[F4]** or **absolute** key in creating this formula. We want the cell references in this formula to be **relative.**

Now let's use the **/Copy** command to copy this formula for the remaining brands.

1.3 Copying the Formula for All Brands

Be sure the cell pointer is at cell I7. In completing this step, we are going to learn a new way to select commands. Press the following keys:

Description	Keys to Press
Display the 1-2-3 command menus:	**/**
Select the /Copy command, this time by pressing the first letter of the command we want:	**C**
(You do not need to press the shift key, just the letter C. We show this letter capitalized, only because that is the way it appears on most PC keyboards.)	
Confirm I7 as the cell to copy:	**[Enter]**
Position the cell pointer to the first cell to copy TO (I8):	**[down]**
Anchor I8 as the first cell:	**.**
Move the cell pointer to the last cell to copy TO (I18):	**[End] [down] [up]**
Confirm I18 as the last cell and perform the /Copy command:	**[Enter]**

Note: This time, we chose the command we wanted by pressing the first letter of the command name. (We did not even need to use the shift key.) This method of choosing commands is often faster than using the arrow keys to move the cursor and then pressing **[Enter].** Additional exercises will help make you more comfortable using this method. Lotus 1-2-3 is programmed to follow either method of entering commands.

Good. Your worksheet should appear as follows:

```
I7:  +E7/C7                                                          READY


        A       B        D        E       F       G       H       I
 1    LESSON 2                           Table 3.1
 2                                                                Average
 3                      Unit    Retail  Dollar  Ounces  Ounce   Retail
 4                      Market  Sales   Market  Sold    Market  Price
 5    Brand            Share   ($mm)    Share   (mm)    Share   Per Unit
 6    --------------   -------- ------- -------- ------- ------- --------
 7    Suave            11.5%   $104.4   9.0%    1,161   13.6%1.711475
 8    Private Label     6.9%    $62.6   5.4%      695    8.1%1.710382
 9    Head & Shoulders 10.4%   $105.5   9.1%      637    7.4%1.914700
10    Flex              6.5%    $74.2   6.4%      563    6.6%2.150724
11    Prell             6.8%    $64.9   5.6%      298    3.5%1.802777
12    Pert              4.7%    $41.7   3.6%      285    3.3%1.674698
13    Silkience         2.6%    $30.1   2.6%      198    2.3%2.181159
14    Agree             2.6%    $25.5   2.2%      196    2.3%1.847826
15    Generic           2.2%    $15.1   1.3%      182    2.1%1.290598
16    Vidal Sassoon     3.4%    $51.0   4.4%      133    1.6%2.833333
17    Jhirmack          4.1%    $39.4   3.4%      124    1.4%1.815668
18    Others           38.3%   $545.1  47.0%    4,088   47.8%2.686545
19    --------------   -------- ------- -------- ------- ------- --------
20    Total           100.0%$1,159.5  100.0%   8,560  100.0%
```

1.4 Creating a Formula for Average Retail Price per Unit for the Market

The formula for calculating the "Average Retail Price per Unit" for the market is simply:

$$\text{Average Retail Price per Unit for the Market} = \frac{\text{Total Retail Sales}}{\text{Total Unit Sales}}$$

Press the following keys:

Description	Keys to Press
Position the cell pointer to I20:	**[F5] I20 [Enter]**

(Notice that we can use the [F5] key here because we have not yet begun the formula.)

Description	Keys to Press
Begin the formula:	+
Point to total retail sales in E20:	[left*4]
Confirm and indicate divison:	/
Point to total unit sales in C20:	[left*6]
Confirm and complete formula:	[Enter]

Good. The value 2.187735 has appeared in cell I20. Having calculated the average retail price per unit for all brands and the market, let's express these results in currency form. This step you can complete on your own.

1.5 Expressing the Results in Currency Form

ON YOUR OWN: Use the **[up]** key to move to cell **I7**. Press **/** to display the command menus. Select the **/Range** command. Select the **Format** command. Select the **Currency** command. (Notice that 1-2-3 initially assumes two decimal places.) Press **[Enter]** to confirm that we do want **two decimals.** Press the **[End]** and then the **[down]** keys to cover all brands and the market, through cell **I20**. Press **[Enter]** to confirm **I20** as the last cell and to perform the formatting command.

Good. You should now see the following:

```
I7: (C2) +E7/C7                                                      READY


          A       B        D        E       F       G       H        I
 1    LESSON 2                    Table 3.1
 2                                                                Average
 3                              Unit    Retail   Dollar  Ounces  Ounce   Retail
 4                              Market  Sales    Market  Sold    Market  Price
 5    Brand                     Share   ($mm)    Share   (mm)    Share   Per Unit
 6    ------------------        ------- -------- ------- ------- ------- --------
 7    Suave                     11.5%   $104.4    9.0%   1,161   13.6%    $1.71
 8    Private Label              6.9%    $62.6    5.4%     695    8.1%    $1.71
 9    Head & Shoulders          10.4%   $105.5    9.1%     637    7.4%    $1.91
10    Flex                       6.5%    $74.2    6.4%     563    6.6%    $2.15
11    Prell                      6.8%    $64.9    5.6%     298    3.5%    $1.80
12    Pert                       4.7%    $41.7    3.6%     285    3.3%    $1.67
13    Silkience                  2.6%    $30.1    2.6%     198    2.3%    $2.18
14    Agree                      2.6%    $25.5    2.2%     196    2.3%    $1.85
15    Generic                    2.2%    $15.1    1.3%     182    2.1%    $1.29
16    Vidal Sassoon              3.4%    $51.0    4.4%     133    1.6%    $2.83
17    Jhirmack                   4.1%    $39.4    3.4%     124    1.4%    $1.82
18    Others                    38.3%   $545.1   47.0%   4,088   47.8%    $2.69
19    ------------------        ------- -------- ------- ------- ------- --------
20    Total                    100.0%$1,159.5   100.0%   8,560  100.0%    $2.19
```

Observation: Doesn't this new format make the numbers clearer? Remember that only the appearance of cells I7 through I20 has changed. The numerical precision in each cell remains the same.

Reviewing What We Learned in Question 1

This question allowed us to practice what we had learned in Lesson 1 and to learn some new capabilities of Lotus 1-2-3:

- The 1-2-3 **/Worksheet Titles** command can be used to freeze one or more adjacent columns as "titles," to prevent them from scrolling off the left side of the screen when you move the cell pointer to the right. Once they are frozen, you cannot normally move the cell pointer left past the rightmost frozen column. The purpose of this command is to keep important information (shampoo brand names in our case) from scrolling off the screen when we need to view columns further to the right.
- We can unfreeze columns by using 1-2-3 **/Worksheet Titles Clear** command.
- We can select commands by either of two methods: (1) by moving the cursor to the command we want and then pressing **[Enter]**, or (2) by simply pressing the first letter of the command we want. This second method can be considerably faster.

Let's move on to Question 2.

QUESTION: **2** What were the average retail prices per ounce for each brand and for the market?

SOLUTION: To answer this question we will:

   2.1 Create a formula for average retail price per ounce for each brand;
   2.2 Copy the formula for all brands;
   2.3 Create a formula for average retail price per ounce for the market; and
   2.4 Express the results in currency form.

Now let's create the formula for average retail price per ounce.

2.1 Creating a Formula for Average Retail Price per Ounce

The formula for calculating "Average Retail Price per Ounce" for each shampoo brand is:

$$\text{Average Retail Price per Ounce} = \frac{\text{Retail Sales}}{\text{Ounces Sold}}$$

Let's enter a formula to calculate this value for Suave shampoo. We'll store the formula in the cell J7. The formula is **J7 = E7/G7.** You can complete this familiar step on your own.

ON YOUR OWN: Move the cell pointer to **J7,** using the arrow keys. Press **+** to begin the formula. Use the arrow keys to point to **E7** for Retail Sales. Press the **/** key to confirm and indicate division. Use the arrow keys to point to **G7** for Ounces Sold. Press **[Enter]** to confirm and to complete the formula.

Good. The value 0.089922 has appeared in cell J7. This tells us that the average retail price per ounce for Suave shampoo is approximately $0.09. Notice again that we used only **relative** cell references in this formula.

Now let's use the **/Copy** command to copy this formula for the remaining brands. You can also complete this familiar step on your own.

2.2 Copying the Formula for All Brands

ON YOUR OWN: Be sure the cell pointer is in cell **J7.** Display the command menus by pressing the **/** key. Select the **/Copy** command. When asked by 1-2-3, confirm **J7** as the cell to **copy FROM** by pressing **[Enter]**. Then when asked by 1-2-3 for range to **copy TO**, use the **[down]** key to move to **J8. Anchor J8** by pressing the **period** key. Use the **[down]** key to move to **J18**, covering all brands. Press **[Enter]** to confirm and complete the copying command.

Good. Your worksheet should now contain a formula for the Average Retail Price per Ounce for each brand. Let's now create a formula for the Average Retail Price per Ounce for the entire market.

2.3 Creating a Formula for Average Retail Price per Ounce for the Market

The formula for calculating the "Average Retail Price per Ounce" for the market is simply:

$$\text{Average Retail Price per Ounce for the Market} = \frac{\text{Total Retail Sales}}{\text{Total Ounces Sold}}$$

We'll store the formula in J20. The formula is **J20 = E20/G20.** You can complete this formula on your own.

ON YOUR OWN: Move the cell pointer to **J20.** Press **+** to begin the formula. Point to **E20** for Total Retail Sales. Press **/** to confirm and indicate division. Point to **G20** for Total Ounces Sold. Press **[Enter]** to confirm and complete the formula.

Good. The value 0.135455 has appeared in cell J20. Having calculated the average retail price per ounce for all brands and the market, let's express these results in currency form.

2.4 Expressing the Results in Currency Form

ON YOUR OWN: Move the cell pointer to **J7**. Press **/** to display the command menus. Select the **/Range** command. Select the **Format** command. Select the **Currency** command. Press **[Enter]** to confirm that we want **two decimals.** Press the **[End]** key and then the [**down**] key to cover all brands and the market. Press [**Enter**] to confirm the cell range and to complete the formatting command.

Good. You should now see the following:

```
J7: (C2) +E7/G7                                                      READY


        A       B        E        F        G        H        I        J
1    LESSON 2           Table 3.1
2                                                           Average  Average
3                       Retail   Dollar   Ounces   Ounce    Retail   Retail
4                       Sales    Market   Sold     Market   Price    Price
5    Brand              ($mm)    Share    (mm)     Share    Per Unit Per Oz.
6    ----------------   -------- -------- -------- -------- -------- --------
7    Suave              $104.4    9.0%    1,161    13.6%    $1.71    $0.09
8    Private Label       $62.6    5.4%      695     8.1%    $1.71    $0.09
9    Head & Shoulders   $105.5    9.1%      637     7.4%    $1.91    $0.17
10   Flex                $74.2    6.4%      563     6.6%    $2.15    $0.13
11   Prell               $64.9    5.6%      298     3.5%    $1.80    $0.22
12   Pert                $41.7    3.6%      285     3.3%    $1.67    $0.15
13   Silkience           $30.1    2.6%      198     2.3%    $2.18    $0.15
14   Agree               $25.5    2.2%      196     2.3%    $1.85    $0.13
15   Generic             $15.1    1.3%      182     2.1%    $1.29    $0.08
16   Vidal Sassoon       $51.0    4.4%      133     1.6%    $2.83    $0.38
17   Jhirmack            $39.4    3.4%      124     1.4%    $1.82    $0.32
18   Others             $545.1   47.0%    4,088    47.8%    $2.69    $0.13
19   ----------------   -------- -------- -------- -------- -------- --------
20   Total            $1,159.5  100.0%    8,560   100.0%    $2.19    $0.14
```

This question allowed us to continue practicing what we already learned. Let's move on to Question 3.

QUESTION: **3** What were the average package sizes (in ounces) for each brand and for the market?

SOLUTION: To answer this question we will:

3.1 Create a formula for average package size for each brand;
3.2 Copy the formula for all brands;
3.3 Create a formula for average package size for the market; and
3.4 Express the results in fixed decimal form.

You should be able to complete all these steps on your own.

3.1 Creating a Formula for Average Package Size

The formula for calculating "Average Package Size" for each shampoo brand is:

$$\text{Average Package Size} = \frac{\text{Ounces Sold}}{\text{Unit Sales}}$$

Let's enter a formula to calculate this value for Suave shampoo. The formula to use is **K7 = G7/C7.** We'll store the formula in the cell K7.

ON YOUR OWN: Move the cell pointer to **K7** using the arrow keys. Press **+** to begin the formula. Use the arrow keys to point to **G7** for Ounces Sold. Press the **/** key to confirm and indicate division. Use the arrow keys to point to **C7** for Unit Sales. Press **[Enter]** to confirm and to complete the formula.

Good. The value of 19.03278 has appeared in cell K7. This tells us that the average package size for Suave shampoo is approximately 19 ounces.

Observation: As we saw above, 1-2-3 will "scroll" the underlying worksheet appropriately so that you may move the cell pointer to any cell when creating a formula.

Note: While in "pointing" mode (that is, while completing a formula), you can position the cell pointer to *any* cell in the worksheet, even those "frozen" using the **/Worksheet Titles** command. Thus, you need not "clear titles" if you create a formula which uses a cell in a "titles" column.

3.2 Copying the Formula for All Brands

ON YOUR OWN: Be sure the cell pointer is in cell **K7.** Display the command menus by pressing the **/** key. Select the **/Copy** command. When asked by 1-2-3, confirm **K7** as the cell to **copy FROM** by pressing **[Enter].** Then when asked by 1-2-3 for the range to **copy TO**, use the **[down]** key to move to **K8. Anchor K8** by pressing the **period** key. Use the **[down]** key to move to **K18** covering all brands. Press **[Enter]** to confirm and complete the copying command.

Good. Your worksheet should now contain a formula for Average Package Size for each brand.

3.3 Creating a Formula for Average Package Size for the Market

The formula for calculating the "Average Package Size for the Market" is simply:

$$\text{Average Package Size for the Market} = \frac{\text{Total Ounces Sold}}{\text{Total Unit Sales}}$$

We'll store the formula in K20. The formula is **K20 = G20/C20.**

ON YOUR OWN: Move to **K20.** Press the **+** key. Point to **G20.** Press **/** to confirm and indicate division. Point to **C20.** Press **[Enter]** to confirm and complete the formula.

Good. The value 16.15094 has appeared in K20. Let's now express our results for all brands and the market in fixed form.

3.4 Expressing the Results in Fixed Form

ON YOUR OWN: Move to **K7.** Press **/** to display the command menus. Select the **/Range** command. Select the **Format** command. Select the **Fixed** command. Press

1 and then **[Enter]** to indicate that we want only **1 decimal** place. Press **[End]** and **[down]** to cover all brands and the market. Press **[Enter]** to confirm the range and perform the formatting command.

Good. You should now see the following:

```
K7:  (F1) +G7/C7                                                        READY


         A        B         F       G       H       I        J        K
1    LESSON 2
2                                                  Average  Average  Average
3                                 Dollar  Ounces  Ounce   Retail   Retail   Package
4                                 Market  Sold    Market  Price    Price    Size
5    Brand                        Share   (mm)    Share   Per Unit Per Oz.  (in oz)
6    -----------------            ------- ------- ------- -------- -------- --------
7    Suave                          9.0%  1,161    13.6%  $1.71    $0.09     19.0
8    Private Label                  5.4%    695     8.1%  $1.71    $0.09     19.0
9    Head & Shoulders               9.1%    637     7.4%  $1.91    $0.17     11.6
10   Flex                           6.4%    563     6.6%  $2.15    $0.13     16.3
11   Prell                          5.6%    298     3.5%  $1.80    $0.22      8.3
12   Pert                           3.6%    285     3.3%  $1.67    $0.15     11.4
13   Silkience                      2.6%    198     2.3%  $2.18    $0.15     14.3
14   Agree                          2.2%    196     2.3%  $1.85    $0.13     14.2
15   Generic                        1.3%    182     2.1%  $1.29    $0.08     15.6
16   Vidal Sassoon                  4.4%    133     1.6%  $2.83    $0.38      7.4
17   Jhirmack                       3.4%    124     1.4%  $1.82    $0.32      5.7
18   Others                        47.0%  4,088    47.8%  $2.69    $0.13     20.1
19   -----------------            ------- ------- ------- -------- -------- --------
20   Total                        100.0%  8,560   100.0%  $2.19    $0.14     16.2
```

The purpose of this question was to continue practicing what we have already learned. In addition, we learned:

- When in the "pointing" mode (e.g., creating a formula), you can position the cell pointer to any cell in the worksheet, even those which are in columns (or rows) "frozen" with the **/Worksheet Titles** command.

Before we move on to Question 4, let's save the work we have completed so far in Lesson 2. You may want to check your results with the completed table beginning at row 101.

Saving Your Worksheet in a File on Diskette

It is a good habit to save your work as often as you like. An electrical plug mistakenly pulled out of the wall socket or a power surge can cause you to lose all the work that has *not* been saved. Once the work is saved, you can shut off your computer; you will always be able to return to your work.

To save your work on Lesson 2, press the following keys:

Description	Keys to Press
Position the cell pointer to C1:	**[Home]**

(Note: Columns A and B are "frozen," so that the cell pointer returns to C1 instead of A1.)

Display the 1-2-3 command menus:	**/**
Select the /File command:	**F**
Select the Save menu choice:	**S**

(The top of the screen will ask for a save file name and will list the presumed name: LESSON02.WK1, which will be used if you press [Enter]. Let's instead use the name LN02—for Lesson 2 completed.)

Enter the name LN02 and confirm:	**LN02 [Enter]**

(The diskette drive should turn on while your worksheet is being saved.)

Now we can continue our work on Lesson 2, knowing that we have saved our answers to the first three questions. As we answer more questions, we can save that work as well, replacing the old LN02 with a new LN02 that contains answers to the first three questions *and* our subsequent work. You can save your work as many times as you like.

Beginning with the fourth question, the instructions will incorporate two changes that will help you to develop further your ability to use 1-2-3 without step-by-step guidance and to gain speed in the use of 1-2-3.

First, when you are directed to complete a familiar task **ON YOUR OWN,** the task will be defined but the specific steps will no longer be outlined. For example, a formula will be given but specific steps (such as to start by pressing the + key) will not be given. You should always feel free to look back at previous instructions to refresh your memory on what steps need to be completed, but you should be developing an ability to complete these tasks without as much guidance.

Second, tasks that you have mastered will be grouped together more concisely. For example, the tasks of creating a formula, copying, and formatting the results will all be included under one heading. You should be gaining speed in completing these tasks and not need to have them described in as much detail in the instructions.

QUESTION: 4 What was the share of industry advertising spending for each brand? Sort in descending order, except "Others."

SOLUTION: To answer this question we will:

    4.1 Create a formula for share of industry advertising spending;
    4.2 Copy the formula for all brands;
    4.3 Create a formula for Total Share of Industry Ad Spending;
    4.4 Express the results in percentage form; and
    4.5 Rank the brands (except "Others") in descending order according to share of industry advertising spending.

The formula for calculating "Share of Industry Advertising Spending" for each shampoo brand is:

$$\text{Share of Industry Advertising Spending} = \frac{\text{Brand Ad Spending}}{\text{Total Industry Ad Spending}}$$

ON YOUR OWN: Create this formula, entering it into cell **M7**. That is, move to cell **M7** and enter the formula:

+L7/$L$20

Be sure to press the **[F4]** key to make the cell reference for **L20 absolute.** (Feel free to review Question 1 in Lesson 1 on how to create formulas with absolute cell references.) After you have completed the formula, look at the top left corner of the screen to be sure that the formula in M7 is exactly as shown here.

Note: Remember, if you make a mistake while creating a formula, use the **[Esc]** key to clear. Also, if you enter a wrong formula, a new one can always be entered to replace the old one. You don't even need to erase the old formula.

Good. The value 0.051063 has appeared in cell M7. This tells us that Suave shampoo accounted for approximately 5.1% of the total advertising dollars spent by the industry.

Now let's use the **/Copy** command to copy this formula for the remaining brands.

ON YOUR OWN: Use the **/Copy** command to copy the formula from cell **M7** to the range of cells **M8 through M18.** That is, the cell range to **copy FROM is M7,** and the cell range to **copy TO is M8..M18.** Remember to **anchor M8** by pressing the **period.**

Good. You should now see the share of industry advertising spending for all brands. Later we will format the results to make them clearer. Let's now sum up all the brand shares and put the total in cell M20.

ON YOUR OWN: Practice using the **@SUM** function by creating a **formula** for Total Share of Industry Ad Spending in **M20.** The formula should add up to **100%,** which of course is equal to **1.** The formula in **M20** should be:

@SUM(M7..M18)

If you wish, review Lesson 1, Question 3, on how to use the @SUM function.

Let's express all these results in percentage form with 1 decimal place.

ON YOUR OWN: Be sure the cell pointer is in **M7.** Use the **/Range Format Percent** command. Specify **1 decimal** place. Cover all brands and the market total by **painting** the range **M7..M20.** Press **[Enter]** to perform the formatting.

The results should be much clearer. Let's now rank the brands in descending order, excluding "Others."

ON YOUR OWN: We've done this before, but since this is a complicated command, here are the specific steps. Invoke the **/Data Sort** command. Select the **Data-Range** command. When 1-2-3 directs you to **Enter Data range,** move to cell **A7.** (Notice that because columns A and B are still "frozen," 1-2-3 will display these columns for a second time to allow us to include them in our data range.) **Anchor A7.** Specify the range to run down to row 17 and across to Column M. That is, paint the range **A7..M17** and press **[Enter]**. Select the **Primary-Key** command. Move to **M7** and press **[Enter]** to specify **Column M** as the primary key. Press **D** and **[Enter]** to select descending order. Press **Go** to perform the sort.

The shampoo brands are now ranked in descending order according to share of industry advertising spending. Your worksheet should appear like this:

```
M7: (P1) +L7/$L$20                                                  READY


        A        B      H       I        J       K        L        M
1    LESSON 2
2                           Average  Average  Average
3                    Ounce   Retail   Retail   Package    Ad     Share of
4                    Market  Price    Price    Size     Spending  Ind. Ad
5    Brand           Share   Per Unit Per Oz.  (in oz)   ($mm)   Spending
6    ---------------  ------- -------  -------  -------  -------  -------
7    Head & Shoulders  7.4%   $1.91    $0.17    11.6    $16.82    14.3%
8    Prell             3.5%   $1.80    $0.22     8.3    $15.95    13.6%
9    Vidal Sassoon     1.6%   $2.83    $0.38     7.4    $13.49    11.5%
10   Pert              3.3%   $1.67    $0.15    11.4     $9.43     8.0%
11   Jhirmack          1.4%   $1.82    $0.32     5.7     $9.40     8.0%
12   Suave            13.6%   $1.71    $0.09    19.0     $6.00     5.1%
13   Agree             2.3%   $1.85    $0.13    14.2     $5.51     4.7%
14   Silkience         2.3%   $2.18    $0.15    14.3     $5.22     4.4%
15   Flex              6.6%   $2.15    $0.13    16.3     $3.48     3.0%
16   Private Label     8.1%   $1.71    $0.09    19.0     ---       0.0%
17   Generic           2.1%   $1.29    $0.08    15.6     ---       0.0%
18   Others           47.8%   $2.69    $0.13    20.1    $32.20    27.4%
19   ---------------  ------- -------  -------  -------  -------  -------
20   Total           100.0%   $2.19    $0.14    16.2   $117.50   100.0%
```

QUESTION: **5** What were the advertising/sales (A/S) ratios for each brand and for the average for the market? Rank in descending order, except for "Others."

SOLUTION: To answer this question, we will:

> **5.1** Create a formula for the advertising to sales ratio;
> **5.2** Copy the formula for all brands;
> **5.3** Create a formula for the advertising to sales ratio for the market;
> **5.4** Express the results in percentage form; and
> **5.5** Rank the brands (except "Others") in descending order according to the advertising to sales ratio.

The formula for calculating "Advertising to Sales Ratio" for each shampoo brand is:

$$\text{Advertising to Sales Ratio} = \frac{\text{Ad Spending}}{\text{Retail Sales}}$$

ON YOUR OWN: Create this formula, entering it into cell **N7**. That is, move to cell **N7** and enter the formula:

$$+ \ L7/E7$$

(Do not use the **[F4]** key, because all cell references are relative.)

Note: You learned about the **[F2]** or **edit** key in the tutorial, where we used it to correct some words or labels. The **[F2]** key can also be used to change or correct a formula. If you wish, try it. Remember to escape "edit mode" by pressing **[Esc]**. The other way to correct a formula, of course, is just to reenter the correct formula.

The value 0.159431 has appeared in cell N7. This tells us that Head & Shoulders advertising represented approximately 15.9% of their retail sales.

Let's now copy this formula to the other brands.

ON YOUR OWN: Use the **/Copy** command to copy the formula from cell **N7** to the range of cells **N8 through N18**. That is, the cell range to **copy FROM is N7,** and the cell range to **copy TO is N8..N18.** Remember to **anchor N8.**

You should see the A/S ratio for each brand. Let's now calculate the average A/S ratio for the entire market. The formula is:

$$\text{Average A/S Ratio for the Market} = \frac{\text{Total Ad Spending}}{\text{Total Retail Sales}}$$

ON YOUR OWN: Create this formula, entering it into cell **N20**. The formula is:

$$+ \ L20/E20$$

The value 0.101336 has appeared in cell N20. Having calculated the average A/S ratio for all brands and the market, let's express all these results in percentage form, with 1 decimal place.

ON YOUR OWN: Be sure the cell pointer is in **N7.** Use the **/Range Format Percent** command. Specify **1 decimal** place. Cover all brands and the market average by **painting** the range **N7..N20,** and then press **[Enter]** to perform the formatting.

The results should be much clearer. Let's now rank the brands in descending order, excluding "Others."

ON YOUR OWN: This time try to perform the sorting with a little less step-by-step guidance. Use the **/Data Sort** command. Select **Data-Range,** and when the old range comes up, **extend** it to the right one column **to cover Column N.** Select **Primary-Key** and move to Column N and press **[Enter].** Confirm **descending** order. Press **Go.**

Note: Many 1-2-3 commands "remember" the last setting used. In **/Data Sort,** the previous Data-Range setting is remembered and can easily be extended to include more data.

Good. The shampoo brands in column A are now ranked in descending order according to their A/S ratios. Your worksheet should now look like:

```
N7: (P1) +L7/E7                                                READY


        A       B       I       J       K       L       M       N
 1    LESSON 2
 2                    Average Average Average
 3                    Retail  Retail  Package   Ad    Share of
 4                    Price   Price   Size    Spending Ind. Ad Ad/Sales
 5    Brand          Per Unit Per Oz. (in oz)  ($mm)  Spending Ratio
 6    ---------------- ------- ------- ------- ------- ------- -------
 7    Vidal Sassoon    $2.83   $0.38    7.4   $13.49   11.5%   26.5%
 8    Prell            $1.80   $0.22    8.3   $15.95   13.6%   24.6%
 9    Jhirmack         $1.82   $0.32    5.7    $9.40    8.0%   23.9%
10    Pert             $1.67   $0.15   11.4    $9.43    8.0%   22.6%
11    Agree            $1.85   $0.13   14.2    $5.51    4.7%   21.6%
12    Silkience        $2.18   $0.15   14.3    $5.22    4.4%   17.3%
13    Head & Shoulders $1.91   $0.17   11.6   $16.82   14.3%   15.9%
14    Suave            $1.71   $0.09   19.0    $6.00    5.1%    5.7%
15    Flex             $2.15   $0.13   16.3    $3.48    3.0%    4.7%
16    Private Label    $1.71   $0.09   19.0    ----     0.0%    0.0%
17    Generic          $1.29   $0.08   15.6    ----     0.0%    0.0%
18    Others           $2.69   $0.13   20.1   $32.20   27.4%    5.9%
19    ---------------- ------- ------- ------- ------- ------- -------
20    Total            $2.19   $0.14   16.2  $117.50  100.0%   10.1%
```

QUESTION: 6 For each brand develop an *index* (base: 100) that compares that brand's share of industry advertising spending with its market share in dollar sales. Sort in descending order, except "Others." Multiply by 100 in the formula.

SOLUTION: To answer this question we will:

6.1 Create a formula for the ad share to market share index;
6.2 Copy the formula for all brands;
6.3 Calculate the index for the entire market (equalling 100.0);
6.4 Express the results in fixed decimal form; and
6.5 Rank the brands (except "Others") in descending order according to the Ad Share to Market Share index.

The formula for calculating the index for "Ad Share to Market Share" for each shampoo brand is:

$$\text{Ad Share to Market Share} = \frac{\text{Share of Industry Ad spending}}{\text{Dollar Market Share}} * 100$$

ON YOUR OWN: Create this formula entering it into cell **O7**. This is the first formula we have seen that requires the use of parentheses. The formula is:

$$+ \ (M7/F7)*100$$

To create this formula, follow these specific steps. Move to cell **07.** Press the **+** key. Press the **(** key, for beginning parenthesis. Move to **M7.** Press **/** to confirm and indicate division. Move to cell **F7.** Press the **)** key, for ending parenthesis. Press ***** for multiplication. Type in the value **100.** Press **[Enter]** to confirm and complete the formula.

Good. The value 261.0205 has appeared in cell O7.

Note: In addition to cell references, we can use numbers (e.g., 100) in formulas. We enter the numbers just by typing them in at the appropriate place. Also, parentheses can be used in Lotus 1-2-3 formulas, just as they are used in regular mathematical formulas, to clarify precisely how a complex formula is constructed. In the absence of parentheses, 1-2-3 follows normal mathematical rules for determining which parts of a formula should be evaluated first. However, it is good practice, just as it is in mathematics, to specify the construction of the formula precisely by using parentheses.

Now let's use the **/Copy** command to copy this formula for the remaining brands. Then copy the formula separately to cell O20, for the entire market.

ON YOUR OWN: Use the **/Copy** command to copy the formula from cell **O7** to cells **O8 through O20.** That is, the cell range to **copy FROM is O7,** and the cell range to **copy TO is O8..O18.** Remember to **anchor O8.**

ON YOUR OWN: Now separately, use **/Copy** to copy the formula **from O7 to O20,** so that the index for the entire market (equalling 100) is entered.

Let's now express all these results in fixed form with 1 decimal place.

ON YOUR OWN: Be sure the cell pointer is in **O7.** Use the **/Range Format Fixed** command. Specify **1 decimal** place. Cover all brands and the market by painting the range **O7..O20,** and press **[Enter]** to perform the formatting.

Once again, the formatting makes our results clearer. Let's now look at the task of ranking the brands (except "Others") in descending order according to the Ad Share to Market Share index.

If you look carefully at the values for the Ad Share to Market Share index (column O), you will notice that they are already in descending order. That is because there is a direct proportional relationship between the A/S ratio and this Ad Share to Market Share index. (This relationship is explained in the section "Management Questions and Discussion.") That was easy!

However, we will want to include column O in our **/Data Sort** data range. In the future, we may want to resort the brands again. If we do not include the data in column O in our data range, these data will not stay aligned with their respective brands, when columns A through N are resorted.

ON YOUR OWN: Invoke the **/Data Sort** command. Select **Data-Range.** When the old range comes up, **extend it to cover Column O,** and then press **[Enter].** Then select the **Quit** menu choice to exit to the **READY** mode (or worksheet).

Note: Several 1-2-3 commands have a Quit menu choice that enables you to exit the command and return directly to the worksheet.

Good. All the work is completed for Question 6. Your worksheet should now look like:

```
07: (F1) (M7/F7)*100                                          READY


         A      B      J        K        L       M       N       O
    1  LESSON 2
    2                Average  Average
    3                Retail   Package    Ad     Share of        Ad Share
    4                Price    Size    Spending Ind. Ad Ad/Sales Mkt Shar
    5  Brand        Per Oz.  (in oz)   ($mm)  Spending Ratio   Index
    6  ----------------  --------  --------  --------  --------  --------  --------
    7  Vidal Sassoon    $0.38    7.4     $13.49   11.5%   26.5%   261.0
    8  Prell            $0.22    8.3     $15.95   13.6%   24.6%   242.5
    9  Jhirmack         $0.32    5.7     $9.40    8.0%    23.9%   235.4
   10  Pert             $0.15   11.4     $9.43    8.0%    22.6%   223.2
   11  Agree            $0.13   14.2     $5.51    4.7%    21.6%   213.2
   12  Silklence        $0.15   14.3     $5.22    4.4%    17.3%   171.1
   13  Head & Shoulders $0.17   11.6     $16.82   14.3%   15.9%   157.3
   14  Suave            $0.09   19.0     $6.00    5.1%    5.7%    56.7
   15  Flex             $0.13   16.3     $3.48    3.0%    4.7%    46.3
   16  Private Label    $0.09   19.0     ---      0.0%    0.0%    0.0
   17  Generic          $0.08   15.6     ---      0.0%    0.0%    0.0
   18  Others           $0.13   20.1     $32.20   27.4%   5.9%    58.3
   19  ----------------  --------  --------  --------  --------  --------  --------
   20  Total            $0.14   16.2     $117.50  100.0%  10.1%   100.0
```

QUESTION: 7 Divide the shampoo market into three segments based on price per ounce: low (below $0.10), medium (between $0.10 and $0.20), and high (above $0.20). Which brands are in each segment, excluding "Others"?

SOLUTION: To answer this question we will:

7.1 Rank the brands in ascending order according to price per ounce;
7.2 Print the Screen; and
7.3 Divide the brands into low, medium, and high segments.

This question is relatively easy to answer. All we need to do is resort our data according to Average Retail Price per Ounce; that is, we just have to change the Primary-key to column J. Then we can print the screen and perform a single segmentation.

ON YOUR OWN: Invoke the **/Data Sort** command. Select **Data-Range** and then press **[Enter]** to confirm the existing range. Select **Primary-key.** Move to a cell in **Column J** and press **[Enter]** to make this column the basis of our new sort. Change to **ascending** order by pressing **A** and then **[Enter].** Press **Go** to perform the sort.

Good. The shampoo brands are now ranked in ascending order according to price per ounce. Your screen should appear as follows:

```
07: (F1) (M7/F7)*100                                                  READY


      A        B      J        K        L        M        N        O
 1  LESSON 2
 2                  Average  Average
 3                  Retail   Package    Ad     Share of          Ad Share
 4                  Price    Size     Spending Ind. Ad  Ad/Sales Mkt Shar
 5  Brand           Per Oz.  (In oz)  ($mm)    Spending Ratio    Index
 6  ---------------  -------  -------  -------  -------  -------  -------
 7  Generic          $0.08    15.6     ----     0.0%     0.0%      0.0
 8  Suave            $0.09    19.0    $6.00     5.1%     5.7%     56.7
 9  Private Label    $0.09    19.0     ----     0.0%     0.0%      0.0
10  Agree            $0.13    14.2    $5.51     4.7%    21.6%    213.2
11  Flex             $0.13    16.3    $3.48     3.0%     4.7%     46.3
12  Pert             $0.15    11.4    $9.43     8.0%    22.6%    223.2
13  Silkience        $0.15    14.3    $5.22     4.4%    17.3%    171.1
14  Head & Shoulders $0.17    11.6   $16.82    14.3%    15.9%    157.3
15  Prell            $0.22     8.3   $15.95    13.6%    24.6%    242.5
16  Jhirmack         $0.32     5.7    $9.40     8.0%    23.9%    235.4
17  Vidal Sassoon    $0.38     7.4   $13.49    11.5%    26.5%    261.0
18  Others           $0.13    20.1   $32.20    27.4%     5.9%     58.3
19  ---------------  -------  -------  -------  -------  -------  -------
20  Total            $0.14    16.2  $117.50   100.0%    10.1%    100.0
```

Let's print this screen out. As we saw in Lesson 1, Lotus 1-2-3 allows us to print out exactly what is showing on our screen with one very easy keystroke. Be sure your printer is turned on and is online. Then press the following keys:

Description	Keys to Press
Press the [PrtSc] key:	**[PrtSc]**
(On many computer keyboards you must press the [Shift] key while you press the [PrtSc] key.)	

Observation: Notice again that everything that appeared on our screen was printed onto the page, including the cell reference in the upper left corner and the word "READY" in the upper-right corner.

Now that we have the brands ranked in ascending order according to price per ounce, it's simple to construct a table by hand using the information on the computer screen, divided according to the following criteria:

- Low (less than $0.10)
- Medium (between $0.10 and $0.20)
- High (above $0.20)

ON YOUR OWN: Divide the brands into price segments just by drawing a few lines on your page at the appropriate places. Draw one line between Private Label and Agree to mark the segmentation between less than versus more than $0.10 per ounce. Draw the second line between Head & Shoulders and Prell to mark the segmentation between less than versus more than $0.20 per ounce. Draw the third line above "Others" to show that we want to separate it out from our analysis.

That's all there is. Let's now answer Question 8, which is even easier.

QUESTION: 8 What was the market share in *unit* sales of each of the three segments, excluding "Others"?

SOLUTION: To answer this question, all we need to do is to look up the unit market share for each brand of shampoo in each segment and then add the shares in each segment. We already calculated unit market shares in column D, so let's examine those results. Press the following keys to see column D:

Description	Keys to Press
Position the cell pointer to D1:	**[F5] D1 [Enter]**

Note: The **[F5]** key normally moves the screen so that the requested cell is displayed in the upper left corner of the worksheet, when moving to a cell *not* on the current screen. Here, however, columns A and B remain on the screen, because they are "frozen."

Finding the values associated with each brand in these segments yields:

Brand	Unit Market Share	Total % for Each Segment	
Generic	2.2%		
Suave	11.5%	20.6%	Low Price
Private Label	6.9%		
Agree	2.6%		
Flex	6.5%		
Pert	4.7%	26.8%	Medium Price (excluding "Others")
Silkience	2.6%		
Head & Shoulders	10.4%		
Prell	6.8%		
Jhirmack	4.1%	14.3%	High Price
Vidal Sassoon	3.4%		

To add each of these segments, we could use the @SUM function or create a formula. But some calculations are easier to do with a hand calculator, or just pencil and paper.

Don't be afraid to take the most efficient route. Using the computer for simple calculations sometimes is more fancy than it is efficient.

QUESTION: 9 Divide the shampoo market into three segments by the A/S ratio: low (below 7%), medium (between 7% and 13%), and high (above 13%). Which brands are in each segment, excluding "Others"?

SOLUTION: To answer the question, we will:

9.1 Rank the brands in ascending order according to the A/S ratio;
9.2 Print the screen; and
9.3 Divide the brands into low, medium, and high segments.

This question is similar to Question 7. All we need to do is resort our data according to A/S ratio. Then we can print the screen and resegment the market.

ON YOUR OWN: Invoke **/Data Sort.** Select **Data-Range** and confirm the existing range by pressing **[Enter]**. Select **Primary-key.** Move the cell pointer to a cell in **Column N** for Ad/Sales Ratio and press **[Enter]** to confirm that this column should be the basis of our sort. Confirm **ascending** order. Then press **Go** to complete the resorting of the data.

Now let's move the table so that column J is lined up next to column B.

ON YOUR OWN: Use the **[right]** key to scroll the table so that **Column J** is aligned next to **Column B.** (Use the **[Scroll-Lock]** key if you scroll too far.)

Good. The shampoo brands are now ranked in ascending order according to their A/S ratios. Your screen should appear like this:

```
07: (F1) (M7/F7)*100                                              READY


          A        B      J        K        L        M        N        O
 1    LESSON 2
 2                      Average  Average
 3                      Retail   Package    Ad     Share of          Ad Share
 4                      Price    Size    Spending Ind. Ad  Ad/Sales Mkt Shar
 5    Brand            Per Oz.  (in oz)   ($mm)   Spending  Ratio    Index
 6    ---------------  -------- -------- -------- -------- -------- --------
 7    Private Label     $0.09    19.0      ---      0.0%     0.0%      0.0
 8    Generic           $0.08    15.6      ---      0.0%     0.0%      0.0
 9    Flex              $0.13    16.3     $3.48     3.0%     4.7%     46.3
10    Suave             $0.09    19.0     $6.00     5.1%     5.7%     56.7
11    Head & Shoulders  $0.17    11.6    $16.82    14.3%    15.9%    157.3
12    Silkience         $0.15    14.3     $5.22     4.4%    17.3%    171.1
13    Agree             $0.13    14.2     $5.51     4.7%    21.6%    213.2
14    Pert              $0.15    11.4     $9.43     8.0%    22.6%    223.2
15    Jhirmack          $0.32     5.7     $9.40     8.0%    23.9%    235.4
16    Prell             $0.22     8.3    $15.95    13.6%    24.6%    242.5
17    Vidal Sassoon     $0.38     7.4    $13.49    11.5%    26.5%    261.0
18    Others            $0.13    20.1    $32.20    27.4%     5.9%     58.3
19    ---------------  -------- -------- -------- -------- -------- --------
20    Total             $0.14    16.2   $117.50   100.0%    10.1%    100.0
```

Let's print this screen out, so we can use it to segment the shampoo brands.

ON YOUR OWN: Be sure your printer is turned on and online. Then press the **[PrtSc]** key.

Now that we have the brand ranked in ascending order according to their A/S ratios, it's simple to construct a table by hand using the information on the computer screen, divided according to the following criteria:

- Low (less than 7%)
- Medium (between 7% and 13%)
- High (above 13%)

ON YOUR OWN: Divide the brands into A/S segments by drawing a couple of lines on your page. Draw one line between Suave and Head & Shoulders. Notice there are no brands between 7% and 13% A/S. Draw another line above "Others" to exclude it from our analysis. That's all we have to do.

Let's now use this segmentation to answer Question 10.

QUESTION: **10** What was the market share in *unit* sales of each of the three segments, excluding "Others"?

SOLUTION: This question is similar to Question 8. To answer it, all we need to do is look up the unit market share figures in column D and then add up the shares in each segment. Press the following keys to see column D:

Description	Keys to Press
Position the cell pointer to D1:	**[F5] D1 [Enter]**

Finding the values associated with each brand in these segments yields:

Brand	Unit Market Share	Total % for Each Segment	
Private Label	6.9%		
Generic	2.2%		
Flex	6.5%	27.1%	Low A/S Ratio (excluding "Others")
Suave	11.5%		
(no brands in segment)		0%	Medium A/S Ratio
Head & Shoulders	10.4%		
Silkience	2.6%		
Agree	2.6%		
Pert	4.7%	34.6%	High A/S Ratio
Jhirmack	4.1%		
Prell	6.8%		
Vidal Sassoon	3.4%		

We could have added up these segments, once again, with the @SUM function or a formula. But if you had a hand calculator available, it was probably easier to use that.

Let's now combine our work in Questions 7 through 10 to produce a segmentation matrix.

QUESTION: **11** Develop a 3-by-3 matrix for segmenting the shampoo market by price and the A/S ratio. Which brands are in each segment?

ON YOUR OWN: Draw a 3-by-3 matrix and label one side **A/S Ratio** and the other side **Price per Ounce.** Then refer to the screens you printed out in Questions 7 and 9 to hand-construct the following table:

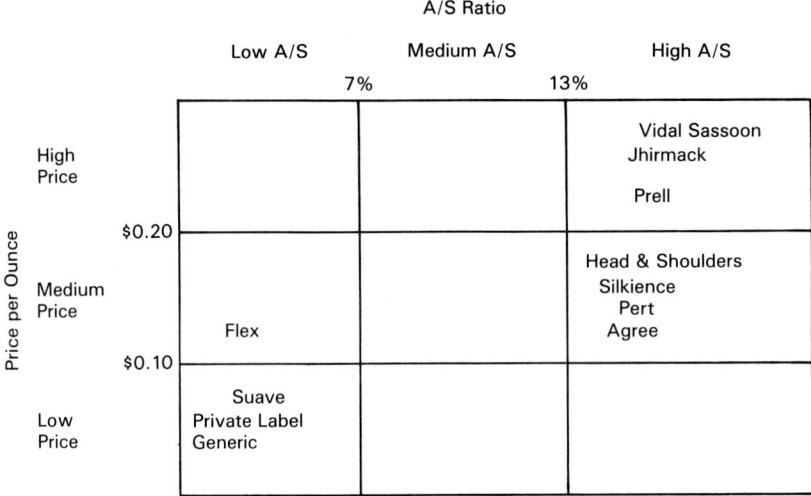

Note: In Lesson 15, we will see how the **Graphics** capability of 1-2-3 could help us to create this table. For now, we need to draw it by hand. Let's now print and save our work.

Printing Your Worksheet on an Attached Printer

The **/Print** command may be used to print any cell range in our worksheet on an attached printer. Let's first clear the "titles" we previously set. Press the following keys:

Description	Keys to Press
Display the 1-2-3 command menus:	**/**
Select the /Worksheet command:	**W**

Description	Keys to Press
Select the Titles command:	**T**
Select the Clear menu choice:	**C**

Observation: Notice that 1-2-3 displays column B again, now that we cleared the **/Worksheet Titles** command.

ON YOUR OWN: Let's make it a little clearer where we are. Press **[Home].** Note that the cell pointer returns to **A1** now that the "titles" have been cleared. Now let's print our work on our printer. Press the following keys:

Description	Keys to Press
Display the 1-2-3 command menus:	**/**
Select the /Print command:	**P**
Select the Printer command:	**P**
(Let's clear all the previous print settings.)	
Select the Clear menu choice:	**C**
Select the All menu choice:	**A**
(We have now cleared all previous settings. Let's now enter a new range.)	
Select the Range menu choice:	**R**
(The top of the screen will ask for the cell range to print. We want to print the entire table.)	
Anchor our position at cell A1:	**.**
Cover our table using the arrow keys and confirm:	**[End] [down] [End] [down] [Tab] [right*7] [Enter]**
(1-2-3 keeps track of the number of lines on each page, making sure that it does not print over the page creases. So we need to tell 1-2-3 that we are starting from the top of a new page.)	
Select the Align menu choice:	**A**
(Make sure that your printer is: 1 Connected to your computer; 2 Turned on; 3 "Online" (Ready indicator on); and 4 Set so that the page crease is just above the printing head.)	
Select the Go menu choice to commence:	**G**
(The printer will now print the cell range specified in Range on your printer.)	
Select the Page menu choice to advance the paper to the next page crease:	**P**
Select the Quit menu choice to return to the worksheet and the READY mode:	**Q**

Good. Your printer should have produced the following two pages of output:

```
LESSON 2                              Table 3.1

                 Unit     Unit     Retail   Dollar   Ounces   Ounce
                 Sales    Market   Sales    Market   Sold     Market
Brand            (mm)     Share    ($mm)    Share    (mm)     Share
----------------  -------- -------- -------- -------- -------- --------
Private Label     36.6      6.9%    $62.6     5.4%      695     8.1%
Generic           11.7      2.2%    $15.1     1.3%      182     2.1%
Flex              34.5      6.5%    $74.2     6.4%      563     6.6%
Suave             61.0     11.5%   $104.4     9.0%    1,161    13.6%
Head & Shoulders  55.1     10.4%   $105.5     9.1%      637     7.4%
Silkience         13.8      2.6%    $30.1     2.6%      198     2.3%
Agree             13.8      2.6%    $25.5     2.2%      196     2.3%
Pert              24.9      4.7%    $41.7     3.6%      285     3.3%
Jhirmack          21.7      4.1%    $39.4     3.4%      124     1.4%
Prell             36.0      6.8%    $64.9     5.6%      298     3.5%
Vidal Sassoon     18.0      3.4%    $51.0     4.4%      133     1.6%
Others           202.9     38.3%   $545.1    47.0%    4,088    47.8%
----------------  -------- -------- -------- -------- -------- --------
Total            530.0    100.0%$1,159.5    100.0%    8,560   100.0%
```

```
     Average  Average  Average
     Retail   Retail   Package    Ad     Share of            Ad Share/
     Price    Price    Size    Spending  Ind. Ad  Ad/Sales Mkt Share
     Per Unit Per Oz.  (in oz)   ($mm)   Spending  Ratio     Index
     -------- -------- -------- -------- -------- -------- --------
       $1.71    $0.09    19.0     ---       0.0%     0.0%      0.0
       $1.29    $0.08    15.6     ---       0.0%     0.0%      0.0
       $2.15    $0.13    16.3    $3.48      3.0%     4.7%     46.3
       $1.71    $0.09    19.0    $6.00      5.1%     5.7%     56.7
       $1.91    $0.17    11.6   $16.82     14.3%    15.9%    157.3
       $2.18    $0.15    14.3    $5.22      4.4%    17.3%    171.1
       $1.85    $0.13    14.2    $5.51      4.7%    21.6%    213.2
       $1.67    $0.15    11.4    $9.43      8.0%    22.6%    223.2
       $1.82    $0.32     5.7    $9.40      8.0%    23.9%    235.4
       $1.80    $0.22     8.3   $15.95     13.6%    24.6%    242.5
       $2.83    $0.38     7.4   $13.49     11.5%    26.5%    261.0
       $2.69    $0.13    20.1   $32.20     27.4%     5.9%     58.3
     -------- -------- -------- -------- -------- -------- --------
       $2.19    $0.14    16.2  $117.50    100.0%    10.1%    100.0
```

Observation: If you examine the printout closely, you will see that the first page contains the columns A through H, and the second contains columns I through P. However, the brand names on the second page are not displayed, making it difficult to read. Let's use the Borders option in the **/Print** command to fix this. We'll explore the Header option, too.

Note: The following set of commands illustrates some relatively sophisticated techniques for printing. This sophistication is not essential. *Feel comfortable skipping this section if you like.*

Press the following keys:

Description	Keys to Press
Be sure the cell pointer is positioned to A1:	**[Home]**
Display the 1-2-3 command menus:	**/**
Select the /Print command:	**P**
Select the Printer command:	**P**
Select the Options command:	**O**
Select the Header menu choice:	**H**

(This option permits you to specify a "header" line which runs across the top of each page. We can use the "|" character to create a three-part heading: left|center|right.)

Enter the "header" line and confirm:	**Lesson 2 Page # [Enter]**

(The "#" character will cause 1-2-3 to number each page sequentially beginning with page 1.)

Select the Borders command:	**B**

(This option is similar to "titles" in that these columns will appear on each page as needed.)

Select the Columns menu choice:	**C**

(We need to indicate which columns will be printed as "borders" on each page—similar to "titles". Let's use columns A and B.)

Anchor the cell pointer in column A, cover column B and confirm:	**. [right] [Enter]**
Select the Quit menu choice to return to the previous menu:	**Q**
Select the Range menu choice:	**R**

(Note that 1-2-3 remembered the settings of the last /Print command! We want to modify the existing Range setting to exclude columns A and B since they are now being printed as "borders." If we don't do this, columns A and B will be printed twice!)

Move to the corners of the existing Range setting (also known as "riding the range"):	**.**

(Note that the blinking underscore has moved from P20 to P1. Whenever 1-2-3 is displaying a cell range, you may use the period (.) to move to the corners of the cell range.)

Move around the existing Range setting some more:	**.**
Reduce and confirm the new Range setting:	**[right*2] [Enter]**
Select the Align menu choice to tell 1-2-3 that the paper is starting on a new page:	**A**

(Make sure the printer is turned on, online, and set to the top of the page.)

Select the Go menu choice to commence:	**G**

Description	Keys to Press
Select the Page menu choice to advance the paper to the next page crease:	**P**
Select the Quit menu choice to return to the worksheet:	**Q**

Good. Your printer should have produced the following three pages of output:

```
Lesson 2 Page 1

LESSON 2                              Table 3.1

                Unit     Unit     Retail   Dollar   Ounces   Ounce
                Sales    Market   Sales    Market   Sold     Market
   Brand        (mm)     Share    ($mm)    Share    (mm)     Share
------------------  --------  --------  --------  --------  --------  --------
Private Label     36.6      6.9%    $62.6      5.4%     695      8.1%
Generic           11.7      2.2%    $15.1      1.3%     182      2.1%
Flex              34.5      6.5%    $74.2      6.4%     563      6.6%
Suave             61.0     11.5%   $104.4      9.0%   1,161     13.6%
Head & Shoulders  55.1     10.4%   $105.5      9.1%     637      7.4%
Silkience         13.8      2.6%    $30.1      2.6%     198      2.3%
Agree             13.8      2.6%    $25.5      2.2%     196      2.3%
Pert              24.9      4.7%    $41.7      3.6%     285      3.3%
Jhirmack          21.7      4.1%    $39.4      3.4%     124      1.4%
Prell             36.0      6.8%    $64.9      5.6%     298      3.5%
Vidal Sassoon     18.0      3.4%    $51.0      4.4%     133      1.6%
Others           202.9     38.3%   $545.1     47.0%   4,088     47.8%
------------------  --------  --------  --------  --------  --------  --------
Total            530.0    100.0%$1,159.5    100.0%   8,560    100.0%
```

```
Lesson 2 Page 2

LESSON 2
                Average  Average  Average
                Retail   Retail   Package    Ad      Share of
                Price    Price    Size     Spending  Ind. Ad  Ad/Sales
   Brand        Per Unit Per Oz.  (in oz)   ($mm)    Spending Ratio
------------------  --------  --------  --------  --------  --------  --------
Private Label     $1.71    $0.09    19.0      ---       0.0%     0.0%
Generic           $1.29    $0.08    15.6      ---       0.0%     0.0%
Flex              $2.15    $0.13    16.3     $3.48      3.0%     4.7%
Suave             $1.71    $0.09    19.0     $6.00      5.1%     5.7%
Head & Shoulders  $1.91    $0.17    11.6    $16.82     14.3%    15.9%
Silkience         $2.18    $0.15    14.3     $5.22      4.4%    17.3%
Agree             $1.85    $0.13    14.2     $5.51      4.7%    21.6%
Pert              $1.67    $0.15    11.4     $9.43      8.0%    22.6%
Jhirmack          $1.82    $0.32     5.7     $9.40      8.0%    23.9%
Prell             $1.80    $0.22     8.3    $15.95     13.6%    24.6%
Vidal Sassoon     $2.83    $0.38     7.4    $13.49     11.5%    26.5%
Others            $2.69    $0.13    20.1    $32.20     27.4%     5.9%
------------------  --------  --------  --------  --------  --------  --------
Total             $2.19    $0.14    16.2   $117.50    100.0%    10.1%
```

```
            Lesson 2 Page 3


            LESSON 2

                             Ad Share/
                             Mkt Share
            Brand              Index
            ----------------  --------
            Private Label        0.0
            Generic              0.0
            Flex                46.3
            Suave               56.7
            Head & Shoulders   157.3
            Silkience          171.1
            Agree              213.2
            Pert               223.2
            Jhirmack           235.4
            Prell              242.5
            Vidal Sassoon      261.0
            Others              58.3
            ----------------  --------
            Total              100.0
```

Observation: The Header option may be used to produce a "header" line at the top of each page. The "#" symbol is used to represent the current page number, beginning with page 1. Also, note that the **/Print** command remembers its previous settings (e.g., Range) just like the **/Data Sort** command. Whenever 1-2-3 is displaying a cell range (as in the Range menu choice of the **/Print** command), you may use the period (.) key to move to the corners of the cell range.

Saving Your Worksheet in a File on Diskette

Just as we did at the end of Lesson 1 and after Question 3 in this lesson, we can use the 1-2-3 **/File Save** command to save our worksheet in a file on diskette. Make sure that *your* data diskette is in the disk drive. Then press the following keys:

Description	Keys to Press
Be sure the cell pointer is positioned to A1:	**[Home]**
Display the 1-2-3 command menus:	**/**
Select the /File command:	**F**
Select the Save menu choice:	**S**

(The top of the screen will ask for a save file name and list the name we used for the first three questions: LN02.WK1, which will be used if you press [Enter].)

Confirm the file name:	**[Enter]**

Description	*Keys to Press*

(Note that 1-2-3 asks whether you want to cancel the command or replace the "old" LN02 with this "new" LN02).

Replace the old file: **R**

Note: The command **/File List Worksheet** will—just as the words indicate—list all the worksheet files on a diskette. This task is easy and very useful if you have a diskette containing many worksheet files. If you are interested, try it. Then press **any key** to return to the **READY** mode.

Reviewing What We've Learned About the /Print and the /File Save Commands

We used both the **/Print** command and the **/File Save** command at the end of Lesson 1. Here at the end of Lesson 2, we practiced what we had learned and saw some new techniques. In summary:

- The **/Print** command may be used to print any cell range in a 1-2-3 worksheet on an attached printer. The use of Align "synchronizes" 1-2-3's internal line counter with the actual physical position of the paper in the printer. For tables which are too large to fit on a single sheet of paper we can use the Borders Columns option to designate certain columns as "print borders" to appear on each page, just as **/Worksheet Titles** permitted us to view the shampoo brand names along with columns I through O. Optional page headers can be created by using the Header option.
- The **/File Save** command may be used to save the current contents of the worksheet in a file on diskette. If a file already exists by a certain name, 1-2-3 permits you to erase the existing file and replace it with a file containing the current contents of the worksheet.
- Whenever 1-2-3 displays a cell range, you may move to the corners of the cell range by successively pressing the period (**.**) key. This capability enables you to save a lot of time if you want to expand or contract the existing cell range.

Let's move on to the analysis of demographic data.

MANAGEMENT DISCUSSION

1 Why is the range for the retail price per unit narrower than the range for the retail price per ounce?

Retail prices per unit ranged from $1.29 to $2.83 in 1983, whereas the average retail price per ounce spread from 8¢ to 38¢ per ounce—nearly a fivefold difference! Brands that were relatively inexpensive per ounce are packaged in large bottle sizes; brands that were relatively expensive, in smaller bottles. One possible explanation is that managers think that consumers consider how much they spend *per bottle* (per unit), not per ounce, so that $2.25 per bottle seems enough to spend at one time, whether the brand of shampoo is expensive or inexpensive.

2 What does the advertising/sales ratio tell you about the relative advertising policy for each brand?

The A/S ratio is a commonly used measure of how important advertising is to the marketing of a particular brand or for an entire industry. Brands with high A/S ratios have a substantial investment in advertising relative to their sales volume; brands with low A/S ratios have little advertising relative to their sales volume.

In 1983, the shampoo market had an A/S ratio over 10%. Shampoo is highly advertised for many reasons, including the nature of the product itself. For example, since shampoo has "hidden" attributes—you can't see if it really works—it will tend to be advertised heavily.

3 What additional information is provided by a measure of a brand's share of industry advertising relative to its market share?

This index is directly proportional to the A/S ratio: Brands with a high A/S ratio have a high index of ad share to market share. This index does provide some additional information, however, because it compares a brand's A/S with the industry's A/S, allowing us to see how intensively a brand is being advertised relative to its competition.

4 Why are some brands priced higher per ounce than others?

Brands which had a high average retail price per ounce in 1983, such as Vidal Sassoon, were being positioned by marketers as premium brands. Marketers of these brands believe that some consumers will decide that these brands provide superior performance or have a desirable image and thereby a higher perceived value than other brands. These consumers may also be more concerned with their hair and therefore will pay a higher price per ounce.

Marketers of brands with a lower price per ounce believe that consumers of those brands are primarily interested in price, that they do not value shampoo enough to pay a higher price per ounce, and that they feel all shampoos are alike.

5 Why do some brands have higher A/S ratios than others?

Brand names can be established and reinforced through advertising. Marketers use advertising to make consumers aware of a new brand, to persuade them that the brand is superior to other brands, or to reinforce the use of that brand. Advertising may also get retailers to carry a brand on their shelves. Brands with a lower A/S ratio may already be well known to consumers or sell on the basis of low price.

It is important to realize that researchers disagree on the role and effects of advertising. Some believe that advertising informs consumers; others believe that it persuades. Suffice it to say here that advertising can be both informative in content and persuasive in intent.

6 Why do higher-priced brands tend to have higher A/S ratios?

To command a higher price for a brand, a marketer must persuade consumers that the brand is superior. For many products, advertising is essential to persuade consumers.

Advertising is not crucial to every industry. In the shampoo market, however, advertising seems extremely important for increasing the perceived product differentiation of several brands. For example, Vidal Sassoon had advertising costs that accounted for 26.5% of total retail sales: 75¢ of the $2.83 price for every bottle. These high advertising expenditures often require higher prices to pay for the advertising.

7 What managerial implications can be drawn from a 3-by-3 matrix segmenting the shampoo market by price and the A/S ratio?

This matrix provides a good introduction to the concept of market segmentation. Managers often divide the market into different parts, since each part or "segment" of the market works differently in some measurable and managerially significant way than the other parts. For example, the types of consumers in the segment might differ in how they buy a product, what they want, or what they can afford. But the type of consumers *within* each segment should be similar in regard to the factor(s) under consideration. For a segment to be economically worthwhile, moreover, it should be substantial in size.

The 3-by-3 matrix shows one way in which the shampoo market might be segmented: according to price and advertising intensity (as measured by the A/S ratio). One interpretation of this matrix is that there are two distinct segments to the shampoo market. In one segment, brands are advertised heavily and are higher priced. In the other segment, brands are not advertised as heavily and they carry a lower price per ounce. Given our previous interpretation of two types of shampoo consumers (Question 4), therefore, there are no brands "in the middle;" consumers either believe some shampoos are superior and are willing to pay more for them or do not believe there are differences and are unwilling to pay more for the higher-priced brands.

This matrix suggests that Suave shampoo competes in a segment with private-label shampoos (under a store's name), generics ("no names"), and Flex.

LESSON 3   CONSUMER ANALYSIS: DEMOGRAPHIC CHARACTERISTICS

OVERVIEW

COMPUTER INSTRUCTIONS

Lesson 3 provides further practice of the essentials of Lotus 1-2-3. In addition, a few new commands are introduced. The instructions periodically require you to complete certain exercises on your own. You can always refer to previous lessons for step-by-step instructions on how to perform these familiar exercises. An index at the back of the book shows where each command was first introduced.

MANAGEMENT ISSUES

Lesson 3 introduces the concepts of consumer analysis, consumer research, and consumer demographic characteristics.

A thorough understanding of consumers is fundamental to marketing success. Different consumers will choose different products. Marketers try to categorize consumers into groups that may share common buying habits. This lesson describes one way in which a manager might categorize consumers: according to demographic characteristics.

MANAGEMENT DISCUSSION QUESTIONS

1 Why do consumer researchers use demographic data?
2 What do the results in Table 3.2 tell you about who disproportionately buys Suave shampoo?
3 What do the results in Table 3.3 tell you about who disproportionately uses Suave shampoo?
4 What is the difference between who *buys* and who *uses* a brand? Since it is usually easier to obtain data on purchase rather than on usage of a product, is it necessary to try to obtain usage data?
5 Which demographic groups do you think a Suave advertising campaign should target?

CASE

Lanznar believed that additional perspective on shampoo consumers, especially the Suave customer, could be gained by examining some demographic data. The comparative demographics for the Suave customer and the total shampoo market would be particularly helpful in assessing Suave's consumer franchise.

TABLE 3.2   DEMOGRAPHIC BUYING DATA

	Percentage of Total Population	Percentage of Total Shampoo Ounces Bought	Percentage of Suave Ounces Bought
Household Income			
Under $8,000	22.0%	10.9%	8.2%
$ 8–11,900	17.5	10.5	12.4
$12–14,900	13.5	10.2	12.1
$15–19,900	18.1	18.1	22.1
$20,000+	28.9	50.2	45.2
Household Size			
1–2	51.9	30.3	22.9
3–4	32.3	41.3	44.9
5+	15.8	28.5	32.2
Age of Female Head of Household			
Under 25	3.9	3.7	4.7
25–34	29.6	31.7	29.2
35–44	15.6	26.9	35.0
45–54	20.0	22.9	20.7
55+	30.9	14.9	10.3
Age of Children			
Oldest under 6	7.3	9.6	11.5
Oldest 6–12	15.7	18.1	19.9
Oldest 13–17	18.4	34.7	39.2
None under 18	58.6	37.5	29.4
Occupation			
Agricultural	3.6	2.9	3.4
Professional/ managerial	33.4	41.4	30.9
Sales/clerical	9.7	14.9	11.7
Skilled blue collar	15.7	16.5	21.5
Unskilled blue collar	15.4	24.5	32.5

Source: Company records; based on research conducted by National Purchase Diary Research, Inc., 1979.

The development of certain indexes would facilitate these comparisons. To create an index, Lanznar needed to divide the figures in one column by the figures in another. Indexes commonly had a base of 100.

The 1979 survey data are shown in Table 3.2. Using the computer, she was able to make repetitive calculations quickly.

Lanznar constructed three indexes for each demographic classification:

1 The percentage of total shampoo ounces bought versus the percentage of the total population represented by the classification.
2 The percentage of Suave ounces bought versus the percentage of total population.
3 The index derived from the ounces in (2) divided by the index derived in (1) (i.e.,

TABLE 3.3 DEMOGRAPHIC USAGE DATA

	Percentage of Shampoo Users	Percentage of Suave Users
Males	46%	45%
Total users 34 and younger	48	62
Users 12 and younger	17	23
Users 17 and younger	24	33
Households of 4+	41	53
Households with $30,000+ income	29	21

an index relating the Suave ounces bought to the total amount of shampoo bought by each group).

The demographic classifications could then be sorted in descending order (within each of the five demographic groupings, e.g., "household income") on the basis of the third index.

Helene Curtis had collected some additional demographic data in a January 1984 consumer survey (Table 3.3). An index based on these data would be useful as well.

COMPUTER INSTRUCTIONS

Retrieving and Examining the Worksheet File for Lesson 3

To begin Lesson 3, we need to retrieve a new worksheet file from the Suave Data Diskette. First, follow these steps, if necessary:

1 Load DOS. Enter date and time.
2 Load the Lotus Access System.
3 Load the 1-2-3 software program.

Insert the Suave Data Diskette into the appropriate disk drive. Then retrieve the worksheet file we need on your own.

ON YOUR OWN: Use the **/File Retrieve** commands to load the worksheet file: **LESSON03.WKS**. Press the **[Home]** key as instructed.

Switch diskettes. Since you have retrieved the file for Lesson 3, you can now switch the diskettes back again. Remove the Suave Data Diskette and replace it with your data diskette.

Let's now see how the data have been organized in this new worksheet. First, notice that the data from Table 3.2 start in the first screen (containing 20 rows) that begins at cell A1.

Press the **[PgDn]** key. The rest of the data from Table 3.2 is located on this screen beginning at cell A21.

Press the **[PgDn]** key twice more. The data from Table 3.3 is located on this screen beginning at cell A61.

Now press the **[Home]** key so that we can begin the lesson.

Pictures of these screens are shown later in the lesson, after some of the exercises have been completed. Let's now move on to Question 1.

QUESTION: **1** Construct the index relating the percentage of total shampoo ounces bought to the percentage of the total population represented by the classification.

SOLUTION: To answer this question we will:

   1.1 Freeze certain rows as "titles" to prevent them from scrolling off the top of the screen;
   1.2 Create a formula for the desired index;
   1.3 Express the result in fixed decimal form; and
   1.4 Copy the formula for all demographic groups.

The lesson will begin with step-by-step instructions for the **/Worksheet Titles** command. It will then ask you to complete most of the remaining exercises on your own.

1.1 Using 1-2-3's Title Capability (Horizontal)

Just as we were able to freeze certain columns, we can do the same thing for certain rows. Let's use the **/Worksheet Titles** command to freeze rows 1 through 7 as "titles." Press the following keys:

Description	*Keys to Press*
Position the cell pointer to any cell in row 8.	
Let's use A8:	**(Use arrow keys or [F5].)**
(We will "freeze" all rows above *this row as "titles.")*	
Display the 1-2-3 command menus:	**/**
Select the /Worksheet command:	**W**
Select the Titles command:	**T**
Select the Horizontal menu choice:	**H**

Good. Now let's move the cell pointer down toward row 21 and see what happens.

Description	Keys to Press
Move to row 21:	**[down*13]**

(Notice that rows 1 through 7 have not moved, but row 8 has disappeared!)

Move to row 22:	**[down]**

(Notice that rows 1 through 7 have not moved, but row 9 has disappeared!)

Note: The **/Worksheet Titles Horizontal** command is used to freeze one or more adjacent rows as "titles" so they do not scroll off the top edge of the screen when the cell pointer moves below the current viewing area (in our example, to rows 21 and 22). This feature permits you to view both the rows of data below row 20 and the column labels entered on top (such as "% of Total Population") on the same screen.

Press the **[Home]** key to return to cell **A8**. Remember, when "titles" are in effect, you cannot position the cell pointer in any of the "frozen" rows. The **[Home]** key will return you to the cell as close as possible to **A1**.

1.2 Creating a Formula for the Desired Index

ON YOUR OWN: Create a **formula** in **F1O** (Household Income under $8,000) which **divides** the "Percent of Total Shampoo Ounces Bought" **(D10) by** the "Percent of Total Population" **(C10) and multiplies** this value **by 100.**

That is, on your own, move to cell **F10;** then use the formula key and the cell pointer to create this formula:

$$+(D10/C10)*100$$

Note: The parentheses are not necessary for this formula, but using parentheses is good practice for complex formulas. If you do not use parentheses, 1-2-3 will follow standard mathematical precedence rules for determining which parts of a complex formula should be calculated first. Using parentheses in the more complex formulas, however, helps to prevent confusion and mistakes.

The value **49.54545** should have appeared in cell **F10.**

1.3 Expressing the Result in Fixed Decimal Form

Instead of copying the formula just created to all demographic groups, let's first express the result in F10 in Fixed format with zero decimal places. We will later see how formatting the result in F10 before copying the formula can save us considerable time.

ON YOUR OWN: Use the **/Range Format Fixed** command to express the result in **F10** in **Fixed** format with **zero decimal** places. The appearance of cell **F10** should have changed to **50.**

Now let's use the **/Copy** command to copy this formula for the remaining demographic groups.

1.4 Copying the Formula for All Demographic Groups

We need to create the same index that we created in F10 for each of the categories in all five demographic groups listed in Table 3.2. That is, we need to copy the formula in F10 over to the following five ranges of cells:

Demographic Group	Cell Range
Household income	F11..F14
Household size	F17..F19
Age of the female head of household	F22..F26
Age of children	F29..F32
Occupation	F35..F39

In each case, you will copy *from cell F10* to one of the five ranges listed above.

Note: You will have to perform the **/Copy** command five separate times, because there are blank cells in between each of these ranges (e.g., F15..F16).

If you copy all at once straight through F11 to F39, the symbol ERR will appear in the cells that should be blank. Just to see what happens, let's copy F10 to a blank cell and find out what we should do if ERR appears. We will learn how to erase the contents of a cell and remove its display format. Press the following keys:

Description	Keys to Press
Position the cell pointer in F10:	**(Use arrow keys, if needed.)**
Display the 1-2-3 command menus:	**/**
Select the /Copy command:	**C**
Confirm F10 as the cell to copy FROM:	**[Enter]**
Move to F11 as the first cell to copy TO:	**[down]**
Anchor F11:	**.**
Paint the range down to F16:	**[down*5]**
(Recall the term "paint the range" is a commonly used phrase for covering a range of cells.)	
Confirm the range and complete the command:	**[Enter]**

Observation: Although appropriate values appear in F11 through F14, ERR appears in F15 and F16. That is because the formulas for F15 and F16 include division by a zero (C15 and C16, respectively). Your screen should look like:

```
 F10: (F0) (D10/C10)*100                                              READY


           A        B        C        D        E        F        G        H
 1      LESSON 3                               Table 3.2
 2
 3                                    % of     % of     -------- Indexes ----------
 4                           % of     Total    Suave    % Shampoo % Suave  % Suave
 5                           Total    Shampoo  Ounces   Oz /     Oz /       /
 6                           Pop.     Oz Bought Bought  % Pop.   % Pop.   % Shampoo
 7                           -------- -------- -------- -------- -------- --------
 8
 9      Household Income (000):
 10     <$8               22.0%    10.9%     8.2%     50
 11     $8-$12            17.5%    10.5%    12.4%     60
 12     $12-$15           13.5%    10.2%    12.1%     76
 13     $15-$20           18.1%    18.1%    22.1%    100
 14     >$20              28.9%    50.2%    45.2%    174
 15                                                  ERR
 16     Household Size:                              ERR
 17     1 - 2             51.9%    30.3%    22.9%
 18     3 - 4             32.3%    41.3%    44.9%
 19     5 +               15.8%    28.5%    32.2%
 20
```

Note: Unlike previous lessons, this time we formatted the cell *before* copying it to other cells. When a cell is copied, the format of the cell (listed in parentheses in the top left corner of the screen) is also copied. Thus, you can do these steps in either order. However, notice that we saved ourselves time by formatting first and copying second because we had to anchor and paint the range only once in the **/Copy** command and not in the **/Range** Format command as well. Here, we can save quite a bit of time because there are five separate ranges of results in Table 3.2.

Now, what should we do about the cells with ERR symbols? Let's erase them. Press the following keys:

Description	Keys to Press
Position the cell pointer in F15:	**[down*5]**
Display the 1-2-3 command menus:	**/**
Select the /Range command:	**R**
Select the Erase menu choice:	**E**
(With /Range Erase, we don't have to anchor F15 before painting the range.)	
Paint the range F15..F16 as the "range to erase":	**[down]**
Confirm this range and complete the command:	**[Enter]**

Well, we took care of that!

There is, however, one peculiarity about Lotus 1-2-3. Even though we erased the contents of cells F15 and F16, 1-2-3 has remembered the display format as Fixed with zero decimal places. [Look at the top left corner of the screen for the format of cell F15. Note that the format indicator (FO) is still displayed.] Try entering the following number into cell F15:

3.14159 [Enter]

Observation: Only the number 3 is displayed. (Remember that the value of F15 when used in any calculation remains at 3.14159, even though its appearance has changed.) 1-2-3 copied the format from cell F10 when the **/Copy** command was used and kept it there even after we erased the contents of the cell.

So, how do we clear a format? We use the **/Range Format** command. Press the following keys:

Description	*Keys to Press*
Display the 1-2-3 command menus:	**/**
Select the /Range command:	**R**
Select the Format command:	**F**
Select the Reset menu choice:	**R**
(Again, with /Range Format Reset command, we don't have to anchor before painting the range.)	
Paint the range F15..F16:	**[down]**
Confirm the range and complete the command:	**[Enter]**

The 3 in cell F15 now appears as 3.14159. By painting the range to include F16, we have reset the format for *both* F15 and F16, even though F16 had no value in it at the time.

ON YOUR OWN: Use **/Range Erase** to **erase** cell **F15.**

Now let's move on to create the index for all demographic groups.

ON YOUR OWN: Use the **/Copy** command to copy the formula (and Fixed format) from **F10** to these ranges:

Demographic Group	*Cell Range*
Household size	F17..F19
Age of the female head of household	F22..F26
Age of children	F29..F32
Occupation	F35..F39

Remember that you will have to select and use the **/Copy** command four separate times, once for each range, so that you do not create any more **ERR** signs. Use the **[PgDn]** and **[PgUp]** keys as you like.

Note: If you make any mistakes doing these exercises, the **/Range Erase** and **/Range Format Reset** commands can be used. Also, the special function **[F2]** key, explained in the "**HBS Tutorial**," can be used to edit the contents of a confirmed cell entry. (A detailed explanation of this **[Edit]** key can also be accessed through the special function **[Help] [F1]** key.) Or you can always start a lesson over.

When you are finished, your worksheet should appear as follows:

```
F10: (F0) (D10/C10)*100                                              READY


         A       B       C       D       E       F       G       H
 1   LESSON 3                            Table 3.2
 2
 3                           % of    % of   -------- Indexes ----------
 4                   % of   Total   Suave   % Shampoo % Suave  % Suave
 5                   Total  Shampoo Ounces    Oz /    Oz /       /
 6                   Pop.   Oz Bought Bought  % Pop.  % Pop.  % Shampoo
 7                   -------- -------- -------- -------- -------- --------
 8
 9   Household Income (000):
10   <$8             22.0%   10.9%    8.2%      50
11   $8-$12          17.5%   10.5%   12.4%      60
12   $12-$15         13.5%   10.2%   12.1%      76
13   $15-$20         18.1%   18.1%   22.1%     100
14   >$20            28.9%   50.2%   45.2%     174
15
16   Household Size:
17   1 - 2           51.9%   30.3%   22.9%      58
18   3 - 4           32.3%   41.3%   44.9%     128
19   5 +             15.8%   28.5%   32.2%     180
20
```

Press **[PgDn]** to view rows 21 through 33; press **[PgDn]** again to view rows 34 through 39.

Reviewing What We've Learned in Question 1

The purpose of this question was to introduce the **/Worksheet Titles Horizontal** command, to cover the **/Range Erase** and **/Range Format Reset** commands, and to continue practicing what we have learned so far.

- The **/Worksheet Titles Horizontal** command may be used to freeze designated rows as "titles" so they do not scroll off the top portion of the screen when the cell pointer is moved below the current viewing area.
- Instead of formatting cells after copying the formula, we can often save time by

reversing the order since the **/Copy** command copies the format of the cell as well as its contents. This is particularly useful when performing multiple copying commands on the same data.

- If you wish to erase the contents (values, formulas, or labels) of any cell, you may use the **/Range Erase** command. If you have not confirmed (by pressing **[Enter]**) the contents, the **[Esc]** key may be used. Furthermore, 1-2-3 automatically replaces the existing contents of a cell when you create a new formula or enter a label or a value.
- If you wish to clear a specific format for a range of cells, you may use the **/Range Format Reset** command.

Let's move on to Question 2.

QUESTION: 2 Construct the index relating the percentage of Suave ounces bought to the percentage of total population represented by the classification.

SOLUTION: To answer this question we will:

2.1 Create a formula for the desired index;
2.2 Express the result in fixed decimal form; and
2.3 Copy the formula for all demographic groups.

Beginning with this question, we will again group together these tasks, which you have already learned. As always, feel free to look back to earlier lessons for step-by-step instructions. Use the index at the back of the book to find out when each function or command was first introduced.

ON YOUR OWN: Create a **formula** in **G10** (Household Income under $8,000) which **divides** the "Percent of Suave Shampoo Ounces Bought" **(E10) by** the "Percent of Total Population" **(C10)** and **multiplies** this value **by 100.**

That is, create this formula for cell **G10:**

$$+(E10/C10)*100$$

The value 37.27272 should have appeared in cell G10. Let's express this result in fixed form.

ON YOUR OWN: Use the **/Range Format Fixed** command to express the result in **G10** in **Fixed** format with **zero decimal** places. The appearance of cell **G10** should have changed to **37.**

Now, let's use the **/Copy** command to copy this formula for the remaining demographic groups.

ON YOUR OWN: Now **copy** the index we've created in **G10** (using the **Fixed** format) to the remaining demographic groups. You will have to use the **/Copy** command five separate times to make sure that no **ERR** is introduced. Make sure that the following groups are included:

Demographic Group	Cell Range
Household income	G11..G14
Household size	G17..G19
Age of the female head of household	G22..G26
Age of children	G29..G32
Occupation	G35..G39

Good. Your worksheet should appear as follows:

```
G10: (F0) (E10/C10)*100                                              READY


         A        B        C        D        E        F        G        H
 1    LESSON 3                              Table 3.2
 2
 3                               % of     % of    --------- Indexes ---------
 4                      % of     Total    Suave   % Shampoo % Suave  % Suave
 5                      Total    Shampoo  Ounces    Oz /      Oz /      /
 6                      Pop.     Oz Bought Bought   % Pop.   % Pop.  % Shampoo
 7                    -------- -------- -------- -------- -------- --------
 8
 9    Household Income (000):
10    <$8              22.0%    10.9%     8.2%      50       37
11    $8-$12           17.5%    10.5%    12.4%      60       71
12    $12-$15          13.5%    10.2%    12.1%      76       90
13    $15-$20          18.1%    18.1%    22.1%     100      122
14    >$20             28.9%    50.2%    45.2%     174      156
15
16    Household Size:
17    1 - 2            51.9%    30.3%    22.9%      58       44
18    3 - 4            32.3%    41.3%    44.9%     128      139
19    5 +              15.8%    28.5%    32.2%     180      204
20
```

Press **[PgDn]** to view rows 21 through 33; press **[PgDn]** again to view rows 34 through 39. Let's move on to Question 3.

QUESTION: 3 Construct the index relating the percentage of Suave ounces bought to the percentage of total shampoo ounces bought for the classification. Create this index by dividing the index derived in Question 2 by the index derived in Question 1.

Sort each of the five demographic groups according to the index calculated above.

SOLUTION: To answer this question we will:

3.1 Create a formula for the desired index;
3.2 Express the result in fixed decimal form;
3.3 Copy the formula for all demographic groups; and
3.4 Rank each of the five demographic groups according to the index calculated.

ON YOUR OWN: Create a **formula** in cell **H10** (Household Income under $8,000) which **divides** the index we derived in Question 2 **(G10) by** the index we derived in Question 1 **(F10) and multiplies** this value **by 100.**

This time, the formula is not spelled out in these instructions, but it is similar to the formulas for F10 and G10. It should be getting easier to see what formula you should create, and how you can create it.

The value **75.22935** should have appeared in cell **H10.** Let's express this result in fixed decimal form.

ON YOUR OWN: Use the **/Range Format Fixed** command to express the result in **H10** in **Fixed** format with **zero decimal** places. The appearance of cell **H10** should have changed to **75.**

Now let's use the **/Copy** command to copy this formula for the remaining demographic groups.

ON YOUR OWN: Now **copy** the index we've created in **H10** for the remaining demographic groups. Once again, you will have to use the **/Copy** command five separate times to make sure no **ERR** is introduced.

Demographic Group	Cell Range
Household income	H11..H14
Household size	H17..H19
Age of the female head of household	H22..H26
Age of children	H29..H32
Occupation	H35..H39

Good. Your worksheet should appear as follows:

```
H10: (F0) (G10/F10)*100                                                    READY


         A        B        C        D        E        F        G        H
1      LESSON 3                            Table 3.2
2
3                                 % of     % of    -------- Indexes ---------
4                        % of     Total    Suave   % Shampoo % Suave  % Suave
5                        Total    Shampoo  Ounces   Oz /     Oz /       /
6                        Pop.     Oz Bought Bought  % Pop.   % Pop.   % Shampoo
7                        -------- -------- -------- -------- -------- --------
8
9      Household Income (000):
10     <$8              22.0%    10.9%     8.2%       50       37       75
11     $8-$12           17.5%    10.5%    12.4%       60       71      118
12     $12-$15          13.5%    10.2%    12.1%       76       90      119
13     $15-$20          18.1%    18.1%    22.1%      100      122      122
14     >$20             28.9%    50.2%    45.2%      174      156       90
15
16     Household Size:
17     1 - 2            51.9%    30.3%    22.9%       58       44       76
18     3 - 4            32.3%    41.3%    44.9%      128      139      109
19     5 +              15.8%    28.5%    32.2%      180      204      113
20
```

Press **[PgDn]** to view rows 21 through 33; press **[PgDn]** again to view rows 34 through 39.

Let's complete one more step and rank each of the five demographic groups according to our new index.

ON YOUR OWN: Use the **/Data Sort** command to rank the demographic group, "Household income." The **Data-Range** should be **A10..H14.** The **Primary-key** should be **Column H.** Choose **descending** order and then press **Go.**

Good. Your worksheet should appear as follows:

```
H10: (F0) (G10/F10)*100                                              READY


          A         B         C         D         E         F         G         H
  1    LESSON 3                              Table 3.2
  2
  3                               % of       % of    ---------  Indexes ----------
  4                     % of      Total      Suave    % Shampoo % Suave   % Suave
  5                     Total    Shampoo    Ounces     Oz /      Oz /       /
  6                     Pop.    Oz Bought   Bought    % Pop.    % Pop.   % Shampoo
  7                    --------  --------   --------  --------  --------  --------
  8
  9    Household Income (000):
 10    $15-$20          18.1%     18.1%      22.1%      100       122       122
 11    $12-$15          13.5%     10.2%      12.1%       76        90       119
 12    $8-$12           17.5%     10.5%      12.4%       60        71       118
 13    >$20             28.9%     50.2%      45.2%      174       156        90
 14    <$8              22.0%     10.9%       8.2%       50        37        75
 15
 16    Household Size:
 17    1 - 2            51.9%     30.3%      22.9%       58        44        76
 18    3 - 4            32.3%     41.3%      44.9%      128       139       109
 19    5 +              15.8%     28.5%      32.2%      180       204       113
 20
```

Let's now rank the next demographic group, "Household size," according to our new index. You can perform the exercise easily; you just have to change the old Data-Range.

ON YOUR OWN: Invoke the **/Data Sort** command. This time, let's clear all previous settings with the **/Data Sort Reset** command. Now **paint** the new range **A17..H19.** The **Primary-key** should be **Column H.** Choose **descending** order and then press **Go** to perform the sort. Notice that the cells in rows 17 through 19 are now properly sorted.

Note: We could have just cleared the old data-range by pressing **[Esc]** and used the previous settings for the Primary-key and order. The **/Data Sort Reset** command, however, is even more useful when all the settings need to be changed.

ON YOUR OWN: Now use **/Data Sort** to rank the remaining demographic groups according to **Column H,** in **descending** order. You will have to use **/Data Sort** three separate times to enter each of the separate data ranges:

Demographic Group	Data-Range
Age of the female head of household	A22..H26
Age of children	A29..H32
Occupation	A35..H39

Good. Let's now move on to our analysis of Table 3.3.

ANALYSIS of TABLE 3.3: SUAVE USERS

4 Construct the index relating the percentage of Suave users to the percentage of shampoo users.

SOLUTION: To analyze Table 3.3 we will:

4.1 Clear the worksheet titles we used for Table 3.2;
4.2 Create a formula for the desired index;
4.3 Express the result in fixed decimal form; and
4.4 Copy the formula for all demographic groups.

Our task here will be easier if we first "unfreeze" rows 1 through 7. Then we will be able to display all of Table 3.3 on one clean screen.

ON YOUR OWN: Invoke the **/Worksheet Titles Clear** command. Now rows 1 through 7 are unfrozen. Return to **A1** by pressing **[Home]**. Press **[PgDn] three times** to move to **A61**, displaying Table 3.3. Let's now create the formula.

ON YOUR OWN: Create a **formula** in **G69** (Males) which divides the "Percent of Suave Users" by the "Percent of Shampoo Users" and multiplies this value by 100. That is, create the formula **G69 = (F69/E69)∗100**.

The value **97.82608** should have appeared in cell **G69**. Let's express this result in fixed decimal form.

ON YOUR OWN: Use the **/Range Format Fixed** command to express the result in **G69** in **Fixed** format with **zero decimal** places. The appearance of cell **G69** should have changed to **98**. Now let's use the **/Copy** command to copy this formula for the remaining demographic groups.

ON YOUR OWN: Now **copy** the index we've created in **G69** for the remaining demographic groups.

Good. Your worksheet should appear as follows:

```
 G69: (F0) (F69/E69)*100                                          READY


             A        B        C        D        E       F       G       H
   61                                           Table 3.3
   62                                                                Index:
   63                                           Percent  Percent Percent of
   64                                           of       of      Suave Users/
   65                                           Shampoo  Suave   Percent of
   66                                           Users    Users   Shampoo Users
   67                                           -------  ------- -------------
   68
   69     Males                                   46%      45%        98
   70     Total Users 34 & Younger                48%      62%       129
   71     Users 12 & Younger                      17%      23%       135
   72     Users 17 & Younger                      24%      33%       138
   73     Households of 4 +                       41%      53%       129
   74     Households w/ $30,000 + Income          29%      21%        72
   75
   76
   77
   78
   79
   80
```

Saving Your Worksheet in a File on Diskette

Let's save your worksheet, with all the completed indexes, under the file name LN03. Press the following keys:

Description	Keys to Press
Return the cell pointer to A1:	**[Home]**
Display the 1-2-3 command menus:	**/**
Select the /File command:	**F**
Select the Save command:	**S**
(The top of the screen will ask for a save file name and will list the presumed name: LESSON03.WK1.)	
Type in the name we want for this completed worksheet file, LN03:	**LN03**
Confirm the worksheet file name:	**[Enter]**
(The disk drive will turn on as your file is being saved.)	

Good. We have now completed Lesson 3.

MANAGEMENT DISCUSSION

1 Why do consumer researchers use demographic data?

Demographic data provide one way that researchers can divide people into types of consumers. If people have similar demographic characteristics (income levels, religion, race, education, etc.) they might behave similarly, as consumers. For example, consumer researchers would want to know if consumers at one level of household income tend to buy certain shampoo brands more than others. If so, then income level becomes an important demographic variable for shampoo marketers to forecast who is likely to buy more of certain shampoos.

2 What do the results in Table 3.2 tell you about who disproportionately buys Suave shampoo?

The indexes that we calculated, based on the data in Table 3.2, suggest a specific pattern: Consumers with medium income, several younger-aged children, in blue-collar occupations, tend to buy Suave shampoo significantly more than other types of consumers. Note that the category on "Age of the Female Head of Household" corresponds with the category on "Age of Children." It is the households with a female head of household under the age of 44 that would be more likely to have children in these younger age groups.

One interpretation is that these families, who have several children and tight household budgets, do not wish to spend the extra money on a higher-priced brand of shampoo. It is also possible that these families have decided that the shampoo they buy for their children does not have to be a premium brand.

3 What do the results in Table 3.3 tell you about who disproportionately uses Suave shampoo?

Data indicate that children and young teens tend to use Suave shampoo disproportionately more than adults do. These data confirm our earlier interpretation that Suave shampoo is often bought for use by children and teenagers. The data also suggest that males tend to use Suave shampoo approximately as much as females do.

4 What is the difference between who *buys* and who *uses* a brand? Since it is usually easier to obtain data on purchase rather than usage of a product, is it necessary to obtain usage data?

Tables 3.2 and 3.3 demonstrate the difference between data on purchase versus usage. Clearly, it is important to try to obtain data on usage. The data in Table 3.2 indicate what type of families tend to buy Suave disproportionately, but it does not tell us who in those families uses it. Therefore, the data in Table 3.2 does not tell us all we would want to know about *why* consumers buy Suave shampoo. The data in Table 3.3 help us to understand that many families buy Suave for usage by their children. In many of these families, the adults may buy a different brand for their own use.

What is of particular importance for marketers is *who makes the decision* to buy _____(Suave shampoo). Many people can be part of the *decision-*

making unit for a product, particularly for a complex business product, such as a corporate jet (think of all the people involved in this decision—CEO, Board, CFO, corporate pilot). Or even the purchase of a pair of boy's jeans may involve the opinions of many in the family (parent buys, boy uses, peers and older brothers influence decision).

Marketers want to select the right marketing tools to reach the decision makers. In the instance of Suave shampoo, young people may use it, but their mothers may make the decision. On the other hand, a supermarket shopping trip often involves the purchase of a number of products to be used by someone at home who had made that selection. Purchase *and* usage data, therefore, are both necessary.

5 Which demographic groups do you think a Suave advertising campaign should target?

The market and demographic data provide information on how Suave was positioned and on which consumers tended to buy the brand most often. Depending on which segment of consumers you choose to target, you would have to decide which message you would use. If you were managing the Suave brand and you decided to aim an advertising campaign toward those consumers who already know and use Suave, the message should remind them why they had made the choice and perhaps persuade them to buy even more. If you decided to target new consumers, the message should persuade them to try the new brand.

LESSON 4   CONSUMER ANALYSIS: PSYCHOGRAPHIC CHARACTERISTICS

OVERVIEW

COMPUTER INSTRUCTIONS

Lesson 4 reinforces the essentials of Lotus 1-2-3. You will be asked to complete most of the exercises on your own. In addition, some new commands are introduced.

MANAGEMENT ISSUES

Lesson 4 introduces the concept of consumer "psychographics"—the analysis of consumer life-styles. Many of the more sophisticated consumer marketing companies have developed an understanding of how consumers can be categorized by their life-styles, attitudes, and values. This lesson shows one psychographic segmentation technique that uses zip-code clusters.

MANAGEMENT DISCUSSION QUESTIONS

1 Why do consumer researchers attempt to gather and analyze psychographic data? Does the use of such data make sense to you?
2 Why is the distinction between "heavy users" and "users" important?
3 What do these results indicate about who disproportionately buys Suave? Who uses Suave?
4 Do these results reinforce your conclusions drawn from the demographic data?
5 Which types of people should the new Suave campaign target? What image should the advertising campaign project?

CASE

Helene Curtis often used PRIZM data[5] to analyze the shampoo market (and Suave, in particular). PRIZM enabled the company to segment the market another way: according to psychographic characteristics. The results were considered very helpful in developing a communications program.

A description of each of the 40 life-style clusters is presented in Chapter 9. Each cluster was examined as a component of: (1) total shampoo users; (2) heavy shampoo users; (3) Suave users; and (4) heavy Suave users. The data are shown in Table 3.4.

---

[5] PRIZM is a geodemographic market segmentation and consumer targeting system developed by Claritas Corporation. Based on the axiom "birds of a feather flock together," PRIZM segments the U.S. market into 40 homogeneous clusters of zip codes. The clusters reflect the socioeconomic status and lifestyles of the people living in the zip-code areas.

TABLE 3.4   PRIZM DATA

Psychographic Cluster	Base: % of Total Population	% Component of Total Shampoo Users	% Component of Heavy Shampoo Users[a]	% Component of Suave Users	% Component of Heavy Suave Users[a]
1. Agribusiness	4.80%	5.68%	4.36%	6.20%	8.54%
2. Back Country Folks	5.92	5.45	4.09	9.09	6.72
3. Black Enterprise	0.85	1.01	1.73	1.01	0.46
4. Blue Blood Estates	0.43	0.41	0.65	0.00	0.00
5. Blue Chip Blues	5.59	5.96	7.02	7.94	9.90
6. Blue Collar Nursery	2.20	2.02	2.37	3.00	3.54
7. Bohemian Mix	0.24	0.17	0.25	0.00	0.00
8. Coalburg and Corntown	3.26	2.96	3.20	4.79	6.47
9. Downtown Dixie-Style	1.05	1.42	1.74	0.69	0.00
10. Emergent Minorities	1.29	1.38	1.31	0.30	0.00
11. Furs and Station Wagons	2.83	3.17	3.86	0.73	1.39
12. God's Country	3.58	3.57	4.45	3.89	1.79
13. Golden Ponds	3.53	3.27	2.81	2.03	2.57
14. Grain Belt	1.94	2.20	2.23	2.63	1.64
15. Gray Power	2.48	2.43	2.91	1.75	1.86
16. Hardscrabble	1.27	1.44	1.49	1.24	1.22
17. Heavy Industry	1.77	1.71	1.06	2.08	0.21
18. Hispanic Mix	0.41	0.40	0.18	0.00	0.00
19. Levittown, U.S.A.	5.51	5.21	5.01	4.21	5.33
20. Middle America	5.94	5.93	7.20	4.08	2.82
21. Mines and Mills	1.94	2.16	1.77	2.08	3.65
22. Money and Brains	0.73	0.59	0.74	0.30	0.57
23. New Beginnings	3.73	3.70	4.11	4.43	3.22
24. New Homesteaders	4.53	4.68	5.56	7.68	7.68
25. New Melting Pot	1.13	0.82	1.14	1.15	0.54
26. Norma Rae-Ville	2.60	2.68	2.06	1.77	2.14
27. Old Brick Factories	1.33	1.57	0.54	0.54	0.00
28. Old Yankee Rows	1.19	1.04	0.96	1.46	0.36
29. Pools and Patios	3.07	2.91	2.51	2.23	1.97
30. Public Assistance	1.02	0.61	0.75	0.39	0.75
31. Rank and File	1.22	1.25	0.79	0.43	0.29
32. Sharecroppers	4.18	4.34	4.44	4.02	2.46
33. Shotguns and Pickups	3.36	3.88	4.18	6.05	6.90
34. Single City Blues	1.17	0.85	1.24	0.88	0.71
35. Tobacco Roads	1.24	0.86	0.33	0.00	0.00
36. Towns and Gowns	2.53	2.54	2.71	1.43	1.57
37. Two More Rungs	1.09	0.85	0.69	1.01	1.11
38. Urban Gold Coast	0.16	0.00	0.00	0.00	0.00
39. Young Influentials	2.04	1.96	2.01	1.88	3.15
40. Young Suburbia	6.85	6.92	5.55	6.61	8.47
Total	100.00%	100.00%	100.00%	100.00%	100.00%

[a]Heavy shampoo (Suave) users were defined as those consumers who purchased shampoo (Suave) at a rate above the average for the entire population.

Lanznar began by developing four indexes to compare each cluster as a component of the four categories listed in Table 3.4 with that cluster as a percentage of the total population. For example, the index for "agribusiness" as a percentage component of "total shampoo users" was 118 (5.68% divided by 4.80%).

Lanznar then used her computer to calculate the following indexes:

1 The index "total shampoo users" divided by "total population." She then compared this index for each cluster with the index for that cluster in the other three categories. For example, indexes for the cluster "Downtown Dixie-Style" would be:

Cluster	Total Shampoo Users Index	Heavy Shampoo Users Index	Suave Users Index	Heavy Suave Users Index
Downtown Dixie-style	136	166	66	0

2 The index "heavy shampoo users" divided by "total population." She then compared this index for each cluster with the indexes for the other three categories.
3 The index "Suave users" divided by "total population." She then compared this index for each cluster with the indexes for the other three categories.
4 The index "heavy Suave users" divided by "total population." She then compared this index for each cluster with the indexes for the other three categories.

Having finished her analysis of the shampoo market, Lanznar put together a market research report and had copies sent to Thomas, Kirk, and Vallera.

COMPUTER INSTRUCTIONS

Retrieving and Examining the Worksheet File for Lesson 4

To begin Lesson 4, we need to retrieve a new worksheet file from the Suave Data Diskette. First, follow these steps, if necessary:

1. Load DOS. Enter date and time.
2. Load the Lotus Access System.
3. Load the 1-2-3 software program.

Insert the Suave Data Diskette into the appropriate disk drive. Then retrieve the worksheet file we need on your own.

ON YOUR OWN: Use the **/File Retrieve** commands to load the worksheet file: **LESSON04.WKS**. Press the **[Home]** key as instructed.

Switch diskettes. Now that you have loaded the worksheet file we need, you should remove the Suave Data Diskette from the disk drive and replace it with your data diskette.

Now let's look at this worksheet. The first screen, beginning at A1, shows only the first part of Table 3.4. Press the **[PgDn]** and **[Tab]** keys to view the rest of Table 3.4. Then press the **[Home]** key to return to cell A1.

Observation: Did you notice that column B is wider than column A? A column in 1-2-3 normally is 9 characters wide, unless you tell 1-2-3 differently. The **/Worksheet Column Set-Width** command allows you to alter the width of any column, so that you can place more or less than 9 characters (anywhere from 1 to 240) in one column. Table 3.4 has columns with the following widths: 4 characters in Column A, 23 characters in Column B, and the conventional 9 characters in Columns C, D, E, F, and G. The width of a column is shown in the top left corner of the screen if the width of at least one of the columns in the worksheet has been altered. For example, the symbols "**[W4]**" appear before the contents of cell A1.

Let's take a moment to see how the **/Worksheet Column Set-Width** command works.

Release 1A Users: The command is called **/Worksheet Column-Width Set** with a maximum column width of 72 characters. The column widths are not noted on your screen.

The /Worksheet Column Set-Width Command

We will go out to column P and then try this new command. Press the following keys:

Description	Keys to Press
Move the cell pointer to column P:	**[Tab] [Tab]**
Display the 1-2-3 command menus:	**/**
Select the /Worksheet command:	**W**
Select the Column command:	**C**
Select the Set-Width menu choice:	**S**
Enter a width of 25 characters:	**25 [Enter]**

Observation: Notice how the width of column P widened. Also notice, however, that the screen now shows only 6 columns (rather than the usual 8). Screens in Lotus 1-2-3 usually contain exactly 72 characters across (which are usually divided into 8 columns with 9 characters each). Since we increased the width of column P, we now cannot see columns V and W on this screen, because columns P through U have used up all 72 characters.

Let's change column P back to the usual 9 characters. Press the following keys:

Description	Keys to Press
Display the 1-2-3 command menus:	**/**
Select the /Worksheet command:	**W**
Select the Column command:	**C**
Select the Reset-Width menu choice:	**R**

Observation: Notice that all the columns on this screen are back to normal.

Note: If you type in a label (word) with more characters than the width of the column, the word will simply spill over into the next column (unless that column is already occupied). However, every value (number) must be displayed within the boundaries of its column's width. Therefore, a very important purpose of the **/Worksheet Column Set-Width** command is to allow the user to enter a number with more than 8 characters in one column. (For clarity, Lotus 1-2-3 always requires one character to be blank in a cell that contains a number.)

Let's see what happens when we enter a number with more than 8 characters (in this case, with 9 characters). Press these keys:

Description	Keys to Press
Enter this number: 123456789	**123456789 [Enter]**
(Note: 1-2-3 displays our number in scientific notation to fit in a column of 9 characters.)	
Display the 1-2-3 command menus:	**/**
Select the /Worksheet command:	**W**
Select the Column command:	**C**
Select the Set-Width menu choice:	**S**
Enter a 10-character width·	**10 [Enter]**

Good. Now you should see 123456789.

Observation: Notice that Lotus 1-2-3 could display the number fully when we widened the column. We entered a 10-character width because the number 123456789 has nine characters and 1-2-3 always requires one character to be blank in a cell that contains a number.

Note: Punctuation or symbols, such as commas or dollar signs, also use some of the characters available in a column. So, you may have to widen a column to make use of a special numerical format.

Note: If you enter a value or calculate a formula and see a line of stars (*********) across the cell, you need to widen the column. If you see these stars, you know that a numerical format must have already been specified for that cell with the use of the

/Range Format command. (Often users specify a format, then erase or change the number and forget that the format is still recorded for that cell.) The line of stars indicates that the combination of the number and the specified format is too long for the column. You can correct the problem just by increasing the width of the column as required.

   ON YOUR OWN: Use the **/Range Erase** command to erase the number in cell P1. Then use the **/Worksheet Column Reset-Width** command to return column P to normal length. Then press **[Home]** to begin Question 1 in Lesson 4.

   Observation: Now you can see that the cell pointer in A1 shows only 4 characters because we had narrowed this column to that width. (Later in the lesson, we will see why we have organized the columns this way.) Also notice that since column B is 23 characters wide, we cannot see column H on this screen.

   Now, let's begin Question 1.

QUESTION: 1 Compute four indexes to compare, for each of the 40 clusters, a cluster's percent of the four categories listed in Table 4 with that cluster's percent of the total population.

   Sort the clusters in descending order by the index, "Percent of Total Shampoo Users" divided by the "Percent of Total Population." Examine the top ten clusters. For each cluster, compare this index with the other three indexes.

SOLUTION: To answer this question we will:

   1.1 Freeze certain columns *and* rows as "titles" to prevent them from "scrolling" off the left and top sides of the screen;
   1.2 Create formulas for the desired indexes;
   1.3 Express the results in fixed decimal form;
   1.4 Copy the formula for all psychographic clusters; and
   1.5 Rank the clusters in descending order and examine the top 10.

   As we have before, we will group together the tasks involved in completing this question. Some new aspects of both the **/Worksheet Titles** command and the **/Copy** command are introduced. However, you have already learned the basic skills necessary for this question.

   In previous lessons we have chosen to freeze either rows or columns as "titles." However, we can also freeze both rows and columns at the same time. Let's try it.

   ON YOUR OWN: Move the cell pointer to **C7**. Invoke the **/Worksheet Titles Both** command. Both the columns to the left and rows above **C7** have now been frozen as "titles." Now let's create the desired indexes.

   ON YOUR OWN: Create a **formula** for each of the four indexes in **Columns H through K**. Place the **four formulas in cells H7, I7, J7, and K7**, respectively, for the cluster "Agribusiness."

   (*Hint:* Use the **[Tab]** and **[Shift-Tab]** keys to move between screens quickly. The **[Tab]** key moves the screen one page to the right. The **[Shift-Tab]** moves the screen one page to the left.)

The formulas to create are:

$$\text{Total Shampoo Users Index} = \frac{\% \text{ Component of Total Shampoo Users}}{\text{Base } \% \text{ of Total Population}} * 100$$
$$\text{(Column H)}$$

$$\text{Heavy Shampoo Users Index} = \frac{\% \text{ Component of Heavy Shampoo Users}}{\text{Base } \% \text{ of Total Population}} * 100$$
$$\text{(Column I)}$$

$$\text{Suave Users Index} = \frac{\% \text{ Component of Suave Users}}{\text{Base } \% \text{ of Total Population}} * 100$$
$$\text{(Column J)}$$

$$\text{Heavy Suave Users Index} = \frac{\% \text{ Component of Heavy Suave Users}}{\text{Base } \% \text{ of Total Population}} * 100$$
$$\text{(Column K)}$$

That is, create the formulas:

$$\textbf{H7} = \textbf{(D7/C7)} * \textbf{100}$$

$$\textbf{I7} = \textbf{(E7/C7)} * \textbf{100}$$

$$\textbf{J7} = \textbf{(F7/C7)} * \textbf{100}$$

$$\textbf{K7} = \textbf{(G7/C7)} * \textbf{100}$$

The values **118.3333**, **90.83333**, **129.1666**, and **177.9166** should have appeared in cells H7, I7, J7, and K7, respectively.

Note: When the **/Worksheet Titles Vertical** command is used, the **[PgUp]** and **[PgDn]** keys move only as many rows as are left "unfrozen" on each screen. Here, we move 14 rows instead of 20, because rows 1–6 appear on every screen. Similarly, when the **/Worksheet Titles Horizontal** command is used, the **[Tab]** and **[Shift-Tab]** keys move only as many characters (columns) as are left "unfrozen" on each screen. Here, we move 45 characters (5 columns of 9 characters each) instead of 72 characters (normally, 8 columns of 9 characters each), because the 27 characters used by columns A and B appear on every screen.

Let's now express these four results in fixed form.

ON YOUR OWN: Use the **/Range Format Fixed** command to express the indexes you just created for "Agribusiness" in **Fixed** format with **zero decimal** places. The values **118**, **91**, **129**, and **178** should have appeared in cells **H7**, **I7**, **J7** and **K7**, respectively.

Now we can copy the four formulas in one single step to all remaining clusters. Let's see how.

ON YOUR OWN: Invoke the **/Copy** command. Then **paint the range to copy FROM: H7..K7.** (This is the first time that we have ever had a range to copy from that was more than one cell.) Move to **H8. Anchor H8** by pressing the **period** key. Then **paint the range to copy TO: H8..K46.** (Use the **[PgDn]** and **arrow** keys to make this easier.) Then press **[Enter]** to perform the copying command.

Good. Your worksheet should appear as follows (Only the first 14 clusters are displayed here.):

```
H7: (F0) (D7/C7)*100                                              READY


      A          B              G        H        I        J        K
 1  LESSON 4
 2                                     Total    Heavy             Heavy
 3                              of Heavy Shampoo  Shampoo  Suave   Suave
 4                              Suave   Users    Users    Users   Users
 5     Psychographic Cluster   Users   Index    Index    Index   Index
 6     ----------------------- -------- -------- -------- ------- --------
 7      1 Agrlbuslness          8.54%    118      91      129     178
 8      2 Back Country Folks    6.72%     92      69      154     114
 9      3 Black Enterprlse      0.46%    119     204      119      54
10      4 Blue Blood Estates    0.00%     95     151        0       0
11      5 Blue Chip Blues       9.90%    107     126      142     177
12      6 Blue Collar Nursery   3.54%     92     108      136     161
13      7 Bohemlan Mlx          0.00%     71     104        0       0
14      8 Coalburg and Corntown 6.47%     91      98      147     198
15      9 Downtown Dlxle-Style  0.00%    135     166       66       0
16     10 Emergent Mlnorltles   0.00%    107     102       23       0
17     11 Furs and Statlon Wagons 1.39%  112     136       26      49
18     12 God's Country         1.79%    100     124      109      50
19     13 Golden Ponds          2.57%     93      80       58      73
20     14 Graln Belt            1.64%    113     115      136      85
```

Press **[PgDn]** to view clusters 15–28; press **[PgDn]** again to view clusters 29–40. Notice how the worksheet is organized so that when we move from one screen to another with **[Tab]** or **[PgDn]**, the table divides neatly into easily comprehensible sections. The structure of your worksheet is very important for working with the data and communicating your work via data diskettes to others.

Note: The exercise above demonstrates how we can copy from a *range* of cells (H7..K7) to another range of cells (H8..K46). This capability can save us a lot of time in completing copy commands.

We can now move on to ranking the clusters according to our first index in column H.

ON YOUR OWN: Our tasks throughout Lesson 4 will be made easier if we include **Columns H, I, J, and K in the Data-Range** right from the start. So, first invoke the **/Data Sort** command. Then select **Data-Range. Paint the range B7..K46.** (Do not include column A, so that the numbers 1 to 40 will remain in order. Notice that even though column B is "frozen," you are able to include it in the range. Momentarily, two column B's are displayed.) Select **Primary-key** and specify **Column H**. Choose **descending** order. Press **Go** to perform the sort.

Note: When painting a large range such as B7..K46, it can save a great deal of time to use the **[End]** key with the **arrow** keys, or to use the **[PgDn]** key.

You should now understand why we made column A only four characters wide. We wanted to use it for the numbers 1 to 40. Therefore, we needed only four characters: two characters for the two digit numbers, one blank character as required by 1-2-3 for any cell containing a number, and an extra blank character for better appearance. Remember that 1-2-3 always uses one extra character for numbers.

The top 14 clusters should appear as follows:

```
H7: (F0) (D7/C7)*100                                                    READY


      A            B              G        H         I         J         K
 1    LESSON 4
 2                                         Total    Heavy
 3                               of Heavy  Shampoo  Shampoo   Suave               Heavy
 4                                Suave    Users    Users     Users     Suave
 5    Psychographic Cluster       Users    Index    Index     Index     Users
 6    ------------------------    -------- -------- --------  --------  --------
 7     1 Downtown Dixie-Style      0.00%    135      166       66        0
 8     2 Black Enterprise          0.46%    119      204      119       54
 9     3 Agribusiness              8.54%    118       91      129      178
10     4 Old Brick Factories       0.00%    118       41       41        0
11     5 Shotguns and Pickups      6.90%    115      124      180      205
12     6 Grain Belt                1.64%    113      115      136       85
13     7 Hardscrabble              1.22%    113      117       98       96
14     8 Furs and Station Wagons   1.39%    112      136       26       49
15     9 Mines and Mills           3.65%    111       91      107      188
16    10 Emergent Minorities       0.00%    107      102       23        0
17    11 Blue Chip Blues           9.90%    107      126      142      177
18    12 Sharecroppers             2.46%    104      106       96       59
19    13 New Homesteaders          7.68%    103      123      170      170
20    14 Norma Rae-Ville           2.14%    103       79       68       82
```

Press **[PgDn]** once and then again if you want to view the remaining clusters.

We have learned several new skills in Lesson 4, so let's now review them.

Reviewing What We've Learned in Lesson 4 So Far

In Question 1, we were able to practice previous skills and we learned the following new commands and techniques:

- The **/Worksheet Column Set-Width** command allows us to alter the number of characters that a column can display. This command is important for two reasons: (1) it allows us to design a worksheet to fit our needs; and (2) it allows us to input a long number precisely and in the desired format.
- The **/Worksheet Titles Both** command allows us to freeze *both* horizontal and vertical titles at the same time. In so doing, the **[PgDn]** and **[PgUp]** keys move only as many rows as are left "unfrozen" on each screen; similarly, the **[Tab]** and **[Shift-**

Tab] keys move only as many characters (columns) as are left "unfrozen" on each screen.
- We can use the **/Copy** command to copy from a range of cells (such as H7..K7) to another range of cells (such as H8..K46).

Let's move on to Question 2.

QUESTION: **2** Sort in descending order the clusters by the index "Percent of Heavy Shampoo Users" divided by the "Percent of Total Population." Examine the top 10 clusters. For each cluster, compare this index with the other three indexes.

SOLUTION: To answer this question we will:

2.1 Resort the clusters in descending order using Column I as the Primary-key, and examine the top 10 clusters.

All we have to do to answer this question is to resort our data range according to a new column. It's that easy. We don't even have to change our existing data range.
ON YOUR OWN: Invoke the **/Data Sort** command. Select **Primary-key**. Move to **Column I** and press **[Enter]**. Reconfirm **descending** order by pressing **[Enter]** again. Then just press **Go** to perform the sort.
Good. Your screen should appear as follows:

```
H7: (F0) (D7/C7)*100                                                  READY


       A              B              G        H        I        J        K
 1     LESSON 4
 2                                           Total    Heavy             Heavy
 3                                 of Heavy Shampoo  Shampoo   Suave    Suave
 4                                  Suave    Users    Users    Users    Users
 5     Psychographic Cluster       Users    Index    Index    Index    Index
 6     ------------------------   -------- -------- -------- -------- --------
 7      1 Black Enterprise          0.46%    119      204      119       54
 8      2 Downtown Dixie-Style      0.00%    135      166       66        0
 9      3 Blue Blood Estates        0.00%     95      151        0        0
10      4 Furs and Station Wagons   1.39%    112      136       26       49
11      5 Blue Chip Blues           9.90%    107      126      142      177
12      6 Shotguns and Pickups      6.90%    115      124      180      205
13      7 God's Country             1.79%    100      124      109       50
14      8 New Homesteaders          7.68%    103      123      170      170
15      9 Middle America            2.82%    100      121       69       47
16     10 Gray Power                1.86%     98      117       71       75
17     11 Hardscrabble              1.22%    113      117       98       96
18     12 Grain Belt                1.64%    113      115      136       85
19     13 New Beginnings            3.22%     99      110      119       86
20     14 Blue Collar Nursery       3.54%     92      108      136      161
```

Examine the top 10 clusters. Then move on to Question 3.

QUESTION: **3** Sort in descending order the clusters by the index "Percent of Suave Shampoo Users" divided by the "Percent of Total Population." Examine the top 10 clusters. For each cluster, compare this index with the other three indexes.

SOLUTION: To answer this question we will:

3.1 Rank the clusters in descending order according to Column J and examine the top 10 clusters.

ON YOUR OWN: Just follow the procedures shown in Question 2 to move the **Primary-key** to **Column J**. When finished, your screen should appear as follows:

```
H7: (F0) (D7/C7)*100                                          READY


      A            B           G        H        I        J        K
 1    LESSON 4
 2                                     Total    Heavy
 3                           of Heavy Shampoo  Shampoo   Suave    Heavy
 4                            Suave    Users    Users    Users    Suave
 5    Psychographic Cluster   Users    Index    Index    Index    Users
 6    --------------------   -------- -------- -------- -------- --------
 7     1 Shotguns and Pickups  6.90%    115      124      180      205
 8     2 New Homesteaders      7.68%    103      123      170      170
 9     3 Back Country Folks    6.72%     92       69      154      114
10     4 Coalburg and Corntown 6.47%     91       98      147      198
11     5 Blue Chip Blues       9.90%    107      126      142      177
12     6 Blue Collar Nursery   3.54%     92      108      136      161
13     7 Grain Belt            1.64%    113      115      136       85
14     8 Agribusiness          8.54%    118       91      129      178
15     9 Old Yankee Rows       0.36%     87       81      123       30
16    10 Black Enterprise      0.46%    119      204      119       54
17    11 New Beginnings        3.22%     99      110      119       86
18    12 Heavy Industry        0.21%     97       60      118       12
19    13 God's Country         1.79%    100      124      109       50
20    14 Mines and Mills       3.65%    111       91      107      188
```

Examine the top 10 clusters. Then move on to Question 4.

QUESTION: **4** Sort in descending order the clusters by the index "Percent of Heavy Suave Shampoo Users" divided by the "Percent of Total Population." Examine the top 10 clusters. For each cluster, compare this index for the other three indexes.

SOLUTION: To answer this question we will:

4.1 Rank the clusters in descending order according to Column K and examine the top 10 clusters.

ON YOUR OWN: Move the **Primary-key** to **Column K**. When finished your screen should appear as follows:

```
H7: (F0) (D7/C7)*100                                          READY


        A            B            G        H        I        J        K
1     LESSON 4
2                                        Total    Heavy             Heavy
3                                of Heavy Shampoo  Shampoo  Suave    Suave
4                                Suave    Users    Users    Users    Users
5     Psychographic Cluster      Users    Index    Index    Index    Index
6     ----------------------     -------- -------- -------- -------- --------
7      1 Shotguns and Pickups     6.90%    115      124      180      205
8      2 Coalburg and Corntown    6.47%     91       98      147      198
9      3 Mines and Mills          3.65%    111       91      107      188
10     4 Agribusiness             8.54%    118       91      129      178
11     5 Blue Chip Blues          9.90%    107      126      142      177
12     6 New Homesteaders         7.68%    103      123      170      170
13     7 Blue Collar Nursery      3.54%     92      108      136      161
14     8 Young Influentials       3.15%     96       99       92      154
15     9 Young Suburbia           8.47%    101       81       96      124
16    10 Back Country Folks       6.72%     92       69      154      114
17    11 Two More Rungs           1.11%     78       63       93      102
18    12 Levittown, U.S.A.        5.33%     95       91       76       97
19    13 Hardscrabble             1.22%    113      117       98       96
20    14 New Beginnings           3.22%     99      110      119       86
```

Examine the top 10 clusters. Then move on to save the work that we completed in Lesson 4.

Saving Your Worksheet in a File on Diskette

ON YOUR OWN: Use the **/File Save** command to save your completed worksheet in a file. Name this file: **LN04**, for Lesson 4 completed. The file name will be displayed as **LN04.WK1** once the file is saved. You can use the **/Worksheet Titles Clear** command first to clear the titles, if you wish.

MANAGEMENT DISCUSSION

1 Why do consumer researchers attempt to gather and analyze psychographic data? Does the use of such data make sense to you?

Recently, researchers have tried to segment consumers not only by demographic characteristics but also by life-style. Patterns of consumer buying behavior, magazines read, television shows watched, propensity to use a coupon in the Sunday newspaper, for example, can be identified based on life-styles. These data are often used in conjunction with demographic data.

This type of research, along with similar research on attitudes and values, remains controversial. Some critics question whether such life-style differences are identifiable, and if so, whether these differences can be translated into a more effective marketing campaign. Supporters of psychographic data argue that major differences can be found even among consumers with similar demographic characteristics. These differences, they maintain, are reflected measurably in psychographic data that explain variations in purchasing behavior.

These particular PRIZM data rely on the assumption: "Birds of a feather flock together." If you agree that similar types of people tend to live within the same zip code, then this type of consumer segmentation scheme should appear useful to you.

2 Why is the distinction between "heavy users" and "users" important?

Marketers often use a form of market segmentation called "volume segmentation" to divide a market into light-, medium-, and heavy-user groups. Heavy users are commonly a small part of the market but can represent a large percentage of total consumption. For example, a little over one-third of households consume 90% of all cola; 17% of all households consume 88% of all beer; and 41% of all households consume 81% of all shampoos. Heavy users also tend to have common demographics, psychographics, media habits, and responses to promotional efforts.

All of these factors make the heavy-user group important not only in terms of consumption, but also for information on the characteristics and motivations of such a consumer group. Often very different from other user groups, heavy users provide insight that may be useful in trying to persuade other users to use more. Still, many companies study their heavy users intensively to ensure the continued loyalty of their franchise.

It should be noted that the data in Table 3.4 are for heavy users and *all* users, which includes heavy users as well.

3 What do these results indicate about who disproportionately buys Suave? Who uses Suave?

These data do not distinguish purchase from usage. The intent is only to determine which types of households use Suave.

The appendix at the end of the lessons provides a description of each "Psychographic Cluster." The indexes calculated indicate that certain psychographic segments of consumers—those with large families do tend to use Suave disproportionately; for example, "Shotguns and Pickups," "New Homesteaders," "Coalburg and Corntown," and "Blue Chip Blues."

4 Do these results reinforce your conclusions drawn from the demographic data?

You should make your own judgment about whether these indexes display a coherent pattern of types that tend to buy Suave most often and use it most heavily. You should also judge whether the results of this psychographic segmentation is consistent with the demographic segmentation data.

5 Which types of people should the new Suave campaign target? What image should the advertising campaign project?

Psychographic segmentation is frequently used to establish the image for a brand. Marketers try to make the image consistent with the life-style of those people the campaign is trying to reach. A family scene may be more appropriate for heavy users; a career-oriented scene for nonusers. Based on your decision on what types of consumers Suave should target, you can determine what image the campaign should project.

CHAPTER 4

Stage 2: Advertising Effectiveness

Ellen Vallera and Gail Lanznar had to reach a consensus about the effectiveness of advertising for Suave shampoo. In completing the next four lessons, you should consider the following questions:

- What do you conclude about the cost effectiveness of a $1 million increase in advertising for Suave shampoo?
- How would you allocate the advertising budget?

Moreover, it may be useful to look at some of Suave's advertisements. Appendix II contains "storyboards" of some representative media advertisements.

INTRODUCTION

Ellen Vallera, brand manager for Suave, had examined Gail Lanznar's research report in great detail. She felt that the report contained important insights into consumer buying behavior and Suave's position in the shampoo market. This information helped Vallera analyze the potential effectiveness of advertising. An assessment of the value of advertising was integral to developing realistic financial projections and well-supported budget requests.

The two decided to meet to discuss the effectiveness of advertising for Suave shampoo. They recognized that the advertising budget would depend on many factors, including: management goals, gross margins, the role of advertising versus other marketing expenditures, competitive advertising levels, and retailers' demands. Furthermore, advertising could have many different effects. Among other effects, it could induce retailers to carry the product and/or increase its shelf-space allocation, prevent other firms from entering the market, and allow the company to realize larger gross margins.

However, Lanznar believed that it was most important to focus on developing a better understanding of the consumer buying process for Suave and other shampoos. She therefore decided to collect more precise behavioral information to help determine the possible responsiveness of new and current users to Suave advertising. In addition, Vallera had pulled her files on the costs of advertising on television and in selected magazines. She would use these data to estimate the costs of reaching different groups of consumers through advertising.

Lanznar and Vallera decided to combine their data, and attempt to estimate more precisely the likely effectiveness of advertising expenditures for Suave shampoo. They organized this stage of the analysis into four sections:

1 The Consumer Buying Process
2 The Costs of Advertising Media
3 Break-Even Analysis of Advertising
4 Break-Even Analysis: New Versus Current Users

The information generated in the first two sections would be used in the following two sections. These latter two sections would lead Vallera to more complete analyses of the financial implications of various advertising budgets for Suave shampoo.

LESSON 5 THE CONSUMER BUYING PROCESS

OVERVIEW

COMPUTER INSTRUCTIONS

Lesson 5 is a very brief Lotus 1-2-3 exercise. The commands used in this lesson have already been introduced. These exercises are included as a separate lesson because they introduce another important marketing concept: the "consumer buying process."

MANAGEMENT ISSUES

The consumer buying process refers to the stages that a consumer goes through from becoming aware of a product to deciding whether to become a "loyal" customer for a particular brand. Managers need to understand the subtleties of this process and how different elements of a marketing program influence a consumer at each stage of the process.

MANAGEMENT DISCUSSION QUESTIONS

1 What do these data on the consumer buying process tell you about how consumers buy shampoo?
2 What do the conversion rates tell you about the consumer buying process?
3 Compare Suave's conversion rate to that of other brands.
4 What do the loyalty rates tell you about the buying process?
5 Does this definition of loyalty make sense to you?
6 Do the conversion and loyalty rates for the shampoo market seem low to you? If so, why do you think they are?

CASE

Lanznar had brought to the meeting data from two consumer surveys conducted for Helene Curtis. These data are shown in Tables 4.1 and 4.2. She felt that the data could be combined to provide a picture of the process that consumers go through when buying shampoo. Marketers sometimes called this mental process the "hierarchy of effects."

The hierarchy of effects concept proposes that a consumer goes through a series of discrete steps from first becoming aware of a product (e.g., advertising and brand awareness) eventually to purchasing and repurchasing the product. Understanding this thought process allows the marketer to be more precise about the intended and actual effects of any marketing program.

TABLE 4.1 AWARENESS AND TRIAL DATA

Brand	Aided Advertising Awareness[a]	Unaided Brand Awareness[b]	Aided Brand Awareness[c]	Ever Having Tried
Suave	29%	19%	88%	45%
Agree	44	10	86	30
Flex	31	24	87	47
Head & Shoulders	52	37	96	53
Jhirmack	66	18	74	14
Pert	43	14	82	34
Prell	41	52	96	59
Silkience	60	17	86	39
Vidal Sassoon	56	13	79	25
Private label/generic[d]	—	—	—	—

[a]The percentage of respondents who replied positively when asked, "Have you seen an advertisement for Suave shampoo lately?"
[b]The percentage of respondents who mentioned Suave when asked, "What shampoos have you heard of?"
[c]The percentage of respondents who replied positively when asked, "Have you heard of Suave shampoo?"
[d]Data not available.
Source: Awareness, Usage, and Attitude Study, June/July 1983; company records.

This fundamental tool of marketing analysis divides the buying process into specific, discrete stages. Four of these stages are suggested by Tables 4.1 and 4.2:

- Awareness of the product;
- Trial of the product;
- Repeat usage; and
- Loyalty, sometimes measured by an index of the rate of usage.

In addition, marketers also talked about "conversion rates." For example, what percentage of consumers who were aware of the Suave brand (or its advertising) had actually tried it?[1] Lanznar thought the conversion rate might be an important measure of the efficacy of advertising for Suave.

Lanznar used the "aided brand awareness" and "ever having tried" measures in Table 4.1 to compute this conversion rate for each brand. She divided the measure of trial by the measure of awareness, and put the conversion rates into percentage form.

One of the most important aspects of consumer buying behavior in the shampoo market is the loyalty of consumers to a brand. Lanznar used the data in Table 4.2 to derive a measure of brand loyalty, defined as the percentage of total shampoo needs

---

[1]The percentage of consumers who have tried a product once and then buy it again within that same year (another measure of loyalty) is another example of a conversion rate. However, the data necessary to calculate this conversion rate appear in both Tables 4.1 and 4.2, and these tables are not based on the same consumer sample. Numerical comparisons based on data from both tables, therefore, could cause problems.

TABLE 4.2   BRAND PURCHASE DATA

Brand	Percentage of Buyers Purchasing at Least Twice (within One Year)	Total Shampoo Ounces (All Brands) per Brand Customer	Brand Shampoo Ounces per Brand Customer
Suave	41%	104.0[a]	38.4[a]
Agree	29	96.9	20.4
Flex	37	90.9	29.9
Dandruff brands[b]	—	67.1	19.2
Jhirmack	32	64.9	14.4
Pert	41	83.5	23.8
Prell	43	67.7	15.6
Silkience	34	87.8	20.8
Vidal Sasson	40	87.1	19.8
Private label/generic	36	100.8	35.2

[a]To be read, "The average customer who had bought Suave last year bought 104.0 ounces of shampoo that year. Of that 104.0 ounces, the average customer bought 38.4 ounces of Suave and 65.6 ounces of all others combined (104.0 − 38.4 = 65.6)."
[b]Includes Head & Shoulders.

Source: Company records; based on research conducted by National Diary Research, Inc., June 1982–May 1983, on a nationally representative sample of 6,500 households.

each brand's customers filled with purchases of that brand. To compute this measure of loyalty, she divided "brand shampoo ounces per brand customer" by "total shampoo ounces (all brands) per brand customer." She then put the loyalty rates in percentage form.

After these calculations were made, Lanznar and Vallera discussed what these and the previous results indicated about the nature of the shampoo market, how consumers buy shampoo, and the role of advertising for Suave. They felt that the survey results, in particular, offered a wealth of information on how advertising affects consumer buying behavior.

COMPUTER INSTRUCTIONS

Retrieving and Examining the Worksheet File for Lesson 5

To begin Lesson 5, we need to retrieve a new worksheet file from the Suave Data Diskette. First, follow these familiar steps, if necessary:

1 Load DOS. Enter date and time.
2 Load the Lotus Access System.
3 Load the 1-2-3 software program.

ON YOUR OWN: Insert the Suave Data Disk into the appropriate disk drive. Use the **/File Retrieve** command to load the worksheet file: **LESSON05.WKS.** After loading the worksheet file, switch diskettes. Remove the Suave Data Diskette and replace it with your data diskette.

After pressing the **[Home]** key, your worksheet will appear with the data from Table 4.1 contained on this first screen. Press the **[PgDn]** key to display the data from Table 4.2.

Now press the **[Home]** key, and let's move on to compute a "conversion rate" and then a "loyalty" measure for each brand.

Computing a Conversion Rate for Each Brand

ON YOUR OWN: Computer a conversion rate for each brand and place the results in **Column G.**

Use this formula:

$$\text{Conversion Rate Percentage} = \frac{\text{Ever Having Tried Percentage}}{\text{Aided Brand Awareness Percentage}}$$

That is, input into cell **G8** the formula: **F8/E8.** Put the result in **Percent** format with **zero decimal** places. **Copy** the result **to all other brands.**

Note: You have to format only cell G8 after inputting the formula for G8. Then when you copy the formula to cells G9..G17, the display format will be copied as well.

Your screen should appear as follows:

```
 G8: (P0) +F8/E8                                                    READY


           A        B        C        D        E        F        G
     1   LESSON 5                              Table 4.1
     2
     3
     4                       Aided    Unaided   Aided    Ever
     5                       Ad       Brand     Brand    Having   Conversion
     6   Brand               Awareness Awareness Awareness Tried    Rate
     7   ---------------     --------- --------- --------- --------- ---------
     8   Suave                 29%      19%       88%      45%      51%
     9   Agree                 44%      10%       86%      30%      35%
    10   Flex                  31%      24%       87%      47%      54%
    11   Head & Shoulders      52%      37%       96%      53%      55%
    12   Jhirmack              66%      18%       74%      14%      19%
    13   Pert                  43%      14%       82%      34%      41%
    14   Prell                 41%      52%       96%      59%      61%
    15   Silkience             60%      17%       86%      39%      45%
    16   Vidal Sassoon         56%      13%       79%      25%      32%
    17   Private Label/        NA       NA        NA       NA       NA
    18      Generic
    19
    20
```

Computing a Brand Loyalty Measure for Each Brand

Now let's compute a loyalty measure for each brand.

ON YOUR OWN: Press the **[PgDn]** key to display the data in Table 4.2. Compute a loyalty measure for each brand and place the results in **Column G.**

Use this formula:

$$\text{Brand Loyalty Measure} = \frac{\text{Brand Shampoo Ounces per Brand Customer}}{\text{Total Shampoo Ounces (All Brands) per Brand Customer}}$$

That is, input into cell **G30** the formula: **F30/E30.** Put the result in **Percent** format with **zero decimal** places. **Copy** the result **to all other brands.**

Your screen should appear as follows:

```
G30:  (P0)  +F30/E30                                            READY


          A        B        C        D        E        F        G
21                                        Table 4.2
22
23                                   % of Buyers  Total    Brand
24                                   Purchasing   Shampoo  Shampoo
25                                   at Least     Oz. (All Ounces
26                                   Twice        Brands)  Per      Brand
27                                   (within      Per Brand Brand   Loyalty
28        Brand                      1 year)      Customer Customer Index
29        ------------------         ----------   -------- -------- --------
30        Suave                         41%        104.0    38.4      37%
31        Agree                         29%         96.9    20.4      21%
32        Flex                          37%         90.9    29.9      33%
33        Dandruff Brands               NA          67.1    19.2      29%
34        Jhirmack                      32%         64.9    14.4      22%
35        Pert                          41%         83.5    23.8      29%
36        Prell                         43%         67.7    15.6      23%
37        Silkience                     34%         87.8    20.8      24%
38        Vidal Sassoon                 40%         87.1    19.8      23%
39        Private Label/                36%        100.8    35.2      35%
40           Generic
```

That's it! Check your results with those starting at row 101, if you like, and then let's save this file.

Saving Your Worksheet in a File on Diskette

ON YOUR OWN: Return to cell A1 and use the **/File Save** command to save the results of our computations. Name the new file: **LN05.**

Good. This lesson has been relatively brief, so let's take a look at how to copy diskettes with Lotus 1-2-3. These methods are different from those discussed in the introductory section, "Using DOS to List and to Copy Files."

Copying Diskettes with Lotus 1-2-3

We've done a lot of work in Lessons 1 through 5 and have created five new files that contain our results. As is discussed in the section on "Using DOS," we should make a copy of our diskettes, so that we don't lose our work in case something happens.

Take out a new, completely blank diskette. You don't even have to worry about formatting this blank diskette.

First, we can always copy a diskette by selecting the **/Quit** command to return to the Lotus Access System and then the **/Exit** menu choice to return to the A> prompt in DOS. Once here, make sure that DOS is loaded and then follow the "diskcopy" instructions in the introductory section of the book on "Using DOS."

Note: When you select the **/Quit** command and confirm **Yes,** you will return to the Lotus Access System. *Before you take these steps, always save the worksheet you had just been working on.* The **/Quit** command (and a confirmed **yes**) will cause you to leave 1-2-3 and will therefore clear the current worksheet. You will have lost your work unless it was saved first. It is best to save your work often. You can easily use the **/File Save Replace** command to make any additions or changes to a saved file, keeping the same file name.

Moreover, Lotus 1-2-3 has the **/System** command to allow you to leave 1-2-3 temporarily and access the operating system, DOS.

ON YOUR OWN: With the Lotus system diskette loaded, invoke the **/System** command. At the A> prompt, make sure DOS is loaded, then follow the normal **diskcopy** procedures. After copying, to return to 1-2-3, type **exit** at the DOS A> prompt. The operating system will return you to 1-2-3 just where you left off in Lesson 5! (If DOS is not loaded, you will get an "error" message. If this happens, press **[Esc]** and then load DOS.)

Release 1A Users: The **/System** command is not available. Release 1A can copy diskettes, however, in a way not available to Release 2 and 2.01 users. The Lotus Access System contains a "Disk-Manager" program, which has a **"Disk-Copy"** command. Use the **/Quit** command to return to the Lotus Access System, select the Disk-Manager program, copy the diskette, and follow the instructions to return to 1-2-3.

Reviewing What We've Learned in Lesson 5

The purpose of this lesson was to practice the skills we have already learned in Lessons 1 through 4. In addition, we learned more about copying:

- The **/Quit** command can be used to end a 1-2-3 session when the first menu line (Worksheet...Quit) is displayed. You will be directed to press Yes to confirm this selection.
- Always save your worksheet before selecting the **/Quit** command and confirming yes.
- Releases 2 and 2.01 have the **/System** command to allow you to leave 1-2-3 temporarily and access the operating system, DOS. Then the normal procedures can be followed to copy a diskette and return to 1-2-3.

- Release 1A allows you to return to the "Lotus Access System" menu, selecting the Disk-Manager program and **Disk-Copy** command to permit you to copy your diskette very easily.

MANAGEMENT DISCUSSION

1. **What do these data on the consumer buying process tell you about how consumers buy shampoo?**

   These data help us to understand the discrete stages, what marketers refer to as a "hierarchy of effects," that consumers go through when deciding what product to buy:

   - Awareness (unaided and aided);
   - Interest;
   - Trial; and
   - Regular use, establishing a certain amount of loyalty

   The data suggest that whereas consumers have trouble remembering the names of shampoos, when helped ("aided"), they are familiar with different brand names. This fact suggests that many shampoo decisions are made in front of the store shelf.

2. **What do the conversion rates tell you about the consumer buying process?**

   This conversion rate measures the percentage of consumers already aware of the shampoo brand that actually try the brand. The rates show that over 40% of people who are aware of a brand will try it at some time. These conversion rates imply that awareness of a brand name often leads to a trial purchase in this market.

3. **Compare Suave's conversion rate to that of other brands.**

   Suave's conversion rate of 51% is slightly above average for the selected brands that are shown in Tables 4.1 and 4.2. The highest conversion rate is for Prell, one of the oldest and most established brands in the shampoo market. The lowest conversion rate is for Jhirmack, which was one of the newest brands in the shampoo market in 1983.

4. **What do the loyalty rates tell you about the buying process?**

   These loyalty rates refer to the ongoing decisions of a customer who buys a brand more than once in a year: How much of that customer's total shampoo purchases are accounted for by that one brand? To calculate this brand loyalty index, divide the brand shampoo ounces bought by a brand customer by the total shampoo ounces bought. These low rates indicate that consumers seem to buy many different brands of shampoo over time, and keep many brands of shampoo on their shelves at the same time.

5. Does this definition of loyalty make sense to you?

This loyalty index is based on the ounces bought by a brand customer. A "brand customer" is defined as someone who has purchased that brand more than once in a year. This definition might be questioned. "Brand loyalty" could be defined as the percentage of total ounces sold to consumers who only buy that brand or who buy that brand twice in a row. Or, it might be argued, a more useful measure would be based on either units or retail dollar value bought by a brand customer. A quantifiable measure for a concept such as "confirmed customer" and "loyalty" rate is difficult to find.

6. Do the conversion and loyalty rates for the shampoo market seem low to you? If so, why do you think they are?

The conversion rates in the shampoo market are relatively normal for consumer household goods. In fact, for established brands like Prell and Head & Shoulders, the conversion rate is higher than it is for many household products.

However, the loyalty index for shampoo brands is relatively low compared to other branded household products. One explanation is that consumers frequently try different brands because they are never fully satisfied with any one brand of shampoo. Also, many shampoo customers believe that they should frequently change brands of shampoo to attain the best appearance for their hair. (There is no conclusive evidence on shampoo efficacy one way or the other.)

In addition, the brand loyalty index is defined based on shampoo purchases by a customer, but if that customer is the head of the household who is buying, for example, one brand of shampoo for the children, another brand for one adult, and a third brand for a second adult, then the brand loyalty index, with a definition based on purchasing, would appear relatively low. The brand loyalty index might be higher if data were based on usage.

LESSON 6   THE COSTS OF ADVERTISING MEDIA

OVERVIEW

COMPUTER INSTRUCTIONS

Lesson 6 is also a relatively brief exercise with functions and commands that have already been introduced. The instructions provide the necessary formulas, but ask you to perform the actual steps on your own. At this point, you should be feeling increasingly confident in your ability to use the basic functions and commands of Lotus 1-2-3.

MANAGEMENT ISSUES

Lesson 6 provides data on media advertising costs and introduces the concepts of audience reach and target audiences. A manager must decide whether an advertising campaign will pay off. The cost of various kinds of advertising and the characteristics of particular media need to be considered. Lesson 6 presents a sampling of media options available for an advertising campaign.

MANAGEMENT DISCUSSION QUESTIONS

1 What does the "cost-per-thousand" (CPM) tell you? Why do managers use CPM as a measure of advertising cost?

2 In choosing media, what factors must be considered other than CPM and the type of delivered audience?

3 Compare the CPM for prime-time versus daytime television. Why is prime-time television more expensive, even measured by CPM?

4 Compare the CPM for television versus print. Why does print in general have higher CPMs?

5 Why would the marketers of certain products use print media?

CASE

Vallera had gathered data on advertising rates for television and selected magazines. Table 4.3 presents data on the costs and audience delivery of a 30-second television commercial. Table 4.4 presents data for the costs and audience delivery of fifteen magazines. She used the data to calculate the cost of an advertising program and match that cost with the audience reached by the different media.

One of the standard measures of media advertising costs is the "cost-per-thou-

TABLE 4.3   TELEVISION: ADVERTISING COSTS AND AUDIENCE DELIVERY[a]

Cost of Average 30-Second Commercial	Estimated Audience Delivery (in millions)				
	Homes	Total Female	Women 25-54	Total Male	Men 25-54
Prime-Time–Network					
$77,975	12.9	13.3	4.9	12.0	4.5
Daytime–Network					
$13,350	5.0	5.1	2.1	4.6	

[a]All numbers are averaged and do not reflect seasonal differences.

Source: Company records, 1983/1984.

sand" (CPM) to reach various audiences. Vallera used Lotus 1-2-3 and the data in Tables 4.3 and 4.4 to compute the CPMs for prime-time television, daytime television, and the fifteen selected magazines.

Vallera was particularly interested in evaluating the effects of a $1 million increase in advertising expenditures. For this purpose, she computed the actual number

TABLE 4.4   SELECTED MAGAZINES: COSTS AND AUDIENCE DELIVERY

Publication	Circulation Rate Base (000s)	Cost of Four-Color Full-Page Ad	Cost of Black and White Full-Page Ad	Average Audience (in thousands)			
				Men 18+	Men 18-49	Women 18+	Women 18-49
General Orientation							
Fortune	690	$36,020	$23,700	1,860	1,376	897	660
National Enquirer	5,075	32,780	26,000	6,987	5,434	11,567	7,724
The New Yorker	480	18,700	11,750	1,311	829	1,238	811
People	2,600	49,200	38,175	7,871	6,479	13,953	10,931
Time	4,600	101,825	65,275	12,322	9,181	9,146	6,500
TV Guide	17,000	85,000	72,000	16,737	12,859	21,101	15,227
Male Orientation							
Playboy	4,400	53,765	38,395	8,422	7,357	—	—
Popular Science	1,800	31,280	22,055	3,801	2,685	—	—
Sports Illustrated	2,425	66,165	42,415	10,786	8,929	—	—
Female Orientation							
Cosmopolitan	2,500	36,575	27,180	—	—	8,253	7,068
Family Circle	7,250	68,150	57,275	—	—	16,613	10,443
Glamour	1,900	31,200	22,100	—	—	5,784	5,145
McCall's	6,200	64,620	52,560	—	—	14,536	9,124
Redbook	3,800	46,940	35,495	—	—	7,743	5,631
Working Mother	500	11,750	8,850	—	—	993	793

Source: Company records, 1983/1984.

of advertisements (on prime-time television, on daytime television, and in each magazine) that Helene Curtis could purchase for each $1 million spent. She decided to compare the level of advertising exposure that $1 million would provide with the results of the break-even analysis. This comparison offered additional insight into whether advertising was likely to be profitable for Suave shampoo. Lanznar's analysis would provide a framework for evaluating how an advertisement might be effective in generating greater sales volume.

COMPUTER INSTRUCTIONS

Retrieving and Examining the Worksheet File for Lesson 6

To begin Lesson 6, we need to retrieve the file for this lesson from the Suave Data Diskette. First, follow these familiar steps, if necessary:

1 Load DOS. Enter date and time.
2 Load the Lotus Access System.
3 Load the 1-2-3 software program.

ON YOUR OWN: Insert the Suave Data Diskette into the appropriate disk drive. Use the **/File Retrieve** command to load the worksheet file: **LESSON06.WKS.** After loading the worksheet file, switch diskettes. Remove the Suave Data Diskette and replace it with your data diskette. Press the **[Home]** key as directed.

ON YOUR OWN: Use the **[PgDn]**, **[PgUp]**, **[Tab]**, and **[Shift-Tab]** keys to examine the worksheet. Note that the data from Table 4.3 start on the first screen at cell **A1** and continue onto the second screen, beginning at **A21**. The data from Table 4.4 begin at cell **A41** and run onto additional screens, both down (to row 67) and to the right (to column T).

Press the **[Home]** key to return to cell A1. Now let's move on to calculate the "Cost Per Thousand" for prime-time and daytime television.

Note: This lesson allows you practice at increasing your speed in performing commands already introduced. To display all the data requires many 1-2-3 screens. *Do only as many repetitive calculations as you feel that you need.* The completed worksheet begins in cell A101.

Creating Formulas to Calculate the CPM of Reaching Various Television Audiences

ON YOUR OWN: The first part of Table 4.3, beginning at cell **A1**, provides data on costs and audiences for prime-time television. First, create the simple **formulas** for "All Viewers" (**B13 = D13+F13**) and for "All Adults" (**H13 = E13+G13).** Put the results in **Fixed** format with **one decimal** place.

Then, calculate the "Cost Per Thousand" for each audience delivered with prime-time television. The formula for cost per thousand is:

$$\text{CPM} = \frac{\text{Cost of Average 30-Second Commercial}}{\text{Audience Delivered (in thousands)}}$$

Since the "audience delivered" figures are displayed in millions, to calculate CPM based on audience in thousands, you should input in cell **B16** the formula:

B16 = $A$13/(B13*1000)

Remember that $A$13 stands for an "absolute" reference to cell **A13**. Press the [**Abs**] key ([**F4**] on most keyboards) to make a cell reference **absolute. Copy** the formula in **B16 to cells C16 through H16** for each audience segment. Put the results in **Currency** format with **two decimal** places.

Good. Your screen should appear as:

```
 B16:  (C2)  +$A$13/(B13*1000)                                          READY


          A        B        C        D        E       F       G        H
 1     LESSON 6                               Table 4.3
 2
 3
 4                              PRIME TIME - NETWORK
 5
 6
 7           <----------Estimated Audience Delivery (in millions)---------->
 8     Cost of
 9     Average                                                          All
10     30-Second   All               Total    Women   Total    Men    Adults
11     Commerc'l  Viewers  Homes    Female     25-54   Male    25-54   25-54
12     --------  --------  -------- --------  -------- -------- ------- --------
13     $77,975     25.3     12.9     13.3      4.9     12.0     4.5     9.4
14
15
16     CPM:       $3.08    $6.04    $5.86    $15.91    $6.50   $17.33   $8.30
17     (Cost Per
18     Thousand)
19
20
```

Then, press the [**PgDn**] key to display the second part of Table 4.3, beginning at cell A21, that provides data on costs and audiences for daytime television. Create a **formula** for "All Viewers" (**C33 = E33 + G33).**

Create a **formula** in cell **C36** for the CPM for "All Viewers, **C36 = $A$33/ (C33*1000),"** and **copy** that formula to cells **D36 through G36** for each audience segment. Use the **same format** as above.

Good. Your screen should appear as:

```
C36: (C2) +$A$33/(C33*1000)                                                    READY


        A          B          C          D          E          F          G          H
 21                                       Table 4.3 (continued)
 22
 23
 24                                       DAYTIME - NETWORK
 25
 26
 27                                <-Estimated Audience Delivery (in millions)->
 28     Cost of
 29     Average
 30     30-Second          All                  Total      Women      Total
 31     Commerc'l          Viewers    Homes     Female     25-54      Male
 32     --------           --------   --------  --------   --------   --------
 33     $13,350            9.7        5.0       5.1        2.1        4.6
 34
 35
 36     CPM:               $1.38      $2.67     $2.62      $6.36      $2.90
 37     (Cost Per
 38     Thousand)
 39
 40
```

Observation: If you get 0 for cells D36 through G36 when you copy, you forgot to key in the absolute cell reference for cell A33.

Now let's move on to calculate the CPM for selected print media.

Creating Formulas to Calculate the CPM of Reaching Various Print Audiences

ON YOUR OWN: The data from Table 4.4 are contained in cells **A41 to T67.** This table provides data on costs and audiences for selected, well-known American magazines. This section will give you practice creating formulas, formatting cells, and copying. Press the **[PgDn]** key to display the beginning of this table.

First, make sure that cell **A41** is the upper left cell in the worksheet. Then position the cell pointer in **D48** and use the **/Worksheet Titles Both** command to freeze both horizontal and vertical titles. This should make it much easier to follow where you are in Table 4.4 as you create and copy formulas.

Second, create the **formulas** for CPM for both four-color and black and white full-page ads for each audience type. Notice that cells with "NA" (or dashes) contain no data, as data are either not applicable or not available. Start by creating the formulas for *Fortune* magazine for each audience segment and put the results in line 49. Notice that the average audience for each segment is listed in Table 4.4 *in thousands.* Therefore, you should create the following formulas for CPM:

$$K49 \;=\; E49/(G49+I49)$$

$$L49 \;=\; F49/(G49+I49)$$

$$M49 = E49/G49$$

$$N49 = F49/G49$$

$$O49 = E49/H49$$

$$P49 = F49/H49$$

$$Q49 = E49/I49$$

$$R49 = F49/I49$$

$$S49 = E49/J49$$

$$T49 = F49/J49$$

Note: When entering a cell address such as E49 in building a formula, you may always type "**E49**" (or "**e49**") instead of "pointing" to the cell.

Third, put all the results in line 49 into **Currency** format with **two decimal** places.

Fourth, **copy** these formulas for all the other magazines listed. Remember, you can save time by making the **range FROM: K49..T49**. Then make the **range TO: K50..T54** using **anchoring.**

Note: As a shortcut, you only need specify a range TO of K50..K54. 1-2-3 will then automatically copy L49..T49 into cells in a similar pattern, i.e., L49 into L50..L54, M49 into M50..M54, etc.

Again, select the **/Copy** command and make the **range FROM: K49..T49**, but this time make **range TO: K57..T59 (or K57..K59).**

Select the **/Copy** command for a third time and make the **range FROM: K49..T49**, but this time make the **range TO: K62..T67 (or K62..K67).**

Keep the Worksheet Titles on for now. Press the [**Home**] key. The cell pointer should return to cell **D48.**

ON YOUR OWN: Use the [**Tab**], [**Shift-Tab**], [**PgUp**], and [**PgDn**] keys to view your results. Check your results with those beginning at row 101, if you wish.

Observation: As we saw in Lesson 4, when we "freeze" titles so that they will appear on every screen, we limit the amount of new data that we can view when we move from screen to screen.

Note: Many people contend that Lotus 1-2-3 works better vertically than horizontally. That is, as we see in this lesson, whereas as many as 20 rows can be displayed on each screen, usually only 8 columns (of 9 characters) can be displayed. Using the **/Worksheet Titles** command further limits our ability to see all the data on as few screens as possible, although it does help us identify what the data pertain to.

Good. Now let's save our results.

Saving Your Worksheet in a File on Diskette

ON YOUR OWN: First, use the **/Worksheet Titles Clear** command to remove the Worksheet Titles. Then press the [**Home**] key to return to cell A1.

Use the **/File Save** command to save your work. Name this new worksheet file: **LN06.**

Reviewing What We've Learned in Lesson 6

This lesson gave us the opportunity to practice the skills we have already learned and perhaps to pick up some speed in performing various steps and commands. We also introduced a sometimes quicker way of building a formula:

- You may type a cell address instead of pointing to that address with the cell pointer.
- When copying FROM a range of cells TO a range of cells, you need not specify the entire range to copy TO in certain instances.

MANAGEMENT DISCUSSION

1 What does "cost-per-thousand" (CPM) tell you? Why do managers use CPM as a measure of advertising cost?

CPM provides a relative measure of advertising costs. It allows managers to compare various advertising media based on a common measure of the cost of reaching one thousand viewers/readers at one time. CPM data are easily obtained and help managers think about the cost effectiveness of the media selected. This measure does not, however, differentiate among types of consumers—some who may be part of the target audience, some who may not be.

2 In choosing media, what factors must be considered other than CPM and the type of delivered audience?

Managers must examine other factors in evaluating the cost effectiveness of advertising media. They usually consider not ony the number of households reached by a campaign (reach) but also the number of times a household needs exposure to a message within a period of time (frequency) and the effect of each ad.

Advertisements in some media have more impact for a certain product or for a certain purpose than they would if other media were used. For example, television ads may be useful to present relatively simple products and to generate awareness, whereas magazine ads are more useful to present more complex products, to provide detailed information, and to encourage consumers to examine these products when shopping. The audience quality, audience attention, and the prestige of the media are additional considerations in selecting and evaluating media.

3 Compare the CPM for prime-time versus daytime television. Why is prime-time television more expensive, even measured by CPM?

Prime-time television is considered more valuable per advertisement than daytime television for a number of reasons. A more valuable demographic group is often reached on prime-time, and viewers tend to pay more attention to prime-time ads than to daytime ads (increased impact).

4 Compare the CPM for television versus print. Why does print in general have higher CPMs?

Print has higher CPMs for at least two reasons. First, because the print media has more well defined, specific audiences, advertisers are able to reach the desired consumer segments more efficiently, without wasting much money on advertising to customers who might not be interested in the product. For example, advertisers who want to reach young women can choose two or three women's magazines, specifically designed to reach that audience.

Second, print advertisements allow the marketer to provide much more detailed information about the product than could a television advertisement. This information may be exposed to the reader (or readers) many times, and at a time convenient for the reader, who will pay more attention to the ad.

5 Why would the marketers of certain products use print media?

Marketers who wish to convey a complex message or who wish to document certain claims about the product, would consider using print advertisements. The printed page allows emphasis of more specific facts than does a 30-second television commercial.

LESSON 7 BREAK-EVEN ANALYSIS OF ADVERTISING

OVERVIEW

COMPUTER INSTRUCTIONS

Lesson 7 asks you to input merely a few formulas. In this way, it is a relatively short lesson. However, the lesson also demonstrates the value of a well-designed worksheet to organize data in such a way that it can be more easily understood and found. In addition, the lesson previews one of the most powerful capabilities of Lotus 1-2-3: the ability to test quickly the effects of changes in the value of a variable when formulas are written using Lotus 1-2-3.

MANAGEMENT ISSUES

Lesson 7 is principally intended to introduce the concept of "break-even analysis"— a fundamental management analysis tool. Break-even calculations are simple to perform, yet often provide a wealth of insight. Using Lotus 1-2-3, one can easily test the financial implications of, for example, different advertising budgets.

MANAGEMENT QUESTIONS

1 What is break-even analysis? Why is it useful?
2 What are the important elements of a break-even formula?
3 Why should a manager perform a break-even analysis in terms of both ounces and market share?
4 What preliminary conclusion might you reach about the feasibility of Helene Curtis breaking even on a $1 million increase in advertising for Suave?

CASE

Vallera was ready to begin the break-even analyses. These analyses would provide further insight into the feasibility of increased advertising spending. Lanznar would help her to interpret the results within the context of the buying behavior and competition in the shampoo market.

Explanation of Break-Even Analysis

Break-even analysis enables managers to determine the sales volume necessary to generate enough "contribution" (or gross margin)[2] to recover the costs of certain expenditures. "Incremental" and "total" break-evens are both common. A manager might be interested in the incremental sales volume required to break even on an increase in expenditures, or in the total sales volume necessary to break even on the total expenditures under consideration.

The basic break-even formula is:

$$\frac{\text{Marketing (Advertising) Expenditures}}{\text{Gross Margin per Unit}} = \text{Units Necessary to Break Even}$$

"Units" may be defined as desired, such as per ounce or per bottle of shampoo.

Basic Break-Even Calculation for Suave Shampoo

Vallera decided to use Lotus 1-2-3 to complete all the break-even calculations and save them in her diskette files. These individual calculations could be carried out just as easily with a calculator. However, by using Lotus 1-2-3 she could run different analyses just by changing one of the numbers in any of the equations.

To begin her financial analysis of advertising effectiveness, Vallera wanted to calculate the results of incremental break-even analyses. Later, as part of a more sophisticated set of financial projections, she would generate several break-even analyses on total marketing expenditures.

Vallera ran the following calculation[3] to determine the additional Suave sales (in ounces) necessary to break even for each incremental $1 million of advertising:

$$\begin{array}{l}\text{Additional Suave} \\ \text{Sales (in Ounces)} \\ \text{Necessary to} \\ \text{Break Even}\end{array} = \frac{\$1 \text{ million}}{\text{Gross Margin per Suave Ounce Sold}}$$

The "gross margin per Suave ounce sold" was calculated as follows:

$$\left[\begin{array}{l}\text{Average Retail} \\ \text{Price per Ounce}\end{array} * \begin{array}{l}1 - \text{Retail Gross} \\ \text{Margin \%}\end{array}\right] * \left[\begin{array}{l}1 - \text{Variable} \\ \text{Cost \%}\end{array}\right]$$

---

[2] Gross margin is defined as dollar sales minus cost of goods sold (commonly the major component of variable costs); to convert it to a percentage, it is then divided by the dollar sales. The terms gross margin and contribution are often used interchangeably; contribution, however, subtracts out *all* variable costs.

[3] For the sake of computational simplicity, break-even analyses are run on a 1-year basis in this case study. Break-even analyses can be run for any number of years. In fact, for many investments and marketing programs, they should be based on a much longer time frame.

which is the same as:

$$\text{Manufacturer Price per Ounce} \times \text{Manufacturer Gross Margin \%}$$

To make this calculation, Vallera compiled three additional pieces of data from her own files and from the Helene Curtis cost-accounting department:

- The average retail price per ounce for Suave in FY 1984 of $0.09;
- An estimated gross margin percentage of 30% for retailers on Suave shampoo; and
- An estimated gross margin percentage of 43% for Helene Curtis on Suave shampoo.

Market-Share Break-Even Calculation

Helene Curtis management was particularly interested in their brands' market shares. Vallera decided, therefore, to compute how much of an increase in market share in ounces (13.6% in FY 1984) would be required to break even, given that 8,560 million ounces of all shampoos were sold in FY 1984.

To compute the necessary increase in market share, she used the following formula:

$$\text{Necessary Increase in Market Share} = \frac{\text{Necessary Additional Ounces}}{8,560 \text{ Million Ounces}}$$

COMPUTER INSTRUCTIONS

Retrieving and Examining the Worksheet File for Lesson 7

To begin Lesson 7, we need to retrieve a new worksheet file from the Suave Data Diskette. First, follow these familiar steps, if necessary:

1 Load DOS. Enter date and time.
2 Load the Lotus Access system.
3 Load the 1-2-3 software program

ON YOUR OWN: Insert the Suave Data Diskette into the appropriate disk drive. Use the **/File Retrieve** command to load the worksheet file: **LESSON07.WKS**. After loading the worksheet file, switch diskettes. Remove the Suave Data Diskette and replace it with your data diskette. Press the **[Home]** key as directed.

Good. Now let's take a look at the data in this worksheet. This first screen contains data on the pricing and cost structure for Suave shampoo. Shortly, we will create three formulas (for cells G13, G17, and G19) that provide additional data about Suave's pricing and margins. We will use these data throughout Lessons 7, 8, 9, and 10.

Press the **[PgDn]** key and look at the screen beginning with cell A21. This screen contains data on the shampoo market in FY 1984. We will use these data in our break-even calculations in Lessons 7, 8, 9, and 10.

Press the **[PgDn]** key once more and look at the screen beginning with cell A41. We will input our break-even formulas onto this screen (in cells G51 and G57).

Observation: Notice that the data have been organized so that specific figures are easy to find. Lotus 1-2-3 provides for an enormous worksheet (8,192 rows [Release 1A Users: 2,048] and 256 columns). It is good practice to make use of as much of this space as necessary to present your data clearly. In Lesson 7, we have organized the different sections of data to begin on new screens. In this way, we can find and use all the data quite easily, just by using the **[PgDn]**, **[PgUp]**, and **[Home]** keys. Such clarity is particularly helpful if co-workers will be using worksheets that you have created. In many companies, diskettes are distributed and exchanged just like memos. *Good organization of data helps others understand and use a worksheet you designed.*

Note: In Lessons 7, 8, 9, and 10, the *completed* lessons will appear on the screens beginning at cell Q1 rather than at the usual cell A101. The other completed screens will run straight downward, on the screens beginning at Q21, Q41, and so forth. To get to the completed lessons, just press **[Tab]** twice. To return, just press **[Shift-Tab]** twice (or **[Home]**). The completed lessons (for Lessons 7, 8, 9, and 10) have been moved because beginning in Lesson 9, we will be using more than the first 100 rows to complete our own work.

Now press the **[Home]** key and let's begin our work.

Creating Formulas for Suave's Pricing and Cost Structure

ON YOUR OWN: We have **three** simple, but important, **formulas** to create for cells **G13, G17,** and **G19** to complete Suave's pricing and gross margin data:

$$1 \quad \begin{array}{l}\text{Manufacturer}\\\text{Price per}\\\text{Ounce for}\\\text{Suave}\end{array} = \begin{array}{l}\text{Retail Price}\\\text{per Ounce}\\\text{for Suave}\end{array} * \left(1 - \begin{array}{l}\text{Retail Gross}\\\text{Margin Percentage}\\\text{for Suave}\end{array}\right)$$

That is:

$$\textbf{G13} \ = \ \textbf{G9}*(1-\textbf{G11})$$

(Format: Currency with 3 decimal places.)

$$2 \quad \begin{array}{l}\text{Manufacturer}\\\text{Gross Margin}\\\text{Percentage}\\\text{for Suave}\end{array} = \left(1 - \begin{array}{l}\text{Variable Cost}\\\text{Margin Percentage}\\\text{for Suave}\end{array}\right)$$

That is:

$$G17 = 1 - G15$$

(Format: Percent with 0 decimal places.)

3   Manufacturer Gross Margin per Ounce for Suave = Manufacturer Price per Ounce for Suave * Manufacturer Gross Margin Percentage for Suave

That is:

$$G19 = G13*G17$$

(Format: Currency with 3 decimal places.)

When you are finished, your screen should appear as:

```
G19: (C3) +G13*G17                                                READY

          A        B        C        D        E      F        G        H
     1  LESSON 7
     2                          BREAK-EVEN ANALYSIS
     3                          -------------------
     4
     5              Pricing and Cost Structure for Suave Shampoo
     6              --------------------------------------------
     7
     8
     9  Retail Price Per Ounce for Suave                   $0.090
    10
    11  Retail Gross Margin Percentage for Suave              30%
    12
    13  Manufacturer Price Per Ounce for Suave             $0.063
    14
    15  Variable Cost Percentage for Suave                    57%
    16
    17  Manufacturer Gross Margin Percentage for Suave        43%
    18
    19  Manufacturer Gross Margin Per Ounce for Suave      $0.027
    20
```

Now we're ready to create some break-even formulas.

Creating Break-Even Formulas

ON YOUR OWN: We need to create in this section **two** break-even **formulas**. (See the case for an "Explanation of Break-Even Analysis.")

Press the **[PgDn]** key twice to display the screen, "Break-Even Analysis: Incremental Advertising Expenditures." Now let's input these two formulas into cells **G51** and **G57**, respectively:

1 Increase in Suave Sales (in millions of ounces) Necessary to Break Even for Each $1 Million Increase in Advertising $= \dfrac{\text{Increase in Advertising for Suave (in millions)}}{\text{Manufacturer Gross Margin per Ounce for Suave}}$

That is:

$$G51 = G45/G19$$

(Format: Fixed with 1 decimal place.)

2 Increase in Market Share Necessary to Break Even for Each $1 Million Increase in Advertising $= \dfrac{\text{Increase in Suave Sales Necessary to Break Even}}{\text{Shampoo Industry Sales in FY 1984}}$

That is:

$$G57 = G51/G26$$

(Format: Percent with 2 decimal places.)

Note: Use the **[PgUp]** or **[PgDn]** keys whenever you like in building a formula.

When you are finished, your screen should look like:

```
G57:  (P2) +G51/G26                                                      READY


            A        B        C        D        E        F        G        H
   41
   42          Break-Even Analysis:  Incremental Advertising Expenditures
   43          ----------------------------------------------------------
   44
   45   Increase in Advertising for Suave (in millions)              $1
   46
   47              SALES NECESSARY TO BREAK EVEN:
   48
   49   Increase in Suave Sales (in millions of ounces)
   50      Necessary to Break Even for Each $1 Million
   51      Increase in Advertising                                  36.9
   52
   53           MARKET SHARE NECESSARY TO BREAK EVEN:
   54
   55   Increase in Market Share Necessary
   56      to Break Even for Each $1 Million
   57      Increase in Advertising                                  0.43%
   58
   59
   60
```

Observation: Why should we use Lotus 1-2-3 to run such important but simple calculations? The answer is that if all we plan to do is run just a few calculations, then we should not bother with Lotus 1-2-3. A calculator or a pencil and "the back of an envelope" is sufficient. *However, we are going to continue using these data and calculations* in Lessons 8, 9, and 10. Then you will see why it made sense to input all these data and formulas into Lotus 1-2-3.

Now let's save our work before we move on.

Saving your Worksheet in a File on Diskette

ON YOUR OWN: Press the **[Home]** key to return to **A1.** Use the **/File Save** command to save your work. Name this new worksheet file: **LN07.**

Reviewing What We've Learned in Lesson 7

This lesson was brief in its use of Lotus 1-2-3, but it introduced the key management concept called "break-even analysis." We practiced the creation of formulas and the formatting of results. We also saw the value of organizing our worksheet so that data are presented clearly and can be accessed easily.

MANAGEMENT DISCUSSION

1 What is break-even analysis? Why is it useful?

Break-even analysis is based on a simple calculation that allows us to determine what sales volume, or market share, is needed to cover a *fixed* business expenditure. Alternatively, some managers calculate what their total revenue must be to cover the total costs of an operation. Either way, the principle is the same: How much do we have to sell to break even on an expenditure of certain resources used for a product?

Break-even analysis provides managers with a way to understand if an investment is likely to pay off. That investment could be buildings and equipment or upfront marketing expenditures, such as advertising. A break-even calculation allows a marketer to analyze the sales volume necessary for a proposed marketing budget to succeed.

2 What are the important elements of a break-even formula?

A formula to determine the additional sales necessary to break even has two principal elements: (1) the amount of the fixed expenditure in the numerator; (2) the gross margin (price less variable cost) per unit sold in the denominator. A break-even calculation to determine the necessary increase in market share would be based on these two elements *plus* the industry's sales volume. Please review the case for further explanations of break-even formulas.

3 Why should a manager perform a break-even analysis in terms of both ounces and market share?

The two break-even formulas based on sales volume (ounces) and market share allow a manager to analyze a proposed marketing expenditure (or capital investment) from different, but related perspectives. The first break-even calculation—sales volume necessary to break even—focuses on the sales of the product itself. It allows the manager to ask whether it is reasonable to expect that the brand's sales volume could increase at the rate necessary to break even. The brand's past sales history would serve as important reference data.

The second calculation—market share necessary to break even—focuses on the brand's competitive position in the market. Certainly, a brand's market share depends on its own sales. However, the overall size and the competitive nature of the industry become more prominent considerations in assessing the feasibility of the break-even sales volume necessary.

4 What preliminary conclusion might you reach about the feasibility of Helene Curtis breaking even on a $1 million increase in advertising for Suave?

Your conclusion about the feasibility of breaking even on a $1 million increase in the advertising for Suave should be based on your analysis of the shampoo market, consumer buying behavior, and cost of advertising media, as detailed in Lessons 1 through 6. This conclusion contains important implications about the effectiveness of advertising for Suave.

LESSON 8 BREAK-EVEN ANALYSIS: NEW VERSUS CURRENT USERS

OVERVIEW

COMPUTER INSTRUCTIONS

Lesson 8 requires you to perform two simple calculations.

MANAGEMENT ISSUES

These two break-even calculations provide considerable insight into the cost effectiveness of increasing the advertising budget for Suave shampoo. These break-even calculations focus directly on how increased advertising might affect either new or current users at two critical stages in the consumer buying process: (1) "conversion" of a new consumer from brand awareness to trial, or (2) repeat purchase by a current consumer.

MANAGEMENT DISCUSSION QUESTIONS

  1 How does an understanding of the consumer buying process add to your ability to determine the feasibility of breaking even on increased advertising for Suave?
  2 Do you think it would be easier to encourage new customers to try Suave or to encourage existing users to use more?
  3 How would your advertising campaign differ if your goal was: (a) to attract new users, or (b) to encourage existing users to use more?
  4 What is the annual value of a Suave customer? Is the annual value of a customer useful information?

CASE

Vallera thought two further calculations might be useful in deciding on the size and objectives of the Suave advertising budget. Two advertising strategies for the fiscal 1985 campaign had been proposed by marketing personnel at Helene Curtis. One was to direct the campaign toward attracting new users. The other strategy was to try to increase the amount purchased (as measured by the "loyalty" index) by current Suave customers.

To decide which strategy to follow, Vallera calculated how much of an increase in trial and, alternatively, how much of an increase in loyalty would be needed to break even for each additional $1 million spent to advertise Suave. She examined the awareness, trial, repeat purchase, and loyalty data, using the number of Suave ounces sold in fiscal 1984.

To calculate the increase in trial (new users)[4] necessary to break even for each additional $1 million in advertising, Vallera used the following data and formula:

- The "ever having tried" rate of 45% for Suave (Table 4.1);
- Suave sales of 1,161 million ounces in FY 1984;
- The number of additional ounces (see previous formula) necessary to break even for the $1 million increase in advertising; and
- This equation:[5]

$$\frac{45\%}{1,161 \text{ Million Ounces}} = \frac{X\%}{\text{Additional Ounces Necessary}}$$

To determine the required increase in loyalty, Vallera used the following data and formula:

- Suave loyalty index of 37% (derived from Table 4.2);
- Suave sales of 1,161 million ounces in FY 1984;
- The number of additional ounces necessary to break even; and
- This equation:[6]

$$\frac{37\%}{1,161 \text{ Million Ounces}} = \frac{X\%}{\text{Additional Ounces Necessary}}$$

Vallera and Lanznar discussed the results of these calculations. They also considered the information they had previously generated, particularly the data on advertising costs. Could enough exposure be purchased with $1 million of advertising to generate the increased trial by new users or the increased loyalty among current users needed to break even?

COMPUTER INSTRUCTIONS

Retrieving and Examining the Worksheet File for Lesson 8

To begin Lesson 8, we need to retrieve a new worksheet file from the Suave Data Diskette. First, follow these familiar steps, if necessary:

1 Load DOS. Enter date and time.
2 Load the Lotus Access System.
3 Load the 1-2-3 software program.

---

[4] Approximately 165 million Americans used shampoo in 1984. Therefore, a 1% increase in trial would mean that 1.65 million people tried Suave for the first time.
[5] The formula assumes that the estimates for "percentage of buyers purchasing at least twice" and the "loyalty index" remain constant.
[6] The formula assumes that the number of Suave customers remains constant.

ON YOUR OWN: Insert the Suave Data Diskette into the appropriate disk drive. Use the **/File Retrieve** command to load the worksheet file: **LESSON08.WKS.** After loading the worksheet file, switch diskettes. Remove the Suave Data Diskette and replace it with your own data diskette. Press the **[Home]** key as directed.

Good. This first screen, of course, is just the same as we left it after Lesson 7. In Lesson 8, we are going to build on our previous work by creating three more break-even formulas.

Let's take a look at the rest of the worksheet. Press the **[PgDn]** key and look at the screen beginning with cell A21. It contains the same market data used in Lesson 7. Press the **[PgDn]** key again. This screen, beginning at A41, is just the same as we left it after Lesson 7. It now includes our two break-even analyses.

Press the **[PgDn]** key one more time. This new screen, entitled "Break-Even Analyses: New vs. Current Users," is where we will place the three new formulas to extend our break-even analysis.

Observation: As you can see, we have continued to organize the worksheet to make it easy to find specific data, to be able to communicate what we are doing clearly, and to move around easily.

We are now ready to create the three new break-even formulas.

Creating Break-Even Formulas: New Versus Current Users

ON YOUR OWN: The **three** new **formulas** we need to construct in cells **G69, G73,** and **G80** are:

1	Increase in Trial Percentage Necessary to Break Even for $1 Million Increase in Advertising	=	"Ever Having Tried" Percentage of Suave Shampoo	*	$\dfrac{\text{Increase in Suave Sales (in millions of ounces) Necessary to Break Even for Each \$1 Million Increase in Advertising}}{\text{Suave Shampoo Sales in FY 1984 (in millions of ounces)}}$

That is:

$$G69 = G66*(G51/G29)$$

(Format: Percent with 2 decimal places.)

2	Increase in Number of New Triers (in millions of people) Necessary to Break Even for $1 Million Increase in Advertising	=	Increase in Trial Percentage Necessary to Break Even for $1 Million Increase in Advertising	*	Estimated Number of Americans Who Used Shampoo in FY 1984 (in millions of people)

That is:

$$G73 = G69*G36$$

(Format: Fixed with 2 decimal places.)

	Increase in Loyalty Percentage Necessary to Break Even for $1 Million Increase in Advertising	=	Suave Loyalty Index	*	Increase in Suave Sales (in millions of ounces) Necessary to Break Even for Each $1 Million Increase in Advertising
3					Suave Shampoo Sales in FY 1984 (in millions of ounces)

That is:

$$G80 = G76*(G51/G29)$$

(Format: Percent with 2 decimal places.)

Good. Check your results with those beginning in column Q, if you like. Your screen should look like:

```
G80: (P2) +G76*(G51/G29)                                        READY


             A        B        C        D        E        F        G        H
   61
   62                      Break-Even Analyses:  New vs. Current Users
   63              ------------------------------------------------
   64                                    NEW USERS:
   65
   66      "Ever Having Tried" Percentage for Suave              45%
   67
   68      Increase in Trial Percentage Necessary to Break Even
   69         for $1 Million Increase in Advertising           1.43%
   70
   71      Increase in Number of New Triers (in millions
   72         of people) Necessary to Break Even for
   73         $1 Million Increase in Advertising                2.36
   74
   75                              CURRENT USERS:
   76      Suave Loyalty Index                                   37%
   77
   78      Increase in Loyalty Percentage Necessary to
   79         Break Even for $1 Million
   80         Increase in Advertising                          1.18%
```

Observation: Notice how easy it was to build on our earlier work to complete these calculations. These three new formulas were based on the results of other formulas that we had already calculated. For example, we used the results of the formula in cell G51, "Increase in Suave Sales Necessary to Break Even," to calculate both the "Increase in Trial Percentage" (G69) and the "Increase in Loyalty Percentage" (G80).

We will continue to build on these results in Lessons 9 and 10. You can see that it becomes very efficient to use Lotus 1-2-3 if the results of some calculations form the basis for additional calculations.

Moreover, by using Lotus 1-2-3, we can easily gain access to both the original data and the results of the formulas if a PC is readily available. Many companies believe that the future lies in paperless files and information systems.

Let's now save our work.

Saving Your Worksheet in a File on Diskette

ON YOUR OWN: Press the **[Home]** key to return to **A1**. Use the **/File Save** command to save our work. Name this new worksheet file: **LN08**.

Reviewing What We've Learned in Lesson 8

This lesson was also very brief in its use of Lotus 1-2-3. We saw, however, how easily we could build on earlier work when creating formulas in 1-2-3 and reemphasized the value of a well-designed worksheet.

MANAGEMENT DISCUSSION

1 How does an understanding of the consumer buying process add to your ability to determine the feasibility of breaking even on increased advertising for Suave?

An understanding of the consumer buying process allows you to focus more precisely on how advertising might influence consumer buying behavior: increase awareness, encourage trial, increase the amount used in a year. This knowledge should help you decide whether you believe it feasible that advertising will influence the consumer's behavior enough to break even. In the case of advertising for Suave shampoo, an understanding of the consumer buying process allows us to calculate: (1) how many new consumers would have to try Suave, or (2) how much of an increase in loyalty would be necessary to break even.

2 Do you think it would be easier to encourage new customers to try Suave or to encourage existing customers to use more?

Your answer to this question should also be based on your analysis of consumer buying behavior in the shampoo market. If you believe that there are segments of consumers who have not tried Suave but could be persuaded to do so, then you might think that advertising might help increase awareness and encourage trial among new customers. On the other hand, if you think that it is more likely that only certain kinds of customers are likely to try and use Suave, then you might argue that it is easier to encourage existing consumers to use more.

3 How would your advertising campaign differ if your goal was (1) to attract new users, or (2) to encourage your existing users to use more?

Your advertising campaign would differ in several ways: first, in the segment of consumers targeted; second, in the message, tailored both to the goal (trial versus more usage) and to an image that would appeal to the targeted segment; third, in the form of media, chosen according to cost effectiveness.

4 What is the annual value of a Suave customer? Is the annual value of a customer useful information?

The "value of a customer" is an important marketing concept, particulary in industrial marketing. The idea is that each customer accounts for a certain amount of profit (or gross margin) every year. The amount of that profit is directly related to the number of times a customer purchases a product in a year. In the shampoo market, loyalty is a key factor in determining the value of a customer. Companies sometimes evaluate a marketing program by its effectiveness in building loyalty over time.

To help us estimate the value of a Suave customer, we have data from Lesson 5 (Table 4.2) on how much a "Suave customer" buys Suave shampoo during one year (38.4 ounces). (We do not have any data on "loyalty" and purchase behavior of Suave customers beyond one year.)

The following formula can be used to estimate the annual value of a Suave customer:

$$\text{Total Shampoo Ounces per Suave Customer} \times \text{Loyalty Rate} \times$$

$$\text{Average Retail Price per Ounce} \times \left(1\text{- }\frac{\text{Retail Gross}}{\text{Margin \%}}\right) \times \frac{\text{Suave's Gross}}{\text{Margin \%}}$$

which is

$$104.0 \times 37\% = 38.4$$

$$0.9 \times (1 - 0.3) \times 43\% = 0.027$$

$$38.4 \times 0.027 = \$1.04$$

The annual value of a Suave customer, therefore, can be estimated quickly: 38.4 times $0.027 (Suave's gross margin per ounce) is $1.04. To break even on $1 million of advertising *in one year* would require that approximately 1 million customers (961,302) be brought in by the advertising. Of course, if a consumer's purchases beyond one year are considered, the value of a Suave customer increases, and the break-even level of customers needed decreases.

CHAPTER 5

Stage 3: Financial Projections

Ellen Vallera had to decide what advertising budget she should recommend for Suave shampoo. In completing the next five lessons, you should consider how you would make the following management decision:

- What advertising budget would you set for Suave shampoo in FY 1985? FY 1986?

INTRODUCTION

Vallera had spent considerable time thinking about the role of advertising for Suave shampoo. She wondered how effective advertising would be in generating sales for Suave. The likely financial results of increased advertising expenditures remained a concern for her.

She had found the work done by Lanznar very useful in helping her to construct assumptions about consumer and competitive response to Suave advertising in the shampoo market. These assumptions were fundamental to her financial projections of the impact of different advertising budgets. Although she would focus on the fiscal 1985 budget, Helene Curtis executives wanted her to consider the fiscal 1986 budget as well.

Helene Curtis was organized according to what was known as a "brand management" system. Under this system, an income statement was prepared for each independent Helene Curtis brand—that is, a separate accounting of the revenues, variable costs, marketing expenditures, and operating profit was made for each brand. The performance evaluation of the brand managers depended heavily on the profits their respective brands achieved.

161

The Suave shampoo brand represented a major source of profits for the company.[1] Under the brand management system, direct responsibility for the performance of Suave was shared by Vallera, the brand manager, and Kirk, the group brand manager for Suave (and related products). They also held primary authority for recommending a marketing program and expenditure level for Suave shampoo.

Their proposals would be reviewed by top management, with Thomas, the vice president of marketing, having the final say. He would consider the budget for the entire Consumer Products Division in his final decision on Suave's marketing program.

To support a proposed marketing budget for Suave, Vallera needed to submit forecasts on the financial performance of Suave shampoo, based on different assumptions about the effects of the budget on sales. Kirk would review her forecasts and arrive at his own conclusions. They would then discuss their analyses in a meeting with Lanznar before putting together a presentation for top management.

USE OF LOTUS 1-2-3 FOR FINANCIAL PROJECTIONS

Helene Curtis executives had begun to use Lotus 1-2-3 to carry out increasingly sophisticated financial analyses and projections. Lotus 1-2-3 permitted multiple financial calculations to be completed rapidly, so that the effects of different assumptions and projections on financial performance could be easily tested.

It was important, however, for managers to recognize that the quality of their conclusions about the financial impact of a marketing program depended on the quality of the marketing analysis behind their assumptions. Too often managers got carried away with the power and ease of Lotus 1-2-3, generating useless printout because of unrealistic assumptions and too little sound thinking beforehand. Lanznar's research, therefore, was very important. It allowed Vallera and other managers to run projections based on realistic assumptions and to interpret the results sensibly.

Vallera felt that she had spent sufficient time talking with Lanznar and analyzing the market research report. To make financial projections for fiscal 1985 and 1986, she organized her analysis into five sections:

1 Break-Even Analysis: Calculating Total Sales Needed
2 Break-Even Analysis: Testing Multiple Assumptions
3 Financial Analysis: Structuring the Spreadsheet
4 Spreadsheet Analysis: Creating Scenarios and Running Sensitivity Tests
5 Financial Analysis: Testing Multiple Assumptions

---

[1] Five products were actually marketed under the Suave brand name (shampoos, hair conditioners/rinses, hair sprays, deodorants/antiperspirants, and hand and body lotions), but shampoo comprised the majority of Suave sales. In fact, all advertising was recorded under shampoos, even though most advertisements included conditioners as well. There was no advertising of other Suave products.

**LESSON 9 BREAK-EVEN ANALYSIS: CALCULATING TOTAL SALES
NEEDED**

OVERVIEW

COMPUTER INSTRUCTIONS

Lesson 9 asks you to create several fairly complicated formulas. In addition, Lesson 9 demonstrates how to "protect" the data in a worksheet against any changes except those specifically desired.

MANAGEMENT ISSUES

This lesson extends the use of break-even calculations to financial analysis. Managers must do more than just break even; they must also seek to maximize profit. Break-even calculations allows managers to analyze the feasibility of obtaining a specific operating profit for a brand.

MANAGEMENT DISCUSSION QUESTIONS

1 Why should a manager examine a break-even calculation based on total sales volume?

2 Why should a manager examine a break-even calculation that includes a certain level of operating profit?

3 When should your analysis include projections of industry growth rates?

4 Can an operating profit of $10.8 million be maintained in FY 1985 with an advertising budget of $7 million? How sensitive is your conclusion to changes in the industry growth rate?

CASE

Vallera wanted to determine the total sales volume necessary to cover the costs of the total amount of marketing expenditures.[2] She knew that:

- FY 1984 marketing expenditures were $20.6 million ($6 million for advertising and $14.6 million for the other marketing expenditures, consumer and trade promotions); and
- FY 1984 operating profit was $10.8 million.

---

[2] Break-even calculations could be run for total advertising expenditures, but management was more interested in the sales level required to cover the entire marketing budget.

She also knew that Helene Curtis management was interested in the amount of Suave sales necessary (1) to break even and (2) to maintain their current operating profit of $10.8 million, if advertising were increased to $7 million in fiscal 1985. (Total marketing expenditures, therefore, would be $21.6 million.)

Using the incremental break-even equations for sales and for market shares that she already had in her diskette files, she ran the following two calculations (the parentheses refer to the second calculation on maintaining operating profit):

$$\text{Suave Sales in Ounces in FY 1985 Necessary to Break Even (Maintain Operating Profit)} = \frac{\$21.6 \text{ Million } (+ \$10.8 \text{ Million})}{\text{Gross Margin per Suave Ounce Sold}}$$

Moreover, management looked at the market share necessary to maintain operating profit. The prevailing wisdom was that industry sales would increase by 2% in fiscal 1985 (that is, FY 1985 industry sales would be 102% of FY 1984 sales). She used the following equation to calculate a $7 million advertising budget (that is, $21.6 million in total marketing):

$$\text{Suave Share of Market (in Ounces) in FY 1985 Necessary to Maintain Operating Profit at \$10.8 Million} = \frac{\dfrac{\$21.6 + \$10.8 \text{ Million}}{\text{Gross Margin per Suave Ounces Sold}}}{\text{Industry Sales (in Ounces)} \times 102\% \text{ in FY 1984}} = \frac{\text{Suave Sales Necessary to Maintain Operating Profit}}{\text{Projected Industry Sales in 1985}}$$

Based on these assumptions, Vallera was now prepared to examine in more detail the break-even relationships between advertising expenditures, sales levels, and market shares.

COMPUTER INSTRUCTIONS

Retrieving and Examining the Worksheet File for Lesson 9

To begin Lesson 9, we need to retrieve a new worksheet file from the Suave Data Diskette. First, follow these familiar steps, if necessary:

1 Load DOS. Enter date and time.
2 Load the Lotus Access System.
3 Load the 1-2-3 software program.

ON YOUR OWN: Insert the Suave Data Diskette into the appropriate disk drive. Use the **/File Retrieve** command to load the worksheet file: **LESSON09.WKS.** After loading the worksheet file, switch diskettes. Remove the Suave Data Diskette and replace it with your data diskette. Press the **[Home]** key as directed.

Good. Once again, we are going to build on what we have already done and add some new analysis.

Let's take a look at the rest of the worksheet. Press the **[PgDn]** key. This screen, beginning at cell A21, contains the same market data we used in Lessons 7 and 8. Press the **[PgDn]** key again. This screen, beginning at cell A41, contains the break-even formulas we created in Lesson 7. Press the **[PgDn]** key once again. This screen, beginning at A61, contains the formulas we created in Lesson 8.

Now press the **[PgDn]** key once again. This screen, beginning at A81, contains some new data on FY 1984 marketing expenditures and operating profit for Suave.

We will use these data to run some new break-even calculations for Suave advertising in FY 1985. Press the **[PgDn]** key once more. On this screen, beginning at cell A101, we will enter some projections for Suave advertising and marketing expenditures and for the industry growth rate and sales volume.

Press the **[PgDn]** key one last time. On this screen, beginning at A121, we will create three new break-even formulas for Suave in FY 1985.

Observation: As you can see, we are beginning to put a lot of data and formulas onto this worksheet. It is becoming increasingly important that the worksheet be designed so that the data are clearly organized and easily found.

Let's move on to complete our new calculations.

Entering Projections for FY 1985

Press the **[PgUp]** key to return to the screen, beginning at A101, that will contain the "Projections for FY 1985."

Let's input the projections that are suggested by the case.

ON YOUR OWN: To enter the projections, follow these steps:

1 Enter into cell **G107** a projection of **$7.0** (in millions). This projection is not based on any formula; it is simply an assumption. Therefore, just type in **7** and press **[Enter]**. Put this value in **Currency** format with **one decimal** place.

2 Create a formula for "Projected Total Marketing Expenditures for Suave Shampoo in FY 1985" in cell G111: **G111 = G107+G89**. Also put this value in **Currency** format with **one decimal** place.

3 Enter into cell **G114** a projection of **2%** for the shampoo industry growth rate. (*Hint:* You can input either **.02** or **2%**. Lotus 1-2-3 can read either entry.) Put in **Percent** format with **zero decimal** places.

4 Create a formula for "Projected Industry Sales in FY 1985" in cell G117: **G117 = G26*(1+G114)**. Put in **Comma** format with **zero decimal** places.

Your screen should appear as follows:

```
G117: (,0) +G26*(1+G114)                                        READY


        A        B        C        D        E        F        G        H
101
102                          Projections for FY 1985
103                          -----------------------
104
105     Projected Advertising Expenditures
106        for Suave Shampoo in FY 1985
107        (in millions)                                      $7.0
108
109     Projected Total Marketing Expenditures
110        for Suave Shampoo in FY 1985
111        (in millions)                                     $21.6
112
113     Projected Shampoo Industry Growth Rate
114        from FY 1984 to FY 1985                             2%
115
116     Projected Industry Sales (in millions
117        of ounces) in FY 1985                             8,731
118
119
120
```

Good. We have entered our projections. Now let's create some new break-even formulas.

Creating Break-Even Formulas: Based on Projections for FY 1985

ON YOUR OWN: The three new break-even formulas we want to construct are explained in the case. In using Lotus 1-2-3, you should create the following three formulas in cells G128, G132, and G138:

1 *Sales Needed to Break Even*

$$G128 = G111/G19$$

(Format: Fixed with 0 decimal places.)

2 *Sales Needed to Maintain Operating Profit*

$$G132 = (G111 + G95)/G19$$

(Format: Comma with 0 decimal places.)

3 *Market Share Needed to Maintain Operating Profit*

$$G138 = G132/G117$$

(Format: Percent with 1 decimal place.)

Check your results with those beginning in column Q, if you like. Your screen should appear as follows:

```
G138: (P1) +G132/G117                                          READY


        A       B       C       D       E       F       G       H
121
122         Break-Even Analysis:  Based on Projections for FY 1985
123         ---------------------------------------------------------
124
125                                 SALES:
126
127     Total Suave Sales (In millions of ounces)
128        In FY 1985 Necessary to Break Even                   797
129
130     Total Suave Sales (In millions of ounces)
131        In FY 1985 Necessary to Maintain
132        Operating Profit of $10.8 Million                  1,196
133
134                              MARKET SHARE:
135
136     Suave Share of Market In FY 1985
137        Necessary to Maintain Operating
138        Profit of $10.8 Million                            13.7%
139
140
```

Observation: Notice once again how these formulas build upon work we had completed earlier. These break-even calculations are based on our earlier calculation of "Manufacturer Gross Margin Per Ounce for Suave" (G19). Also, notice how neatly we can organize and file our work in Lotus 1-2-3, so that it can be transferred on a diskette to co-workers or easily retrieved by ourselves later.

Note: There are two reasons to consider using Lotus 1-2-3 to run a series of related calculations:

1 Lotus 1-2-3 allows you to build upon your work, using the results of calculations as the basis for further calculations.
2 Lotus 1-2-3 allows you to organize and file work so that it can be easily transferred or retrieved.

Now we'll introduce a third benefit of using 1-2-3 for calculations. It is one of the most important uses of Lotus 1-2-3: sensitivity analysis.

Using Lotus 1-2-3 to Run Sensitivity Tests

ON YOUR OWN: Let's take a look at what happens if we change some key assumptions that form the basis of our break-even analysis for FY 1985. The break-even calculations for FY 1985 have two key assumptions:

- Projected advertising expenditures for Suave in FY 1985; and
- Projected shampoo industry growth rate in FY 1985.

First, let's try some new projections for Suave advertising expenditures in FY 1985. For example, enter **8** (for $8.0 million) into cell **G107.** Then press **[PgDn]** and see how the results of the break-even calculations have all changed: 797 to 834; 1,196 to 1,233; and 13.7% to 14.1%, respectively. Let's press **[PgUp]** and enter **9** into cell **G107.** Again press **[PgDn]** and see how the results have changed.

Observation: See how much quicker it is to test the effects of these changes in assumptions using Lotus 1-2-3, rather than to calculate each result for each new assumption by hand.

Note: Let's now take a closer look at this third reason to use Lotus 1-2-3 for a series of related calculations:

> **3** Lotus 1-2-3 allows you to run "sensitivity tests" by quickly recalculating the results when you change key assumptions.

What we just did was conduct a sensitivity test to see how sensitive the results of our break-even calculations are to changes in projected Suave advertising expenditures for FY 1985 (i.e., $7 to $8 to $9 million).

ON YOUR OWN: Now let's run a sensitivity test on the effect of different industry growth rates. Reset Suave advertising in cell **G107** to **$7** million, and let's try a "no-growth" assumption **(0%)** in cell **G114.** Then press **[PgDn]** and see how the "Suave Share of Market in FY 1985 Necessary to Maintain Operating Profit of $10.8 Million" has changed (13.7% share to 14.0% share). Then go back and enter **4%** (type in **.04** or **4%**) into **G114** and look at the results. (The share necessary went down to 13.4%.)

Note: If the results of several formulas change by just adjusting one key number, isn't it likely we might accidentally change a number that we do not want to change and cause all our results to be faulty? It is possible, and worse, we might not notice the mistake. Fortunately, 1-2-3 provides a mechanism to protect the data we do not want to change. Let's take a look.

Using the Protect Command to Prevent Inadvertent Changes to Data

We can protect our worksheet from inadvertent changes to data by using the **/Worksheet Global Protect** command. Press the following keys:

Description	Keys to Press
Display the 1-2-3 command menus:	**/**
Select the /Worksheet command:	**W**

Description	Keys to Press
Select the Global command:	G
Select the Protection command:	P
Confirm that you want to Enable the worksheet protection:	E

ON YOUR OWN: Go to cell **G95,** where the figure on Suave Operating Profit in FY 1984 ($10.8 million) is stored. This number is an "historical fact" that we do not want to change, and it is important to our break-even analysis.

Try to change it, perhaps by trying to input **$12.0** into cell **G95.**

Observation: See what happened. Lotus 1-2-3 said that the cell is protected. That is we cannot make any changes in the cell. Notice that in the upper left corner of the screen, the symbols "PR" are now displayed after the cell's display format and before its contents [Release 1A Users: no symbols]. The PC sounded a beep indicating that we cannot input a new number into the cell, and the words "Protected Cell" appeared in the bottom left corner of the screen. In fact, the entire worksheet is protected. We cannot make any changes, additions, or deletions at all.

But what happens if we really *do* want to enter, delete, or change some data? In particular, how can we run sensitivity tests if the worksheet is protected?

Unprotecting Specific Cells

Lotus 1-2-3 allows us to "unprotect" the specific cells that we do want to change. Let's see how by unprotecting our two projections of FY 1985 Suave advertising and of the industry growth rate. Press the following keys:

Description	Keys to Press
Press the [Esc] key to clear the entry we tried to make in cell G95:	[Esc]
(Notice that the words "Protected Cell" have disappeared.)	
Go to cell G107:	[PgDn] [up*8]
Display the 1-2-3 command menus:	/
Select the /Range command:	R
Select the Unprotect command:	U
Confirm that cell G107 is the range that we want to unprotect:	[Enter]

The cell G107 will be highlighted to indicate that changes can be made in the cell. In the upper left corner of the screen the symbol "U" is now displayed. [Release 2 Users: Unprotected cells are only highlighted as long as the cell pointer is located in that cell.]

ON YOUR OWN: Let's try some new projections for Suave advertising in FY 1985. Enter **$8.0** into cell **G107.** Then press **[PgDn]** to see the results.

Observation: Notice that we were able to make changes in G107, since we had unprotected the cell. *By changing the FY 1985 Suave advertising projection in cell G107, sales and market share requirements in cells G128, G132, and G138 all changed. Lotus 1-2-3 recalculates results when the values in a formula are changed, even though the cells containing the formulas may be protected.* For example, the formula for cell G128 (G111/G19) is protected. We cannot change it unless we first unprotect cell G128. However, because we changed the data in cell G107, the value in G111 (G111 = G107 + G89) changed, causing the value in G128 to change.

ON YOUR OWN: The one other cell that we want to unprotect now is **G114,** the cell that contains the projections for the shampoo industry growth rate. Use the **/Range Unprotect** command to unprotect cell **G114.** Try some new projections for the industry growth rate then see how the results of the formulas in **G117** and **G138** also change. For example, test the effects of projections of **0%** and then of **4%** for the shampoo industry growth rate.

Note: We can also use the **/Range Protect** command to reprotect some specific range of cells after that range has been unprotected. Still, the **/Range Unprotect** and **/Range Protect** commands must be used with the **/Worksheet Global Protection Enable** command. That is, you must follow *both* steps to use this protection capability of Lotus 1-2-3:

1 Use the **/Worksheet Global Protection Enable** command to activate the protection capability.
2 Use the **/Range Unprotect** and **/Range Protect** commands to specify exactly what cells should be left protected and unprotected.

However, the two sets of commands can be used *in either order.* In a new worksheet, all cells are protected. You might want to unprotect some cells (**/Range Unprotect**), enter formulas in these cells, and then turn on the protection facility (**/Worksheet Global Protection Enable**) to protect the rest of the worksheet. Or you may follow the order used in this exercise.

Saving Your Worksheet in a File on Diskette

We can save this worksheet with the Protection system on the worksheet. In fact, managers often purposely leave the Protection system on a worksheet before it is filed in order to protect the worksheet before it is transferred to another manager.

ON YOUR OWN: First, return the projection for cell **G107** to **$7.0** (million) and for cell **G114** to **2%.** Then, press the **[Home]** key to return to **A1.**

Use the **/File Save** command to save our work. Name the new worksheet file: **LN09.**

Reviewing What We Learned in Lesson 9

We saw once again how we can build on previous work by constructing a series of related formulas in Lotus 1-2-3. We also saw how helpful it is to organize the data in our worksheet clearly.

In addition, we learned the following new capabilities of 1-2-3:

- Lotus 1-2-3 allows us to run sensitivity tests quickly so that we can see the effects of changes in key assumptions or projections.
- Lotus 1-2-3 allows us to protect the data in our worksheet. However, 1-2-3 also allows us to unprotect specific cells so that we can change data that we do want to change. Using this protection capability requires two steps (in any order):
  1. Use the **/Worksheet Global Protection Enable** command to protect the entire worksheet.
  2. Use the **/Range Unprotect** command to unprotect those cells in which the data will be changed. (Use **/Range Protect** if you then want to reprotect some or all of these cells.)
- Lotus 1-2-3 will protect the formulas in cells once this global protection power is enabled. However, the results of the formulas will change if the values in the formulas are changed. This allows us to protect the actual formulas but then to run sensitivity tests and see how the results are affected.

MANAGEMENT DISCUSSION

1 Why should a manager examine a break-even calculation based on total sales volume?

A manager should understand what total sales volume is necessary for a product or division to break even. Incremental break-even calculations are important to analyze the cost effectiveness of an additional expenditure or investment. A manager must also be aware, however, of the overall sales level necessary to cover the expense of a marketing budget.

2 Why should a manager examine a break-even calculation that includes a certain level of operating profit?

A manager responsible for profit and loss is usually required to project what level of profit will be achieved. Often, to avoid the complexities of depreciation schedules, interest, and taxation, managers focus on projecting what level of operating profit can be achieved. A break-even calculation that accounts for a certain level of operating profit allows a manager to gauge the feasibility of attaining the sales volume necessary to reach that operating profit.

3 When should your analysis include projections of industry growth rates?

Break-even formulas that calculate the share of market needed to break even or to reach a certain level of operating profit require industry sales volume to be forecast. To do so, a manager must project the growth rate for the industry. It is particularly important to look at the share of market necessary to break even (or to reach a certain operating profit) when the growth rate of an industry is either high or very uncertain. If the projections of the industry growth rate vary greatly, the market share necessary to break even will have a wide range as well.

4 Can an operating profit of $10.8 million be maintained in FY 1985 with an advertising budget of $7 million? Is your conclusion sensitive to changes in the industry growth rate?

Your answer should be based on your analysis of the shampoo market and Suave's position in that market. The sensitivity tests that Lotus 1-2-3 allows us to run indicate that any conclusion is indeed very sensitive to changes in projections of the industry growth rate. If the industry grows at 0%, then Suave needs a 14.0% share of the market. If the shampoo market grows at a 10% rate, then Suave needs only 12.7% of the market. That difference of 1.3% of the market is an enormous difference for a market as large, mature, and competitive as the shampoo market.

LESSON 10   BREAK-EVEN ANALYSIS: TESTING MULTIPLE ASSUMPTIONS

OVERVIEW

COMPUTER INSTRUCTIONS

Lesson 10 introduces perhaps the most powerful, sophisticated, but complicated command in Lotus 1-2-3: the Data-Table command, often referred to as the What-If command. The Data-Table command allows you to test the effects of many different values for a variable at the same time, answering such questions as, What if advertising ranged from $3 million to $10 million?

MANAGEMENT ISSUES

Using the Data-Table command, you can determine the Suave sales volume necessary to maintain operating profit under different assumptions about (1) Suave advertising expenditures and (2) the shampoo industry growth rate. These calculations should help you understand the sensitivity of a brand's financial performance to management decisions and market forces.

MANAGEMENT DISCUSSION QUESTIONS

1 When is what-if analysis useful?
2 What are the dangers for managers using the Data-Table command?
3 What useful information is provided by break-even calculations that are based on a range of advertising levels?
4 What useful information is provided by break-even calculations based on a range of industry growth rates as well as advertising levels?

CASE

Helene Curtis brand managers had learned how to use a powerful Lotus 1-2-3 function that enabled them to run multiple calculations at once. Using this feature (called the Data Table, or sometimes the what-if, function), they could vary one or two assumptions at a time (e.g., the amount of advertising and the projected industry sales level) and compare the results. For example, break-even calculations could be computed on several different levels of marketing expenditures simultaneously. The results would be displayed on one screen, making it easier to compare the various marketing expenditure levels and their assumptions.

Varying the Level of Advertising Expenditures

Vallera knew that it was important to understand the range of sales levels and of market shares necessary to maintain Suave's operating profit ($10.8 million) at different levels of advertising in fiscal 1985. As before, she assumed that industry sales would increase by 2% from fiscal 1984 to fiscal 1985 and that other marketing expenditures would remain constant at $14.6 million. She decided to make these calculations for advertising levels ranging from $3 million to /$10 million, at increments of $1 million.

Varying Advertising Levels and Industry Growth Rates

Vallera was also interested in what the market share break-evens would be if, in fact, industry sales grew at a different rate. Using the Data Table function and the same range of projections for advertising expenditures, she generated calculations on the basis of changes in both variables. She calculated market shares necessary to maintain operating profit in fiscal 1985, given industry growth rates of -1%, 0%, 1%, 2%, 3%, 4%, and 5%. These projections of industry growth, she thought, covered the range of possibilities for the coming year.

These calculations would generate an extensive amount of data to assist Vallera in her break-even analyses for Suave shampoo. Once she finished analyzing these results, she would be ready to apply them to financial scenarios that allowed fluctuations in operating profit. She realized that any analysis would need to include *explicitly* her assumptions about the effects of advertising in the market.

Introduction to Data Table

In Lesson 9 we ran sensitivity tests by changing our assumptions about the values of two of the key variables in our break-even calculations. First, we varied our projections for Suave advertising expenditures in FY 1985 and examined how the results of our break-even formulas changed with each new projection. Then we varied the projections for the shampoo industry growth rate from FY 1984 to FY 1985 and examined how the result of our market-share break-even formula changed.

To perform these sensitivity tests, we had to enter new assumptions *one at a time* and then examine the effect of each new assumption. Wouldn't it be great if we could list on a single screen a whole series of assumptions about the value of a key variable and then see right on that same screen the different results generated by each of these assumptions, simultaneously?!

The architects of 1-2-3 thought so, too. Lotus 1-2-3 has a very powerful command called *Data Table* that allows us to do just that. In fact, the **/Data Table** command allows us to test the effects of varying assumptions about the value of either one or two key variables at the same time.

Just as it is powerful, Data Table is also one of the most sophisticated and complicated commands in 1-2-3. To learn how to use the **/Data Table** command, we will start with a special example. Then we will use Data Table to augment our financial analysis of Suave shampoo.

COMPUTER INSTRUCTIONS

Retrieving and Preparing the Worksheet for Lesson 10

To begin Lesson 10, we need to retrieve a new worksheet file from the Suave Data Diskette. First, follow these familiar steps, if necessary:

1 Load DOS. Enter date and time.
2 Load the Lotus Access System.
3 Load the 1-2-3 software program.

ON YOUR OWN: Insert the Suave Data Diskette into the appropriate disk drive. Use the **/File Retrieve** command to retrieve from the Suave Data Diskette the file named: **LESSON10.WKS**. After you have retrieved the file, switch diskettes. Remove the Suave Data Diskette and replace it with your data diskette. Press the **[Home]** key as directed.

Observation: The worksheet has global protection on it to be consistent with Lesson 9. Therefore, we cannot put any additional information into the worksheet until we remove the global protection. Fortunately it is easy to remove the global protection. Press the following keys:

Description	Keys to Press
Display the 1-2-3 command menus:	**/**
Select the /Worksheet command:	**W**
Select the Global command:	**G**
Select the Protection command:	**P**
Select the Disable menu choice:	**D**

Now we can begin our special example for the **/Data Table** command. Recall that a completed worksheet begins in column Q, for your convenience.

Data Table Example: Altering 1 Variable

ON YOUR OWN: Move the cell pointer (use the **[F5]** or **[PgDn]** keys) so that cell **A201** is in the upper left corner of the screen. (The completed example starts in cell Q201.) Your screen should appear as follows:

```
A201:  ' WHAT IF 1                                                    READY


           A       B       C       D       E       F       G       H
    201  WHAT IF 1                           "WHAT IF"
    202                          (Using the Data Table Command)
    203
    204
    205                     Price per unit        $100
    206                     Cost per unit         $80
    207                                         --------
    208                     Profit per unit       $20
    209
    210
    211
    212                                    PROFIT PER UNIT
    213
    214
    215                     Price       $110
    216                     per         $100
    217                     unit        $90
    218
    219
    220
```

Note: The **/Data Table** command is commonly called *what if* because it allows us to answer questions such as, What if we assume a different price per unit? What will the profit per unit be?

Observation: This screen contains a simple formula in cell E208 for the profit per unit (price per unit minus cost per unit). It also includes three different assumptions about price per unit ($110, $100, and $90) in cells D215, D216, and D217, respectively.

Let's now see how **/Data Table** works. We will use **/Data Table** to calculate what profit per unit would be under each of the three different assumptions about price per unit.

To complete the first step necessary to set up a data table, press the following keys:

Description	Keys to Press
Move the cell pointer to cell E214:	**(Use the arrow keys or [F5].)**
Indicate that a formula will be entered:	**+**
Move the cell pointer to the Profit-per-unit formula in cell E208:	**(Use the arrow keys.)**
Confirm that we want to "duplicate" the formula of cell E208 in cell E214:	**[Enter]**
(This step has directed 1-2-3 that the value in E214 should be the same as the result of the formula in E208.)	

The value **20** should appear in cell **E214**.

Note: To create a data table for 1 variable, 1-2-3 specifically requires that we enter the formula in the cell one **[up]** and one to the **[right]** from the top of the column of assumptions—that is, one **[up]** and to the **[right]** from cell D215, which is cell E214. This specific structure for a data table with 1 variable is shown below:

Unused	**Formula**
Assumptions	Results

This first step created a link between the data table and our model (here, a simple equation for profit per unit).

Now that we have completed this first necessary step, we are ready to use the **/Data Table** command. Press the following keys:

Description	Keys to Press
Display the 1-2-3 command menus:	**/**
Select the /Data command:	**D**
Select the Table command:	**T**

(1-2-3 will ask whether we want to alter 1 or 2 variables or whether we want to "Reset" previous ranges. Since we have no previous ranges recorded, we can move directly on to choosing 1 input variable.)

Indicate that we want to test different values for 1 variable (Price per unit):	**1**

(Later in this lesson we will see how to test different values for 2 variables.)
(1-2-3 will now direct us to "Enter Table range.")

Move the cell pointer to D214 so that we can include the different prices in the range:	**(Use the arrow keys.)**
Anchor D214 as the beginning of our range:	**.**
Paint the Table range D214..E217:	**[down*3] [right]**

(Note: We have painted a rectangular range that includes: (1) the three different assumptions in D215, D216, and D217; (2) the formula we entered in E214; and (3) the blank cells E215, E216, and E217 that will eventually contain our results. Since any range in 1-2-3 must be rectangular, we have also included a blank cell, D214, that won't be used.)

Description	*Keys to Press*

Confirm the range: **[Enter]**

(1-2-3 will ask us to "Enter Input cell," that is, the cell in the formula that contains the 1 variable for which we are testing alternative values.)

Move the cell pointer to E205 to indicate that the
variable "Price per unit" is the "input cell":   **[up*9]**

Confirm that E205 is the input cell we want: **[Enter]**

(This is the final step. Watch 1-2-3 complete the calculations!)

ON YOUR OWN: Use **/Range Format** to put the three results into **Currency** format with **zero decimal** places. (We suggest that you leave the value in E214 unformatted, so that it is clear that this value is neither an assumption nor a result.)

Good. Your screen should appear as follows:

```
E215: (CO) 30                                                           READY


         A        B        C        D        E        F        G        H
201   WHAT IF 1                              "WHAT IF"
202                              (Using the Data Table Command)
203
204
205                     Price per unit          $100
206                     Cost per unit            $80
207                                            ---------
208                     Profit per unit          $20
209
210
211
212                                       PROFIT PER UNIT
213
214                                            20
215                     Price       $110        $30
216                     per         $100        $20
217                     unit         $90        $10
218
219
220
```

Observation: You have now constructed a *data table* that lists a set of assumptions about the price per unit and the resulting profit per unit for each respective assumption. 1-2-3 has quickly calculated what the profit per unit would be if the price per unit were, alternatively, $110, $100, or $90. The profit per unit results calculated (in cells E215, E216, and E217, respectively) are based on the formula you entered in cell E214.

Note: The effect of each assumption is listed in the cell *immediately to the right* of that assumption. For example, if the price per unit were $110 (as listed in cell D215), then the profit per unit would be $30 (as listed in cell E215). We included the blank cells E215, E216, and E217 in the rectangular table range because we knew that eventually those cells would contain the results.

Note: Instead of moving the cell pointer to the cell that contains the formula (here, E208) or the input cell (E205), you can always type in the cell address. Still, you should find it good practice to point to these cells, particularly the one that contains the formula, so that you can always "see" the formula.

The steps for creating a 1-variable data table are reviewed on the following page for your reference.

Summary of Steps for Using Data Table with 1 Variable

Lotus 1-2-3 requires you to follow certain steps and to use a specific structure when constructing a data table. Let's review the steps for creating a data table with 1 variable. Use the following diagram to follow:

1 *List in a column* the values for the one variable that you want to test. (In the preceding example, the alternative values [the assumptions] for the price per unit were already listed in the column from D215 to D217, so you did not need to complete this step.)

2 *Create a formula* that will form the basis of your data table in the cell that is one [up] and one to the [right] from the top of the column of values that were entered in step 1. (Before, we entered into cell E214 the formula for "Profit per unit," which had originally been created in cell E208.)

3 *Invoke the /Data Table command.* Confirm that the data table will have *1* input cell. (Later we will see how to reset the ranges when necessary before creating a new data table.)

4 *Paint the range* that forms a rectangle that includes: (a) the series of assumptions, (b) the formula created to compute the data table results, and (c) the cells immediately to the right of the assumptions. (Before, the range was D214..E217.)

5 *Move the cell pointer to the "input cell."* It contains the variable for which we want to test alternative assumptions. (Before, the input cell was E205 because that cell contained the variable for "Price per unit," and we wanted to test these different assumptions about the value of that variable.)

6 *Press [Enter]* and watch the results appear.

Based upon these steps, a data table with 1 variable will always have this specific structure:

[unused]   +

testing result

testing result

testing result

testing result

The word *testing* refers to the different assumptions about the values of the 1 variable that the data table is designed to test. The symbol **+** refers to the formula that is created to form the basis of the data table. The word *result* refers to the values that the data table will eventually produce using that formula.

   Note: While the assumptions must be listed in a column, they do not have to be listed in sequential order. Any order is acceptable to 1-2-3. Also, both the assumptions to be tested and the results can be formatted any way you like.

   Now let's see how 1-2-3 creates a data table when we want to test multiple assumptions about the values of 2 variables.

Data Table Introduction: Altering 2 Variables

Lotus 1-2-3 also has the power to calculate in a data table the effects of changing the values of 2 variables at a time. Let's introduce this use of the **/Data Table** command with a special example as well. Move the cell pointer to A221. (The completed example starts in cell Q221.) Your screen should appear as follows:

```
A221: ' WHAT IF 2                                                 READY


         A       B       C       D       E       F       G       H
221  WHAT IF 2                         "WHAT IF"
222                           (Using the Data Table Command)
223
224
225                     Price per unit         $100
226                     Cost per unit          $80
227                                           --------
228                     Profit per unit        $20
229
230
231
232                                    PROFIT PER UNIT
233
234                                        Cost per unit
235
236                                    $70      $80      $90
237                     Price     $110
238                     per       $100
239                     unit       $90
240
```

   Observation: This example looks very similar to the one we just completed. Now, however, we are going to test alternative assumptions about the values of *both*:

   1 Price per unit; and
   2 Cost per unit.

Let's see how 1-2-3 handles this task.
   Observation: This screen contains the same simple formula in cell E228 for the

profit per unit as well as our three different assumptions for the price per unit ($110, $100, and $90) in cells D237, D238, and D239, respectively. In addition, this screen contains three different assumptions about the cost per unit ($70, $80, and $90) in cells E236, F236, and G236, respectively.

Note: Lotus 1-2-3 requires that the assumptions about the *second* variable run *across a row* and that those assumptions begin in the cell that is one [**up**] and one to the [**right**] from the top of the column that contains the assumptions about the first variable. That is, the first set of assumptions begin in cell D237, the second set of assumptions must begin in cell E236. In this manner the results generated can be displayed in a rectangular range between the two sets of assumptions. The specific structure for a data table with 2 variables is shown below:

Formula	Assumptions 1
Assumptions 2	Results

By testing these assumptions simultaneously, we should get nine different results (three assumptions *times* three other assumptions). Let's use the **/Data Table** command to calculate the effect on the profit per unit of these simultaneous changes in both the price per unit and the cost per unit.

To complete the first step necessary to set up the data table, press the following keys:

Description	Keys to Press
Move the cell pointer to cell D236:	(Use the arrow keys or [F5].)
Indicate that a formula will be entered:	+
Move the cell pointer to the profit-per-unit formula in cell E228:	(Use the arrow keys.)
Confirm that we want to "duplicate" the formula of cell E228 in cell D236:	[Enter]
(This step has directed 1-2-3 that the value in D236 should be the same as the result of the formula in E228.)	

The value **20** should appear in cell **D236**, the same as appeared in cell E214 in the 1-variable data table. This is because whether there are one or two input variables, the *formula* remains unchanged.

Note: To create a data table for 2 variables, 1-2-3 specifically requires that we enter the formula in the cell exactly one **[up]** from the top of the column containing the assumptions for the first variable. This cell forms the upper left corner of the data table and creates a link between the data table and the profit equation.

Now that we have completed this necessary first step, we are ready to use the **/Data Table** command. Here we will repeat the step-by-step instructions but will omit some of the explanation provided earlier. Press the following keys:

Description	Keys to Press
Display the 1-2-3 command menus:	**/**
Select the /Data command:	**D**
Select the Table command:	**T**
Indicate that we want to test different values for each of 2 variables:	**2**
(Note: 1-2-3 now displays the Table range from our previous data table. But we don't want to use the previous setting, so let's go back two steps and then reset the Table range.)	
Escape from the previous setting:	**[Esc]**
(Notice that the "range" is removed, but the cell pointer remains at cell D214.)	
Now back up again:	**[Esc]**
(Notice that the cell pointer has returned to D236. Also, the command menu has returned to where we can select "Reset.")	
Select the Reset menu choice:	**R**
(Note: When you press "Reset," you are returned to READY mode. We have now reset all previous ranges, and we are ready to use Data Table again.)	

We are now ready to set up a new Data Table. Be sure the cell pointer is in D236. Then press the following keys:

Description	Keys to Press
Display the 1-2-3 command menus:	**/**
Select the /Data command:	**D**
Select the Table command:	**T**
Indicate that we want to test different values for each of 2 variables (Price per unit and Cost per unit):	**2**
Anchor D236 as the beginning of our range:	**.**
Paint the Table range D236..G239:	**[down*3] [right*3]**
Confirm the range:	**[Enter]**

Description	Keys to Press
Move the cell pointer to E225 to indicate that the variable "Price per unit" is the input cell for the first variable:	**(Use the arrow keys.)**
(Note: The first variable is always for the assumption listed in the column.)	
Confirm E225 as the input cell for the first variable:	**[Enter]**
(1-2-3 will now ask us to enter the input cell for the second variable.)	
Move the cell pointer to E226 to indicate that the variable "Cost per unit" is the input cell for the second variable:	**(Use the arrow keys.)**
(Note: The second variable is always for the assumption listed across the row.)	
Confirm that E226 is the input cell for the second variable:	**[Enter]**
(This is the final step. Watch 1-2-3 complete the calculations!)	

ON YOUR OWN: Use **/Range Format** to put the nine results in the range **E237..G239** into **Currency** format with **zero decimal** places. (We suggest that you leave the value in cell D236 unformatted, so that it is clear that this value is neither an assumption nor a result.)

Good. Your screen should appear as follows:

```
E237: (CO) 40                                                        READY


         A        B        C        D        E        F        G        H
221   WHAT IF 2                             "WHAT IF"
222                          (Using the Data Table Command)
223
224
225                       Price per unit        $100
226                       Cost per unit         $80
227                                          --------
228                       Profit per unit       $20
229
230
231
232                                 PROFIT PER UNIT
233
234                                       Cost per unit
235
236                           20     $70      $80      $90
237                       Price    $110     $40      $30      $20
238                       per      $100     $30      $20      $10
239                       unit      $90     $20      $10      $0
240
```

Observation: Lotus 1-2-3 has quickly calculated the effects on the profit per unit of changes in assumptions about *both* the price per unit and cost per unit. We now have nine separate results, which show that depending on our assumptions, the profit per unit could range from $40 ($110-$70) to $0 ($90-$90). Notice that the results for cells F237–F239 are the same as we obtained in the previous 1-variable data table analysis. This is because for these cells, the cost per unit was assumed to be $80, just as it was in the formula.

Let's now review the steps for creating a 2-variable data table.

Summary of Steps for Using Data Table with 2 Variables

Using the **/Data Table** command to test the effect of changes in 2 variables involves the following steps. Use the diagram below as is helpful:

1 *List in a column* the alternative values that will be tested for the first variable (the alternative assumptions about the price per unit in our example).

2 *List across a row* the alternative values that will be tested for the second variable (the alternative assumptions for the cost per unit in our example). This row of values must begin in the cell one [up] and one to the [right] from the top cell in the column that contains the assumptions about the first variable.

3 *Create a formula* that will form the basis of your data table in the cell in the upper left corner of the data table. This cell will be one [up] from the uppermost cell in the column that contains the assumptions about the first variable. (In the example above, we entered into cell D236 the formula for "Profit per unit" which had originally been created in cell E228.)

4 *Invoke the /Data Table command.*

5 *Use "Reset"* to clear any previous ranges. If you reset, then invoke the /Data Table command again and confirm that a *2*-variable data table will be created. (If you did not use reset but found you should have, press [Esc] twice. Then use reset and invoke the /Data Table command again.)

6 *Paint the range* that forms a rectangle, beginning at the cell with the newly created formula from Step 3 and then covering all the assumptions for both the first variable and the second variable. The cells where our results will eventually appear will also be covered.

7 *Move the cell pointer to the first input cell.* It contains the variable used for the first set of assumptions. (Earlier, the first input cell was E225, the "Price per unit.") Press [Enter].

8 *Move the cell pointer to the second input cell.* It contains the variable used for the second set of assumptions. (Earlier, the second input cell was E226, the "Cost per Unit.") Press [Enter] and watch the results appear.

Based upon these steps, a data table with 2 variables will always have this specific structure:

+	test 2	test 2	test 2	test 2
test 1	result	result	result	result
test 1	result	result	result	result
test 1	result	result	result	result
test 1	result	result	result	result

The word **test 1** refers to the different assumptions about the values of the first variable that the data table is designed to test. The word **test 2** refers to the different assumptions about the values of the second variable that the data table is to test. The symbol **+** refers to the formula that is created to form the basis of the data table. The word **result** refers to the results that the data table will eventually produce using that formula.

Note: We can see that **/Data Table** is a powerful command that allows us to list the results of multiple sensitivity tests in one compact table. We can create a data table to test the effect of changes in the values of either one or two variables.

However, **/Data Table** is also a complicated command. Like other commands in 1-2-3, it is best learned by actually using it.

In the remainder of Lesson 10, we will create first a 1-variable and then a 2-variable data table to test different assumptions about the values of variables in our break-even formulas. We will create the data tables that are described in the case.

You should refer to these examples and, specifically, the summary pages to help answer any questions you might have as we proceed along in Lesson 10. The instructions for the remainder of Lesson 10 will not contain as much detailed explanation as did the instructions for these two examples.

Creating 1-Variable Data Tables for Break-Even Analysis

ON YOUR OWN: Press **[Home]** to return to the beginning of our worksheet for break-even analysis. Press the **[PgDn]** key seven times to get to the screen beginning with cell **A141**. It is on this screen that we will create our 1-variable data tables. (Notice that the first seven screens are just as we left them after Lesson 9.)

Observation: The values in Column C represent different assumptions (or projections) about Ad Spending for Suave in FY 1985. These are the assumptions that we will test by using the **/Data Table** command.

Notice that we have included labels for two blank columns (D and E). Why are we including room for results in two columns? We are going to test the effects of different projections about Ad Spending in FY 1985 on *both* "SUAVE SALES NEEDED" *and* "SUAVE SHARE OF MARKET NEEDED" to maintain an operating profit of $10.8 million.

Let's see how we can do this. We will first prepare the column for "SUAVE SALES NEEDED" by creating a link from the data table to our break-even sales model. Press the following keys:

Description	Keys to Press
Move the cell pointer to cell D152:	(Use the arrow keys or [F5].)
Indicate that a formula will be entered:	+
Move the cell pointer to G132, the cell containing the formula for Suave Sales Needed to maintain the $10.8 million operating profit:	[PgUp] [right*3]
Confirm that the formula in G132 is the one we want to duplicate in cell D152:	[Enter]

The value **1196.013** should appear in cell **D152**.

Observation: We have now created the formula that will form the basis for the data table results in Column D. This column will list the effects of different assumptions about Suave Ad Spending on the Suave Sales Needed (in millions of ounces) to maintain an operating profit of $10.8 million.

Now let's create the formula that will form the basis for the data table results in Column E. This column will list the effects of different assumptions about Suave Ad Spending on the Suave Share of Market Needed to maintain an operating profit of $10.8 million.

Press these keys:

Description	Keys to Press
Move the cell pointer to E152:	**[right]**
Indicate that a formula is to be entered:	**+**
Move the cell pointer to G138, the cell containing the formula we want:	**[PgUp] [down*6] [right*2]**
Confirm that G138 is the cell we want:	**[Enter]**

The value **0.136981** should appear in cell **E152**.

Note: We are now ready to create a data table that tests the effects of different assumptions about *1 input variable* (Suave Ad Spending in FY 1985, as listed in Column C) *on the results of two different formulas* (the break-even formula listed in D152 *and* the break-even formula listed in E152.)

Press the following keys:

Description	Keys to Press
Display the 1-2-3 command menus:	**/**
Select the /Data command:	**D**
Select the Table command:	**T**
Clear the previous data table range:	**R**
(We know that previous ranges exist, so we can just reset them right away.)	
Display the 1-2-3 command menus again:	**/**
Select the /Data command again:	**D**
Select the Table command again:	**T**
Indicate that there is 1 input variable:	**1**
Move the cell pointer to C152:	**(Use the arrow keys.)**
Anchor C152 as the beginning of our range:	**.**

Description	Keys to Press
Paint the Table range C152..E160:	**[down*8] [right*2]**
Confirm the range:	**[Enter]**
(1-2-3 will ask us to enter the input cell.)	
Move the cell pointer to G107, the cell that contains projections for Suave Ad Spending in our break-even formulas:	**(Use the [PgUp] and arrow keys.)**
Confirm that cell G107 is the cell we want:	**[Enter]**
(Watch 1-2-3 calculate the effects of our different assumptions!)	

ON YOUR OWN: Put the sales results in cells **D153..D160** into **Comma** format with **zero decimal** places. Put the share results in cell **E153..E160** into **Percent** format with **one decimal** place. Notice how this formatting makes our results much clearer. (Leave cells **D152** and **E152** unformatted, so that they are not confused with assumptions or results.)

Good. Your screen should appear as follows:

```
E153: (P1) 0.1200702455                                          READY


       A      B      C      D      E      F      G      H
141 ------------------------------------------------------------------
142                            TO MAINTAIN AN OPERATING PROFIT OF
143                            $10.8 MILLION IN FY 1985
144                            ------------------------------------
145
146                 Projected SUAVE    SUAVE
147                     Ad    SALES    SHARE
148                 Spending NEEDED    OF
149                 FY 1985 (OUNCES)   MARKET
150                  ($mm)    (mm)     NEEDED
151                 -------- -------- --------
152                          1196.013 0.136981
153                   $3.0    1,048    12.0%
154                   $4.0    1,085    12.4%
155                   $5.0    1,122    12.9%
156                   $6.0    1,159    13.3%
157                   $7.0    1,196    13.7%
158                   $8.0    1,233    14.1%
159                   $9.0    1,270    14.5%
160                  $10.0    1,307    15.0%
```

Note: This exercise showed that we can test the effects of changes in the value of one variable on the results of more than one formula. To do so, the additional formulas for the data table must all be lined up immediately to the right of the first formula—just as the formula in E152 was lined up immediately to the right of the formula in D152.

Now let's create a data table that tests the effects of different assumptions about the values of two variables in our break-even formula for "SHARE OF MARKET IN FY 1985 NECESSARY TO MAINTAIN AN OPERATING PROFIT OF $10.8 MILLION." This time, however, you will enter the assumptions on your own.

Entering the Assumptions for a 2-Variable Data Table

We have explained the steps and structure for creating data tables that test different assumptions about 2 variables. However, learning this complicated command requires practice. Let's create a data table testing different assumptions about 2 variables in our break-even formulas.

ON YOUR OWN: Press the **[PgDn]** key to display the screen that will contain our new data table. This screen, beginning at cell **A161**, is the screen on which we will create our 2-variable data table.

This time, we will leave it up to you to enter the assumptions that we want to test. First, we will enter different assumptions about Suave Ad Spending in FY 1985. So, enter the following values into the corresponding cells (and put into **Currency** format with **one decimal** place):

Cell	Value
C170	$3.0
C171	$4.0
C172	$5.0
C173	$6.0
C174	$7.0
C175	$8.0
C176	$9.0
C177	$10.0

Observation: These are the same values we tested in the 1-variable exercise.

The second variable to test is the Industry Growth Rate. Enter the following values into the corresponding cells (and put into **Percent** format with **zero decimal** places):

Cell	Value
D169	− 1%
E169	0%
F169	1%
G169	2%
H169	3%
I169	4%
J169	5%

Note: You can enter a percentage by typing in either **0.01** or **1%**, for example.

Good. We have now entered the different assumptions about the industry growth rate that we wish to test. Your screen should appear as follows:

```
D169: (P0) -0.01                                                    READY


        A        B        C        D        E        F        G        H
 161 ------------------------------------------------------------------------
 162  SHARE OF MARKET IN FY 1985 NECESSARY TO MAINTAIN OPERATING PROFIT
 163                       OF $10.8 MILLION
 164
 165
 166                              Projected Industry Growth Rate
 167                                 from FY 1984 to FY 1985
 168
 169                          -1%       0%       1%       2%       3%
 170  Projected        $3.0
 171  Advertising      $4.0
 172  Expenditures     $5.0
 173  for Suave        $6.0
 174  Shampoo          $7.0
 175  In FY 1985       $8.0
 176  (in millions)    $9.0
 177                  $10.0
 178
 179
 180
```

Note: Cells I169 and J169 are not visible on this screen. Press the **[Tab]** key if you wish to view them.

Creating a 2-Variable Data Table for Break-Even Analysis

To complete the first step necessary to set up the data table, let's create the formula that will form the basis of our data table. Then let's use the **/Data Table** command. Press the following keys:

Description	Keys to Press
Move the cell pointer to cell C169:	**(Use the arrow keys and re-align screen so that A161 is in top left corner.)**
Indicate that a formula will be entered:	**+**
Move the cell pointer to G138, the cell containing the formula for Suave Share of Market Necessary:	**[PgUp] [PgUp] [down*9] [right*4]**

Description	*Keys to Press*
Confirm that the formula in G138 is the one we want to duplicate in cell C169:	**[Enter]**

(Note: The value 0.136981 should appear in cell C169, the same as appeared in cell E152 in the 1-variable data table.)
(Now let's move directly to performing the /Data Table command.)

Invoke the /Data Table command:	**/D T**

(We saved some space here by including all 3 keys on this one line.)

Clear the previous data table range:	**R**
Invoke the /Data Table command again:	**/D T**
Indicate that 2 variables will be input:	**2**
Anchor C169 as the beginning of our range:	**.**
Paint the Table range C169..J177:	**[End] [down] [right*7]**
Confirm the range:	**[Enter]**
Move the cell pointer to G107, the cell containing the formula for the first input variable (Suave Ad Spending in FY 1985):	**(Use the [PgUp] and arrow keys.)**
Confirm that G107 is the input cell for the first variable:	**[Enter]**

(Note that the cell pointer returns to cell C169.)

Move the cell pointer to G114, the cell containing the formula for the second input cell (Industry Growth Rate):	**(Use the [PgUp] and arrow keys.)**
Confirm that G114 is the input cell for the second variable:	**[Enter]**

(Watch 1-2-3 calculate the effects of our different assumptions! Press [Tab] once to see the rest of the results.)

ON YOUR OWN: Put the share results in the range **D170..J117** into **Percent** format with **one decimal** place.

Good. Your screens should appear as follows:

D170: (P1) 0.1237087378   READY

	A	B	C	D	E	F	G	H
161	---	---	---	---	---	---	---	---
162	SHARE OF MARKET IN FY 1985 NECESSARY TO MAINTAIN OPERATING PROFIT							
163			OF $10.8 MILLION					
164								
165								
166					Projected Industry Growth Rate			
167					from FY 1984 to FY 1985			
168								
169		0.136981		−1%	0%	1%	2%	3%
170	Projected		$3.0	12.4%	12.2%	12.1%	12.0%	11.9%
171	Advertising		$4.0	12.8%	12.7%	12.6%	12.4%	12.3%
172	Expenditures		$5.0	13.2%	13.1%	13.0%	12.9%	12.7%
173	for Suave		$6.0	13.7%	13.5%	13.4%	13.3%	13.1%
174	Shampoo		$7.0	14.1%	14.0%	13.8%	13.7%	13.6%
175	In FY 1985		$8.0	14.5%	14.4%	14.3%	14.1%	14.0%
176	(In millions)		$9.0	15.0%	14.8%	14.7%	14.5%	14.4%
177			$10.0	15.4%	15.3%	15.1%	15.0%	14.8%
178								
179								
180								

I170: (P1) 0.1177612023   READY

	I	J	K	L	M	N	O	P
161								
162								
163								
164								
165								
166								
167								
168								
169	4%	5%						
170	11.8%	11.7%						
171	12.2%	12.1%						
172	12.6%	12.5%						
173	13.0%	12.9%						
174	13.4%	13.3%						
175	13.8%	13.7%						
176	14.3%	14.1%						
177	14.7%	14.5%						
178								
179								
180								

Note: If you want to view the results in columns I and J on the same screen as the assumptions in column C, you can use the **/Worksheet Titles Vertical** command.

We have now completed a great deal of complex work in this lesson. Check your results with the completed tables beginning in column Q, if you like. Then, let's save all this work.

Saving Your Worksheet in a File on Diskette

ON YOUR OWN: Press the **[Home]** key. Use the **/File Save** command to save our work in Lesson 10. Name the file: **LN10**.

Review of Lesson 10

In this lesson, we learned one of the most powerful but complicated commands in 1-2-3: the **/Data Table** command. Lesson 13 presents an opportunity for additional practice using this command.

To reexamine the steps and structure for creating a data table (with either 1 or 2 variables), it is best to review the two special examples that began this lesson. In addition, the summary discussions following these examples may be helpful.

MANAGEMENT DISCUSSION

1 When is what-if analysis useful?

What-if analysis is useful when the effects of assumptions on key variables provide valuable information. Lotus 1-2-3 can process a range of assumptions about the values of either one or two variables. To analyze the effects of these different assumptions, managers can use the powerful **Data-Table** command of Lotus 1-2-3.

2 What are the dangers for managers using the Data-Table command?

The dangers are that managers might get involved in the calculations and numbers themselves, losing sight of the consumer and the dynamics of the market—data that form the foundation of any projections. An important question to ask repeatedly is, Does this projection make sense?

3 What useful information is provided by break-even calculations that are based on a range of advertising levels?

This series of break-even calculations allows a manager to understand how sensitive the break-even market shares or sales volumes are to different levels of advertising expenditures. The data table that was calculated indicates that if the advertising level is set at $3.0 million, then a Suave market share of 12.0% is needed to maintain the operating profit of $10.8 million. However, if the advertising level is set at $10.0 million, then a market share of 15.0% is needed to maintain the operating profit of $10.8 million.

4 What useful information is provided by break-even calculations based on a range of industry growth rates as well as industry's advertising levels?

These break-even calculations, which are generated in the 2-variable data table, allow a manager to gauge the relative importance of these 2 variables. Although both variables are important, the results seem to indicate that the level of advertising expenditures is more critical.

A change in advertising expenditure of $1 million requires approximately a 0.4% to 0.5% increase in market share to maintain the same operating profit. However, a change in the projected industry of growth rate of 1% requires only approximately a 0.1% to 0.2% increase in market share to maintain the operating profit. As a rule, break-even sales volumes are more sensitive to internal changes (brand expenditures, margins, etc.) than changes in the environment external to the brand.

This data table allows a manager to examine the effects of simultaneous changes in 2 variables on a single matrix. A manager can look at each level of advertising spending and then examine, across a range of industry growth rates, the feasibility of achieving the market share necessary to maintain an operating profit of $10.8 million.

LESSON 11   FINANCIAL ANALYSIS: STRUCTURING THE SPREADSHEET

OVERVIEW

COMPUTER INSTRUCTIONS

Lesson 11 introduces the concept of a spreadsheet and demonstrates how a spreadsheet may be organized.

MANAGEMENT ISSUES

Lessons 11, 12, and 13 introduce the use of Lotus 1-2-3 in financial management. Spreadsheet analysis is a tool frequently used for financial management. Managers who have profit and loss responsibility need to examine the range of feasible financial results for their business.

Lesson 11 specifically addresses how to structure a spreadsheet so that assumptions, revenues and costs, and projected results are all presented clearly.

MANAGEMENT DISCUSSION QUESTIONS

1. Why is the structure of a spreadsheet important?
2 What are the key elements of a spreadsheet?
3 Do the assumptions presented in Lesson 11 appear reasonable to you?
4 Which assumptions should most concern a brand manager?

CASE

Vallera knew that any successful brand manager must be concerned with more than just breaking even on marketing expenditures. Over time, she would be expected to do better than merely maintain operating profit. She had profit responsibility, which often superseded any other considerations.

Brand managers at Helene Curtis reported profits and losses in annual statements. Managers could use these statements and Lotus 1-2-3 to analyze various assumptions. A "spreadsheet" could be developed to test changes in the level of advertising expenditures, for instance, within an organized profit and loss structure.

Break-even analyses were only one type of sensitivity analysis. Vallera could also develop financial projections without a specific, predetermined profit requirement. Operating profit would be determined by the assumptions and the fundamental economic relationships in the spreadsheet.

All managers at Helene Curtis were required to use the same in-house format for structuring a spreadsheet. Since a spreadsheet was often used by many managers and diskettes were commonly passed around, the person using a spreadsheet often did not develop it. It was important, therefore, that the originator of a spreadsheet document the assumptions behind various projections, protect valuable data from being changed, and display any changes in assumptions and the results of sensitivity analyses together on the monitor's screen. A well-structured spreadsheet made it possible to transfer, interpret, and communicate results about a vast array of possible scenarios within the company more easily.

Vallera was prepared to design a spreadsheet that would clearly document her assumptions and identify the accepted accounting relationships among the financial variables. She also wanted to separate out the brand performance measures to show clearly the effects of her sensitivity analyses. She included space for fiscal 1985 and fiscal 1986 projections.

Table 5.1 shows the various screens that made up the spreadsheet structure. She divided the spreadsheet into three screens: (1) assumptions, (2) revenues and expenditures, and (3) performance measures.

TABLE 5.1   THE ASSUMPTIONS SCREEN

```
A1: ' LESSON 11                                                    READY


          A       B       C       D       E       F       G       H
1    LESSON 11           THE SUAVE BRAND MANAGEMENT ACCOUNT
2              (dollar figures in millions, except retail price per ounce)
3    ------------------------------------------------------------------
4                    Assumptions Fixed Under All Scenarios
5    1)Industry annual growth %          SUAVE MKTING EXPENDITURES
6    2)Industry advertising              8)Annual trade promotion:
7      expenditures in FY 85:            9)Annual consumer promo:
8    3)Industry advertising
9      expenditures in FY 86:            ADVERTISING ALLOCATIONS
10                                       10)Prime Time TV:
11   4)Suave retail price/oz.:           11)Daytime TV:
12   5)Retail gross margin % :           12)Print:
13   6)Variable cost % :
14   7)Mfg. gross margin % :             ALL FIGURES IN CONSTANT '84 DOLLARS
15   ------------------------------------------------------------------
16                    Assumptions Made Under Specific Scenarios
17
18
19
20
```

TABLE 5.1 (continued) THE REVENUES AND EXPENDITURES SCREEN[a]

```
A21: ' INDUSTRY                                                          READY


          A        B        C        D        E        F        G        H
    21  INDUSTRY INDUSTRY INDUSTRY                     SUAVE    SUAVE    SUAVE
    22  FY 1984  FY 1985  FY 1986                      FY 1984  FY 1985  FY 1986
    23           (proj.)  (proj.)   CATEGORIES                  (proj.)  (proj.)
    24  -------- -------- --------                    -------- -------- --------
    25  8,560.0                     Sales In Ounces     1,161.0
    26  $1,159.5                    Retail Dollar Sls.  $104.4
    27                              Retail Margin       $31.3
    28                                                 --------
    29                              Mfg. Dollar Sales   $73.1
    30                              Variable Costs      $41.7
    31                                                 --------
    32                              Gross Margin        $31.4
    33                                                 --------
    34                              Trade Promotion     $12.7
    35                              Consumer Promotion  $1.9
    36  $117.5                      Total Advertising   $6.0
    37                                Prime Time TV     $3.5
    38                                Daytime TV        $2.5
    39                                Print             $0.0
    40                              Total Marketing     $20.6
```

[a]These data have been disguised; nevertheless, the fundamental relationships hold. Numbers were rounded off to simplify calculations.

TABLE 5.1 (continued) THE PERFORMANCE MEASURES SCREEN

```
A41:                                                                     READY


          A        B        C        D        E        F        G        H
    41                                                 --------
    42                              Operating Profit    $10.8
    43
    44                              Mkt. Share:Ounces   13.6%
    45                              Mkt. Share:Dollars  9.0%
    46                              Industry Ad Share   5.1%
    47                              Ad/Sales Ratio      5.7%
    48
    49
    50
    51
    52
    53
    54
    55
    56
    57
    58
    59
    60
```

The Assumptions Screen

One screen displayed the assumptions behind each scenario. The assumptions fixed under all scenarios were developed using data from the production and accounting departments. Helene Curtis had decided to assume that prices, margins, promotions, and the allocation of advertising dollars would remain constant from fiscal 1984 to fiscal 1986. Management believed that these assumptions were reasonable, because the inflation rate for these 12 months was likely to be very low and all revenues and costs would probably be affected equally by any inflation that did occur.

There was room at the bottom of this screen shown in Table 5.1 for assumptions specific to each scenario. For example, the amount of Suave advertising might be placed in this area so sensitivity analysis could be carried out on its relationship with market share and operating profit.

The Revenues and Expenditures Screen

Another screen displayed a variation of the standard income statement that Helene Curtis used for all its brands, excluding only operating profit. Table 5.1 shows the Suave income statement for fiscal 1984.

The Performance Measures Screen

The third screen displayed the five primary measures of brand performance that Helene Curtis management used to evaluate the success of its brands. Table 5.1 shows the brand performance for fiscal 1984.

Vallera was now ready to construct sensitivity analyses based on what she had learned from Gail Lanznar and her own work to date.

Introduction to Spreadsheet Structures

In Lesson 11, we will introduce the use of 1-2-3 for spreadsheet analysis. Our instructions on using 1-2-3 in spreadsheet analysis will continue in Lessons 12 and 13.

The spreadsheet is one of the most commonly used tools in financial management. The Lotus 1-2-3 worksheet, in fact, was purposely designed to look like a blank spreadsheet: a matrix of columns and rows with individual cells where either numbers or words could be entered.

The Lotus Development Corporation lists three principal capabilities of 1-2-3: (1) database management; (2) spreadsheet analysis; and (3) graphics. (These three capabilities are the reason the software was named "1-2-3.") In Lessons 1 through 10, we saw how 1-2-3 could facilitate database management. In Lessons 11 through 13, we will see how 1-2-3 assists spreadsheet analysis. In Lessons 14 through 18, we will learn how to create graphs with 1-2-3.

Using 1-2-3 for Spreadsheet Analysis

We have already learned all the functions and commands that are essential for using 1-2-3 in spreadsheet analysis. In Lessons 11 through 13, we will learn:

1 How to structure a spreadsheet;
2 How to apply all that we have learned to creating a spreadsheet; and
3 A few new techniques that facilitate spreadsheet analysis with 1-2-3.

Let's see what a spreadsheet is all about.

COMPUTER INSTRUCTIONS

Retrieving the Worksheet File for Lesson 11 and Examining the Spreadsheet Structure

First, follow these familiar steps, if necessary:

1 Load DOS. Enter date and time.
2 Load the Lotus Access System.
3 Load the 1-2-3 software program.

ON YOUR OWN: Insert the Suave Data Diskette into the appropriate disk drive. Use the **/File Retrieve** command to retrieve from the Suave Data Diskette the file named **LESSON11.WKS**. After you have retrieved the file, switch diskettes. Remove the Suave Data Diskette and replace it with your diskette. Press **[Home]** as directed. The screens beginning at cell A1 contain the spreadsheet displayed in Table 5.1 of the case. Use the **[PgDn]** key to view the rest of the spreadsheet. Return to cell **Al** by pressing the **[Home]** key.
Note: The completed worksheet starts at row 101 for Lessons 11 through 18. Let's examine the structure of this spreadsheet more closely.

The Assumptions Screen

The first screen, beginning at **A1**, contains space for us to list explicitly the assumptions that will form the foundation of our pro forma forecasts and spreadsheet analysis. We saw in Lessons 9 and 10 how important it is for us to understand the effects of different assumptions about key projections or variables.

Understanding our assumptions is just as important in spreadsheet analysis as it is in break-even analysis. That is why we have designed the spreadsheet so that we can display on one screen exactly what assumptions underlie our spreadsheet analysis. Later in this lesson, we will enter most of these assumptions.

The Revenues and Expenditures Screen

Press the **[PgDn]** key again to display the second screen beginning at **A21**. This screen displays the FY 1984 income statement for the Suave brand management account. In addition, it contains the columns into which we will enter projections to create pro formas for FY 1985 and FY 1986. Industry projections will be entered into columns B and C. Suave projections will be entered into columns G and H. These projections will be "driven" by the assumptions that we entered earlier in the first screen, just as we saw in Lessons 9 and 10.

The Performance Measures Screen

Press the **[PgDn]** key again to display the third screen beginning at **A41**. This screen displays the key performance measures for the Suave brand management account. We will input formulas into the corresponding cells in columns G and H for Suave's projected performance in FY 1985 and FY 1986.

Note: This spreadsheet has been structured so that its components can be easily found and are clearly understood. However, we have here provided just one example for you of how a spreadsheet could be structured. Therefore, before we go on, it is important to mention two points:

1 This particular spreadsheet has been designed to be very compact, using only 3 screens. The worksheet in 1-2-3, however, is enormous. This spreadsheet could have been designed so that its components were still displayed clearly but were much more spread out. For example, the assumptions could be displayed across several screens. As we move through Lessons 11, 12, and 13, decide for yourself how the spreadsheet might be designed differently for your purposes.
2 Many managers create spreadsheets that contain projections for more than just 2 years. The appropriateness of the number of years depends on the decision that is being analyzed. [See the Management Questions and Discussion.]

Observation: After we create our projections for FY 1985 and FY 1986, we will display the projected performance measures for Suave in columns G and H, from line 42 to 47. However, the assumptions that underlie that projected performance are located 2 screens above. It would be helpful, therefore, if we could display on one screen both the key assumptions and the performance effects. The **/Worksheet Window** command will allow us to do just that.

To see how (1) the *Assumptions Screen* works and (2) how the **/Worksheet Window** command works, let's first input some assumptions and then try *windowing*.

Entering Fixed Assumptions

ON YOUR OWN: Press the **[Home]** key to return to the first screen. The first set of assumptions, located in lines 5 through 14, will remain unchanged throughout our entire spreadsheet analysis. We will not test different values for them under sensitivity analysis. As the case describes, the values of the first three assumptions were set by senior Helene Curtis management. **Input the following values:**

Assumption	Cell	Entry	Value	Format
1	D5	Industry Annual Growth %	.02	Percent with 0 decimals
2	D7	Industry Advertising in FY 85	145	Currency with 1 decimal
3	D9	Industry Advertising in FY 86	170	Currency with 1 decimal

Assumptions 4 through 12 are based upon the figures for FY 1984. That is, Helene Curtis management assumed that these figures would remain constant throughout FY 1985 and FY 1986.

ON YOUR OWN: To enter these assumptions, **create the following formulas** based upon the figures in FY 1984:

Assumption	Cell	Formula	1-2-3 Equation	Format
4	D11	Retail Dollar Sales/ Sales in Ounces	$+ F26/F25$	Currency with 2 decimals
5	D12	Retail Margin/ Retail Dollar Sales	$+ F27/F26$	Percent with 0 decimals
6	D13	Variable Costs/ Mfg. Dollar Sales	$+ F30/F29$	Percent with 0 decimals
7	D14	Gross Margin/ Mfg. Dollar Sales	$+ F32/F29$	Percent with 0 decimals
8	H6	Trade Promotion	$+ F34$	Currency with 1 decimal
9	H7	Consumer Promotion	$+ F35$	Currency with 1 decimal
10	H10	Prime Time TV/ Total Advertising	$+ F37/F36$	Percent with 0 decimals
11	H11	Daytime TV/ Total Advertising	$+ F38/F36$	Percent with 0 decimals
12	H12	Print/ Total Advertising	$+ F39/F36$	Percent with 0 decimals

Entering Assumptions for Specific Scenarios

The second part of the screen (lines 16 through 20) will be used to enter assumptions for specific scenarios. These are the assumptions that we will vary in Lesson 12 to run our sensitivity tests.

Right now we do not need to know what exactly a scenario is. We'll learn that in Lesson 12. However, for now, let's input two key assumptions so that we can see how to use this part of the Assumptions Screen.

ON YOUR OWN: **Type in** the following, beginning in each respective cell:

Cell	Entry	Format
A18	**Suave advertising, FY 1985**	—
A19	**Suave advertising, FY 1986**	—
D18	**$7.0**	Currency with 1 decimal
D19	**$8.0**	Currency with 1 decimal

Good. Your screen should appear as:

```
A1: ' LESSON 11                                                    READY


      A       B       C       D       E       F       G       H
1  LESSON 11              THE SUAVE BRAND MANAGEMENT ACCOUNT
2              (dollar figures In millions, except retail price per ounce)
3  --------------------------------------------------------------------
4                  Assumptions Fixed Under All Scenarios
5   1)Industry annual growth %      2%  SUAVE MKTING EXPENDITURES
6   2)Industry advertising              8)Annual trade promotion:   $12.7
7     expenditures In FY 85:   $145.0  9)Annual consumer promo:     $1.9
8   3)Industry advertising
9     expenditures In FY 86:   $170.0  ADVERTISING ALLOCATIONS
10                                     10)Prime Time TV:             58%
11  4)Suave retail price/oz.:   $0.09  11)Daytime TV:                42%
12  5)Retail gross margin % :     30%  12)Print:                      0%
13  6)Variable cost % :           57%
14  7)Mfg. gross margin % :       43% ALL FIGURES IN CONSTANT '84 DOLLARS
15 --------------------------------------------------------------------
16                  Assumptions Made Under Specific Scenarios
17
18 Suave advertising, FY 1985   $7.0
19 Suave advertising, FY 1986   $8.0
20
```

We have now seen how to enter assumptions into this part of our spreadsheet. In Lesson 12, we will see how to use these assumptions in creating our spreadsheet scenarios.

To complete this lesson on the spreadsheet structure, let's see how we can use windowing to display on a single screen our key assumptions *and* our performance measures.

Using Windowing

To see how the **/Worksheet Window** command works, press the following keys:

Description	Keys to Press
Return to cell A1:	**[Home]**
Move the cell pointer, using the [PgDn] key and the [down] key only, until the performance measures are at the bottom of the screen, with three lines left at the very bottom:	**[PgDn] [down*29]**
(Cell A31 should be in the top left corner of the screen, and the cell pointer should be in cell A50.)	

Now let's see how to use the **/Worksheet Window** command. Press the following keys:

Description	*Keys to Press*
Move the cell pointer to line 41, on top of the per- formance measures:	**[up*9]**

(Notice that we have not altered the screen. We have just moved the cell pointer.)

Display the 1-2-3 command menus:	**/**
Select the /Worksheet command:	**W**
Select the Window command:	**W**
Select the Horizontal command:	**H**

(Note that this command indicates that we will "split the screen horizontally at the current row.")

Observation: Notice that 1-2-3 has displayed a second heading for columns A through H. This shows that we have split the screen into an upper part and a lower part.

Concerning the upper part, notice that the cell pointer is located right above the second column heading, in cell A40. This means that we can move the cell pointer around the upper part of the screen.

Concerning the lower part, notice that 1-2-3 has taken away the very last line that we had left at the bottom (line 50). It did so in order to make room for the second column heading.

Observation: When we use windowing to split a screen horizontally, we must remember that we will lose the last line and therefore must allow room to avoid losing a line of data we want.

Note: Pressing the **[Window]** key (the **[F6]** function key) will move the cell pointer to A41 in the lower part of the screen. We can then move the cell pointer around the lower part of the screen. Try it. Pressing **[F6]** again returns the cell pointer to the upper part of the screen.

Note: The **[Scroll Lock]** key can be very useful when windowing is used. For example, if you advance the screen too far **[down]** or **[up]**, the **[Scroll Lock]** key allows you to realign the screen quickly.

Let's move the cell pointer so that we display the key assumptions in the upper part. Press the following keys:

Description	*Keys to Press*
Move the cell pointer to A20:	**[PgUp] [PgUp]**

(Note that the [PgUp] key now moves only 10 lines each time. This is because the upper half of the screen contains only 10 lines.)

| Use the arrow keys to move line 15 to the top of the
screen: | **[down*4]** |

Your screen should appear as:

```
A24: (C1) " --------                                                    READY


        A       B       C       D       E       F       G       H
15    -----------------------------------------------------------------
16                      Assumptions Made Under Specific Scenarios
17
18    Suave advertising, FY 1985       $7.0
19    Suave advertising, FY 1986       $8.0
20
21    INDUSTRY INDUSTRY INDUSTRY                       SUAVE   SUAVE   SUAVE
22    FY 1984 FY 1985 FY 1986                          FY 1984 FY 1985 FY 1986
23            (proj.) (proj.)        CATEGORIES                (proj.) (proj.)
24    -------- -------- --------                       -------- -------- --------
        A       B       C       D       E       F       G       H
41                                                     --------
42                              Operating Profit       $10.8
43
44                              Mkt. Share:Ounces      13.6%
45                              Mkt. Share:Dollars      9.0%
46                              Industry Ad Share       5.1%
47                              Ad/Sales Ratio          5.7%
48
49
```

Observation: We have now split the screen so that we can show on one screen the "Assumptions Made Under Specific Scenarios" and the projected "Performance Measures." Also note that we have designed our "windowed" screen so that the category headings from the "Revenues and Expenditures Screen" are displayed (lines 21 to 24). These headings will help us see that the results in column G will be the projected FY 1985 performance and the results in column H will be the projected FY 1986 performance.

Note: You can also use **/Worksheet Window** to split a screen vertically. The steps are analogous to splitting the screen horizontally. You can also use **/Worksheet Window Clear** to remove a split screen. Many times you will find that you want to rearrange how you split a screen. Just use **/Worksheet Window Clear** and then start over.

Let's now save this spreadsheet, which contains the assumptions we entered earlier.

Saving Your Work in a File on Diskette

ON YOUR OWN: Use **/Worksheet Window Clear** to remove the split screen. If we did not first clear the windowing, the screen would still be split when we retrieved it later. Of course, we could clear the windowing then, if desired.

Press the **[Home]** key to return to cell A1. Use **/File Save** to save the worksheet. Name the file: **LN11**.

Reviewing What We Learned in Lesson 11

In Lesson 11, we learned:

- A spreadsheet is a collection of rows and columns that is commonly used in management analysis, especially for financial projections.
- The Lotus 1-2-3 worksheet was designed to look like and be used as a spreadsheet.
- For the sake of understanding and clarity, it is important to design a spreadsheet so that the assumptions underlying our spreadsheet projections are clearly listed.
- We can use the **/Worksheet Window** command to split a screen, either horizontally or vertically.

Good. Let's now move on and create some financial projections for Suave in FY 1985 and FY 1986.

MANAGEMENT DISCUSSION

1 Why is the structure of a spreadsheet important?

The structure of a spreadsheet determine whethers the key elements are presented clearly. These key elements should be presented as clearly as possible so that both the managers who create it and other managers who use or examine it can understand how the spreadsheet works.

2 What are the key elements of a spreadsheet?

There are three key elements to a spreadsheet: (1) the assumptions that underlie the spreadsheet projections, (2) the revenue and cost structure that form the heart of the spreadsheet projections, and (3) the performance results that are calculated based on variations in the assumptions.

There are two types of assumptions. *Fixed* assumptions are predetermined market or brand data. *Variable* assumptions are either future uncertainties or are under the manager's control. When varied, they test different performance results. These assumptions include elements such as industry growth rates or advertising levels.

3 Do the assumptions presented in Lesson 11 appear reasonable to you?

Your answer to this question depends on your analysis of the shampoo market. There are two sets of assumptions in Lesson 11: (1) the first three, related to the industry as a whole, and (2) the next nine (numbers 4 through 12), for Suave, specifically. In addition, assumptions will be made about the level of Suave advertising. The Suave Budgeting Case provides more information useful in assessing how reasonable are the different market projections.

4 Which assumptions should most concern a brand manager?

The answer depends on which assumptions are most uncertain and have the greatest influence on profitability. If a brand manager believes that the growth rate and level of advertising spending of the industry are highly unpredictable, then the manager should be most concerned about industry-specific assumptions. However, if the manager believes that the revenue and the cost structure of the brand itself is subject to great change, then the manager should be most concerned about these assumptions. Lastly, if a manager believes that the "fixed" assumptions are fairly reliable, then the manager should be most concerned about projections for Suave advertising expenditures and the effects of the various levels of advertising on either Suave's growth rate or its market share.

**LESSON 12   SPREADSHEET ANALYSIS: CREATING SCENARIOS AND
RUNNING SENSITIVITY TESTS**

OVERVIEW

COMPUTER INSTRUCTIONS

Lesson 12 uses the spreadsheet structure developed in the previous lesson to construct
financial projections. This exercise provides you with a new application of familiar
functions and commands. Lesson 12 also contains a special section on Lotus 1-2-3
financial functions, with an example using "Net Present Value" (NPV) analysis.

MANAGEMENT ISSUES

In Lesson 12, you will learn how to define and construct spreadsheet scenarios and
then how to run sensitivity tests based on each scenario. The differences among an
assumption, a scenario, and a sensitivity test should become clearer as you complete
the lesson. Understanding these concepts will greatly assist you in interpreting the
results of spreadsheet projections.

MANAGEMENT DISCUSSION QUESTIONS

1 What is a scenario?
2 What is the difference between a scenario driven by a brand's growth rate and
one that is driven by a brand's market share? Which scenario provides a sounder
basis for financial projections for Suave?
3 Scenario A: What conclusions would you draw from the sensitivity tests that were
based on this scenario?
4 Scenario B: What conclusions would you draw from the sensitivity tests that were
based on this scenario?

CASE

Management believed that advertising Suave shampoo would have an effect on sales.
The key question, of course, was how much of an effect.

Managers at Helene Curtis differed in their assumptions about the effect of
advertising. They had different interpretations of the data on the marketing environment, and a variety of opinions on what would occur in the future in the shampoo
industry.

Whatever their assumptions were, managers at Helene Curtis derived sales fore-casts for Suave shampoo usually in one of two ways:

- *By examining the brand's sales history*
  (For example, projected Suave fiscal 1985 sales calculated as Suave fiscal 1984 sales plus its expected growth), that is, the forecast for Suave future sales was assumed to be "driven" by an expected growth rate in brand sales; or,
- *By examining the brand's share of industry sales*
  (For example, projected Suave fiscal 1985 sales calculated as projected industry sales in fiscal 1985 times Suave's expected market share), that is, the forecast for Suave future sales was assumed to be "driven" by an expected Suave share position in the industry.

These were two similar but still decidedly different perspectives. Suave sales might be projected to increase, but its share of market might not if the shampoo industry as a whole expanded by a greater percentage. Suave's market share might be projected to increase, but its sales might not if sales in the shampoo industry as a whole declined by a greater percentage.

Under the first perspective, managers focused on *the rate of growth of Suave's sales.* Under the second perspective, other managers focused on Suave's competitive position in the shampoo market, as measured by Suave's *share of market.*

At Helene Curtis, these two perspectives were represented as "Scenario A" and "Scenario B" for the purposes of spreadsheet analysis. Management used a system of equations in the spreadsheet to define a scenario. The scenario was intended to capture the chain of cause and effect between a management action (e.g., advertising) and a projected result (Suave sales).

Under *each* scenario, Vallera could run a variety of tests on the spreadsheet to determine how sensitive the brand's performance was to changes in assumptions about advertising's effectiveness for Suave. For example, having chosen a particular level of advertising spending, she could postulate different market shares and see what the effect on operating profit would be. The key, of course, was for her to figure out which market share projection was most likely—given a particular advertising level and her understanding of all the factors affecting Suave's market share.

Vallera had determined that two scenarios would be sufficient at this time. For each scenario, she decided to choose what she believed were the three most feasible levels of fiscal 1985 and 1986 advertising spending. Then for each advertising level, she would project three realistic growth rates for brand sales (Scenario A) or for market shares (Scenario B) for Suave shampoo.

As a result, she would run nine sensitivity analyses under each scenario (3 by 3). These analyses would allow her not only to speculate about the effects of advertising but also to view the level of operating profit calculated for various amounts of ad-vertising expenditures under different assumptions.

Scenario A and its nine sensitivity analyses are described in Table 5.2. Three advertising budgets were chosen. Vallera described them as moderate, aggresive, and

TABLE 5.2 SENSITIVITY ANALYSES UNDER SCENARIO A

Bases of the Scenario:

1. Suave advertising expenditures are assumed to be set by budget in advance.
2. Suave shampoo sales in an upcoming year are assumed to be determined by sales in the previous year times a projected rate of growth.

$$
\begin{matrix}
\text{Suave} \\
\text{FY 1985} \\
\text{Sales}
\end{matrix}
=
\begin{matrix}
\text{Suave} \\
\text{FY 1984} \\
\text{Sales}
\end{matrix}
+
\begin{bmatrix}
\text{Suave} & \text{Percentage} \\
\text{FY 1984} \times & \text{Growth} \\
\text{Sales} & \text{Rate}
\end{bmatrix}
$$

Sensitivity Analysis Tests to Be Run:

1. Assuming that a "moderate" advertising budget is set:

    $7.0 million in FY 1985
    $8.0 million in FY 1986

    The following growth rates for Suave sales will be tested:

    - 0%
    - 2%
    - 4%

2. Assuming that an "aggressive" advertising budget is set:

    $8.0 million in FY 1985
    $10.0 million in FY 1986

    The following growth rates for Suave shampoo sales will be tested:

    - 2%
    - 4%
    - 6%

3. Assuming that a "conservative" advertising budget is set:

    $6.0 million in FY 1985
    $6.0 million in FY 1986

    The following growth rates for Suave shampoo sales will be tested:

    - − 2%
    - 0%
    - 2%

conservative. Under each budget are the three assumptions about the annual sales growth rate that she believed were most plausible.

Scenario B and its nine sensitivity analyses are described in Table 5.3. The same three advertising budgets were chosen. Under each budget are the three assumptions about Suave's market share that Vallera believed were most reasonable.

TABLE 5.3   SENSITIVITY ANALYSES UNDER SCENARIO B

Bases of the Scenario:

1. Suave advertising expenditures are assumed to be set by budget in advance.
2. Suave shampoo sales in a given year are assumed to be determined by industry sales in that year times the market share that Suave can command.

$$\frac{\text{Suave Sales}}{\text{in FY 1985}} = \frac{\text{Industry Sales}}{\text{in FY 1985}} \times \frac{\text{Suave Market}}{\text{Share in FY 1985}}$$

Sensitivity Analysis Tests to Be Run:

1. Assuming that a "moderate" advertising budget is set:

   $7.0 million in FY 1985
   $8.0 million in FY 1986

   The following market share percentages for Suave shampoo (FY 1984 = 13.6%) will be tested:

FY 1985	*FY 1986*
• 13.1%	12.1%
• 13.6%	13.6%
• 14.1%	15.1%

2. Assuming that an "aggressive" advertising budget is set:

   $8.0 million in FY 1985
   $10.0 million in FY 1986

   The following market share percentages for Suave shampoo will be tested:

FY 1985	*FY 1986*
• 13.6%	13.6%
• 14.1%	15.1%
• 14.6%	16.1%

3. Assuming that a "conservative" advertising budget is set:

   $6.0 million in FY 1985
   $6.0 million in FY 1986

   The following market share percentages for Suave shampoo will be tested:

FY 1985	*FY 1986*
• 12.5%	11.1%
• 13.1%	12.1%
• 13.6%	13.6%

For the first sensitivity test under Scenario A, the "Assumptions" screen on the spreadsheet would read:

```
A1:  ' LESSON 12                                                          READY


          A        B        C        D        E        F        G        H
1    LESSON 12            THE SUAVE BRAND MANAGEMENT ACCOUNT
2             (dollar figures in millions, except retail price per ounce)
3    -----------------------------------------------------------------------
4                    Assumptions Fixed Under All Scenarios
5    1)Industry annual growth %        2%  SUAVE MKTING EXPENDITURES
6    2)Industry advertising                8)Annual trade promotion:    $12.7
7      expenditures in FY 85:    $145.0    9)Annual consumer promo:     $1.9
8    3)Industry advertising
9      expenditures in FY 86:    $170.0    ADVERTISING ALLOCATIONS
10                                         10)Prime Time TV:              58%
11   4)Suave retail price/oz.:    $0.09    11)Daytime TV:                 42%
12   5)Retail gross margin % :      30%    12)Print:                       0%
13   6)Variable cost % :            57%
14   7)Mfg. gross margin % :        43% ALL FIGURES IN CONSTANT '84 DOLLARS
15   -----------------------------------------------------------------------
16                    Assumptions Made Under Specific Scenarios
17
18   Suave advertising, FY 1985    $7.0 Suave annual growth rate          0%
19   Suave advertising, FY 1986    $8.0
20
```

For the first sensitivity test under Scenario B, the "Assumptions" screen on the spreadsheet would read:

```
A1:  ' LESSON 12                                                          READY


          A        B        C        D        E        F        G        H
1    LESSON 12            THE SUAVE BRAND MANAGEMENT ACCOUNT
2             (dollar figures in millions, except retail price per ounce)
3    -----------------------------------------------------------------------
4                    Assumptions Fixed Under All Scenarios
5    1)Industry annual growth %        2%  SUAVE MKTING EXPENDITURES
6    2)Industry advertising                8)Annual trade promotion:    $12.7
7      expenditures in FY 85:    $145.0    9)Annual consumer promo:     $1.9
8    3)Industry advertising
9      expenditures in FY 86:    $170.0    ADVERTISING ALLOCATIONS
10                                         10)Prime Time TV:              58%
11   4)Suave retail price/oz.:    $0.09    11)Daytime TV:                 42%
12   5)Retail gross margin % :      30%    12)Print:                       0%
13   6)Variable cost % :            57%
14   7)Mfg. gross margin % :        43% ALL FIGURES IN CONSTANT '84 DOLLARS
15   -----------------------------------------------------------------------
16                    Assumptions Made Under Specific Scenarios
17
18   Suave advertising, FY 1985    $7.0 Suave share (ounces) FY 85      13.1%
19   Suave advertising, FY 1986    $8.0 Suave share (ounces) FY 86      12.1%
20
```

Vallera realized that many more sensitivity analyses could be run under each scenario and that no one set could encompass all the useful tests.

COMPUTER INSTRUCTIONS

Introduction to Spreadsheet Analysis

Now that we have learned how to structure a spreadsheet, let's use the spreadsheet to create pro forma forecasts for Suave's financial performance in FY 1985 and FY 1986. We will then test the effects of changing the key assumptions that underlie our projections. In particular, we will test different assumptions about the effect of Suave advertising on Suave's financial performance.

Helene Curtis management held two similar, but still markedly different, perspectives on how advertising worked to affect Suave sales. (See the case for further explanation). Each of these perspectives implied a "scenario" about the "cause-and-effect chain" between advertising and the performance results.

Let's see how we can represent these scenarios with 1-2-3 for our spreadsheet analysis.

Representing Scenarios When Using 1-2-3 for Spreadsheet Analysis

A scenario is represented in 1-2-3 spreadsheet analysis as a set or *system of equations* that captures the "cause-and-effect chain." After each set of equations has been entered into the spreadsheet, sensitivity tests can then be run within each scenario. In this lesson, we will create two scenarios:

Scenario A: Projections of Suave sales are based upon the *annual rate of growth* for the Suave brand from FY 1984 to FY 1986.

Scenario B: Projections of Suave sales are based upon Suave's *market share* (in ounces) in FY 1985 and FY 1986.

So, let's begin by retrieving and examining the worksheet file for Lesson 12.

Retrieving and Examining the Worksheet File for Lesson 12

First, follow these familiar steps, if necessary:

1 Load DOS. Enter date and time.
2 Load the Lotus Access System.
3 Load the 1-2-3 software program.

ON YOUR OWN: Insert the Suave Data Diskette into the appropriate disk drive. Use the **/File Retrieve** command to retrieve the file named: **LESSON12.WKS.** After you have retrieved the file, switch diskettes. Remove the Suave Data Diskette and replace it with your data diskette. Press the **[Home]** key as directed.

Use the **[PgDn]** and **[PgUp]** keys to examine the worksheet. As you can see, the spreadsheet appears just as we left it at the end of Lesson 11. Press the **[Home]** key again, and let's create our first scenario.

Note: The screens beginning at cell A101 contain Scenario A, as completed. The screens beginning at cell Q101 contain Scenario B, as completed. As always, the completed results are just for reference. All our work in Lesson 12—for both Scenario A and Scenario B—will be performed on the screens beginning at cells A1, A21, and A41.

Creating Scenario A

Scenario A will be based on our assumptions about Suave's annual growth rate. Therefore, let's display our assumptions about this key factor in our Assumptions Screen.

ON YOUR OWN: **Type in** the following, beginning in each respective cell:

Cell	Entry	Format
E18	Suave annual growth rate	—
H18	.02	Percent with 0 decimals

Observation: We have entered an assumption of 2% for Suave's annual growth rate. Later we will project different growth rates and test the impact of these different rates on Suave's performance.

Now we can create the set of equations that comprise Scenario A. While the creation of the spreadsheet may seem like a lot of work at first, once it has been set up, the spreadsheet becomes a powerful tool for financial analysis. For clarity, the instructions here specify each of the separate steps that need to be completed to create the spreadsheet.

Entering Industry Projections for FY 1985 and FY 1986

We will begin by entering projections for the entire shampoo industry.

ON YOUR OWN: Complete the following steps. Note that the formulas often require the use of the **[F4]** Absolute key. When entering the formulas, make sure you are aware of what the cell references represent.

1 Enter a projection into cell B25 for Industry Sales (in ounces) in FY 1985. Use our first assumption about industry annual growth rate:

$$B25 = A25*(1 + \$D\$5) \qquad \text{Format: } \textbf{Comma with 1 decimal place}$$

Copy the formula from cell **B25 to C25**.

2 Enter a projection into cell B26 for Industry Retail Dollar Sales in FY 1985. Again use the assumption about industry annual growth rate:

$$B26 = A26*(1+\$D\$5) \qquad \text{Format: } \textbf{Comma with 1 decimal place}$$

Copy the formula from cell **B26 to C26.**

3 Enter a projection into cell B36 for Industry Advertising in FY 1985. Use our second assumption from the screen above:

$$B36 = D7 \qquad \text{Format: } \textbf{Currency with 1 decimal place}$$

4 Enter a projection into cell C36 for Industry Advertising in FY 1986. Use our third assumption from the screen above:

$$C36 = D9 \qquad \text{Format: } \textbf{Currency with 1 decimal place}$$

Entering Projections for Suave in FY 1985: Creating a Pro Forma Forecast

ON YOUR OWN: Now you will enter projections for Suave shampoo specifically. To save time, format all the results after you have completed all the projections. Complete the following steps:

5 Enter a projection into cell G25 for Suave Sales (in ounces) in FY 1985. Use the assumption that we entered earlier about the Suave annual growth rate:

$$G25 = F25*(1+\$H\$18)$$

6 Enter a projection into cell G26 for Suave Retail Dollar Sales in FY 1985. Use the fixed assumption about Suave retail price per ounce:

$$G26 = G25*\$D\$11$$

7 Enter a projection into cell G27 for the Retail Margin on Suave in FY 1985. Use the fixed assumption about Suave's retail margin:

$$G27 = G26*\$D\$12$$

8 Enter a **dashed line** across cell **G28** by copying the dashed line in cell F28.

9 Enter into cell G29 a formula for Manufacturer Dollar Sales:

$$G29 = G26-G27$$

10 Enter into cell G30 a formula for Suave Variable Costs. Use the fixed assumption about Suave variable cost percentage:

$$G30 = G29*\$D\$13$$

11 Enter a **dashed line** into cell **G31** by copying cell F31.

12 Enter into cell G32 a formula for Suave Gross Margin:

$$G32 = G29 - G30$$

13 Enter a **dashed line** into cell **G33** by copying cell F33.

14 Enter into cell G34 the fixed assumption about Suave Trade Promotion:

$$G34 = \$H\$6$$

15 Enter into cell G35 the fixed assumption about Suave Consumer Promotion:

$$G35 = \$H\$7$$

16 Enter into cell G36 our assumption about Suave Advertising for FY 1985:

$$G36 = \$D\$18$$

17 Enter into cells G37, G38, and G39 the respective allocations of total advertising. Use the fixed assumptions about advertising allocation percentages:

$$G37 = G36*\$H\$10$$

$$G38 = G36*\$H\$11$$

$$G39 = G36*\$H\$12$$

18 Enter into cell G40 a formula for Total Marketing Expenditures:

$$G40 = @SUM(G34..G36)$$

19 Enter a **dashed line** into cell **G41** by copying cell F41.

20 Enter a formula into cell G42 for Suave Operating Profit:

$$G42 = G32 - G40$$

ON YOUR OWN: Now that you have completed all the projections, format the results in cell G25 in **Comma** with **1 decimal** and for the range **G26..G42** in **Currency** with **1 decimal**.

Entering Formulas for Measuring Suave Performance

ON YOUR OWN: Now you will enter the formulas for measuring Suave performance in FY 1985. Again, to save time, format all the results at the end. Complete the following steps:

21 Enter into cell G44 a formula for the projected Suave Market Share (in Ounces):

$$G44 = G25/B25$$

22 Enter into cell G45 a formula for the projected Suave Market Share (in Dollars):

$$G45 = G26/B26$$

23 Enter into cell G46 a formula for Suave's projected Share of Industry Advertising:

$$G46 = G36/B36$$

24 Enter into cell G47 a formula for Suave's projected Ad/Sales Ratio:

$$G47 = G36/G26$$

ON YOUR OWN: Format the results in the range **G44..G47** in **Percent** with **1 decimal**.

Good. Your screens should now appear as:

```
A1:  ' LESSON 12                                                    READY


        A       B        C        D        E        F        G        H
 1    LESSON 12            THE SUAVE BRAND MANAGEMENT ACCOUNT
 2           (dollar figures in millions, except retail price per ounce)
 3    -------------------------------------------------------------------
 4                    Assumptions Fixed Under All Scenarios
 5    1)Industry annual growth %      2% SUAVE MKTING EXPENDITURES
 6    2)Industry advertising             8)Annual trade promotion:    $12.7
 7      expenditures in FY 85:   $145.0 9)Annual consumer promo:       $1.9
 8    3)Industry advertising
 9      expenditures in FY 86:   $170.0 ADVERTISING ALLOCATIONS
10                                      10)Prime Time TV:               58%
11    4)Suave retail price/oz.:   $0.09 11)Daytime TV:                  42%
12    5)Retail gross margin % :     30% 12)Print:                        0%
13    6)Variable cost % :           57%
14    7)Mfg. gross margin % :       43% ALL FIGURES IN CONSTANT '84 DOLLARS
15    -------------------------------------------------------------------
16                  Assumptions Made Under Specific Scenarios
17
18    Suave advertising, FY 1985   $7.0 Suave annual growth rate         2%
19    Suave advertising, FY 1986   $8.0
20
```

```
A21:  ' INDUSTRY                                                                          READY


          A          B          C          D          E          F          G          H
21     INDUSTRY  INDUSTRY  INDUSTRY                               SUAVE     SUAVE     SUAVE
22     FY 1984   FY 1985   FY 1986                              FY 1984   FY 1985   FY 1986
23               (proj.)   (proj.)   CATEGORIES                           (proj.)   (proj.)
24     --------  --------  --------                              --------  --------  --------
25     8,560.0   8,731.2   8,905.8  Sales In Ounces             1,161.0   1,184.2
26     $1,159.5  1,182.7   1,206.3  Retail Dollar Sls.           $104.4    $106.5
27                                  Retail Margin                 $31.3     $31.9
28                                                              --------  --------
29                                  Mfg. Dollar Sales             $73.1     $74.6
30                                  Variable Costs                $41.7     $42.5
31                                                              --------  --------
32                                  Gross Margin                  $31.4     $32.0
33                                                              --------  --------
34                                  Trade Promotion               $12.7     $12.7
35                                  Consumer Promotion             $1.9      $1.9
36     $117.5    $145.0    $170.0  Total Advertising              $6.0      $7.0
37                                    Prime Time TV                $3.5      $4.1
38                                    Daytime TV                   $2.5      $2.9
39                                    Print                        $0.0      $0.0
40                                  Total Marketing               $20.6     $21.6
```

```
A41:                                                                                      READY


          A          B          C          D          E          F          G          H
41                                                              --------  --------
42                                  Operating Profit             $10.8     $10.4
43
44                                  Mkt. Share:Ounces            13.6%     13.6%
45                                  Mkt. Share:Dollars            9.0%      9.0%
46                                  Industry Ad Share             5.1%      4.8%
47                                  Ad/Sales Ratio                5.7%      6.6%
48
49
50
51
52
53
54
55
56
57
58
59
60
```

Observation: That was a lot of work. It takes many equations to create a spreadsheet, especially when we are trying to be precise about what assumptions we are

using. However, once we have entered the basic equations for the spreadsheet, we can then easily complete two final tasks:

1 We can run out projections for as many years into the future as we want.
2 We can test the effects of changes in key variables.

Let's see how easy it is to extend our projections from FY 1985 to a pro forma for FY 1986.

Copying Your Projections from FY 1985 to FY 1986

Although you have seen the **/Copy** command many times by now, follow these specific steps to see how easy it is to extend our projections:

Description	*Keys to Press*
Move the cell pointer to G25:	**(Use the arrow keys.)**
Display the 1-2-3 command menus:	**/**
Select the /Copy command:	**C**
Specify the range to copy FROM, by pressing these four keys:	**[End]**
	[down]
	[down*5]
	[Enter]
(Notice how easy that was, using the [End] key.)	
Move the cell pointer to H25:	**[right]**
(Note: We have to move only to the cell that begins the range TO. Lotus 1-2-3 understands that we mean the whole range.)	
Confirm that this cell begins the range TO:	**[Enter]**

Observation: Lotus 1-2-3 copied everything for us: the formulas, the formats, even the dashed lines.

Note: When using the **/Copy** command (as well as the **/Move** command), we do not have to paint the entire range TO. We only have to move the cell pointer to the beginning of the range. If we had extended the projections beyond FY 1986, we would have had to paint only the first cell (in line 25) for each year.

Note: We need to make one change in our projection for FY 1986, however. When we copied the formulas, we also copied the value for Suave advertising in FY 1985 into the cell for Suave advertising in FY 1986.

We want to enter a separate assumption about Suave advertising in FY 1986. So, let's do so.

ON YOUR OWN: Move the cell pointer to **H36** and enter our assumption about Suave advertising in FY 1986:

$$H36 = \$D\$19$$

Good. Your screens should appear as:

```
A21: ' INDUSTRY                                                       READY


        A         B         C         D         E         F         G         H
21   INDUSTRY  INDUSTRY  INDUSTRY                            SUAVE     SUAVE     SUAVE
22   FY 1984   FY 1985   FY 1986                           FY 1984   FY 1985   FY 1986
23             (proj.)   (proj.)     CATEGORIES                      (proj.)   (proj.)
24   --------  --------  --------                          --------  --------  --------
25    8,560.0   8,731.2   8,905.8  Sales In Ounces          1,161.0   1,184.2   1,207.9
26   $1,159.5   1,182.7   1,206.3  Retail Dollar Sls.        $104.4    $106.5    $108.6
27                                 Retail Margin              $31.3     $31.9     $32.6
28                                                          --------  --------  --------
29                                 Mfg. Dollar Sales          $73.1     $74.6     $76.1
30                                 Variable Costs             $41.7     $42.5     $43.4
31                                                          --------  --------  --------
32                                 Gross Margin               $31.4     $32.0     $32.7
33                                                          --------  --------  --------
34                                 Trade Promotion            $12.7     $12.7     $12.7
35                                 Consumer Promotion          $1.9      $1.9      $1.9
36    $117.5    $145.0    $170.0  Total Advertising           $6.0      $7.0      $8.0
37                                  'Prime Time TV             $3.5      $4.1      $4.7
38                                  Daytime TV                 $2.5      $2.9      $3.3
39                                  Print                      $0.0      $0.0      $0.0
40                                 Total Marketing            $20.6     $21.6     $22.6
```

```
A41:                                                                  READY


        A         B         C         D         E         F         G         H
41                                                         --------  --------  --------
42                                 Operating Profit          $10.8     $10.4     $10.1
43
44                                 Mkt. Share:Ounces         13.6%     13.6%     13.6%
45                                 Mkt. Share:Dollars         9.0%      9.0%      9.0%
46                                 Industry Ad Share          5.1%      4.8%      4.7%
47                                 Ad/Sales Ratio             5.7%      6.6%      7.4%
48
49
50
51
52
53
54
55
56
57
58
59
60
```

Notice that since we have projected advertising spending of $8.0 million instead of $7.0 million for FY 1986, advertising allocations, total marketing expenditures, and the performance measures have now all changed for FY 1986.

We are now ready to run the sensitivity tests that are described in the case.

Sensitivity Tests Under Scenario A

Table 5.2 in the case lists nine sensitivity tests to be run under Scenario A. Each of these tests involves specific assumptions about both the Suave advertising spending levels and the Suave annual growth rate.

Because of the way we constructed our spreadsheet, we can change our projections directly simply by inputting the new values for Suave advertising levels and annual growth rate into the Assumptions Screen.

ON YOUR OWN: Run one of the sensitivity tests that are described in Table 5.2 of the case. Input the new values and then use the **[PgDn]** key to see the effects of each change.

Observation: Wouldn't it be great if we could see both our assumptions and the performance measures on one screen? As we saw in Lesson 11, we can use the **/Worksheet Window Horizontal** command to do just that.

Using Windowing to Run the Sensitivity Results Under Scenario A

Follow these steps to create a horizontal window that displays both the assumptions and performance measures on one screen. (If you need to, review the keystroke-by-keystroke instructions from Lesson 11 on how to use windowing.) Here we will use the **[Scroll Lock]** key. The steps to complete are:

1 Press **[Home]** to return to cell A1. Press **[PgDn]** once, press the **[Scroll Lock]** key, and then press the **[down]** key 8 times so that row 48 is at the bottom of the screen.
2 Press the **[Scroll Lock]** key again to deactivate it and then the **[down]** key until the cell pointer is in row 41. Then invoke the **/Worksheet Window Horizontal** command.
3 Press the **[up]** key until row 15 is at the top of the screen and the "Assumptions Made Under Specific Scenarios" are displayed.

Your screen should appear as follows:

```
A15:  "---------------------------------------------------------------  READY


        A        B        C        D        E        F        G        H
 15  --------------------------------------------------------------------------
 16                    Assumptions Made Under Specific Scenarios
 17
 18  Suave advertising, FY 1985    $7.0 Suave annual growth rate            2%
 19  Suave advertising, FY 1986    $8.0
 20
 21  INDUSTRY INDUSTRY INDUSTRY                     SUAVE    SUAVE    SUAVE
 22  FY 1984  FY 1985  FY 1986                      FY 1984  FY 1985  FY 1986
 23           (proj.)  (proj.)   CATEGORIES                  (proj.)  (proj.)
 24  -------- -------- --------                     -------- -------- --------
 25  8,560.0  8,731.2  8,905.8 Sales In Ounces      1,161.0 $1,184.2 $1,207.9
 26  $1,159.5 1,182.7  1,206.3 Retail Dollar Sls.    $104.4   $106.5   $108.6
        A        B        C        D        E        F        G        H
 41                                                 -------- -------- --------
 42                           Operating Profit        $10.8    $10.4    $10.1
 43
 44                           Mkt. Share:Ounces       13.6%    13.6%    13.6%
 45                           Mkt. Share:Dollars       9.0%     9.0%     9.0%
 46                           Industry Ad Share        5.1%     4.8%     4.7%
 47                           Ad/Sales Ratio           5.7%     6.6%     7.4%
```

Now you can run the sensitivity tests described in Table 5.2 of the case and see on one screen both the different assumptions and the effects of those assumptions on performance. A manager would also probably want to keep a printed copy of the results of each sensitivity test, as displayed on this windowed screen.

ON YOUR OWN: Using the windowed screen, run each of the nine sensitivity tests described in Table 5.2. After each sensitivity test, use the **[PrtSc]** key to print out a copy of the results of that test (totaling nine printouts). A manager would also probably want to save Scenario A in a file on diskette. So, let's do that before proceeding to Scenario B.

Saving Scenario A in a File on Diskette

First, a manager might want to clear the windowed screen before saving the file. (This step is not necessary. If the file were saved with the split screen still displayed, that is just how the file would appear when it was later retrieved. Of course, a window can be cleared at any time.)

ON YOUR OWN: Use the **/Worksheet Window Clear** command to remove the windowed screen. Press the **[Home]** key.

Now we are ready to save Scenario A in a file.

Note: Lesson 12 differs from other lessons because we will save two files in this one lesson—one file will be for Scenario A, and one for Scenario B.

ON YOUR OWN: Use the **/File Save** command to save Scenario A. Name the file: **LN12A**. This file name is an abbreviation for Lesson 12, Scenario A.

Good. We can now move on to Scenario B. But watch how much easier our work will be since we have already constructed the spreadsheet for Scenario A.

Creating Scenario B

Scenario B will be based on our assumptions about Suave's competitive position in the shampoo market. In particular, the effectiveness of Suave advertising will be interpreted as what market share that advertising helps Suave to attain.

This scenario sounds quite different than Scenario A. From the standpoint of management analysis, it is different in many respects. However, from the standpoint of using 1-2-3, it is very similar, because all but a few of the equations used in Scenario A will be used in Scenario B.

So, don't worry. Now that we have constructed the spreadsheet for Scenario A, Scenario B is easy to create. Let's see how.

ON YOUR OWN: Complete the following steps: (The first four steps will make the necessary changes in the assumptions screen. The fifth and sixth steps will make the necessary changes in the spreadsheet formulas.)

1 Type in, beginning in cell E18, the following:

Suave share (ounces) FY 85

2 Type in, beginning in cell E19, the following

Suave share (ounces) FY 86

3 Enter into cell H18:   **.131**   .   Format in **Percent** with **1 decimal**
4 Enter in cell H19:   **.121**   . Format in **Percent** with **1 decimal**
5 Enter into cell G25 a formula for determining Suave Sales in FY 1985 based upon projected market share, rather than upon projected annual growth rate:

G25 = B25*H18

6 Now enter a formula for Suave Sales in FY 1986 based upon projected market share:

H25 = C25*H19

That's it! We have now transformed this copy of Scenario A into Scenario B. Your screens should appear as:

```
A1: ' LESSON 12                                                          READY


        A         B         C         D         E         F         G         H
 1   LESSON 12           THE SUAVE BRAND MANAGEMENT ACCOUNT
 2        (dollar figures in millions, except retail price per ounce)
 3   --------------------------------------------------------------------------
 4                  Assumptions Fixed Under All Scenarios
 5   1)Industry annual growth %       2%  SUAVE MKTING EXPENDITURES
 6   2)Industry advertising                8)Annual trade promotion:     $12.7
 7     expenditures in FY 85:   $145.0     9)Annual consumer promo:       $1.9
 8   3)Industry advertising
 9     expenditures in FY 86:   $170.0  ADVERTISING ALLOCATIONS
10                                      10)Prime Time TV:                  58%
11   4)Suave retail price/oz.:  $0.09  11)Daytime TV:                     42%
12   5)Retail gross margin % :    30%  12)Print:                           0%
13   6)Variable cost % :          57%
14   7)Mfg. gross margin % :      43% ALL FIGURES IN CONSTANT '84 DOLLARS
15   --------------------------------------------------------------------------
16                  Assumptions Made Under Specific Scenarios
17
18   Suave advertising, FY 1985      $7.0 Suave share (ounces) FY 85      13.1%
19   Suave advertising, FY 1986      $8.0 Suave share (ounces) FY 86      12.1%
20
```

```
A21: ' INDUSTRY                                                          READY


        A         B         C         D         E         F         G         H
21   INDUSTRY  INDUSTRY  INDUSTRY                      SUAVE     SUAVE     SUAVE
22   FY 1984   FY 1985   FY 1986                      FY 1984   FY 1985   FY 1986
23             (proj.)   (proj.)   CATEGORIES                   (proj.)   (proj.)
24   --------  --------  --------                      --------  --------  --------
25   8,560.0   8,731.2   8,905.8 Sales In Ounces      1,161.0   1,143.8   1,077.6
26  $1,159.5   1,182.7   1,206.3 Retail Dollar Sls.   $104.4    $102.9    $96.9
27                               Retail Margin         $31.3     $30.8    $29.1
28                                                    --------  --------  --------
29                               Mfg. Dollar Sales     $73.1     $72.0    $67.8
30                               Variable Costs        $41.7     $41.1    $38.7
31                                                    --------  --------  --------
32                               Gross Margin          $31.4     $30.9    $29.1
33                                                    --------  --------  --------
34                               Trade Promotion       $12.7     $12.7    $12.7
35                               Consumer Promotion     $1.9      $1.9     $1.9
36   $117.5    $145.0    $170.0 Total Advertising      $6.0      $7.0     $8.0
37                                Prime Time TV         $3.5      $4.1     $4.7
38                                Daytime TV            $2.5      $2.9     $3.3
39                                Print                 $0.0      $0.0     $0.0
40                               Total Marketing       $20.6     $21.6    $22.6
```

```
A41:                                                                    READY


            A         B         C         D         E         F         G         H
41                                                             ——————    ——————    ——————
42                                        Operating Profit     $10.8     $9.3      $6.5
43
44                                        Mkt. Share:Ounces    13.6%     13.1%     12.1%
45                                        Mkt. Share:Dollars    9.0%      8.7%      8.0%
46                                        Industry Ad Share     5.1%      4.8%      4.7%
47                                        Ad/Sales Ratio        5.7%      6.8%      8.3%
48
49
50
51
52
53
54
55
56
57
58
59
60
```

Observation: We were able to complete these steps so quickly because the rest of the equations in Scenario A are the same for Scenario B. We did not even have to reformat the results in cells G25 and H25. (Remember that the example of the completed Scenario B begins at cell Q101. The example of the completed Scenario A begins as usual at A101.)

Sensitivity Tests Under Scenario B

Table 5.3 in the case lists the sensitivity tests to be run under Scenario B.
ON YOUR OWN: Run these sensitivity tests by entering the various values for both Suave advertising and Suave market share in FY 1985 and FY 1986. Use the **[PgDn]** key to examine the effect of each change in the pro forma forecasts.

Also on your own, use the **/Worksheet Window Horizontal** command to display both the Assumptions Made Under Specific Scenarios and the Performance Measures. Using the windowed screen, run each sensitivity test again so that you can see how the performance measures change under the different assumptions. After each sensitivity test, use the **[PrtSc]** key to print out a copy of the results of that test.

A manager might also want to protect all the data except the specific assumptions used to run these sensitivity tests. Let's practice using the protection command in Scenario B. (We could have used it in Scenario A as well.)

Protecting These Spreadsheet Scenarios

Let's use the **/Worksheet Global Protection** command to protect these scenarios.
Note: We do not even have to clear the windowed screen before we use the

protection command. You can put the protection on whether the screen is windowed or not.

ON YOUR OWN: Complete these steps:

1 Invoke the **/Worksheet Global Protection Enable** command to protect the work-sheet.
2 Use the **/Range Unprotect** command to unprotect the range where we have placed the assumptions that we wish to test. Specifically **unprotect** the range **A15..H20**.

Observation: The worksheet is now protected. But we can still run sensitivity tests on our key assumptions because the range that contains our assumptions was specifically unprotected under Step 2.

A manager would also probably want to save Scenario B in a file on diskette. So, let's do that as well.

Saving Scenario B in a File on Diskette

ON YOUR OWN: Press [**Home**] to return to cell A1. Use the **/File Save** command to save Scenario B. Name the file: **LN12B**. This file name is an abbreviation for Lesson 12, Scenario B.

LOTUS 1-2-3 FINANCIAL FUNCTIONS

Lesson 12 has shown how to construct a spreadsheet and how to run sensitivity tests using 1-2-3. Lotus 1-2-3 is also able to run commonly used financial functions, such as "Net Present Value" (NPV) or "Internal Rate of Return" (IRR) calculations.

The Lotus manuals provide a list of all the functions that 1-2-3 can run. Most of these functions are reasonably self-explanatory, *if you already understand the management concept or technique.* That is, the NPV function is reasonably self-explanatory, if you already understand what NPV analysis is all about.

This book is not designed to teach sophisticated financial techniques. However, it is easy to show generally how to use Lotus 1-2-3 financial functions. We will just use the NPV function as an example.

Using the NPV Function: An Example

Our Suave financial analysis has been performed on a one-year basis, with all marketing costs expensed in that year. If a longer time frame were used, NPV would become an important function.

ON YOUR OWN: Move the cell pointer to the screen beginning at cell **A201**.

This worksheet shows a simple projected income statement for a $2,000 investment in Year 1. Row 216 contains the projected **Net Profit** that the investment will deliver. Your screen should appear as follows:

```
 A201: ' NPV EXAMPLE                                              READY


        A        B        C      D       E       F       G       H
 201 NPV EXAMPLE
 202                             YEAR 1  YEAR 2  YEAR 3  YEAR 4  YEAR 5
 203                             ------- ------- ------- ------- -------
 204
 205 Investment                 ($2,000)
 206
 207
 208 Revenue                     $2,000  $2,000  $2,000  $2,000  $2,000
 209
 210 Cost                       ($3,000)($1,000)($1,000)($1,000)($1,000)
 211                             ------- ------- ------- ------- -------
 212 Profit Before Tax          ($1,000) $1,000  $1,000  $1,000  $1,000
 213
 214 Tax at 25% Rate                 $0 ($250)  ($250)  ($250)  ($250)
 215                             ------- ------- ------- ------- -------
 216 Net Profit                 ($1,000)  $750    $750    $750    $750
 217
 218 NET PRESENT VALUE
 219 AT YEAR 0 (WITH 10%
 220 DISCOUNT RATE)
```

In this simple NPV example, it is assumed that the investment produces revenues of $2,000 with an operating cost of $1,000 in each of the five years. It is further assumed that the investment of $2,000 is expensed entirely in Year 1. The resultant Profit Before Tax is assumed to be subject to a 25% tax rate (with no tax loss carry forward for the loss in Year 1).

Let's see how we can calculate the NPV of this investment at Year 0 (today). This calculation requires a discount rate and a range of values to be discounted. Here we will use a 10% rate to value the projected five-year stream of net profits.

ON YOUR OWN: Let's place the net present value in cell D220. Since our worksheet is protected, we must unprotect cell D220. Move the cell pointer to **D220** and use the **/Range Unprotect** command. Then press the following keys:

Description	Keys to Press
Move the cell pointer to D220:	**(Use the arrow keys.)**
Type in the symbols to indicate that we will use the NPV function:	**@NPV(**
(1-2-3 now needs to know what discount rate we are using. Let's use 10%.)	
Enter the 10% discount rate:	**.1**
Confirm the discount rate with a comma:	**,**
(1-2-3 now needs to know what range of values to discount.)	

Description	Keys to Press
Move the cell pointer to D216:	[up]*4
Anchor D216 and paint the range D216..H216:	. [right]*4
Close the range D216..H216:	)
Confirm the @NPV entries and calculate the net present value:	[Enter]

The value **1252.180** should appear in cell **D220**.

ON YOUR OWN: Put the result in **Currency** format with **zero decimal** places. Save the calculation in the worksheet file LN12B, if you like.

ON YOUR OWN: If you have a Lotus 1-2-3 manual available, look up what financial functions are available. The Release 1A manual shows the financial functions on p. 282. The Release 2.01 manual shows them on pp. 232–233. The manuals also show other 1-2-3 functions available, such as mathematical, logical, statistical, string, and date and time functions. As you become more sophisticated in your use of 1-2-3, you might try exploring some of these special functions.

Reviewing What We Learned in Lesson 12

In Lesson 12, we learned an important new application of Lotus 1-2-3: spreadsheet analysis.

- We learned how to represent a "scenario" through a system of equations.
- We learned how easy it is, once we have constructed a scenario, to run projections out for as many years as appropriate.
- We learned how easy it is to run sensitivity tests based on each scenario. As-sumptions can be varied with the corresponding pro forma forecasts quickly cal-culated by 1-2-3.
- We learned how easy it can be to create an entirely new scenario when it involves changing only a few formulas in a scenario we have already created.
- We reviewed the use of windowing and of worksheet protection.
- We learned how to use the 1-2-3 financial functions through an example using the @NPV function.

Let's move on to our last lesson in spreadsheet analysis.

MANAGEMENT DISCUSSION

1 What is a scenario?

A scenario is a road map, in a sense, of the chain of cause and effect from an action, such as advertising, to a projected result, such as sales. A set of equations are used to relate the various relevant economic and marketing elements to each other. Each scenario contains explicit or implicit assumptions about how the market works.

2 **What is the difference between a scenario driven by a brand's growth rate and one that is driven by a brand's market share? Which scenario provides a sounder basis for financial projections for Suave?**

A scenario driven by a brand's growth rate is based on the assumption that the overall condition of the shampoo industry forms the context in which advertising influences consumers to buy the brand. The condition of the industry (and the industry growth rate) is not, however, a primary consideration for determining the sales of that particular brand.

Alternatively, a scenario that is driven by a brand's market share is based more explicitly on the assumption that advertising influences consumers to choose a particular brand over other brands. The condition of the industry (it's growth rate and it's competitiveness) is therefore considered *directly* in determining whether advertising is likely to increase a brand's sales.

3 **Scenario A: What conclusions would you draw from the sensitivity tests that were based on this scenario?**

Your answer to this question should be based on your analysis of the shampoo market, consumer buying behavior in the market, and the cost effectiveness of advertising for Suave shampoo.

4 **Scenario B: What conclusions would you draw from the sensitivity tests that were based upon this scenario?**

Your answer to this question should be based on your analysis of the shampoo market, consumer buying behavior in the market, and the cost effectiveness of advertising. In addition, your conclusion should directly consider how competitive the shampoo industry is and what level of market share Suave shampoo is likely to achieve.

LESSON 13   FINANCIAL ANALYSIS: TESTING MULTIPLE ASSUMPTIONS

OVERVIEW

COMPUTER INSTRUCTIONS

Lesson 13 demonstrates the use of the **/Data Table** command in spreadsheet analysis. Since you already learned this command in Lesson 10, the instructions will ask you to complete most of the steps on your own. In addition, you will learn how to use the **/Data Fill** command.

MANAGEMENT ISSUES

Lesson 13 helps clarify the difference between spreadsheet and break-even analysis. In this instance, the level of operating profit is not assumed but rather is projected.

MANAGEMENT DISCUSSION QUESTIONS

1 In this lesson, what-if analysis is used to project different levels of operating profit (based on different levels of advertising for Suave and on variations in the industry growth rate or Suave's market share). In Lesson 10, what-if analysis was used to calculate different levels of sales volume and of market share necessary to maintain a fixed operating profit of $10.8 million.

   Why would a manager run both break-even calculations and financial projections?

2 What is your best projection for Suave operating profit in FY 1985? Make any assumptions explicit. Why are these assumptions reasonable, in your opinion?

CASE

To complete her financial analysis, Vallera wanted to use the Data Table function to project operating profit for fiscal 1985. This function would allow her to run several sensitivity tests under these two scenarios. First, she would set advertising expenditures for fiscal 1985 at $7.0 million. She would then recreate the two scenarios by varying:

- Suave's annual growth rate; and
- Suave's market share (in ounces), FY 1985

One-Variable Analyses

   Scenario A: Annual growth rate varied from −1% to 5% (−1%, 0%, 1%, 2%, 3%, 4%, 5%)
   Calculate the seven levels of fiscal 1985 operating profit.

> *Scenario B*: Market share varied from 12.1% to 15.1% (12.1%, 12.6%, 13.1%, 13.6%,
> 14.1%, 14.6%, 15.1%)
> Calculate the seven levels of fiscal 1985 operating profit.

After understanding the implications of these results, she was ready to generate one last set of sensitivity analyses with different levels of advertising expenditures.

Two-Variable Analyses

Using the same two scenarios but also allowing Suave fiscal 1985 advertising expenditures to vary between $3 million and $10 million, Ellen Vallera created two matrices of projected operating profit.

Vallera's extensive analysis of the potential impact of different advertising budgets on the performance of Suave shampoo was now finished. She would put together a written report, send copies to the other members of the Suave management team, and prepare for their meeting to discuss how to present the results to top management.

COMPUTER INSTRUCTIONS

Introduction

In Lesson 10, we learned how to use the **/Data Table** command. We tested how our break-even points would change under different assumptions about both Suave ad spending in FY 1985 and the shampoo industry growth rate.

In Lesson 13, we will again use the **/Data Table** command. This time, we will combine spreadsheet with sensitivity analysis. We will test how Suave's projected operating profit for FY 1985 would change under different assumptions. Under Scenario A, we create a 1-variable data table to test the effects on operating profit of different assumptions about Suave's annual growth rate. Then we will create a 2-variable data table to test the effects of different assumptions about both Suave's annual growth rate and Suave's ad spending in FY 1985.

Under Scenario B, we will create a 1-variable data table to test the effects on operating profit of different assumptions about Suave's ounce market share. Then we will create a 2-variable data table to test the effects of different assumptions about both Suave's ounce market share and its ad spending in FY 1985.

Because **/Data Table** is a complicated command, the instructions for the data tables under Scenario A are specially designed to help you practice the use of the **/Data Table** command.

Lesson 13 also teaches one new technique that is helpful in the creation of data tables: the **/Data Fill** command. This command will help us enter the different assumptions more rapidly than we did in Lesson 10.

For the data tables under Scenario B, the instructions will ask you to perform all the necessary steps on your own. In this way, creating these data tables can help you to gain self-sufficiency in the use of the **/Data Table** command.

Let's begin.

Retrieving, Preparing, and Examining the Worksheet File for Lesson 13

First, we need to retrieve the worksheet for Lesson 13. Follow these familiar steps, if necessary:

1 Load DOS. Enter date and time.
2 Load the Lotus Access System.
3 Load the 1-2-3 software program.

ON YOUR OWN: Insert the Suave Data Diskette in the appropriate disk drive. Use the **/File Retrieve** command to retrieve from the Suave Data Diskette the file named: **LESSON13.WKS**. After you have retrieved the file, switch diskettes. Remove the Suave Data Diskette and replace it with your data diskette. Press the **[Home]** key as directed.

Observation: The worksheet has global protection on it to be consistent with Lesson 12. Therefore, we cannot put any additional information into the worksheet until we remove the Global Protection. Use the **/Worksheet Global Protection Disable** command to remove the global protection.

Now let's take a look at the worksheet.

ON YOUR OWN: Use the **[PgDn]** key to display the screen beginning at cell **A61**. On this screen, we will create the 1-variable data table that tests, under Scenario A, the effects on Suave's operating profit of different assumptions about Suave's annual growth rate.

Now press the **[PgDn]** key again to display the screen that begins at cell **A81**. On this screen, we will create the 2-variable data table that tests, under Scenario A, the effects of different assumptions about both Suave's annual growth rate and Suave's ad spending in FY 1985. [Completed worksheet begins at cell A101.]

Next, use the **[PgUp]** and **[Tab]** keys to display the screen that begins at cell **Q61**. On this screen, we will create the 1-variable data table that tests, under Scenario B, the effects of different assumptions about Suave's ounce share in FY 1985.

Now press the **[PgDn]** key to display the screen that begins at cell **Q81**. On this screen, we will create the 2-variable data table that tests, under Scenario A, the effects of different assumptions about both Suave's ounce share and Suave's ad spending in FY 1985. [Completed worksheet begins at cell Q101.]

Return to the screen that begins at cell **A61** so that we can create the 1-variable data table under Scenario A.

Note: In contrast to Lesson 12, in which we built Scenario B from Scenario A in the same area of the worksheet (and consequently saved *two* files, LN12A and LN12B), here the two scenarios appear in separate areas of the worksheet.

Entering the Assumptions for the 1-Variable Data Table Under Scenario A

We first need to enter the assumptions that we want to test about Suave's annual growth rate. The following seven values need to be entered into the corresponding cells (and put into **Percent** format with **zero decimal** places):

Cell	Value
C69	−1%
C70	0%
C71	1%
C72	2%
C73	3%
C74	4%
C75	5%

We can do this by typing in each of the seven values one by one. However, 1-2-3 has a command that may make this task easier: the **/Data Fill** command. This command allows you to enter sequential values quickly by specifying the first value, the amount of increase for each value in the sequence, and the highest value.

Let's try it. Press the following keys:

Description	Keys to Press
Move the cell pointer to cell C69:	**(Use the arrow keys or [F5].)**
Display the 1-2-3 command menus:	**/**
Select the /Data command:	**D**
Select the Fill command:	**F**

(1-2-3 will ask us to "Enter Fill range.")

Anchor C69 as the cell that begins the Fill range:	**.**
Paint the range C69..C75:	**[down*6]**

(Note: This step tells 1-2-3 that we will enter seven different values in cells C69 through C75.)

Confirm the range C69..C75:	**[Enter]**

(1-2-3 now needs to know the value to "start" the sequential order. If you make a mistake at any time after pressing [Enter], just press [Esc] and input the correct number.)

Enter the first assumption that we will test (−1%):	**−1% [Enter]**

(1-2-3 has now been told to fill in sequential order our seven cell range with values beginning at −1%.)
(1-2-3 now needs to know by what "step" that sequential order should increase.)

Indicate that the values should increase by 1% at a time:	**1%[Enter]**

(1-2-3 now asks where the sequential order of numbers should "stop.")

Description	*Keys to Press*
Indicate that the values should "stop" at the end of the Fill range:	[Enter]
(Watch 1-2-3 fill the range just as we directed.)	

Note: When 1-2-3 asked at what value the sequential order should "stop," it listed "8191" as a possible entry. (The designers of 1-2-3 had in mind filling a range 0..8191, using all 8192 rows.) If we had just pressed 5% [Enter] instead of [Enter], we would have obtained the same result because 1-2-3 would have just filled up the range we had specified earlier (C69..C75) in sequential order. Of course, 5% would have automatically become the last value in the range. So, the entry "8191" directs 1-2-3 just to fill up the range specified earlier.

Release 1A Users: 8191 is replaced by 2047, as there are 2048 rows.

ON YOUR OWN: Use the **/Range Format** command to put the values in cells **C69..C75** in **Percent** format with **zero decimal** places.

Creating the 1-Variable Data Table Under Scenario A

Now let's create the 1-variable data table under Scenario A. These instructions will guide you on what steps need to be performed. However, in order to give you a chance to practice using the **/Data Table** command on your own, keystroke-by-keystroke instructions will not be provided. In this way, Lesson 13 should help you to attain self-sufficiency in using this powerful but complicated command. If you wish, you may review the "Summary of Steps for Using Data Table with 1 Variable" that is contained in Lesson 10.

Create the Formula that Forms the Basis of the Data Table

ON YOUR OWN: Move the cell pointer to **D68**. Press the **+** key to indicate that a formula will be entered. Move to **G42**, the cell containing the projection for Suave Operating Profit in FY 85. Press [Enter] to confirm that we want to **duplicate** the formula from G42 into D68.

The value **10.428** should appear in **D68**. We have completed the first step. Now, we are ready to use **/Data Table**.

Build the New Data Table

ON YOUR OWN: Invoke the **/Data Table** command. (Since we have created no previous data tables in Lesson 13, we do not have to Reset.) Press **1** to indicate that we want to test different values for one variable. Move to **C68**, press the **.** key to anchor, and **paint** the range **C68..D75**. (We have now painted the rectangular data table range.) Press [Enter] to confirm the range. Move to **H18** to indicate that the variable "Suave Annual Growth Rate" is the input cell. Press **[Enter]** to confirm H18 and to perform the data table calculations.

Good. Your screen should appear as follows:

```
D68:  +G42                                                      READY

          A       B       C       D       E       F       G       H
61  --------------------------------------------------------------------
62
63                              *   PROJECTIONS OF SUAVE
64                                  OPERATING PROFIT
65                                  FOR FY 1985
66                                  (IN MILLIONS)
67
68                                  10.428
69                         -1%       9.486
70                Suave     0%       9.8
71                Annual    1%      10.114
72                Growth    2%      10.428
73                Rate      3%      10.742
74                (proj.)   4%      11.056
75                          5%      11.37
76
77
78                              *   These projections assume advertising
79                                  expenditures of $7.0 million
80                                  for Suave in FY 1985.
```

Observation: You have now constructed a data table that lists a set of assumptions about the Suave annual growth rate and the resulting operating profit for each respective assumption.

Note: The effect of each assumption is listed in the cell *immediately to the right* of that assumption. For example, if the Suave annual growth rate were 4% (as listed in cell C74), then the operating profit would be $11.056 million (as listed in cell D74).

ON YOUR OWN: Put the results in **D69..D75** into **Currency** format with **one decimal** place to make it clearer that these values refer to dollar amounts. However, we suggest that you leave the value in D68 unformatted, so that you do not confuse it with one of the results.

Entering the Assumptions for the 2-Variable Data Table Under Scenario A

Now let's create a 2-variable data table to test the effects of different assumptions about both Suave's annual growth rate and Suave's projected ad spending in FY 1985.

ON YOUR OWN: Press the **[PgDn]** key to display the screen beginning at cell **A81** that will contain our new data table.

We first need to enter the assumptions that we want to test about Suave's annual growth rate. The following seven values need to be entered into the corresponding cells (and put into **Percent** format with **zero decimal** places):

Cell	Value
C89	− 1%
C90	0%
C91	1%
C92	2%
C93	3%
C94	4%
C95	5%

We have three options for entering these data. First, we can type in each of the seven values one at a time. Second, since we already have these values in C69..C75, we could just use the **/Copy** command. In this situation, copying the values from C69..C75 to C89..C95 would probably be the easiest way to enter the assumptions.

Note: If you decide to copy the values from C69..C75 to C89..C95, it is easier if you move the cell pointer to cell C69 before invoking the **/Copy** command. Move the cell pointer to cell C69. Then invoke the command, paint the range by pressing **[End][down]**, and press **[Enter]** to confirm the range to copy FROM. To enter the range to copy TO, just press **[PgDn]** and **[Enter]**. You need not paint the entire range when using the **/Copy** command if you want the data to be entered into the same pattern of cells as exists in the range to copy FROM. Press **[PgDn]** to return the cell pointer to cell C89 and view the results.

The third method is using the **/Data Fill** command. The instructions here will guide you on what steps need to be performed to use this method, so that you can gain practice with this new command.

ON YOUR OWN: Move the cell pointer to **C89**. Invoke the **/Data Fill** command. (1-2-3 now displays the last fill range. Unfortunately, 1-2-3 does not have "Reset" for **/Data Fill**, so we need to escape from the previous range.) Press **[Esc]** to clear the old range. Move to **C89** to begin our new range, press the **.** key to anchor, and **paint** the range **C89..C95**. (1-2-3 now needs to know where to start, and it displays the "Start" value for the previous range.) Press **[Enter]** to confirm **− .01** as our first value. (1-2-3 now needs to know at which the values should increase, and it displays the "Step" from the previous range.) Press **[Enter]** to confirm **.01**. (1-2-3 now needs to know where to "Stop" and it displays .05 from the previous range.) Press **[Enter]** to confirm **8191** and watch the range get filled up.

Note: All we had to do was enter the Fill range and confirm the previous settings. The **[Scroll Lock]** key is useful in realigning the screen.

ON YOUR OWN: Use the **/Range Format** command to put the values in cells **C89..C95** in **Percent** format with **zero decimal** places.

Now let's use the **/Data Fill** command to enter the different assumptions about Suave's projected ad spending in FY 1985. The following eight values should be entered into the corresponding cells (and put in **Currency** format with **one decimal** place):

Cell	Value
D88	$3.0
E88	$4.0
F88	$5.0
G88	$6.0
H88	$7.0
I88	$8.0
J88	$9.0
K88	$10.0

You can either type in each of the eight values or use **/Data Fill**, whichever you find easier.

Note: If you use **/Data Fill**, follow these guidelines: Invoke **/Data Fill**. Press **[Esc]** to clear the old range. Move to **D88, anchor, paint D88..K88**. Enter **3** as the "Start." (Type in the **number 3** and press **[Enter]**.) Enter **1** as the "Step." Press **[Enter]** for the "Stop."

ON YOUR OWN: Use the **/Range Format** command to put the values in cells **D88..K88** in **Currency** format with **one decimal** place.

Good. Your screen should appear as follows:

```
 D88: (C1) 3                                                    READY


         A         B         C         D         E         F         G         H
 81  ------------------------------------------------------------------------------
 82      PROJECTIONS OF SUAVE OPERATING PROFIT FOR FY 1985 (IN MILLIONS)
 83
 84                                         Projected Advertising Expenditures
 85                                           for Suave Shampoo in FY 1985
 86                                                   (in millions)
 87
 88                               $3.0      $4.0      $5.0      $6.0      $7.0
 89                     -1%
 90      Suave          0%
 91      Annual         1%
 92      Growth         2%
 93      Rate           3%
 94      (proj.)        4%
 95                     5%
 96
 97
 98
 99
100
```

Creating the 2-Variable Data Table Under Scenario A

Once again, the instructions will guide you on what steps need to be performed, but keystroke-by-keystroke instructions will not be provided. If you wish, review the "Summary of Steps for Using Data Table with 2 Variables" that is contained in Lesson 10.

Create the Formula that Forms the Basis of the Data Table

ON YOUR OWN: Move the cell pointer to **C88**. Press the **+** key to indicate that a formula will be entered. Move to **G42** and press **[Enter]** to **duplicate** the formula in G42 into G88.

The value **10.428** should appear in **C88**, the same as appeared in D68 in the 1-variable data table. Both data tables use the same formula.

Build the New Data Table

ON YOUR OWN: Invoke **/Data Table. Reset** the old table ranges and references. Invoke **/Data Table** again. Press **2** to indicate that a 2-variable data table will be created. **Anchor C88** and **paint C88..K95**. Press **[Enter]** to confirm. Move to **H18** and press **[Enter]** so that "Suave Annual Growth Rate" becomes the first input variable. Move to **D18** and press **[Enter]**, so that "Suave Advertising, FY 1985" becomes the second input variable. Watch 1-2-3 calculate the results.

ON YOUR OWN: Put the results in the range **D89..K95** into **Currency** format with **one decimal** place.

Good. Your screens should appear as follows:

```
D89: (C1) 13.486                                                           READY

          A      B        C       D       E       F       G       H
 81  -------------------------------------------------------------------
 82      PROJECTIONS OF SUAVE OPERATING PROFIT FOR FY 1985 (IN MILLIONS)
 83
 84                                    Projected Advertising Expenditures
 85                                       for Suave Shampoo in FY 1985
 86                                              (in millions)
 87
 88                   10.428    $3.0    $4.0    $5.0    $6.0    $7.0
 89                      -1%   $13.5   $12.5   $11.5   $10.5    $9.5
 90           Suave       0%   $13.8   $12.8   $11.8   $10.8    $9.8
 91           Annual      1%   $14.1   $13.1   $12.1   $11.1   $10.1
 92           Growth      2%   $14.4   $13.4   $12.4   $11.4   $10.4
 93           Rate        3%   $14.7   $13.7   $12.7   $11.7   $10.7
 94           (proj.)     4%   $15.1   $14.1   $13.1   $12.1   $11.1
 95                       5%   $15.4   $14.4   $13.4   $12.4   $11.4
 96
 97
 98
 99
100
```

```
I89: (C1) 8.486                                                      READY


              I         J         K         L       M       N       O       P
   81
   82
   83
   84
   85
   86
   87
   88        $8.0      $9.0     $10.0
   89        $8.5      $7.5      $6.5
   90        $8.8      $7.8      $6.8
   91        $9.1      $8.1      $7.1
   92        $9.4      $8.4      $7.4
   93        $9.7      $8.7      $7.7
   94       $10.1      $9.1      $8.1
   95       $10.4      $9.4      $8.4
   96
   97
   98
   99
  100
```

Note: You can use the **/Worksheet Titles Vertical** command, if you like, for viewing the results in columns I, J, and K on the same screen as the assumptions listed in column C.

Saving Your Worksheet in a File on Diskette

We have completed a great deal of work on Lesson 13. We should protect this work by saving it right now. Later, when we have completed the data tables under Scenario B, we can just save the worksheet again.

ON YOUR OWN: Press the **[Home]** key. Use the **/File Save** command to save your work in Lesson 13. Name the file: **LN13**.

Note: There is no need to create two files here, as there was in Lesson 12, since the two scenarios are stored in two separate places on the worksheet (beginning at column A and column Q) and therefore can be saved in one file.

Now let's move on to create the data tables under Scenario B.

Creating the 1-Variable Data Table Under Scenario B

Once again, follow these steps to complete for this 1-variable data table:

Step 1: Fill in the Assumptions to Be Tested

ON YOUR OWN: Use the **[Tab]** key to move to the screen beginning at **Q1**. As you remember from Lesson 12, the spreadsheet analysis for Scenario B will use the columns in this screen. Next, use the **[PgDn]** key to display the screen beginning at cell **Q61**. We will create the 1-variable data table on this screen. In this data table, we will test the effect of different assumptions about Suave's ounce share in FY 1985 on Suave's projected operating profit in FY 1985.

ON YOUR OWN: Enter the following seven assumptions about Suave's ounce share in FY 1985:

Cell	Value
S69	12.1%
S70	12.6%
S71	13.1%
S72	13.6%
S73	14.1%
S74	14.6%
S75	15.1%

You can either use the **/Data Fill** command to enter these values or input them one by one into each cell. (If you use the **/Data Fill** command, first **escape** the previous Fill range and then return the cell pointer to cell S69. The "Fill range" should be **S69..S75**; the "Start" should be **.121**; the "Step" should be **.005**.) Put these assumptions in **Percent** format with **one decimal** place.

Step 2: Create the Formula that Forms the Basis of the Data Table

ON YOUR OWN: Move the cell pointer to **T68**. Use the + key and the **[PgUp]** and arrow keys to enter the **formula** for Suave Operating Profit in FY 1985 (from cell **W42**) into cell **T68** (10.51517 should appear in the cell).

Step 3: Build the New Data Table

ON YOUR OWN: Clear the previous Table range with the **/Data Table Reset** command. Invoke the **/Data Table** command and indicate that you want to create a **1-variable** data table. Move the cell pointer to **S68**; **anchor** that cell; **paint** the Table range **S68..T75**; and press **[Enter]** to confirm that range.

Then use the **[PgUp]** and arrow keys to move to cell **X18** (containing the value for Suave's ounce share in FY 1985) as the **input cell**. Press **[Enter]** and watch 1-2-3 calculate the data table results. Put the results in **Currency** format with **one decimal** place.

Your screen should appear as:

```
T69: (C1) 6.9730588114                                          READY


        Q        R        S        T        U        V        W        X
61  -----------------------------------------------------------------------
62
63                               *   PROJECTIONS OF SUAVE
64                                   OPERATING PROFIT
65                                   FOR FY 1985
66                                   (IN MILLIONS)
67
68                               10.51517
69                      12.1%    $7.0
70           Suave      12.6%    $8.2
71           Ounce      13.1%    $9.3
72           Share      13.6%    $10.5
73           In FY 85   14.1%    $11.7
74           (proj.)    14.6%    $12.9
75                      15.1%    $14.1
76
77
78                               *   These projections assume advertising
79                                   expenditures of $7.0 million
80                                   for Suave in FY 1985.
```

Creating the 2-Variable Data Table Under Scenario B

Follow these steps to complete for this 2-variable data table:

Step 1: Fill in the Assumptions to Be Tested

ON YOUR OWN: Use the **[PgDn]** key to display the screen beginning at cell **Q81**. We will create the **2-variable** data table on this screen. In this data table, we will test the effect on Suave's projected operating profit in FY 1985 of different assumptions about both Suave's ounce share in FY 1985 and Suave's ad spending in FY 1985.

ON YOUR OWN: Enter the following seven assumptions about Suave's ounce share in FY 1985:

Cell	Value
S89	12.1%
S90	12.6%
S91	13.1%
S92	13.6%
S93	14.1%
S94	14.6%
S95	15.1%

You can use the **/Data Fill** command to enter these values, invoke the **/Copy** command to copy these values from cells S69..S75, or input them one by one into each cell. (If you use the **/Data Fill** command, the "Fill range" should be **S89..S95**; the "Start" should be **0.121**; the "Step" should be **.005**.) Put these assumptions in **Percent** format with **one decimal** place.

Then enter the following eight assumptions about Suave's ad spending in FY 1985:

Cell	Value
T88	$3.0
U88	$4.0
V88	$5.0
W88	$6.0
X88	$7.0
Y88	$8.0
Z88	$9.0
AA88	$10.0

Again you can use the **/Data Fill** command to enter these values, invoke the **/Copy** command to copy these values from cells D88..K88, or input them one by one into each cell. (If you use the **/Data Fill** command, the "Fill range" should be **T88..AA88**; the "Start" should be **3**; the "Step" should be **1**.) Put these assumptions in **Currency** format with **one decimal** place.

Step 2: Create the Formula that Forms the Basis of the Data Table

ON YOUR OWN: Move the cell pointer to **S88**. Use the **+** key and the **[PgUp]** and arrow keys to enter the **formula** for Suave Operating Profit in FY 1985 (from cell **W42**) into cell **S88**.

Step 3: Build the New Data Table

ON YOUR OWN: Clear the previous Table range with the **/Data Table Reset** command. Invoke the **/Data Table** command and indicate that you want to create a **2-variable** data table. Be sure the cell pointer is in **S88; anchor** that cell; **paint** the Table range **S88..AA95**; and press **[Enter]** to confirm that range.

Then use the **[PgUp]** and arrow keys to move to cell **X18** (containing the value for Suave's ounce share in FY 1985) as the **first input** cell. Press **[Enter]** to confirm. Then use the **[PgUp]** and arrow keys to move to cell **T18** (containing the value for Suave's ad spending in FY 1985) as the **second input** cell. Press **[Enter]** and watch 1-2-3 calculate the data table results. (Press **[Tab]** to see the rest of the results.) Put the results (in T89..AA95) in **Currency** format with **one decimal** place.

Your screens should appear as:

```
T89: (C1) 10.9730588114                                                    READY


        Q        R        S        T        U        V        W        X
81   ---------------------------------------------------------------------
82        PROJECTIONS OF SUAVE OPERATING PROFIT FOR FY 1985 (IN MILLIONS)
83
84                                     Projected Advertising Expenditures
85                                       for Suave Shampoo in FY 1985
86                                               (in millions)
87
88                      10.51517    $3.0     $4.0     $5.0     $6.0     $7.0
89                        12.1%    $11.0    $10.0     $9.0     $8.0     $7.0
90          Suave         12.6%    $12.2    $11.2    $10.2     $9.2     $8.2
91          Ounce         13.1%    $13.3    $12.3    $11.3    $10.3     $9.3
92          Share         13.6%    $14.5    $13.5    $12.5    $11.5    $10.5
93          in FY 85      14.1%    $15.7    $14.7    $13.7    $12.7    $11.7
94          (proj.)       14.6%    $16.9    $15.9    $14.9    $13.9    $12.9
95                        15.1%    $18.1    $17.1    $16.1    $15.1    $14.1
96
97
98
99
100
```

```
Y89: (C1) 5.9730588114                                                     READY


        Y        Z       AA       AB       AC       AD       AE       AF
81
82
83
84
85
86
87
88     $8.0     $9.0    $10.0
89     $6.0     $5.0     $4.0
90     $7.2     $6.2     $5.2
91     $8.3     $7.3     $6.3
92     $9.5     $8.5     $7.5
93    $10.7     $9.7     $8.7
94    $11.9    $10.9     $9.9
95    $13.1    $12.1    $11.1
96
97
98
99
100
```

Note: Use the **/Worksheet Titles Vertical** command, if you wish to see on one screen the assumptions with the results in Columns Y, Z, and AA.

Saving Your Worksheet in a File on Diskette

We have now completed Lesson 13. Let's save our new work along with the file that we had created earlier: **LN13**.

ON YOUR OWN: Press the **[Home]** key. Use the **/File Save** command. When 1-2-3 lists "Enter save file name: **LN13**," press **[Enter]** to indicate that we want to save our fully completed worksheet under the file name we had created earlier. When 1-2-3 asks whether we want "Cancel" or "Replace," press **R** to indicate that we want the new fully completed worksheet to replace the previous worksheet as the file named **LN13**.

Review of Lesson 13

In this extensive lesson, we practiced the use of the sophisticated **/Data Table** command. We also learned how to use the **/Data Fill** command and a shortcut in using the **/Copy** command was reintroduced: When copying TO, only the first cell needs to be entered into the range if you want the data to be entered into the same pattern as cells as exists in the range to copy FROM. (In our first example, we copied from the range C69..C75 to the range C89..C95. Only C89 needed to be specified in the range to copy TO.)

To review the steps and structure for creating a data table (with either 1 or 2 variables), you can reexamine the summary discussions that are included in the instructions for Lesson 10.

MANAGEMENT DISCUSSION

1 Why would a manager run both break-even calculations and financial projections?

A manager should run break-even calculations to help analyze the cost effectiveness of a marketing expenditures (or a fixed investment). Also, a manager can run break-even calculations to help analyze the feasibility of achieving a certain level of operating profit.

However, a manager who has profit and loss responsibilities usually must project what level of operating profit will be achieved. Spreadsheet analysis allows a manager to determine and commit to precise levels of operating profit.

2 What is your best projection for Suave operating profit in FY 1985?

Your answer to this question should be based on your analysis of the shampoo market, consumer-buying behavior in the market, and the cost effectiveness of advertising for Suave.

CHAPTER **6**

Stage 4: Graphics

The Suave marketing team had to present their final recommendations on an advertising budget for Suave shampoo to Bob Thomas. They decided to create several graphs using Lotus 1-2-3 to help communicate some of the most important findings and conclusions that they had reached. In completing the next five lessons, you should consider the following questions:

- How can graphs be useful to managers?
- Which of the graphs do you think are most useful?
- What other graphs would you create if you were a brand manager for Suave shampoo?

INTRODUCTION

Ellen Vallera and Gail Lanznar had compiled an extensive body of information to help Helene Curtis management decide on an advertising budget for Suave shampoo. Two reports had been written and sent to the appropriate managers. These reports contained an analysis of the shampoo market and its consumers, a preliminary evaluation of the effectiveness of advertising for Suave, and a series of financial projections, break-evens, and sensitivity analyses.

Brad Kirk had finished reading the market-research and financial reports. He found them extremely informative but recognized that different conclusions about the size of Suave's advertising budget could still be reached. It would be the responsibility of the Suave management team to put together a presentation for top management that would clarify the issues and lead to a productive discussion of advertising for

Suave shampoo. Then Bob Thomas and other corporate managers could arrive at a decision.

The Suave management team met in Kirk's office. First, they outlined what they believed to be the two most important tasks left to the team:

1 A final analysis of the relationships among the data to prioritize the various findings and to shed new light, if possible, on the significance of the marketing and financial relationships uncovered.
2 A reorganization of their work to communicate effectively their analysis and findings.

USE OF GRAPHICS

The members of the Suave management team agreed that graphs could be extremely useful in business management. Graphs served two purposes: to enlighten and to illustrate. As *a analytical* tool, graphs could clarify for managers relationships that were contained in the data but that were not otherwise obvious upon inspection. As a *communications* tool, graphs could also depict relationships among data more clearly and communicate that information more forcefully to management.

The team used the graphics capabilities of Lotus 1-2-3 to help them prepare their presentation. Lotus 1-2-3 was capable of creating and printing five types of graphs: pie, *XY*, line, bar, and stacked bar. Each type of graph could be generated with varying amounts of detail. However, a graph containing significant detail took a considerable amount of time to produce.

SELECTED GRAPHS

The Suave management team knew that the senior management group demanded pointed presentations that provided only the most relevant findings in the most concise manner. They decided to use graphics, therefore, to examine five important issues and illustrate the relationships among that data:

1 The Ad Share-Market Share Relationship
2 Market Segmentation
3 Demographic Characteristics of Suave Consumers
4 Projected Revenues for Suave Shampoo
5 Revenue Structure for Suave Shampoo

The team decided to develop the graphs in some detail so that their findings would be clearly communicated. Care was taken in organizing the presentation to ensure that the graphs illustrated effectively the important points.

After the presentation was given, Kirk and Vallera would each have the opportunity to recommend an advertising budget for Suave.

LESSON 14 GRAPHICS: THE AD SHARE-MARKET SHARE RELATIONSHIP

OVERVIEW

COMPUTER INSTRUCTIONS

Lesson 14 shows how to create pie charts and an *XY* graph. You will also learn how to save graph files.

MANAGEMENT ISSUES

As discussed in the case, there are two managerial purposes for the use of graphs: analysis and communication. You should consider whether the graphs presented in these lessons are worth the effort to create them and whether there are other graphs that would be more useful.

MANAGEMENT DISCUSSION QUESTIONS

1 What is the managerial usefulness of these two pie charts?
2 What does the *XY* graph show about the relative importance of advertising for the Suave brand?
3 Should the *XY* graph be used to analyze the relative effectiveness of Suave advertising?

CASE

The Suave team decided to create three graphs that were related to their analysis of the relationship between the market share and advertising share for each brand:

1 A *pie chart* to depict market shares (in dollars) for Suave and other shampoo brands;
2 A *pie chart* to depict advertising shares for Suave and other shampoo brands; and
3 An *XY graph* to plot the relationship between the market share and advertising share for each of the different brands of shampoo.

COMPUTER INSTRUCTIONS

Introduction to Lotus 1-2-3 Graphics

Lotus 1-2-3 has three general capabilities: database management, spreadsheet analysis, and graphics. In Lessons 1 through 13, we have learned how to use the database management and spreadsheet analysis capabilities. In Lessons 14 through 18, we will learn how to create graphs using 1-2-3.

Let's first take a look at how the graphics capability of Lotus 1-2-3 works. This overview will help us understand better what we do later to construct different types of graphs.

Types of Graphs that Lotus 1-2-3 Can Create

Lotus 1-2-3 is able to create five types of graphs:

1 Pie charts
2 *XY* graphs
3 Line graphs
4 Bar graphs
5 Stacked bar graphs

In Lessons 14 through 18, we introduce each of these types of graphs, creating two graphs of the same type in certain instances. The lessons are organized according to the management issues outlined in the case. Specifically, the lessons, management issues, and types of graphs that we will create are:

Lesson	Management Issue	Graph Types
14	The Ad Share-Market Share Relationship	2 pie charts 1 *XY* graph
15	Market Segmentation	1 *XY* graph
16	Demographic Characteristics of Suave Consumers	1 bar graph
17	Projected Revenues for Suave Shampoo	1 line graph
18	Revenue Structure for Suave Shampoo	1 bar graph 1 stacked bar graph

The Structure of 1-2-3 Graphics: Graph Names, Worksheet Files, and Print Files

Lotus 1-2-3 uses a specific structure for creating, filing, and naming graphs. This structure appears repeatedly in Lessons 14 through 18. It can be summarized as follows:

- A graph always uses data that are present in a worksheet.
- As many graphs as are desired can be created out of the data present in a work-

sheet. However, a graph can never be created from data that must be accessed from more than one worksheet. Each graph can access data only from a single worksheet.

- Each graph in a worksheet must receive its own name—whether only one or many graphs are created from data in the worksheet.
- Once a graph has been created and named, the worksheet must be saved using **/File Save** if the graph is to be saved along with the data. (If the graph is not saved in the worksheet, it will be lost when you leave 1-2-3.) If the worksheet was saved before the graph was created, then the worksheet must be saved again after the graph is created. This process saves the specifications used to produce the graph. When the worksheet is subsequently retrieved from the disk, any associated graphs in the worksheet file will also be retrieved and can be displayed.
- Each graph must also be saved in its own "picture" file. This type of file is required to print a "presentation-quality" graph. A special program must be used: the Lotus PrintGraph program.

Simply stated, we will always follow these three steps after we create a graph:

1 Name the graph.
2 Save the worksheet that contains the graph in a worksheet file. If we wish simply to add a graph to an existing worksheet file and keep that file's existing name, we will use the **/File Save Replace** command for this step. In fact, graphs can be thought of just like worksheet data in this regard: If you change the data, you must resave the worksheet or the change(s) will be lost.
3 Save the graph in its own "graph" or "picture" file.

The first step identifies the data (graph), the second allows the graph to be retrieved and displayed, and the third is necessary to make a high-quality printed copy of the graph.

The Process of Creating Graphs: "Try It, View It, and Change It"

Graphs are created in Lotus 1-2-3 through an iterative process of trial and error. The instructions are designed to simulate this process because that is how all users create graphs once they begin to use 1-2-3 on their own. We will use the **/Graph** commands to:

- Try creating a particular graph;
- View what we created and determine whether we want to change or improve it; and then
- Make changes and view the new graph to see if more changes are needed.

Specific Steps that Need to Be Remembered or Looked Up

The graphics commands in Lotus 1-2-3 are often not as intuitive or easily remembered for many users as are other parts of 1-2-3. At various places, the instructions will point out a particular step or detail that may not be intuitive, but that just has to be remembered or looked up when creating that graph. The index at the back of the book will assist you in using these instructions as a reference.

The Options Command: Deciding How to Allocate Your Time

One particular command that we will use frequently in the trial-and-error process is the **/Graph Options** command. This command allows us to improve the presentation and clarity of the graph through titles, data labels, legends, or formatting and scale changes.

Using this **Options** command to enhance the details of the graph can be very time consuming. The instructions for Lessons 14 through 18 will help you to learn how to use the **Options** command. However, managers who use 1-2-3 to create graphs must always judge whether it is worth the time to specify carefully how the details (and how many details) should appear on each graph. That judgment usually depends on the purpose of the graph, the number of people who will view it, and who those people will be.

Now that we have read this introduction to Lotus 1-2-3 graphics, let's move on and actually create some graphs.

Retrieving the File that Contains the Data on Ad Shares and Market Shares

In Lesson 14, we will create three graphs out of the data that we had previously compiled in Lesson 2. If you completed Lesson 2 thoroughly, then these data are contained on *your data diskette* under the file name **LN02.WK1**. Therefore, the instructions will direct you to retrieve this file from your data diskette.

However, you may also use the worksheet file **LESSON02.WKS** from the *Suave Data Diskette* to create the graphs described in this lesson. You may wish to use the file **LESSON02.WKS** if you did not save your work after completing Lesson 2 or if the file you did save is not sufficiently complete. As you remember, the completed worksheet for Lesson 2 begins at cell A101 in the file **LESSON02.WKS**.

Note on Using the File LN02.WK1 from Your Data Diskette: Load DOS. Enter date and time. Load the Lotus Access System. Then load the 1-2-3 software program. Insert your data diskette into the appropriate disk drive. Use the **/File Retrieve** command to load the file **LN02.WK1**.

Note on Using the File LESSON02.WKS from the Suave Data Diskette: If you prefer to use the completed worksheet for Lesson 2 as contained on the Suave Data Diskette, load DOS, the Lotus Access System, and the 1-2-3 software program. Insert the Suave Data Diskette into the appropriate disk drive. Use the **/File Retrieve** command to load the file **LESSON02.WKS**. Then remove the Suave Data Diskette and replace it with your data diskette, so that you can learn how to save the graphs. (Remember, that the Suave Data Diskette is permanently protected so that nothing can be saved or changed on it.)

To use the file **LESSON02.WKS**, you need to move the cell pointer to the completed worksheet that begins at cell **A101**. As you follow the instructions for Lesson 14, *add 100 to each cell reference* in the instructions. For example, if the instructions direct you to move to the cell pointer to *G7*, you need to move the cell pointer to cell *G107*.

Note: The worksheet files **LESSON14.WKS** through **LESSON18.WKS** on the

Suave Data Diskette contain the eight completed graphs. These files are for reference purposes only. You should not use these files in order to follow the instructions. However, if you wish, these lessons may be retrieved to see how the graphs should appear.

We are now ready to create and save three graphs in Lesson 14.

GRAPH 1: PIE GRAPH COMPARING SUAVE'S MARKET SHARE WITH ITS COMPETITORS' MARKET SHARES

To create and save this graph, we'll complete the following steps:

1.1 Create the initial graph and then view it to see how it looks;
1.2 Improve the appearance of the graph;
1.3 Name the graph;
1.4 Save the worksheet that contains the graph; and
1.5 Save a "picture" of the graph for later printing.

1.1 Creating and Viewing the Initial Graph to Compare Suave's Market Share with Its Competitors' Market Shares

To create a picture of this comparison, we will start by using the **/Graph** command. With this command we are able to create pie graphs (often called *pie charts*). Press the following keys:

Description	*Keys to Press*
Display the 1-2-3 command menus:	**/**
Select the /Graph command:	**G**
(We now need to tell 1-2-3 what type of graph we're building.)	
Select the Type command:	**T**
(Let's build a pie graph to see the market shares of the various brands.)	
Select the Pie menu choice:	**P**
(For pie graphs, the "X-axis" will always refer to the range of cells containing the labels for each slice of the pie. This is just one of the many details you will have to remember or look up later when you create graphs on your own.)	
Select the X menu choice to specify the cell range of shampoo names for each pie slice:	**X**
(1-2-3 will direct us to enter the X-axis range.)	
Use the cell pointer to paint the cell range of shampoo names (A7..B18):	**[down*6]**
	.
	[End]

Description	Keys to Press
	[down]
	[up*2]
	[right]
Confirm the range A7..B18 as the X-axis range:	[Enter]

(Now we need to tell 1-2-3 how to divide up the pie—according to market share (in dollars). For pie graphs, the A-axis will always refer to the range of cells containing the values for each slice of the pie. Again, this is just a detail you will have to remember or look up.)

Select the A menu choice to specify that we will enter the cell range containing the Dollar Market Share values: **A**

(1-2-3 will direct us to enter the "first data range." Only this first data range is used for pie graphs.)

Use the cell pointer to paint the cell range containing the Dollar Market Share values (F7..F18) and confirm:

	[right*5]
	[down*6]
	.
	[End]
	[down]
	[up*2]
	[Enter]

(We have now created the initial graph. Let's see how it looks.)

Select the View command: **V**

(You should see a pie graph labeled with each shampoo name along with its dollar market share.)

Observation: Notice that this pie graph is not completely clear. Some of the names may overlap each other, and some of the shampoo brand names (and market shares) may also be cut off from the screen. The names will also be cut off if we later try to print the graph. So, what can we do about clarifying this pie graph?

1.2 Improving the Appearance of the Graph

One way to fix the problem is by using abbreviations for the brand names. Let's see how.

Press the following keys:

Description	Keys to Press
Press any key to return to the Graph menu:	[Space]
Escape from the /Graph command:	[Esc] [Esc]

Description	Keys to Press
Move the cell pointer to column C:	**[right*2]**

(Now let's insert a new column where we can put the brand name abbreviations.)

Display the 1-2-3 command menus:	**/**
Select the /Worksheet command:	**W**
Select the Insert command:	**I**
Select the Column menu choice:	**C**

(Watch column H "Ounce Market Share" disappear. These values will now be in column I.)

Confirm that the column insert range is C1..C1:	**[Enter]**

We are now ready to enter the abbreviations.

ON YOUR OWN: In column C, in the cell immediately to the right of each brand name, **type in** the following abbreviations for each respective shampoo brand name.

Brand Name	Abbreviation for Brand Name
Private Label	PL
Generic	GC
Flex	FX
Suave	SV
Head & Shoulders	HS
Silkience	SL
Agree	AG
Pert	PT
Jhirmack	JK
Prell	PR
Vidal Sassoon	VS
Others	OT

Note: You may, if you wish, just type in each of these abbreviations and then press **[Enter]**. In that case, each abbreviation will automatically be left-justified in column C. Or, if you wish, you may press the ^ character before typing each abbreviation in order to center these abbreviations in column C. Or, you may use the **/Range Label** command and choose how you would like the labels displayed ("left," "right," or "center"). Whether the abbreviations are left-justified or centered in column C, they will appear exactly the same on the graph.

Now we are ready to use these abbreviations in creating the pie chart. Press the following keys:

Description	Keys to Press
Display the 1-2-3 command menus:	/
Select the /Graph command:	**G**
(Now let's change the X-axis range that contains the labels for the pie chart.)	
Select the X command:	**X**
(1-2-3 will display the range A7..B18.)	
Escape from this range:	**[Esc]**
(The cell pointer should now be in A7.)	
Move the cell pointer to the beginning of the new range at cell C7:	**[right*2]**
Anchor C7 as the beginning of the new range:	**.**
Paint the range C7..C18:	**[End]** **[down]**
Confirm the range C7..C18:	**[Enter]**
(We have now made all the necessary changes. Let's escape from the /Graph command.)	
Escape from the /Graph command:	**[Esc] [Esc]**
(Now let's display the graph using a new key, so that we can see how the graph looks using the abbreviations.)	
Press the [Graph] key (the [F10] function key on most keyboards) to display the graph, without having to use the /Graph command:	**[F10]**

Observation: Notice how much clearer the graph looks and how all the brand name abbreviations and market share percentages are fully displayed.

Note: Pressing the **[Graph]** (**[F10]**) key will display whatever graph we most recently created or viewed. The **[Graph]** (**[F10]**) key can be used only if we are in the worksheet and the command menu is not displayed.

This special function key, **[F10]**, allows us to review the most recently accessed graph without having to go through the **/Graph View** menu. Therefore, when the command menu is not displayed, we need to press only one key rather than three to review the previous graph.

This exercise helps to demonstrate the iterative process that is inherent in creating graphs. After we create a graph, if the graph does not appear as we wish or if small presentation problems arise, we should make whatever changes are appropriate and then review the graph to see if the correct changes have been made. Sometimes we will return to the worksheet to make changes in labels or range. Other times, as we shall soon see, we will make changes in the "Graph Options."

Now let's continue to improve the graph by adding some titles to the pie graph we have created. Press the following keys:

Description	**Keys to Press**
Press any key to return to the worksheet:	**[Space]**
Display the 1-2-3 command menus:	**/**
Select the /Graph command:	**G**
Select the Options command:	**O**

(1-2-3 provides a long set of options. We will learn many of these in Lessons 14 through 18.)

Select the Titles menu choice:	**T**

(1-2-3 permits up to two title lines for each graph.)

Select the First menu choice:	**F**
Type in the title (use the Caps Lock key):	**DOLLAR MARKET SHARE PERCENTAGE**

(A graph title can contain up to 40 characters. It can begin with numbers or symbols and can contain spaces. 1-2-3 will automatically center the title.)

Confirm the title:	**[Enter]**

(Let's return to the previous menu so we can View the pie graph again.)

Select the Quit menu choice:	**Q**
Select the View command:	**V**

(You should now see the title.)

Press any key to return to the Graph menu:	**[Space]**

(Now let's add a subtitle for the pie graph.)

Select the Options command:	**O**
Select the Titles menu choice:	**T**

(Since 1-2-3 permits up to two title lines for each graph, let's use the second line for the subtitle.)

Select the Second menu choice:	**S**

(The second title line, like the first, can contain up to 40 characters, can begin with numbers or symbols, can contain spaces, and will be automatically centered.)

Type in the subtitle, all in small letters, and put in parentheses. (Make sure the Caps Lock key is off. If not, press the key once more.):	**(for leading shampoo brands)**
Confirm the second title line:	**[Enter]**

(Let's return to the previous menu so we can View the graph again.)

Select the Quit menu choice:	**Q**
Select the View command:	**V**

Good. You have completed your first graph. It should look similar to this:

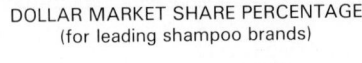

DOLLAR MARKET SHARE PERCENTAGE
(for leading shampoo brands)

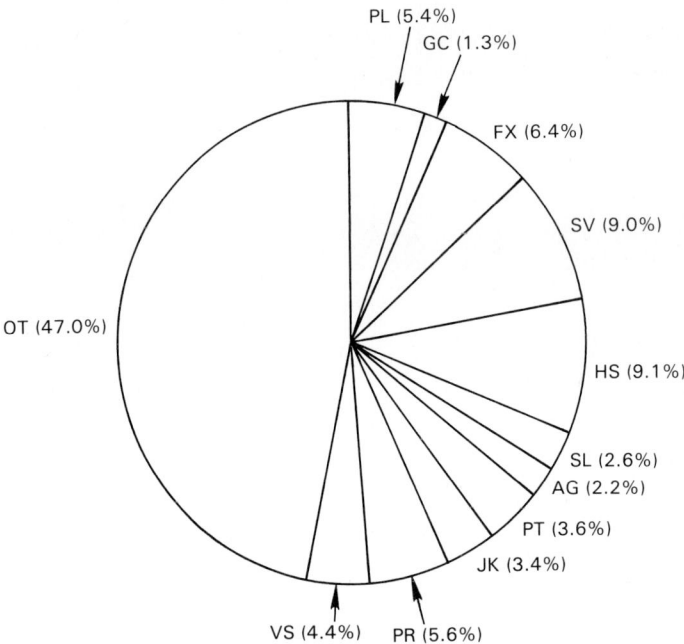

Note: This exercise demonstrates that using **/Graph Options** also involves an iterative process, just as creating the original graph involves an iterative process. Now that we have created the graph we want, we need to:

1 Name the graph to identify it.
2 Save the worksheet with the graph in it for display.
3 Save the "picture" file of the graph for later printing.

1.3 Naming the Graph in the Worksheet

Now that you've created a pie graph, let's save it in the worksheet so that we may proceed to the next graph. (If you are using LESSON02.WKS from the Suave Data Diskette, be sure you have removed the Suave Data Diskette and replaced it with your data diskette. Do it now if you have not done so already.) Press the following keys:

Description	Keys to Press
Press any key to return to the Graph menu:	**[Space]**
Select the Name command:	**N**

Description	*Keys to Press*

(We want to save this graph under a "name" within the worksheet. So we need to "create" a name.)

Select the Create menu choice: **C**

(Let's call this graph MKTSHARE).
(A graph name can contain up to 15 characters. The name can begin with a number and can contain spaces.)

Type in the name for this graph and confirm: **MKTSHARE [Enter]**

(Now you have a graph stored within your worksheet named "MKTSHARE." You may recall this graph at any time by using the /Graph Name Use command.)

Note: The graph is stored *within* your worksheet. However, the "new" worksheet file itself has not yet been saved on the diskette, nor has the graph been saved for later printing with the PrintGraph program. Therefore, we have two more steps to complete. *You must be sure to complete these two additional steps before you leave this worksheet, or else you will either not be able to print the graph conveniently, or, worse, you will lose it completely.*

1.4 Saving the Worksheet that Contains the Graph

Now that the graph has been named, we need to save this worksheet to be able to display and retrieve the graph later. Let's give this new file (containing the graph and the brand name abbreviations) a different name, **LN14**, referring to Lesson 14.

    ON YOUR OWN: If necessary, press the **[Esc]** key as many times as necessary to clear completely the **/Graph** command menu. Then press the **[Home]** key to return the cell pointer to A1. Use the **/File Save** command to save this worksheet file. When 1-2-3 displays the file name, **LN02.WK1**, type in **LN14**. Then press **[Enter]** to confirm this new file name.

    Now we are ready to complete Step 3: Saving a "picture" of the graph on file for later printing.

1.5 Saving a "Picture" of the Graph for Later Printing

As we will see later, printing a presentation quality graph requires the use of the PrintGraph program. In order to be able to use this program, we need to save a separate "picture" file of the graph. These files are called "PIC" files by 1-2-3, so that the file name will be the name you provide plus the extension .PIC.

    Because we are not used to creating "picture" files, this extra step may not be intuitive. It also makes for more work. Unfortunately, this is just a step that we have to remember to complete in order to be able to print the graph later. Just remember that for graphs, we must name the graph, save it in a worksheet file in order to be able to retrieve it later, *and* then save it in a separate picture file in order to make a high-quality print of it later.

    So, let's see how to complete this third step. Press the following keys:

Description	Keys to Press
Display the 1-2-3 command menus:	**/**
Select the /Graph command:	**G**
Select the Save menu choice:	**S**
(1-2-3 now needs a name for the special "picture" file.)	
Let's name this picture file just as we named the graph. Type in the file name and enter:	**MKTSHARE [Enter]**
(A picture file name can contain up to only 8 characters, must begin with a letter, and cannot contain any spaces.) *(We have now completed this necessary additional step!)*	
Select the Quit menu choice to exit the command menus and to return to the worksheet:	**Q**

Note: The names you choose for "named graphs" (using **/Graph Name Create**), which are stored within the worksheet (using **/File Save**), and those you choose for "picture" files (using **/Graph Save**) are completely independent. However, to minimize the number of names you need to remember, it might often be wise to use the same names. In this instance, we used the name MKTSHARE both to "name" the graph and to save the "picture" file. (This suggestion—to use the same name both to name the graph and to save the picture file—means of course that this common name is limited to only 8 characters, must begin with a letter, and cannot contain any spaces.)

We are now ready to move on to create the second pie graph to compare the ad spending for Suave versus for other brands.

GRAPH 2: PIE GRAPH COMPARING SUAVE'S AD SHARE WITH ITS COMPETITORS' AD SHARES

To create and save this graph, we'll complete the following steps:

2.1 Create the initial graph and then view it to see how it looks;
2.2 Improve the appearance of the graph;
2.3 Name the graph;
2.4 "Replace" the existing worksheet file with a new file that contains the new pie graph; and
2.5 Save a "picture" of the graph for later printing.

2.1 Creating the Initial Graph to Compare Sauve's Ad Share with Its Competitor's Ad Shares

In completing the first part of this, you should have saved a new worksheet file named LN14.WK1. We will be using this worksheet file to create another graph. If you have left this file for any reason, then retrieve the file LN14.WK1 from your data diskette.

(Remember, if appropriate, to add 100 to the cell references in the instructions.)

This pie chart provides a visual comparison of shampoo brands according to their respective advertising shares. It should be easier to create this graph now that we have already used the **/Graph** command. Accordingly, follow the step-by-step instructions only as closely as is necessary. The steps for creating graphs are only learned through repetition. *The more you do on your own, the quicker you will learn.* Press the following keys:

Description	*Keys to Press*
Display 1-2-3 command menus:	**/**
Select the /Graph command:	**G**
(Before continuing, we want to reset all the settings from the previous graph.)	
Select the Reset command:	**R**
(1-2-3 "remembers" all ranges from the previous graph. Although we will use one of the previous ranges again, it is good practice to avoid any possible confusion and reset everything.)	
(The /Graph Reset Graph command works just like the /Data Table Reset command.)	
Select the Graph menu choice:	**G**
(This step confirms that we want to reset all previous settings. We now need to tell 1-2-3 what type of graph we're building.)	
Select the Type command:	**T**
(Let's build a pie graph to see the shares of industry ad spending for Suave and the other brands.)	
Select the Pie menu choice:	**P**
Select the X menu choice to specify the cell range of shampoo names for each pie slice:	**X**
Move the cell pointer to C7:	**(Use the arrow keys.)**
Anchor C7 and then paint the range C7..C18:	**.**
	[End]
	[down]
Confirm the range C7..C18 as the *X*-axis range:	**[Enter]**
(We now need to enter the "values" for the pie graph.)	
Select the A menu choice to specify the cell range containing the Share of Industry Ad Spending values for each brand:	**A**
Move the cell pointer to N7, which contains the first Share of Industry Ad Spending value:	**(Use the [Tab] and the arrow keys.)**
Anchor N7 and then paint the range N7..N18:	**.**
	[End]

Description	Keys to Press
	[down]
	[up*2]
Confirm the range N7..N18 as the "first data range":	**[Enter]**
(Let's take a look at what we have created so far.)	
Select the View command:	**V**
(You should see a pie graph labeled with the abbreviation for each shampoo name along with its share of ad spending.)	

Let's now improve the appearance of the graph. Fortunately, this step will not entail as much work as did the first pie graph because we have already used the abbreviations for the brand names.

2.2 Improving the Appearance of the Graph

All we have to do now is add the titles to the graph. Press the following keys:

Description	Keys to Press
Press any key to return to the Graph menu:	**[Space]**
Select the Options command:	**O**
Select the Titles menu choice:	**T**
(Remember that 1-2-3 permits up to two title lines for each graph.)	
Select the First menu choice:	**F**
Type in the title (use the Caps Lock key):	**INDUSTRY AD SHARE**
Confirm the title:	**[Enter]**
(Now let's add a subtitle.)	
Select the Titles menu choice:	**T**
Select the Second menu choice:	**S**
Type in the subtitle, all in small letters and put in parentheses (take the Caps Lock key off):	**(for leading shampoo brands)**
Confirm the subtitle:	**[Enter]**
(Let's return to the previous menu so we can view the pie graph again.)	
Select the Quit menu choice:	**Q**
Select the View command:	**V**

Good. We have now created our second graph. The graph should look like this:

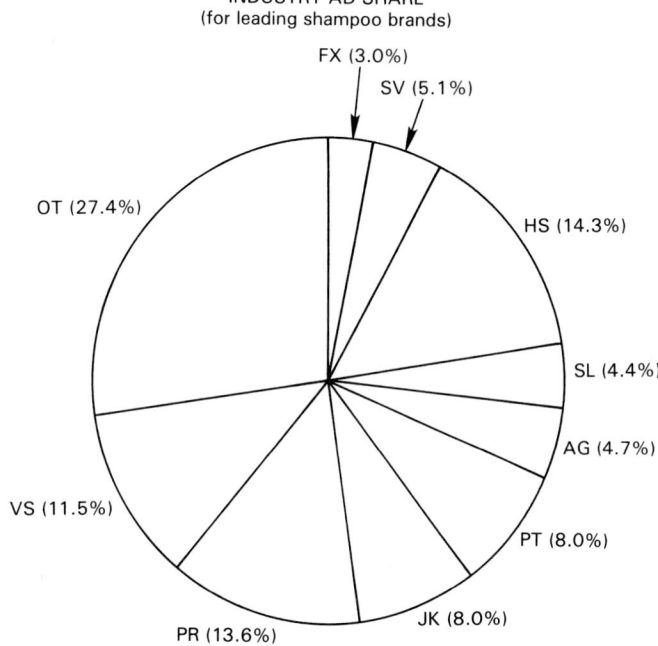

INDUSTRY AD SHARE
(for leading shampoo brands)

Observation: That seemed a lot easier. Also, remember that if you make a mistake inputting a title, you can always use the **[backspace]** keys.

We now must complete again the necessary three steps to save our work:

1 Name the graph to identify it and distinguish it from the other pie graph.
2 "Replace" the existing worksheet file with this new file containing the graph so that the graph can be displayed and retrieved.
3 Save a "picture" of the graph for later printing.

2.3 Naming the Graph in the Worksheet

Now that you've created another pie graph, let's save it in the worksheet along with the data and the first pie graph so that we may proceed to the next graph. Press the following keys:

Description	Keys to Press
Press any key to return to the Graph menu:	**[Space]**
Select the Name command:	**N**

Description	Keys to Press
(We want to save this graph under a "name" within the worksheet. So we need to "create" a name.)	
Select the Create menu choice:	**C**
(Let's call this graph ADSHARE.)	
Type in the name for this graph and confirm:	**ADSHARE [Enter]**

Now we have a graph stored *within* our worksheet named "ADSHARE." We also have a graph named "MKTSHARE." To recall a graph from the worksheet at any time, we must make it the "current" graph. ADSHARE is the current graph. [Use the **View** command to check and then press any key to return to the Graph menu.]

Revisiting a Previously Named Graph

Now that we have created two graphs in one worksheet, how can we go back to another graph? How do we specify which of the graphs we want?

Fortunately, we gave a different name to each graph. Let's see how we can use the name of the first graph, MKTSHARE, to go back to that graph. Press the following keys (the Graph menu should be displayed):

Description	Keys to Press
Select the Name command:	**N**
Select the Use menu choice:	**U**
(You should see the two graph names listed.)	
Use the arrow keys to move the cursor to the MKTSHARE graph and confirm:	**(Use the arrow keys.) [Enter]**
(The MKTSHARE graph should now appear on your screen. It is now the current graph.)	
Press any key to return to the Graph menu:	**[Space]**

Note: We can go back to any graph on the worksheet file by using the **/Graph Name Use** command. Once you go back to a graph, 1-2-3 makes that graph the "current" graph. This allows you, if you want, to make further changes in the graph. Practice this command again by making ADSHARE the current graph.

Remember that we can create and name as many graphs as we want within a single worksheet. However, we still must complete the steps of saving the worksheet with this new graph in it and of saving a "picture" file of the graph for later printing.

2.4 "Replacing" the Existing Worksheet File with a New File that Contains the New Pie Graph

Now that the graph has been named, we need to save it in a worksheet file. In this case, we should "Replace" the worksheet file that we created earlier in this lesson with a new file that contains the new graph. The new file will also be named LN14. It will contain the first graph plus this new second graph.

ON YOUR OWN: Press the **[Esc]** key as many times as necessary to clear completely the **/Graph** command menu. Then, press the **[Home]** key to return to cell A1. Use the **/File Save Replace** command to save this worksheet file under the name: **LN14**.

The worksheet file now contains both the MKTSHARE and the ADSHARE graphs. Use the **/Graph Name Use** command to check that both of these graphs are part of the worksheet. Then press the **[Esc]** key as many times as necessary to return to the worksheet. Press the **[F10]** key to see the current graph, ADSHARE.

Now we are ready to complete Step 3: Saving a "picture" of the graph on file for later printing.

2.5 Saving a "Picture" of the Graph for Later Printing

Just as we did with the MKTSHARE graph, we now need to create a picture file of the ADSHARE graph, so that the PrintGraph program can be used to create a presentation quality print of the graph. Before starting, **make sure that ADSHARE is the current graph**. Use the **/Graph Name Use** command if necessary.

Press the following keys:

Description	Keys to Press
Display the 1-2-3 command menus:	**/**
Select the /Graph command:	**G**
Select the Save menu choice:	**S**
(1-2-3 now needs a name for the special picture file.)	
Let's name this picture file just as we named the graph. Type in the file name and enter:	**ADSHARE [Enter]**
(We have now completed this necessary additional step.)	
Select the Quit menu choice to return to the worksheet:	**Q**

Note: Once again we have minimized the number of names we need to remember by using "ADSHARE" both to "name" the graph in the worksheet file and to save the "picture" file.

We are now ready to create the *XY* graph that compares the ad share to the market share for each shampoo brand.

GRAPH 3: *XY* GRAPH COMPARING THE AD SHARE TO THE MARKET SHARE FOR EACH SHAMPOO BRAND

To create and save this graph, we'll complete the following steps:

3.1 Create the initial graph and then view it to see how it looks;

3.2 Improve the appearance of the graph;

3.3 Name the graph; save the worksheet file with the new graph; save a "picture" for later printing.

Beginning with this graph, we will combine the three steps necessary for saving the graph into one section. The instructions will also direct you to complete these steps on your own. You should be completing these steps almost as a reflex once you have finished a graph that you want to save.

3.1 Creating the Initial Graph to Compare the Ad Share to the Market Share for Each Shampoo Brand

Once again, we will be using the worksheet file LN14.WK1 to create another graph. If you have left this file for any reason, then just retrieve the file from your data diskette. (Remember, if appropriate, to add 100 to cell references in the instructions.)

This graph will be our first attempt at creating an *XY* graph. An *XY* graph allows us to plot data on two sets of axes (vertical and horizontal). Let's see how. Press the following keys:

Description	Keys to Press
Display the 1-2-3 command menus:	*I*
Select the /Graph command:	**G**
(Before continuing, we want to reset all the settings from the previous graph.)	
Select the Reset command:	**R**
Select the Graph menu choice:	**G**
Select the Type command:	**T**
(Let's build an XY graph. The X-axis, or horizontal axis, will display each brand's share of industry ad spending and the Y-axis, or vertical axis, will display each brand's dollar market share.)	
Select the XY menu choice:	**X**
(We now need to specify the data for each of the axes.)	

Description	Keys to Press
Select the X menu choice to indicate that we want to specify the data for the *X*-axis:	**X**

(Let's put the Share of Industry Ad Spending for each brand on the X-axis. Therefore, we need to paint the range of values in column N for each brand. However, let's leave out "Others.")

Description	Keys to Press
Move the cell pointer to N7:	**(Use the [Tab] and the arrow keys.)**
Anchor N7 and the paint range N7..N17 (leaving out "Others"):	**.** **[down*10]**
Confirm the range N7..N17 as the *X*-axis range:	**[Enter]**

(We now need to specify the data for the Y-axis.)
(With XY graphs, the A range choice represents the Y-axis. We need only the X range and A range in XY graphs.)

Description	Keys to Press
Select the A menu choice to specify the data for the *Y*-axis:	**A**

(Let's put the Dollar Market Share for each brand on the Y-axis. Therefore, we need to paint the range of values in column G. Again, let's leave out "Others.")

Description	Keys to Press
Move the cell pointer to G7, which contains the first Dollar Market Share value:	**(Use the arrow keys.)**
Anchor G7 and then paint the range G7..G17 (leaving out "Others"):	**.** **[down*10]**
Confirm the range G7..G17 as the *Y*-axis data range:	**[Enter]**

(Let's take a look at what we have created so far.)

Description	Keys to Press
Select the View command:	**V**

Let's now improve the appearance of the graph. In this instance, we have a fair amount of work to do to make this graph provide insight on the ad share-market share relationship.

3.2 Improving the Appearance of the Graph

Let's see how we can make this graph more presentable. Press the following keys:

Description	Keys to Press

(Notice that the graph contains lines that connect squares, but we don't know what each square represents. Those squares represent shampoo brands. Let's first replace them with the brand abbreviations.)

Description	Keys to Press
Press any key to return to the Graph menu:	**[Space]**
(Now let's see how the options command can help us.)	
Select the Options command:	**O**
(We first need to label the data in the graph, so that we know what each data point represents.)	
Select the Data-Labels menu choice:	**D**
(Remember that with an XY graph, we use only the X or A range choices.)	
Select the A menu choice:	**A**
(We now want to paint the range of brand name abbreviations, excluding "Others.")	
Move the cell pointer to C7:	**(Use the arrow keys.)**
Anchor C7 and paint the range C7..C17:	**.**
	[End]
	[down]
	[up]
Confirm the range C7..C17:	**[Enter]**
(1-2-3 can place the data-labels you just specified in a variety of places. Let's center the label over each data point.)	
Select the Center menu choice:	**C**
Select the Quit menu choice to return to the Options menu:	**Q**
Select the Quit menu choice once more to return to the Graph menu:	**Q**
(Let's see what we have now.)	
Select the View command:	**V**
(Notice that the brand name abbreviations now appear, but the lines and symbols on the graph still remain. These lines and symbols are inappropriate for our purpose here, so let's remove them.)	
Press any key to return to the Graph command:	**[Space]**
Select the Options command:	**O**
(The Options Format menu choice deals with lines and symbols on the graph. If you like, press [right] and see a brief explanation of the Format menu choice on the second line.)	
Select the Format menu choice:	**F**
Select the Graph menu choice to indicate that we want to set the format for the entire graph:	**G**
(We are now given a choice of whether we want lines, symbols both or neither. We want neither.)	
Select the menu choice Neither:	**N**

Description	Keys to Press
Select the Quit menu choice to return to the Options menu:	Q
Select the Quit menu choice to return to the Graph menu:	Q
Select the View command to see what you have now:	V

Observation: The graph now looks better. Notice that 1-2-3 has automatically scaled both the X-axis and the Y-axis (0..0.16 for the X-axis; 0..0.1 for the Y-axis). We could change these scales using the **Options Scale** command (the lower and upper boundaries; the intervals between data points). However, the scales that 1-2-3 set automatically seem about right. We would like to put the numbers on the scales in percentages.

Let's see how we can change the format of the numbers on the X-axis and the Y-axis. Press the following keys:

Description	Keys to Press
Press any key to return to the Graph menu:	**[Space]**
Select the Options command:	**O**
Select the Scale menu choice:	**S**
(Let's now set the format for the numbers on the X-axis, the share of industry spending.) (Just as we can set the "display format" for any cell in the worksheet, we can also set the "display format" for the values which appear alongside each axis. Do not confuse this "Format" with "Graph Format," which controls the use of lines and/or symbols in our graphs!)	
Select the X scale menu choice:	**X**
Select the Format menu choice:	**F**
Select the Percent menu choice:	**P**
Use 0 decimal places and confirm:	**0 [Enter]**
Select the Quit menu choice to return to the Options menu:	**Q**
(Let's now set the format for the number on the Y-axis, the dollar market shares of the brands. We will put these in percent format, with 0 decimal places.)	
Select the Scale menu choice again:	**S**
Select the Y Scale menu choice:	**Y**
Select the Format menu choice:	**F**
Select the Percent menu choice:	**P**
Use 0 decimal places and confirm:	**0 [Enter]**

Description	Keys to Press
(Let's take a look at what we have created so far.)	
Escape all the way to the first Graph menu:	**[Esc*3]**
Select the View command:	**V**

Observation: The graph now looks even better. Let's give the graph a title, and let's give a title to each of the axes.

Description	Keys to Press
Press any key to return to the Graph menu:	**[Space]**
Select the Options command:	**O**
Select the Titles menu choice:	**T**
(1-2-3 permits up to two title lines for each graph.)	
Select the First menu choice:	**F**
Type in the title (use the Caps Lock key) and confirm:	**AD SHARE VS. MKT SHARE [Enter]**
(Remember that a graph title can contain up to 40 characters.)	
Select the Titles menu choice again:	**T**
Select the Second menu choice:	**S**
Type in the subtitle (use all small letters and parentheses) and confirm (take Caps Lock key off):	**(for leading shampoo brands) [Enter]**
(Let's now put titles on the axes themselves. These will be in addition to the titles for the overall graph.)	
Select the Titles menu choice again:	**T**
(Let's first enter a title for the X-axis.)	
Select the X-Axis menu choice:	**X**
Type in the X-Axis title and confirm:	**Industry Ad Share [Enter]**
(Now let's enter a title for the Y-axis.)	
Select the Titles menu choice again:	**T**
Select the Y-Axis menu choice:	**Y**
Enter the Y-Axis title and confirm:	**Dollar Market Share [Enter]**
Select the Quit menu choice to return to the Graph menu:	**Q**
Select the View command to see what you have now:	**V**

Good! That was quite a bit of work, but now the graph clearly shows how each shampoo brand is positioned in terms of its advertising and market shares. A copy of how the graph should appear is printed below:

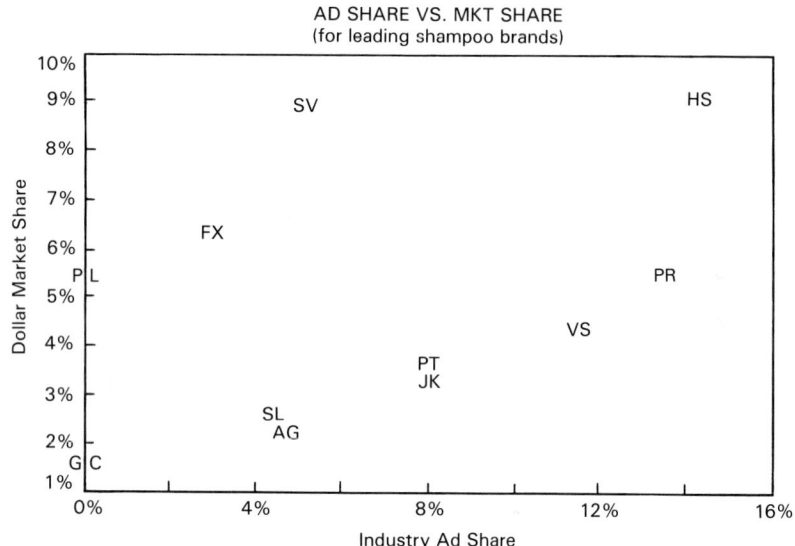

Observation: This exercise is a good example of how time-consuming it can be to specify all the details of the graph. However, in this instance, the time seems well spent. Other times, depending on your objectives, it may be that you only want a "rough" graph.

Let's now move on to the three steps that we know we have to complete:

1 Name the graph.
2 "Replace" the existing worksheet file with the new file.
3 Save a "picture" of the graph for later printing.

3.3 Name the Graph; Save the Worksheet File; Save a Picture File

ON YOUR OWN: First, name the graph. Press **any key** to return to the Graph menu. Select the **Name** command. Select the **Create** command. Type in the name: **ADMKT**. Press **[Enter]** to confirm the name.

Now that the graph has been named, we need to save it in a worksheet file. Once again, let's "Replace" the worksheet file, LN14.

ON YOUR OWN: If necessary, press the **[Esc]** key as many times as necessary to clear completely the **/Graph** command menu. Then press the **[Home]** key to return to cell A1. Use the **/File Save Replace** command to save this worksheet file under the name: **LN14**. The worksheet file now contains three graphs (the MKTSHARE, AD-SHARE, and ADMKT graphs). Use the **/Graph Name Use** command to check that all three of these graphs are part of the worksheet. Press the **[Esc]** key as many times as necessary to return to the worksheet. Check that ADMKT is the current graph.

Lets's now save a "picture" of the graph on file for later printing.

ON YOUR OWN: Select the **/Graph** command, and then the **Save** command. Type in the picture file name: **ADMKT**. Press **[Enter]** to confirm the name. Press **Quit** to return to the worksheet.

Note: Once again we have minimized the number of names we need to re-member by using "ADMKT" both to "name" the graph and to save the "picture" file. Also, if you like, you can retrieve the LESSON14.WKS file from the Suave Data Diskette and use the **/Graph Name Use** command to view any or all of the three completed graphs.

Let's now review what we learned in this lesson.

Reviewing What We Learned in Lesson 14

In Lesson 14, we learned all the essential steps necessary for creating pie and *XY* graphs, with one exception—printing graphs. We will learn how to print graphs in Lesson 15.

In Lessons 16, 17, and 18, we will learn how to create, save, and print three other types of graphs: bar graphs, line graphs, and stacked bar graphs.

To understand how to construct graphs using Lotus 1-2-3, it is best to review the introductory overview at the beginning of this lesson. In addition, we learned the following specific steps for creating graphs:

- Creating graphs is an iterative process. You should make frequent use of the **View** command to display the current state of the graph.
- To create a graph, you need to tell 1-2-3: (1) what kind of graph to create (Type), and (2) what data to display (*X, A*, etc.). Options in the **/Graph** command are used to improve the appearance of the graph.
- A pie graph uses the "X Range" to label each slice of the pie and uses the "A Range" to measure the size of each slice of the pie.
- An *XY* graph uses the "X Range" for the values on the *X*-axis and the "A Range" for the values on the *Y*-axis.
- "Data-Labels" allows you to put labels on each of the data points.
- The "format" of a graph (not to be confused with the "display format" of the axes) permits you to use symbols, lines, both, or neither to connect the data points. If you do not set the "format" of a graph, 1-2-3 automatically uses both symbols and lines.
- 1-2-3 automatically "scales" the graph so that all the data points are displayed. However, by using the Scale option, you can specify the lower and upper bounds for either axis. You can also set the format for the scales.
- A graph may be "named" and stored in the worksheet using the **/Graph Name Create** command and later recalled by using the **/Graph Name Use** command.

Let's now move on to Lesson 15 to learn how to print graphs.

MANAGEMENT DISCUSSION

1 What is the managerial usefulness of these two pie charts?

These two pie charts are primarily useful to show visibly and quickly how the shampoo industry is divided in terms of market shares and advertising spending.

2 What does the *XY* graph show about the relative importance of advertising for the Suave brand?

This graph demonstrates clearly that advertising is relatively less important for Suave than it is for most brands of shampoo. Many brands with a much lower dollar market share have a higher ad share than Suave.

3 Should the *XY* graph be used to analyze the relative effectiveness of Suave advertising?

It would be inappropriate to use this *XY* graph to analyze the relative effectiveness of advertising for Suave. The fact that Suave has higher dollar market share than brands that advertise more does not mean that advertising is relatively more effective for Suave. No conclusion can be drawn about the relative effectiveness of advertising for different shampoos by comparing their dollar market share and industry ad shares at one point in time. This comparison allows us to understand only the relative importance of advertising to different brands at a particular point in time.

LESSON 15   GRAPHICS: MARKET SEGMENTATION

OVERVIEW

COMPUTER INSTRUCTIONS

Lesson 15 contains instructions for the creation of another *XY* graph. In addition, this lesson provides the first instructions for printing graphs. Printing graphs in Lotus 1-2-3 is a bit complicated and requires the use of the PrintGraph program. It also requires specific instructions for the type of printer that you are using.

MANAGEMENT ISSUES

This particular *XY* graph, which compares the price per ounce and the A/S ratio for each brand of shampoo, seems to be an extremely useful graph for both analyzing and communicating the segmentation of the shampoo market and the positioning of the various brands within the market. However, this graph certainly does not cover all the factors that should be considered in analyzing the market segmentation of Suave's positioning.

MANAGEMENT DISCUSSION QUESTIONS

1 What does this *XY* graph tell you about segmentation of the shampoo market?
2 How else might you want to segment the market?
3 What does the *XY* graph tell you about Suave's positioning in the market?
4 What other factors should you consider in analyzing Suave's positioning in the market?

CASE

The Suave team decided to create a second *XY* graph to plot the relationship between (1) the A/S ratio, and (2) the retail price per ounce for Suave and for each of the other shampoo brands. They thought that important insights could be gained by segmenting the shampoo market based on these two factors. In addition, they thought that, for this segmentation analysis, an *XY* graph would be particularly useful for showing the positioning of each brand in the shampoo market.

COMPUTER INSTRUCTIONS

Overview of Computer Instructions for Lesson 15

Lesson 15 provides instructions for the creation of a new *XY* graph. These instructions will allow you to practice what you learned in Lesson 14.

Most important, Lesson 15 also provides instructions on how to print graphs, which is a particularly complicated aspect of Lotus 1-2-3. A special introduction to the printing of graphs begins this lesson. Instructions for the creation of the new *XY* graph then follows. The lesson concludes with several sections that provide step-by-step instructions on how you should go about printing the graphs that you have created and saved.

The instructions for Lesson 15 assume that you have fully completed Lesson 14. If you have not done so, it is probably best to complete Lesson 14 before proceeding with Lesson 15. Completing Lesson 14 ensures not only that your file is consistent with the instructions for Lesson 15 but also that you understand the essentials of 1-2-3 graphics to prevent any confusion in Lesson 15.

To begin this lesson, please make sure that:

1 You know what brand of printer you are using. Later in the lesson, you will need to specify this brand so that Lotus 1-2-3 can "talk to" your printer.
2 Your printer is connected to your computer, the power for your printer is turned on, and the printer is *online*, i.e., ready to receive data from your computer.
3 The paper is loaded into the printer and the paper is set so that the page crease is just above the printing head.

Let's now move on to the introduction to the printing of the graphs with Lotus 1-2-3.

INTRODUCTION TO THE PRINTING OF GRAPHS WITH LOTUS 1-2-3

Graphs can be printed with Lotus 1-2-3 through two methods:

1 With certain kinds of printers only, a *draft-quality* graph can be printed just by pressing the **[PrtSc]** key while the graph is displayed on your screen.
2 With all kinds of printers, a *presentation-quality* graph can be printed by using the Lotus 1-2-3 Print Graph program, which contains special software separate from the 1-2-3 system software. This method requires several steps to complete.

Let's take an introductory look at each of these methods.

Printing a Draft-Quality Graph

If you are using certain brands of printers (and Releases 2 or 2.01, DOS 2.0 or above), you can print a draft-quality graph very easily. Once you complete some brief setup (explained next), you just display the graph on your screen and then press the **[PrtSc]** key.

You can use this method if you are using one of these printers:

- Most IBM printers (any of several types); or
- Most Epson printers (any of several types).

Most IBM and Epson printers are specifically designed to be able to handle this convenient, simple method for printing graphs. Other printers usually require the use of the PrintGraph program (discussed later).

It is easy to find out whether your printer can print a graph in this way. Just follow the steps explained later in the lesson for setting up this method. When you press the **[PrtSc]** key, if your printer prints nothing (or worse, garbage), then this method cannot be used. (If your printer continues feeding paper, just turn the printer off for a moment and then turn it back on.) Don't worry, however. Just use the PrintGraph method explained later. It will take a little more time, but it will print out a better-quality graph.

This method requires some brief setup. When you load DOS, you will also load a special DOS graphics software. Then you will load the Lotus 1-2-3 software. We will see these steps shortly.

No matter what kind of printer you are using, you will also want at times to print a presentation-quality graph.

Printing a Presentation-Quality Graph

To print a presentation-quality graph requires the use of the special PrintGraph software that is contained on the separate Lotus PrintGraph disk. (If you have a PC that uses $3\frac{1}{2}$-inch diskettes, read the following note.) To use this software, you need to complete the steps listed next. Just read the steps for now to preview how the PrintGraph disk is used. This lesson provides detailed instructions later on how to complete these steps for the graphs that you have created.

1 After you have created the graph, you must save the graph in a special "picture" file. We learned how to do this in Lesson 14.

2 Then use the **/Quit** command to return to the Lotus Access System. Be sure to insert the Lotus System Disk in Drive A before using the **/Quit** command.

3 When you are back at the Lotus Access System screen, press **P** to specify that you want to access the special PrintGraph software.

4 Lotus will direct you to insert the separate Lotus PrintGraph disk. Do so, and then press **[Enter]** to load the PrintGraph software.

5 You will use a special PrintGraph menu to specify what kind of hardware you are using and what printing options you want.

6 Select which graphs you want to print.

7 Align the paper, and then press **Go** to begin printing.

Note for Users of $3\frac{1}{2}$-Inch Diskettes: Because $3\frac{1}{2}$-inch diskettes have more storage space for data than $5\frac{1}{4}$-inch diskettes, Lotus puts both the 1-2-3 software program *and* the PrintGraph program on the $3\frac{1}{2}$-inch Lotus System Disk. Therefore, if you are using a $3\frac{1}{2}$-inch disk system (such as an IBM Convertible PC), then you will not need to switch from the System Disk to a separate PrintGraph disk when the instructions direct you to do so. Therefore, ignore the references to the PrintGraph "disk" and the need for others to switch diskettes from time to time.

The Lotus PrintGraph software reads how to print the graphs from the special "picture" files that we had saved. That is why we had to save each graph in Lesson 14 not only as part of a worksheet but also under a separate picture file.

Let's begin by loading the software and files necessary to complete this lesson.

Loading the Necessary Software and Files

Let's first set up the use of the **[PrtSc]** key. (All readers should complete this setup in order to see whether your printer can handle this method of printing graphs.) Complete these familiar steps, if necessary:

1 Insert the DOS disk. Load DOS. Enter date and time.
2 At the A> prompt, type   **graphics**   and then press **[Enter]**.
(This step loads a special DOS graphics software that allows the **[PrtSc]** key to print a graph on certain types of printers.)
3 When the **A**> prompt appears again, insert the Lotus 1-2-3 System Disk. Then type   **lotus**   and press **[Enter]**.
4 When the Lotus Access System screen appears, press **[Enter]** to select the 1-2-3 software.
5 Insert *your data diskette* into the appropriate disk drive; it contains the worksheet file LN14.WK1 that you saved as part of Lesson 14. This file should contain the data from the completed Lesson 2; the abbreviations for the shampoo brand names; and the three graphs we created in Lesson 14.

ON YOUR OWN: Use the **/File Retrieve** command to retrieve the file **LN14.WK1** from your data diskette. Press **[Home]** if you have been using the set of data that begins at cell A1. (Press **[F5] A101 [Enter]** if you have been using the data that begins at cell A101, and remember to add 100 to any cell reference in the instructions.)

Let's now create a new *XY* graph to improve our understanding of the segmentation of the shampoo market.

XY GRAPH SEGMENTING THE SHAMPOO MARKET BY THE PRICE PER OUNCE AND THE A/S RATIO

To create and save this graph, we'll complete the following familiar steps:

1.1 Create the initial graph and view it;
1.2 Improve the appearance of the graph;
1.3 Name the graph; save the worksheet file; save the picture file of the graph.

1.1 Creating the Initial Graph to Segment the Shampoo Market by the Price per Ounce and the A/S Ratio for Each Brand

We have already seen how to create an *XY* graph and have already entered abbreviations for the shampoo brands. It should be getting easier, therefore, to create this new graph. Follow the step-by-step instructions only as closely as is necessary. The more you do on your own, the quicker you will learn. Press the following keys:

Description	Keys to Press
Display the 1-2-3 command menus:	/
Select the /Graph command:	G
(Before continuing, we want to reset all the settings from the previous graphs that we created in Lesson 14.)	
Select the Reset command:	R
Select the Graph menu choice:	G
Select the Type command:	T
(We are building a new XY graph. The X-axis, or horizontal axis, will display each brand's A/S ratio and the Y-axis, or vertical axis, will display each brand's retail price per ounce.)	
Select the XY menu choice:	X
Select the X menu choice to indicate that we want to specify the data for the *X*-axis:	X
(Let's put the A/S Ratio for each shampoo brand on the X-axis. So, we need to paint the range of values in column O for each brand. Let's again leave out "Others.")	
Move the cell pointer to O7:	**(Use the [Tab] and the arrow keys.)**
Anchor O7 and then paint the range O7..O17 (leaving out "Others"):	.
	[down*10]
Confirm the range O7..O17 as the *X*-axis range:	**[Enter]**
Select the A menu choice to specify the data for the *Y*-axis:	A
(Let's put the Average Retail Price per Ounce for each brand on the Y-axis. So, we need to paint the range of values in column K for each brand. Let's again leave out "Others.")	
Move the cell pointer to K7:	**(Use the [Tab] and the arrow keys.)**
Anchor K7 and then paint the range K7..K17 (leaving out "Others"):	.
	[down*10]

Description	Keys to Press
Confirm the range K7..K17 as the *Y*-axis data range:	**[Enter]**
Select the View command:	**V**

Let's now improve the appearance and clarity of the graph.

1.2 Improving the Appearance of the Graph

Notice that, just like with our first *XY* graph, this graph contains lines that connect squares. Those squares represent shampoo brands, but we don't know which branch each square represents. Let's make the graph clearer. We'll first replace the squares with brand abbreviations. Press the following keys:

Description	Keys to Press
Press any key to return to the Graph menu:	**[Space]**
Select the Options command:	**O**
(We first need to label the data in the graph, so that we know what each square, or data point, represents.)	
Select the Data-Labels menu choice:	**D**
(Remember that with an XY graph, we use only the X or A range choices.)	
Select the A menu choice:	**A**
(We now want to paint the range of brand name abbreviations, excluding "Others.")	
Move the cell pointer to C7:	**(Use the arrow keys.)**
Anchor C7 and paint the range C7..C17:	**.**
	[End]
	[down]
	[up]
Confirm the range C7..C17:	**[Enter]**
(1-2-3 can place the data-labels you just specified in a variety of places. Let's center the label over each data point.)	
Select the Center menu choice:	**C**
Select the Quit menu choice to return to the Options menu:	**Q**
Select the Quit menu choice once more to return to Graph menu:	**Q**
Select the View command:	**V**

Description	Keys to Press
(Just as with the first XY graph, the brand name abbreviations now appear, but the lines and symbols on the graph still remain. These lines and symbols are inappropriate for our purposes here, so let's remove them.)	
Press any key to return to the Graph command:	**[Space]**
Select the Options command:	**O**
(The Options Format menu choice deals with lines and symbols on the graph. If you like, press [right] and see a brief explanation of the Format menu choice on the second menu line.)	
Select the Format menu choice:	**F**
Select the Graph menu choice to indicate that we want to set the format for the entire graph:	**G**
(We are now given a choice of whether we want lines, symbols, both, or neither. We want neither.)	
Select the menu choice Neither:	**N**
Select the Quit menu choice to return to the Options menu:	**Q**
Select the Quit menu choice to return to the Graph menu:	**Q**
Select the View command:	**V**

Observation: The graph now looks much better. Notice that 1-2-3 has automatically scaled both the *X*-axis and the *Y*-axis. These scales seem about right. So, we don't want to set the scales manually, but we do want to format the numbers on the scales. We also want to add titles to the graph.

Let's move on to format the numbers on the *X*- and *Y*-axes. Then we will add titles. Press the following keys:

Description	Keys to Press
Press any key to return to the Graph menu:	**[Space]**
Select the Options command:	**O**
Select the Scale menu choice:	**S**
(Let's now set the format for the numbers on the X-axis. We will put these numbers in percent format, with 0 decimal places.)	
Select the X Scale menu choice:	**X**
Select the Format menu choice:	**F**
Select the Percent menu choice:	**P**
Use 0 decimal places and confirm:	**0 [Enter]**

Description	Keys to Press
Select the Quit menu choice to return to the Options menu:	**Q**
(Let's now set the format for the numbers on the Y-axis. We will also put these numbers in percent format, with 0 decimal places.)	
Select the Scale menu choice:	**S**
Select the Y Scale menu choice:	**Y**
Select the Format menu choice:	**F**
Select the Percent menu choice:	**P**
Use 0 decimal places and confirm:	**0 [Enter]**
(Now let's add titles to the graph.)	
Select the Quit menu choice to return to the Options menu:	**Q**
Select the Titles menu choice:	**T**
Select the First menu choice:	**F**
Type in the title (use the Caps Lock key) and confirm:	**A/S VS. PRICE/OZ. [Enter]**
Select the Titles menu choice again:	**T**
Select the Second menu choice:	**S**
Type in the subtitle (use all small letters and parentheses) and confirm (take Caps Lock key off):	**(for leading shampoo brands) [Enter]**
(Let's now put titles on the axes themselves. These will be in addition to the titles for the overall graph.)	
Select the Titles menu choice again:	**T**
Select the *X*-Axis menu choice:	**X**
Type in the *X*-Axis title and confirm:	**A/S Ratio [Enter]**
Select the Titles menu choice again:	**T**
Select the *Y*-Axis menu choice:	**Y**
Type in the *Y*-Axis title and confirm:	**Retail Price per Ounce [Enter]**
Select the Quit men choice to return to the Graph menu:	**Q**
Select the View command to see what you have now:	**V**

Good. We have now completed a new *XY* graph that will help us to analyze how the shampoo market could be segmented by the A/S ratio and the retail price per ounce. A copy of the graph is printed below:

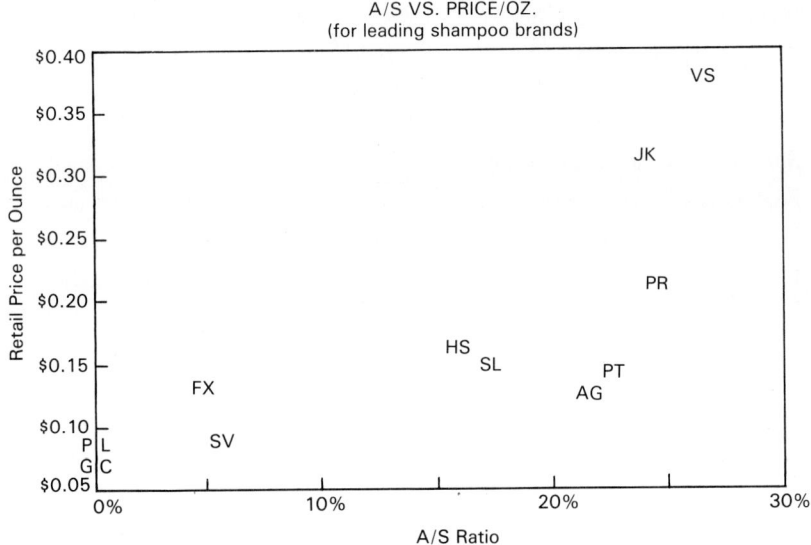

A/S VS. PRICE/OZ.
(for leading shampoo brands)

Observation: This exercise once again shows how it can take a fair amount of time to specify all the details of the graph. However, the graph now clearly shows each brand of shampoo according to its A/S ratio and retail price per ounce.

Before we move on to printing, we must complete the three steps needed to save the graph:

1 Name the graph.
2 Save the worksheet containing the graph.
3 Save a "picture" of the graph for later printing.

1.3 Name the Graph; Save the Worksheet File; Save a Picture File

ON YOUR OWN: First, name the file. Press **any key** to return to the Graph menu. Select the **Name Create** command. Type in the name: **ADPRICE**. Press **[Enter]** to confirm the name. Now that the graph has been named, we need to save it in a worksheet file. This worksheet will contain not only the new *XY* graph but also the three graphs that we completed in Lesson 14 because we retrieved the file LN14.WK1 at the beginning of Lesson 15 to use in creating this new graph. To distinguish this new worksheet file (containing our new *XY* graph), let's give it a new name, LN15, indicating that it belongs to Lesson 15. (The file LN14.WK1 will also remain on your data diskette.)

ON YOUR OWN: If necessary, press the **[Esc]** key as many times as necessary to clear completely the **/Graph** command menu. Then press the **[Home]** key to return to cell A1. Use just the **/File Save** command to resave this worksheet file under the name: **LN15.** The worksheet file now contains the three graphs from Lesson 14 (the MKTSHARE, ADSHARE, and ADMKT graphs) and the new *XY* graph from Lesson 15 (ADPRICE). Use the **/Graph Name Use** command to check that all four of these graphs are part of the worksheet. Then press the **[Esc]** key as many times as necessary to return to the worksheet.

Let's now save a "picture" of the graph on file for later printing.

ON YOUR OWN: Select the **/Graph** command, and then the **Save** command. Type in the picture file name: **ADPRICE.** Press **[Enter]** to confirm the name. Press **Quit** to return to the worksheet.

Note: Once again we have minimized the number of names we need to re-member by using "ADPRICE" both to "name" the graph and to save the "picture" file. (Remember that the file LESSON15.WKS on the Suave Data Diskette also contains the completed ADPRICE graph.)

Now we're ready to learn how to print these graphs.

THE PRINTING OF GRAPHS

The remainder of this lesson will be devoted to providing instructions on how to print the four graphs that we have already created. These instructions will be divided into the following sections:

A Printing a draft-quality graph with the **[PrtSc]** key.
B Printing a presentation-quality graph with PrintGraph:
  1 Loading the PrintGraph software.
  2 Specifying the hardware settings.
  3 Specifying certain printing options.
  4 Selecting what graphs (or images) are to be printed.
  5 Aligning the page and pressing **Go** to begin printing.

In addition, Lesson 15 will provide these special addenda:

Addendum 1:   An optional section on using the **/System** command with Releases 2.01 and 2 for loading the PrintGraph software.
Addendum 2:   A section on using PrintGraph with a PC that has only one disk drive.
Addendum 3:   A section for Release 1A users on how to follow these instructions while using the Release 1A PrintGraph software.

Release 1A Users: The instructions for this section are based on Release 2.01 of Lotus 1-2-3. The PrintGraph menu for Release 2.01 is different from the PrintGraph menu for Release 1A. Read Addendum 3 before continuing with these instructions.

A. Printing a Draft-Quality Graph with the [PrtSc] Key

Printing a graph with the **[PrtSc]** key is convenient and quick. However, as noted in the introduction to printing, you need to remember the following:

1 Only certain brands of printers can print a graph using this **[PrtSc]** method (most IBM and Epson printers). All printers can work with the PrintGraph method that we will use later.
2 The DOS "graphics" software must be loaded before you load Lotus and the worksheet file. Remember when you typed "graphics" at the DOS A> prompt? If not, review the steps that we described in the introduction to printing.
3 This method will print only a draft-quality graph. The PrintGraph method will print a presentation-quality graph.
4 Try this method. If your printer cannot use this method, your printer will simply not print the graph when you press the **[PrtSc]** key. That will not cause any harm. [The paper is likely to move up one sheet. If it continues, just turn the printer off for a moment and then turn it back on.]

Note: This method uses a separate DOS graphics software. You should have loaded this software at the beginning of the lesson, as described earlier. If for some reason you did not load the DOS graphics software at the beginning of the lesson, do so now. Just follow the instructions at the beginning of this lesson in the section "Loading the Necessary Software and Files." Remember to retrieve the worksheet file, LN14.WK1, and then return to these instructions.

The reason that this method can work with only certain printers is that printing graphs requires a lot of complex information to be transmitted from the PC to the printer using specific codes. Printers are designed to read different codes. Only certain printers (such as IBM and Epson) are capable of using DOS graphics software. When we use the more powerful PrintGraph software, we will be able to specify which type of printer we are using, from a long list of different brands of printers. The PrintGraph program will then use whatever codes are appropriate for your printer to transmit the information about the graph to your printer.

Well, let's try this method. First, be sure that DOS, the DOS graphics software, Lotus, and the worksheet file you just saved, LSN15.WK1, are all loaded into the PC. Then press the following keys:

Description	Keys to Press
Clear 1-2-3 command menus:	**[Esc] as many times as is necessary.**
(This step will ensure that we are all at the same point in the instructions.)	
Display the 1-2-3 command menus:	/
Select the /Graph command:	**G**
Select the Name command:	**N**
Select the Use menu choice:	**U**

Description	*Keys to Press*

(Note: As we saw in Lesson 14, the /Graph Name Use command allows us to revisit graphs that we had already created.)
(You should see four graph names listed: ADMKT, ADPRICE, ADSHARE, and MKTSHARE. Let's print the graph that we most-recently created: ADPRICE.)

Select the ADPRICE graph: **(Move the cursor to the ADPRICE choice.)**

Confirm that we want to display the ADPRICE graph: **[Enter]**

(Good. The ADPRICE graph should now be displayed.)
(Before we actually begin printing, again be sure that your printer is:
1 Connected to your PC;
2 Turned on;
3 Online; and
4 Set so that the page crease is just above the printing head.)

Commence printing. Hold the [Shift] key down while
you press the [PrtSc] key: **[PrtSc]**

(This should take about a minute. If you do not get a print of the graph, don't worry. Just turn off the printer for a second to stop the paper from feeding. Then turn the printer back on and put it online. Then move on to the PrintGraph sections.)

Observation: This method can be particularly convenient. Unfortunately, this method cannot always be used. However, the PrintGraph method can always be used and is the method that delivers a presentation quality of the graph. Let's see how.

B. Printing a Presentation-Quality Graph with PrintGraph

Printing a presentation-quality graph with PrintGraph may seem complicated at first, but with a little practice, it will become much easier.

B.1. Loading the PrintGraph Software

There are two methods for loading PrintGraph software:

1 We can return to the Lotus Access System using **/Quit** and select PrintGraph. This method can be used with Release 2.01, Release 2, or Release 1A of Lotus 1-2-3.
2 We can return to the PrintGraph program as a "subprocess" under 1-2-3 using the **/System** menu choice. This method is not available with Release 1A.

The instructions use the first method. Addendum 1 discusses the second method.
We will be using the Lotus PrintGraph disk. Be sure you have it available. Then press the following keys:

Description	Keys to Press

Clear the ADPRICE graph from the screen by pressing any key: **[Space]**

Escape from the Graph command menu: **[Esc]**

*(You should now see the first line of 1-2-3 command menus. We want to use the /Quit
command to return to the Lotus Access System.)*

*(Note: At this point, if you have the data diskette in Drive A and you are not using a
hard disk system, be sure to remove the data diskette from Drive A and insert the Lotus
System Disk.)*

Select the /Quit command: **Q**

*(1-2-3 will ask us whether we really want to end the 1-2-3 session. This step will clear
the 1-2-3 program from the PC memory cells. We do want to.)*

Indicate that we do want to leave 1-2-3 and return
to the Lotus Access System screen: **Y**

(The Lotus Access System screen will now be displayed.)

*(This time we want to choose the PrintGraph software—which is a separate software
program from the 1-2-3 program.)*

Choose the PrintGraph software: **P**

*(Lotus will direct us to insert the PrintGraph disk in Drive A. So, remove the 1-2-3
System disk and insert the PrintGraph disk.)*

Press [Enter] as directed: **[Enter]**

Good. You should now see the following screen:

```
Copyright 1986 Lotus Development Corp.  All Rights Reserved. Release 2.01  MENU
-------------------------------------------------------------------------------
Select graphs for printing
Image-Select  Settings  Go  Align  Page  Exit
===============================================================================
    GRAPH     IMAGE OPTIONS                      HARDWARE SETUP
    IMAGES    Size               Range Colors    Graphs Directory:
    SELECTED   Top      .395     X                 A:\
               Left     .750     A               Fonts Directory:
               Width   6.500     B                 A:\
               Height  4.691     C               Interface:
               Rotate   .000     D                 Parallel 1
                                 E               Printer Type:
               Font              F
               1  BLOCK1                         Paper Size
               2  BLOCK1                           Width      8.500
                                                   Length    11.000

                                                ACTION OPTIONS
                                                Pause: No    Eject: No
```

This screen looks complicated and technical. Let's see if we can make it simpler.

We are now using the Lotus *PrintGraph* software. (Remember, we "Quit" the *Lotus 1-2-3 Program*, inserted the PrintGraph disk, and chose the PrintGraph software.) This screen deals with how to print graphs using the PrintGraph software.

There are two general parts to the screen:

1 There is a special command menu system for the PrintGraph software. We will use the PrintGraph command menu to specify what hardware we are using, to indicate how the graph should look, and to select what graphs to print.
2 Below the command menu is a summary of the: "GRAPH IMAGES SELECTED," "IMAGE OPTIONS," "HARDWARE SETUP," and "ACTION OPTIONS" specified.

Lotus assumes that we want to use certain hardware setups and printing options *unless we specify otherwise*. The specifications that Lotus assumes are listed on your screen. For example, look under "HARDWARE SETUP" at "Paper Size." Lotus assumes that we are using $8\frac{1}{2}$-inch by 11-inch paper. We could change that specification if we were using another size of paper.

We will use most of the specifications that Lotus assumes. However, we will change a few of them. We will also list the graphs we want printed ("GRAPH IMAGES SELECTED"). We will use the PrintGraph command menu to make these changes and selections. In each instance, our specific choices will then be summarized on the screen.

We are now ready to use the PrintGraph command menu to:

• Specify the hardware settings;
• Specify certain printing options;
• Select what graphs we want to print; and
• Align the paper and then begin printing by pressing "Go."

Release 1A Users:　　Please look at Addendum 3.

B.2. Specifying the Hardware Settings

There are several possible questions that we could answer in specifying what hardware we are using. For our purposes in Lesson 15, we really need to answer only two questions:

1 What disk drive contains your data diskette on which the "picture" files were saved?
2 What kind of printer are you using?

Answer these questions for your particular hardware by pressing the following keys and making the appropriate selections for your hardware:

Description　　　　　　　　　　　　　　　　　　　　　　　　　*Keys to Press*

(The "Settings" command deals with both hardware questions and printing options.)

Select the Settings command:　　　　　　　　　　　　**S**

Description	*Keys to Press*

(A new menu will now be displayed. The "Hardware" menu choice allows you to specify the HARDWARE SETUP.)

Select the Hardware menu choice: **H**

Specifying the Disk Drive that Contains the Data Diskette

Observation: Look under HARDWARE SETUP. Note that Lotus assumes that the diskette that contains the data and graphs is in disk drive A. That is, Lotus assumes:

Graphs Directory:
**A: **

If you are using a PC with either one disk drive or with a hard disk, you will want to keep that specification (see Addendum 2). So, you don't have to do anything.

However, if you are using a PC with two disk drives, it will be much easier if you can keep the PrintGraph in drive A and load the data diskette in drive B.

ON YOUR OWN: If you are using a PC with two disk drives, complete the following steps:

1 Select the "Graphs-Directory" menu choice.
2 When Lotus directs you to "Enter directory containing picture files," type **b:** .
3 Put the data diskette in Drive B.
4 Press **[Enter]** to confirm that the data diskette that contains our picture files will be in Drive B.

Note: If you followed these steps, the screen will now change to show, under HARDWARE SETUP:

Graphs Directory:
**B: **

Let's now specify what type of printer we are using.

Specifying the Printer

Observation: Look under HARDWARE SETUP again. Lotus might or might not have made an assumption about your "Printer Type," depending on what type of printer you specified when you used the "Install" program to set the drives for your Lotus disks.

ON YOUR OWN: If a "Printer Type" is not listed, or if you wish to change the listing, complete the following steps:

1 Select the "Printer" menu choice.
2 When the choices of "Type of Graphic Output" are listed, follow the directions to specify your choice.

Note: If you are using a printer that includes a choice of "low-density" or "high-density," then you have a choice of the clarity and resolution of the graph to be printed. Low-density printing is not as bold and clear, but the printing is completed relatively quickly. High-density printing is much clearer, but it takes considerably more time. We suggest that, for now, you select low-density printing.

Most likely, the assumptions that Lotus listed, for "Fonts Directory," "Interface," and "Paper Size" are all correct. Lotus has made these assumptions based upon the hardware that you specified when you used the Install program. (The Fonts Directory simply refers to the disk drive that contains the PrintGraph disk. If you are using a PC with one or two disk drives, **A**: will be listed. If you are using a PC with a hard disk, then **C**: will be listed.)

Let's move on to specify the printing options.

B.3. Specifying the Printing or "Image" Options

Lotus allows us to specify exactly how the graph should be printed according to three options:

1 Size of the graph;
2 The "Fonts"—or type or print—used; and
3 The colors used (if you have a color printer).

We could accept the standard printing specifications that Lotus currently lists. Let's change just the size of the graph, which is the easiest option to specify. Press the following keys:

Description	*Keys to Press*
Return to the Settings command menu (which includes the Image, Hardware, Action, Save, Reset, and Quit choices):	**Q**
Select the Image menu choice:	**I**
(This menu choice allows us to specify the printing options.) *(Our three options should now appear. We can change the (1) size; (2) fonts; and (3) range colors. Let's just change the size of the graph.)*	
Select the Size menu choice:	**S**

Description	Keys to Press

(Lotus assumes the settings for a graph that will cover Half *of an 8½-by-11 inch page.* [*Release 1A Users:8-by-11 inch*] *The measurements currently displayed by "Top, Left, Width, Height, Rotate" refer to a half-page graph.)*
(Let's specify a Full-page graph.)

Select the Full menu choice: **F**

Observation: Notice how the numbers under IMAGE OPTIONS SIZE have changed. The numbers now refer to the measurements for a graph that will cover a full 8½-by-11-inch page.

As mentioned, "Fonts" refers to the type of print and "Range Colors" refer to your choice if you are using a color printer. We suggest that you experiment with these more-sophisticated options when you become more comfortable with Lotus PrintGraph.

Let's now select the graphs that we want to print.

B.4. Selecting the Graphs, or "Images," to Print

Let's print all four graphs that we created and saved. To see how we select these graphs or images to be printed, press the following keys:

Description	Keys to Press

Return to the first PrintGraph command menu (which
   contains the choices "Image-Select, Settings, Go,
   Align, Page, Exit"):   **Q Q Q**
     (The Image-Select command allows us to list the graphs we want to print.)
Select the Image-Select command: **I**

Observation: Notice that all four graphs are listed: ADMKT, ADPRICE, AD-SHARE, MKTSHARE. Let's specify that we want to print all four graphs.

ON YOUR OWN: Follow the steps to specify that all four graphs should be printed:

   1 Press the **[Space]** bar to mark **ADMKT** with a # sign, designating **ADMKT** as a graph to be printed.
   2 Press the **[down]** key to move to **ADPRICE**. Press the **[Space]** bar to mark **ADPRICE** (note the # sign).
   3 Press the **[down]** key to move to **ADSHARE**. Press the **[Space]** bar to mark **ADSHARE** (note the # sign).

4 Press the **[down]** key to move to **MKTSHARE**. Press the **[Space]** bar to mark **MKTSHARE** (note the # sign).

5 Press the **[Return]** key to confirm our selections and to return to the command menu.

Observation: Note that the four graphs are now listed below GRAPH IMAGES SELECTED. This listing means that all four graphs will be printed when we press "Go." All we have to do now is to align the paper and press Go.

B.5. Aligning the Paper and Pressing Go

Once again, be sure that your printer is:

1 Connected to your computer;
2 Turned on; and
3 Online

To prepare to begin printing, press the following keys:

Description	Keys to Press

(The Align menu choice will align the "paper settings" specifications in the PrintGraph program with the actual setting on your printer.)

Select the Align menu choice:	**A**

(The Go menu choice will print all the graph images that you selected, one immediately following the other in the order that you selected them.)

Select the Go menu choice:	**G**

(These four graphs will probably take several minutes to print.)
(The Page menu choice advances the paper to the top of the next page when done. This makes it easier to remove the pages of printed graphs.)

Select the Page menu choice:	**P**

(May need to hit "P" twice. Tear off the printed graphs.)
(We are done with the PrintGraph software. Let's now see how to return to the 1-2-3 System software.)

Select the Exit menu choice:	**E**

(Lotus will ask whether we really want to leave the PrintGraph session.)

Select the Yes menu choice to exit PrintGraph:	**Y**

(Lotus will return us to the Lotus Access System.)
(If you are using a two-disk drive system, remove the PrintGraph disk and load the 1-2-3 System disk.)

Choose the 1-2-3 System software:	**1**

(That's it! You are now back in Lotus 1-2-3.)

This is the end of the main part of the lesson. (Feel free to check your graphs with those in LESSON15.WKS on the Suave Data Diskette.)

The following three sections form an addendum to the lesson:

Addendum 1:   Using the /**System** command with Release 2.01 or Release 2.
Addendum 2:   Using PrintGraph with a PC that has only one disk drive.
Addendum 3:   Using PrintGraph with Release 1A.

A review section is provided after the three addenda.

Addendum 1: Using the /System Command with Release 2.01 (or Release 2)

Release 2.01 (or Release 2) allows you to run the PrintGraph software while keeping the 1-2-3 System software and your worksheet in memory.

The method requires extra memory because DOS, the 1-2-3 System software, your worksheet files, and the PrintGraph software all will be loaded in the computer at once. Specifically, a PC with 256 K memory cannot handle this method. You should consider having 512K memory to use this method.

This system, if there is sufficient memory to use it, can save some steps both in loading the PrintGraph software and in exiting from PrintGraph.

To load PrintGraph through this method, you should complete these steps:

1 Invoke the 1-2-3 command menus with /.
2 Select the System menu choice. 1-2-3 will remain in memory, as will DOS and your worksheet files. However, the PC will reinvoke DOS and the A> prompt will appear.
3 At the A> prompt, remove the 1-2-3 System disk (if you are using a disk drive system) and insert the PrintGraph disk.
4 Then type in **PGRAPH** and press **[Enter]**.

Note: Using this method, you did not have to Quit 1-2-3 first. You did not even have to save the current worksheet file because the data on that file has been left in memory as well until you return to 1-2-3.

This method also saves some time when you return to 1-2-3. To exit from PrintGraph, you follow these steps when you are in the PrintGraph menu:

1 Select the **Exit** menu choice.
2 Select the **Yes** menu choice to leave PrintGraph.
3 The DOS A> prompt will appear. Type in **exit** and press **[Enter]**. You will now be back directly in 1-2-3 exactly where you left!

Note: While this method is somewhat faster, it can be more confusing because Lotus will no longer be flashing directions on the screen at each step of the process. If you are going to use this method, be sure you have enough memory. Also, be sure you remember what to type and enter each time the DOS A> prompt appears.

Observation: As discussed in Lesson 5, the **/System** command can also be used at any time instead of the **/Quit** command to temporarily leave 1-2-3 and execute DOS commands. (However, no DOS command that loads another program into memory, such as "graphics" or "Set Clock," can be used, or you will not be able to return to 1-2-3.) To return to 1-2-3, type **exit** at the DOS prompt. You will return to exactly where you left 1-2-3. This use of the **/System** command does *not* require additional memory.

Addendum 2: Using PrintGraph with a PC that Has Only One Disk Drive (and No Hard Disk)

Using PrintGraph with a PC that has only one disk drive (and no hard disk) is, in most ways, exactly the same as using a PC with two disk drives.

There is, however, one major difference. It will become necessary for you to switch diskettes frequently—from the 1-2-3 System Disk to the PrintGraph disk to your data diskette. If the wrong disk is loaded, the PC will let you know that the file or commands cannot be read. However, you will have to figure out which disk or diskette should be loaded. It probably will be clear to you which disk should be loaded, depending upon what task Lotus needs to complete at that moment.

Note: If you are using a PC with two disk drives, be sure to specify that Lotus should read the "picture files" from the B drive. Then insert the data diskette that contains the picture files into the B drive. Use the A drive for the System disk and the PrintGraph disk. This will save you a lot of steps in switching disks.

Addendum 3: Using PrintGraph with Release 1A

If you are using Release 1A with a newer printer, you should select whatever man-ufacturer and type of printer listed on the PrintGraph menu that comes closest to the type of printer you are actually using. (For example, if you are using an IBM ProPrinter, select the IBM Graphics Printer that is listed on the Release 1A menu.)

Differences in the Release 1A PrintGraph Menu

There are several differences between the Release 1A PrintGraph menu and the Release 2.01 PrintGraph menu. These differences involve the command systems and the screen layout. The layout of the initial Release 1A screen is shown next:

```
┌────────────────────────────────────────────────────────────────────┐
│  Copyright 1982, 1983 Lotus Development Corp.  All Rights Reserved.      MENU │
│  ------------------------------------------------------------------------ │
│  Select  Options  Go  Configure  Align  Page  Quit                   │
│  Select pictures                                                     │
│  ════════════════════════════════════════════════════════════════════  │
│   SELECTED GRAPHS    COLORS              SIZE    HALF         DIRECTORIES │
│                                                                      │
│                      Grid:      Black    Left Margin:    .750   Pictures │
│                      A Range:   Black    Top Margin:     .395   B:\      │
│                      B Range:   Black    Width:         6.500   Fonts    │
│                      C Range:   Black    Height:        4.691   A:\      │
│                      D Range:   Black    Rotation:       .000            │
│                      E Range:   Black                           GRAPHICS DEVICE │
│                      F Range:   Black    MODES                           │
│                                                                Epson FX80/1 │
│                      FONTS               Eject: No             Parallel  │
│                                          Pause: No                      │
│                      1: BLOCK1                                 PAGE SIZE │
│                      2: BLOCK1                                           │
│                                                               Length   11.000 │
│                                                               Width     8.000 │
└────────────────────────────────────────────────────────────────────┘
```

The command menus differ from Release 2.01 primarily as follows:

1 Instead of using the command "Settings Hardware," Release 1A uses the command "Configure" for specifying the hardware (under the headings "Directories" and "Graph Device" on screen).

2 Instead of using the command "Settings Options," Release 1A uses the command "Options" to set the optional printing specifications (under "Size" on screen).

3 Instead of using the command "Image-Select," Release 1A uses the command "Select" to specify which graphs should be printed (under "Selected Graphs" on screen).

4 Instead of assuming that the picture files are in Drive A, Release 1A assumes they are in the Drive B unless specified otherwise.

If you keep these and the other minor differences in mind, you should be able to follow the instructions in Lesson 15 and figure out the keystrokes that you should press.

Reviewing What We Learned in Lesson 15

Lesson 15 provided us practice in creating an XY graph. More important, it provided instructions on how to print graphs.

Using the [PrtSc] Key

You may be able to print a draft-quality graph just by pressing the **[PrtSc]** key while the graph is displayed on your screen. To use this method you must load a special DOS graphics software. Therefore, when you are loading DOS and graphics, follow these steps:

1 Insert the DOS disk. Load DOS. Enter date and time.
2 At the A> prompt, type **graphics** and press **[Enter]**. This step loads the special DOS graphics software for using the **[PrtSc]** key.
3 When the A> prompt appears again, insert the Lotus 1-2-3 system disk. Then type **lotus** and press **[Enter]**.
4 When the Lotus Access System appears, press **[Enter]** to select the 1-2-3 software.

If your printer cannot use this method, don't worry. You can always use the Lotus PrintGraph program.

Using the PrintGraph Program

To print a presentation-quality graph on any printer, follow these steps:

1 After you have created the graph, you must save the graph in a special "picture" file. We learned how to do this in Lesson 14.
2 Then use the **/Quit** command to return to the Lotus Access System. Be sure to insert the Lotus System Disk in Drive A before using the **/Quit** command.
3 When you are back at the Lotus Access System screen, press **P** to specify that you want to access the special PrintGraph software.
4 Lotus will direct you to insert the separate Lotus PrintGraph disk. Do so, and then press **[Enter]** to load the PrintGraph software.
5 Specify which disk drive contains the diskette on which the "picture" files are saved.
6 Specify which type of printer you are using from a range of choices provided by Lotus 1-2-3.
7 Specify the options for how the graph should be printed (for example, full page or half page).
8 Select which graphs you want to print.
9 Align the paper.
10 Press **Go** to begin the printing.

In the next lesson, we will learn how to create a bar graph.

MANAGEMENT DISCUSSION

1 What does this *XY* graph tell you about segmentation of the shampoo market?

This graph is extremely useful for analyzing segmentation of the shampoo market. It demonstrates quite visibly that the shampoo market can be segmented into two types of brands: (1) those that have a relatively low A/S ratio and a relatively low price per ounce; (2) those that have a relatively high A/S ratio and a relatively high retail price per ounce. The first type of brand is targeted toward consumers who are primarily interested in price. The second type of brand is targeted toward consumers who are primarily interested in the performance (perceived or actual) of shampoo.

2 How else might you segment the market?

The market might be segmented by the type of shampoo, such as dandruff shampoo, conditioning shampoo, or all-purpose shampoo. Or, markets are sometimes segmented by the type of retail stores that sell the product, e.g., supermarket, drugstore, etc. Other methods were shown in Lessons 3 and 4: demographics and psychographics. It is the manager's job to decide what are the most important factors that determine the structure of the market, and then to segment the market based on those factors.

3 What does the *XY* graph tell you about Suave's positioning in the market?

This graph clearly demonstrates that Suave is positioned to appeal to price-sensitive consumers and retailers who want to carry a branded, low-price shampoo. Suave competes primarily against generic and private label brands and the Flex brand. It is not the lowest-priced brand. Therefore, one could argue that it is positioned to provide a perceived assurance of quality that generic and private label brands might not provide, but still at a relatively low price per ounce.

4 What other factors should you consider in analyzing Suave's positioning in the market?

Our analysis has not yet considered, for example, that Helene Curtis markets many different types of shampoo under the Suave name: dandruff shampoo, conditioning shampoo, herbal shampoo, and baby shampoo. In this way, Helene Curtis positions the Suave brand to provide the assurance of quality for price-sensitive consumers—no matter what type of shampoo they might be interested in buying. Other factors could be the level of perceived quality or the average package size sold.

LESSON 16	GRAPHICS: DEMOGRAPHIC CHARACTERISTICS OF SUAVE CONSUMERS

OVERVIEW

COMPUTER INSTRUCTIONS

Lesson 16 is a relatively brief lesson that shows how to create and save a bar graph.

MANAGEMENT ISSUES

This bar graph is intended to help communicate some of the demographic information about consumers that was derived in Lesson 3. This particular graph deals with income levels among Suave consumers. You should consider whether this type of graph would be useful in making a presentation about consumer segmentation and the targeting of advertising.

MANAGEMENT DISCUSSION QUESTIONS

1 How is a bar graph useful?
2 Assess the usefulness of this particular bar graph.
3 What other demographic characteristics would be most useful to graph?

CASE

The Suave team decided to create a bar graph to illustrate the relationships between categories of consumer household income and the relative amount of Suave purchased by consumers in each category. The team recognized that many bar graphs could be created based on both the demographics and other data. They had to decide how helpful these bar graphs would be in making their presentation to Bob Thomas.

COMPUTER INSTRUCTIONS

Overview of Computer Instructions for Lesson 16

Lesson 16 is a relatively brief lesson. It provides instructions on how to create a bar graph. We will use the data that we compiled in Lesson 3 to create this bar graph. Therefore, if you completed Lesson 3 as the instructions directed, you will begin this lesson by retrieving the worksheet file LN3.WK1 from your data diskette. As we always do in creating graphs, we will: (1) Create the initial graph and view it; (2) Improve the appearance of the graph; (3) Name the graph; (4) Save the worksheet; and (5) Save a "picture" of the graph.

Lesson 16 also explains how, if you make a mistake, you can delete a graph name from a worksheet file and erase a picture file.

Loading the Necessary Software and Files

First, we need to load DOS and Lotus 1-2-3. If you found that your printer can print a draft quality graph when you press the **[PrtSc]** key, then you should also load the DOS graphics software at the A> prompt. So, complete these familiar steps, if necessary:

1 Load DOS. Enter date and time.
2 If your printer can use it, load the DOS graphics software. (Refer to Lesson 15 if you need to review this step.)
3 Load the Lotus Access System.
4 Load the 1-2-3 software program.

Now we need to retrieve the worksheet file that contains the indexes we calculated in Lesson 3.

ON YOUR OWN: If you completed Lesson 3 as the instructions directed, insert your data diskette into the appropriate disk drive. Use the **/File Retrieve** command to load the file **LN03.WK1**.

If you wish, you may alternatively retrieve the worksheet file **LESSON03.WKS** from the Suave Data Diskette. This file contains, beginning at cell **A101**, the completed worksheet for Lesson 3. If you use this worksheet file to create the bar graph, remember to add 100 to any cell references in the Lesson 16 computer instructions.

Let's move on and create our first bar graph.

BAR GRAPH SEGMENTING SUAVE CONSUMERS BY HOUSEHOLD INCOME

We will follow these familiar general steps:

1.1 Create the initial graph and view it;
1.2 Improve the appearance and clarity of the graph;
1.3 Name the graph; save the worksheet file; save the picture file of the graph.

1.1 Creating the Initial Graph to Segment Suave Consumers by Household Income

Building a bar graph is similar to building an *XY* graph. In both cases, we use the X menu choice to specify what data or labels go on the *X*-axis. However, whereas we use only the A range in *XY* graphs to specify data for the *Y*-axis, with bar graphs we can specify up to six ranges of data for the *Y*-axis, using the A, B, C, D, E, and F ranges. To keep Lesson 16 simple we will specify only one set of data using just the A range. In Lesson 18, we will use the A, B, and C ranges for a "stacked" bar graph.

Let's see how to create a bar graph. Follow the step-by-step instructions only as closely as is necessary. Press the following keys:

Description	*Keys to Press*
Display the 1-2-3 command menus:	/
Select the /Graph command:	**G**
(Since we have not created any graphs in this worksheet before, we do not have to reset any settings.)	
Select the Type command:	**T**
(We are building a bar graph. The X-axis or horizontal axis will display the five categories of Household Income shown in Table 2, and the Y-axis, or vertical axis, will display the index in Column H corresponding to each of these categories.)	
Select the Bar menu choice:	**B**
(We now need to specify the data for each of the axes.)	
Select the X menu choice to indicate that we want to specify the data for the *X*-axis:	**X**
(Let's put the Household Income categories on the X-axis. So, we need to paint the categories listed in the range A10..A14.)	
Move the cell pointer to A10:	**(Use [End] [down] and the arrow keys.)**
Anchor A10 and then paint the range A10..A14:	**.** **[End] [down]**
Confirm the range A10..A14 as the *X*-axis range:	**[Enter]**
(We now need to specify the data for the Y-axis. We will specify only one set of data for the Y-axis and, therefore, use only the A range.)	
Select the A menu choice to specify the data for the *Y*-axis:	**A**
(Let's put the values from the third index in Column H on the Y-axis)	
Move the cell pointer to H10:	**(Use the arrow keys.)**
Anchor H10 and then paint the range H10..H14:	**.** **[End] [down]**
Confirm the range H10..H14 as the *Y*-axis data range:	**[Enter]**
Select the View command:	**V**
(You should see a bar graph that still needs some work.)	

Let's now improve the appearance of the graph.

1.2 Improving the Appearance of the Graph

Let's first add some titles for the graph and for each of the axes. These titles will help us to remember what the bars represent. We will also label the bars and then adjust manually the scale of the *Y*-axis. Press the following keys:

Description	Keys to Press
Press any key to return to the Graph menu:	**[Space]**
(Let's first type in a title for the entire graph. We will use the Options command.)	
Select the Options command:	**O**
(Now let's use the Titles menu command.)	
Select the Titles menu choice:	**T**
Select the First menu choice:	**F**
Type in the title (use the Caps Lock key) and confirm:	**DEMOGRAPHIC ANALYSIS OF SUAVE CONSUMERS** **[Enter]**
Select the Titles menu choice again:	**T**
Select the Second menu choice:	**S**
Type in the subtitle (use parentheses and take Caps Lock key off), then confirm:	**(segmentation by household income)** **[Enter]**
(Let's now put titles on the axes themselves.)	
Select the Titles menu choice again:	**T**
(Let's first enter a title for the X-axis.)	
Select the *X*-Axis menu choice:	**X**
Type in the *X*-Axis title and confirm:	**Household Income (000)** **[Enter]**
(Now let's enter a title for the Y-axis).	
Select the Titles menu choice again:	**T**
Select the *Y*-Axis menu choice:	**Y**
Type in the *Y*-Axis title and confirm:	**Index: Suave Oz./Shampoo Oz.** **[Enter]**
Select the Quit menu choice to return to the Graph menu:	**Q**
Select the View command to see what you have now:	**V**

Observation: Now it's a lot clearer what the bars on the graph represent. However, wouldn't it be nice to see right on the graph the exact index figure for each household income category (for example, that the category $15,000–$20,000 has an index of 122)?

We can put a label on each individual bar. To see how, press the following keys:

Description	Keys to Press
Press any key to return to the Graph menu:	**[Space]**
(We will use the Options command again.)	
Select the Options command:	**O**
(We now need to indicate that we will be adding data-labels for each of the bars.)	
Select the Data-Labels menu choice:	**D**
(Remember that we used only the A range for this bar graph.)	
Select the A menu choice:	**A**
(We now want to paint the index figures in column H.)	
Move the cell pointer to H10:	**(Use the arrow keys.)**
Anchor H10 and paint the range H10..H14:	**.**
	[End] [down]
Confirm the range H10..H14:	**[Enter]**
(1-2-3 now asks where we want the data-labels to go.)	
(Note: With a bar graph, the data-labels go only above each bar, regardless of what choice you make.)	
Confirm that we want the data-labels to go above each bar (even though we can choose any alignment and will still get "above"):	**A**
(Let's see what we have now.)	
Return to the Graph menu:	**Q Q**
Select the View command:	**V**

Observation: Notice that the index figures for each income category are now listed above each graph. However, some of the figures run off the graph. We can correct that by "manually" setting the scale for the *Y*-axis. This procedure will override the scale that 1-2-3 had set for us automatically.

To see how to change the scales of an axis, press the following keys:

Description	Keys to Press
Press any key to return to Graph menu:	**[Space]**
Select the Options command:	**O**
(The Scale menu choice allows us to set the scales manually.)	

Description	Keys to Press
Select the Scale menu choice:	**S**
(We want to adjust the Y-axis scale.)	
Select the *Y* Scale menu choice:	**Y**
(In Lesson 15, we used the Format choice. Here we want to use the Manual choice.)	
Select the Manual menu choice:	**M**
(Notice that the cursor moves to Manual, but the same menu remains on the first line.) *(We now need to set the lower and upper boundaries of the scale.)*	
Select the Lower menu choice:	**L**
(1-2-3 lists 0 until we specify otherwise. Here we actually do want 0 to be the lower scale boundary.)	
Confirm that the lower scale boundary should be 0:	**[Enter]**
(Now we will change the upper scale boundary.)	
Select the Upper menu choice:	**U**
(1-2-3 also lists 0 for the upper scale boundary. Before 1-2-3 had "automatically" set 130 as the upper boundary. Let's manually set 160 as the upper boundary.)	
Type in 160 as the upper boundary and confirm:	**160** **[Enter]**
Return to the Graph menu:	**Q Q**
Select the View command:	**V**

Observation: That looks much better. The data-labels are now all listed within the upper boundary of the graph. A copy of the graph is shown below:

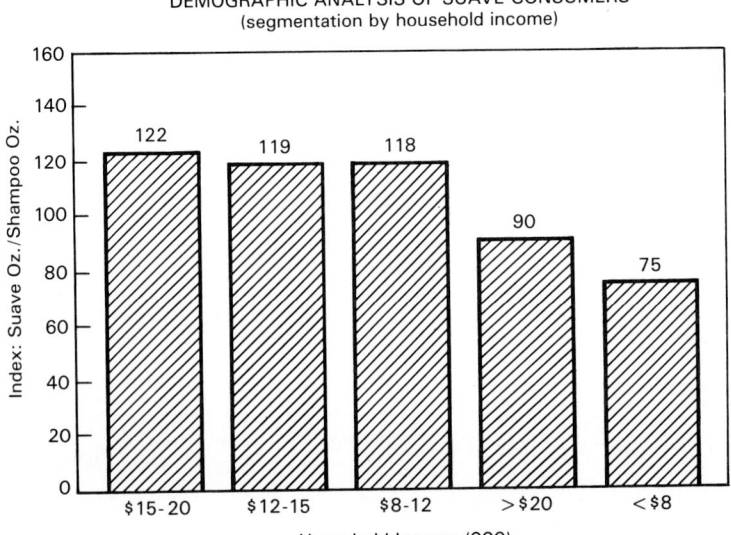

DEMOGRAPHIC ANALYSIS OF SUAVE CONSUMERS
(segmentation by household income)

ON YOUR OWN: If you found in Lesson 15 that your printer can print a copy of the graph when you press **[PrtSc]**, use the **[PrtSc]** key to print out a copy of the graph.

We are now ready to complete the three steps needed to save the graph:

1 Name the graph.
2 Save the worksheet containing the graph.
3 Save a "picture" of the graph for later printing.

1.3 Name the Graph; Save the Worksheet File; Save the Picture File

ON YOUR OWN: First, name the graph. Press **any key** to return to the **Graph** menu. Use the **/Graph Name Create** command to enter the name **DEMOGR** (abbreviation for "Demographic" Analysis) for the graph. We are now ready to save the worksheet file that contains this new bar graph on demographic market segmentation.

ON YOUR OWN: If necessary, press the **[Esc]** key as many times as necessary to clear completely the **/Graph** command menu. Then press the **[Home]** key to return to cell A1. Use the **/File Save** command to save this worksheet on your data diskette. Name the file: **LN16**.

This worksheet file will contain only this one bar graph. Let's now save a "picture" of the graph on file for later printing.

ON YOUR OWN: Use the **/Graph Save** command to save this bar graph in a picture file. Name the file: **DEMOGR**.

Note: Once again we have minimized the number of names we need to remember by using "DEMOGR" both to "name" the graph and to save the "picture" file. (Completed graph also in **LESSON16.WKS** file of the Suave Data Diskette.)

We are now done with this lesson. However, before we go to Lesson 17, let's see how we can delete a named graph and erase a picture file.

Deleting a Named Graph and Erasing a Picture File

What do we do if we give a graph the wrong name? Or, if we make a typographical error in typing the name and don't see it until after we have entered the name? What do we do if we make similar mistakes while saving a picture file? Or if we just want to eliminate a graph we had named or saved?

If You Make a Mistake Entering a Graph Name or a Picture File Name

If you find that you made such a mistake but have already created the graph name or saved the picture file, then:

1 Make that graph "current" again by using the **/Graph Name Use** command.
2 Use the **/Graph Name Create** command to enter the correct graph name, or use the **/Graph Save** command to save the picture file under the correct file name.
3 Then delete the mistaken graph name or erase the mistaken picture file. (See the sections below.)

Deleting a "Named" Graph Name from the Worksheet

To delete a named graph from the worksheet, just use the **/Graph Name Delete** command. When the menu of graph names appears, move the cursor to the name that you want to delete and press **[Enter]**.

Note: If you wish to keep the graph but just place it under a different name, be sure to create the correct name first before you delete the other name. Every graph should have some name in order to be retained when the worksheet file is later saved.

Also, be sure to use the **/File Save** or **/File Save Replace** command to save the worksheet file that contains the correct graph names.

Erasing a Picture (or Graph) File

If you wish to erase a picture file, just use the **/File Erase Command**. 1-2-3 will then provide a menu of "Worksheet Print Graph Other." Be sure your data diskette is in the appropriate disk drive. Move the cursor to "Graph" and press **[Enter]** to indicate that you want to erase a picture file. 1-2-3 will display the list of picture files that you saved. Move the cursor to the file that you wish to erase and press **[Enter]**. 1-2-3 will ask you to confirm that you really want to erase that file.

Note: If you do erase a picture file name but you want to save that graph under a different picture file name, be sure to use the **/Graph Save** command to save the graph for later printing under the correct picture file name.

Remember that once a graph has been saved in a picture file (using **/Graph Save**), *it cannot be retrieved back into 1-2-3*. At this point the picture file can *only* be printed with PrintGraph. Thus, any time you create a graph in 1-2-3, be sure to name it (using **/Graph Name Create**) and also to save it within your worksheet (using **/File Save**). Then the graph can always be retrieved and displayed (and possibly printed using **[PrtSc]**).

Reviewing What We Learned in Lesson 16

In Lesson 16, we built on what we had learned in Lessons 14 and 15. We also learned the following new points:

- Creating a bar graph, like creating an *XY* graph, involves setting the data for the *X*-axis and the *Y*-axis. However, with a bar graph we can specify up to six sets of data for the *Y*-axis, using the A, B, C, D, E, and F ranges. In this lesson, we used only the A range.
- We can improve the appearance of a bar graph by entering titles for the graph, titles for the axes, and data-labels for the bars.
- The **/Graph Options Scale Manual** command allows us to set the scale for the axes exactly as we wish. Using this command, we can change the scales that 1-2-3 had set for the graph automatically.
- The **/Graph Name Delete** command allows us to delete a named graph from the worksheet.
- The **/File Erase Graph** command allows us to erase a picture file from our data diskette.

MANAGEMENT DISCUSSION

1 How is a bar graph useful?

A bar graph helps to demonstrate visibly any comparison of the values of a certain factor that can be divided into a small number of discrete categories, e.g., five income ranges, four age ranges, etc.

2 Assess the usefulness of this particular bar graph.

This particular bar graph clearly and quickly shows the category of households—based upon household income—that are most likely, more likely, less likely, and least likely to buy Suave shampoo.

3 What other demographic characteristics would be most useful to graph?

Essentially, a bar graph could demonstrate this comparison for each of the demographic characteristics in Table 3.2. However, a bar graph allows only a limited number of categories at one time. Therefore, whereas the bar graph is useful in demonstrating the results of our demographic index, it would not be useful to demonstrate our results in our psychographic indexes.

LESSON 17   GRAPHICS: PROJECTED REVENUES FOR SUAVE SHAMPOO

OVERVIEW

COMPUTER INSTRUCTIONS

Lesson 17 is a relatively brief lesson that shows how to create and save a line graph.

MANAGEMENT ISSUES

This line graph is intended to help in both the analysis and communication of some of the revenue projections for Suave that were made using spreadsheet analysis. Line graphs are frequently used in business and financial management.

MANAGEMENT DISCUSSION QUESTIONS

1 How is a line graph useful?
2 Assess the usefulness of this particular graph.
3 Is a line graph the most appropriate type of graph for depicting revenue projections?

CASE

The Suave team decided to create a line graph to chart different Suave revenue projections that had resulted from their spreadsheet analysis. In particular, they created a line graph that demonstrated the effect on Suave revenues in FY 1985 and FY 1986 of different assumptions about Suave's annual growth rate, based on Scenario A. They knew that a line graph could be created to illustrate many of the elements of their spreadsheet analysis.

COMPUTER INSTRUCTIONS

Overview of the Lesson and Loading the Necessary Software and Files

Lesson 17 provides instructions on how to create a line graph. We will use the data that we compiled in Lesson 12 to create this line graph.

The instructions for creating this line graph will be similar to those that we followed in Lessons 14, 15, and 16. The only significant difference is that this time we will use the X range and the A, B, and C ranges—rather than just the X and A ranges. We will need to specify the data that correspond to each of these ranges. To specify these data in the worksheet *at one time* requires an extra step in this instance. Then, as we always do in creating graphs, we will: (1) create the initial graph; (2) improve its appearance; (3) name the graph; save the worksheet; and save a picture of the graph.

First, of course, we need to load the necessary software.

ON YOUR OWN: Complete these familiar steps, if necessary:

1 Load DOS. Enter date and time.
2 If your printer can print a graph with **[PrtSc]**, at the A> prompt load the DOS graphics software.
3 Load the Lotus Access System.
4 Load the 1-2-3 software program.

Now we need to retrieve the worksheet file that contains our spreadsheet analysis in Lesson 12 on projected revenues for Suave Shampoo under Scenario A.

ON YOUR OWN: If you completed Lesson 12 as the instructions directed, insert your data diskette into the appropriate disk drive. Use the **/File Retrieve** command to load the file **LN12A.WK1**.

If you wish, you may alternatively retrieve the worksheet file LESSON12.WKS from the Suave Data Diskette. This file contains, beginning at cell A101, the completed worksheet for Lesson 12, Scenario A. If you use this worksheet file, remember to add 100 to any cell references in the Lesson 17 computer instructions.

Let's first specify the data we will need for the line graph. Here, we need to construct a separate table for the data in the worksheet before we can create the graph.

Creating a Separate Set of Data for the Line Graph in the Worksheet

To build a line graph, we will use the X range to specify what data or categories should go on the *X*-axis. In this case we will put the three fiscal years 1984, 1985, and 1986 on the *X*-axis.

Then we can specify up to six lines of data that correspond to the *Y*-axis. We would use the A, B, C, D, E, or F ranges to specify each line of data. In this case we will input three lines of data, corresponding to the following three assumptions about the Suave annual growth rate: 0%, 2%, or 4%. Specifically, we will use the A, B, and C ranges to correspond to the Suave retail dollar sales that results in the various fiscal years from each of the three assumptions.

First, let's make sure that we have the data we need in our spreadsheet. We have entered in cell H18 our assumption about the Suave annual growth rate. Then we have displayed in cell F26 the Suave Retail Dollar Sales for FY 1984. In cells G26 and H26 are the projections for Suave Retail Dollar Sales for FY 1985 and FY 1986. These projections are based on our assumption about the Suave annual growth rate. When we change the assumption in cell H18, our projections in cells G26 and H26 change.

To create this line graph, we need to capture on the worksheet, all at once, the FY 1984 through FY 1986 Suave retail dollar sales that result from each of three assumptions about the Suave annual growth rate. Let's first build a framework for our 3 × 3 table of revenue projections to make it easier to know just where to enter the different values from our spreadsheet. So that we will know what the numbers represent, **type** the label "Suave Revenue Projections" across cell F49. Then **type** "Suave Growth Rate" downward in cells D52, D53, and D54, respectively. Finally, **enter** our three assumptions about the growth rate (0%, 2%, 4%) into cells E52, E53, and E54, respectively, and put in **Percent** format with **zero decimals**.

Now we are ready to put all the data for this line graph in one area of the worksheet. The instructions will document *two* methods for doing so: by "hand-copying" data and by using the **/Data Table** command.

Note: Creating this line graph allows us the opportunity to consolidate some of the 1-2-3 skills we have acquired for database management, spreadsheet analysis, sensitivity analysis (Data Table), and graphics. Shown next are two methods for creating this line graph. We suggest that you use just the first method only if you have not used the **/Data Table** command before (Lessons 10 and 13). If you have, we suggest you try *both* methods. The first method is simpler but more limited and will deepen your understanding of **/Data Table**. Then erase your results and use the **/Data Table** method. This method will allow you to change your assumption values later on and generate new graphs easily.

To create the line graph under the hand-copy method, we need to complete the following steps:

1 Enter the assumption 0% into cell H18. Press **[PgDn]** to see the resulting Retail Dollar Sales in cells G26 and H26 [should be same as F26].

2 Enter the value from F26 into cell F52; enter the value from G26 into cell G52; enter the value from cell H26 into H52. *Type in these figures. Do not use the* **/Copy command.** (Of course, use the **[PgDn]** and **[PgUp]** keys to make these steps easier.)

   (*Note*: Use the **/Range Value** command if you like (not available in Release 1A). This command allows you to copy the *values* of formulas, not the formulas themselves. In this way, you can enter the values three at a time and do not need to format.)

3 Enter the assumption 2% into H18.

4 Enter the values that are now in cells F26, G26, and H26 into cells F53, G53, and H53, respectively.

5 Enter the assumption 4% into H18.

6 Enter the values that are now in cells F26, G26, and H26 into cells F54, G54, and H54, respectively.

ON YOUR OWN: If necessary, use the **/Range Format** command to format the values in cells **F52..H54** into **Currency** format with **one decimal** place.

Good. The screen beginning at cell A41 should appear as:

```
F52: (C1) 104.4                                                 READY

          A         B         C         D         E         F         G         H
41
42                                      Operating Profit       $10.8     $11.1     $11.4
43
44                                      Mkt. Share:Ounces      13.6%     13.8%     14.1%
45                                      Mkt. Share:Dollars      9.0%      9.2%      9.4%
46                                      Industry Ad Share       5.1%      4.8%      4.7%
47                                      Ad/Sales Ratio          5.7%      6.4%      7.1%
48
49                                              Suave Revenue Projections
50
51
52                                      Suave        0%   $104.4    $104.4    $104.4
53                                      Growth       2%   $104.4    $106.5    $108.6
54                                      Rate         4%   $104.4    $108.6    $112.9
55
56
57
58
59
60
22-Oct-87   10:39 AM
```

Note: The reason that we need to type in these values (or use the **/Range Value** command) rather than use the **/Copy** command is that the **/Copy** command copies the *formulas* themselves. Therefore, just as the values in cells G26 and H26 change when we enter new assumptions into cell H18, so too would the values change in cells G52..H54. We need to capture the Suave retail dollar sales values for each assumption, so that they will not change when we change the value of the assumption.

Now we are ready to try another method, using **/Data Table** (skip this section, if desired).

Creating a Set of Data for a Line Graph Using /Data Table

ON YOUR OWN: Erase the results using the **/Range Erase** (and **/Range Format Reset**) command for cells **F52..H54**.

In the first method, we "hand-copied" (or used **/Range Value**) the spreadsheet data to a separate table for each of three assumptions about Suave's growth rate. In fact, *we actually hand-simulated how the* **/Data Table** *command works!*

Let's now use the **/Data Table** command. (Refer to the detailed instructions in Lessons 10 or 13, if necessary.) To do so, complete the following steps:

1 Move to cell F51 and indicate that a formula will be created (+). Move the cell pointer to cell F26 and enter the result of that cell into cell F51. Do the same for cell G51 (enter the formula from cell G26) and cell H51 (from cell H26).

2 Invoke the **/Data Table** command for 1 variable. Set and confirm the range to

include the assumptions, the three formulas, and the cells that will contain our results. (E51..H54)

3 Move the cell pointer to H18 and confirm that the variable "Suave annual growth rate" is the input cell. (Watch 1-2-3 complete the calculations!)

4 Put the results in cells F52..H54 into **Currency** format with **one decimal** place. Leave cells F51..H51 unformatted so that you do not confuse them with your results.

Good. The screen beginning at cell A41 should appear as:

```
F52: (C1) 104.4                                              READY

          A         B        C        D       E       F        G         H
41                                                   ──────── ──────── ────────
42                                      Operating Profit   $10.8    $11.1    $11.4
43
44                                      Mkt. Share:Ounces   13.6%    13.8%    14.1%
45                                      Mkt. Share:Dollars   9.0%     9.2%     9.4%
46                                      Industry Ad Share    5.1%     4.8%     4.7%
47                                      Ad/Sales Ratio       5.7%     6.4%     7.1%
48
49                                         Suave Revenue Projections
50
51                                               104.4  108.576 112.9190
52                                      Suave   0%  $104.4   $104.4    $104.4
53                                      Growth  2%  $104.4   $106.5    $108.6
54                                      Rate    4%  $104.4   $108.6    $112.9
55
56
57
58
59
60
22-Oct-87   10:43 AM
```

Note: The only difference between this screen and the previously "hand-copied" screen is the value of the formulas in cells F51..H51. The inclusion of these formulas in the table will allow us to change our assumption values later on and generate new graphs easily.

Let's now create our first line graph.

LINE GRAPH TO DISPLAY PROJECTED SUAVE REVENUES UNDER DIFFERENT ASSUMPTIONS

To create this graph, we will follow these familiar general steps:

1.1 Create the initial graph;

1.2 Improve the appearance of the graph;

1.3 Name the graph; save the worksheet file; save the picture file.

1.1 Creating the Initial Graph to Display Projected Suave Revenues under Different Assumptions about the Suave Annual Growth Rate

Now we are ready to create the actual line graph. Follow the step-by-step instructions as closely as is necessary. Press the **[Home]** key and then the following keys:

Description	Keys to Press
Display the 1-2-3 command menus:	**/**
Select the /Graph command:	**G**
Select the Type command:	**T**
Select the Line menu choice:	**L**
(We now need to specify the data for each of the axes.)	
Select the X menu choice to indicate that we want to specify the data for the *X*-axis:	**X**
(Let's put the fiscal years 1984, 1985, and 1986 on the X-axis. So, we need to paint the range F22..H22.)	
Move the cell pointer to F22:	**(Use the [PgDn] and the arrow keys.)**
Anchor F22 and then paint the range F22..H22:	**.** **[right*2]**
Confirm the range F22..H22 as the *X*-axis range:	**[Enter]**
(We now need to specify the data for each of the lines on the graph. The first line will represent the "A range" and will correspond to the Suave retail dollar sales that result from an assumption of 0% for the Suave annual growth rate.)	
Select the A menu choice to specify the data for the first line:	**A**
(We now need to paint the range of data that we entered in cells F52, G52, and H52.)	
Move the cell pointer to F52:	**(Use the [PgDn] and arrow keys.)**
Anchor F52 and then paint the range F52..H52:	**.** **[right*2]**
Confirm the range F52..H52 as containing the data for the first line:	**[Enter]**
(We now need to specify the data for the second line, representing the "B range" and corresponding to the Suave retail dollar sales that result from an assumption of 2% for the Suave annual growth rate.)	
Select the B menu choice to specify the data for second line:	**B**
(We now need to paint the range of data that we entered in cells F53, G53, and H53.)	

Description	Keys to Press
Move the cell pointer to F53:	**(Use the [PgDn] and arrow keys.)**
Anchor F53 and then paint the range F53..H53:	. **[right*2]**
Confirm the range F53..H53 as containing the data for the second line:	**[Enter]**

(Finally, we need to specify the data for the third line, representing the "C range" and corresponding to the Suave retail dollar sales that result from an assumption of 4% for the Suave annual growth rate.)

Select the C menu choice to specify the data for the third line:	**C**

(We now need to paint the range of data that we entered in cells F54, G54, and H54.)

Move the cell pointer to F54:	**(Use the [PgDn] and arrow keys.)**
Anchor F54 and then paint the range F54..H54:	. **[right*2]**
Confirm the range F54..H54 as containing the data for the third line:	**[Enter]**
Select the View command:	**V**

Observation: You should see an initial line graph. Let's now improve the appearance and clarity of this graph.

Note: You should see now why we used the A, B, and C ranges. Each range corresponds to the data that is represented by one of the lines.

1.2 Improving the Appearance of the Graph

Just as we did with the bar graph in Lesson 16, let's first add some titles for this line graph and for the *Y*-axis. As we already see, the *X*-axis is self-explanatory. It represents the three fiscal years. We will also add some data-labels for the lines and then adjust manually the scale on the *Y*-axis. This lesson will continue to provide keystroke-by-keystroke instructions. However, if you feel confident, you should try completing some of these steps on your own. Press the following keys:

Description	Keys to Press
Press any key to return to the Graph menu:	**[Space]**

(Let's first type in a title for the entire graph. We will use the Options Titles command.)

Select the Options command:	**O**
Select the Titles menu choice:	**T**

Description	Keys to Press
Select the First menu choice:	**F**
Type in the title (use the Caps Lock key) and confirm:	**PROJECTIONS OF SUAVE REVENUES** **[Enter]**
Select the Titles menu choice again:	**T**
Select the Second menu choice:	**S**
Type in the subtitle (use parentheses and take Caps Lock key off), then confirm:	**(varying Suave's annual growth rate)** **[Enter]**
(Let's now put titles on the Y-axis.)	
Select the Titles menu choice again:	**T**
Select the Y-axis menu choice:	**Y**
Type in the Y-axis title and confirm:	**Suave Revenues (in millions)** **[Enter]**
Select the Quit menu choice to return to the Graph menu:	**Q**
Select the View command to see what you have now:	**V**

(This view of the graph suggests that we should change the scales on the Y-axis. We saw how to use the Options Scale Manual command in Lesson 15.)

Press any key to return to the Graph command:	**[Space]**
Select the Options command:	**O**
Select the Scale menu choice:	**S**
(We want to adjust the Y-axis scale.)	
Select the Y scale menu choice:	**Y**
Select the Manual menu choice:	**M**
(Let's set the lower boundary of the scale at 100.)	
Select the Lower menu choice:	**L**
Type in 100 as the lower boundary and confirm:	**100 [Enter]**
(Let's set the upper boundary of the scale at 116.)	
Select the Upper menu choice:	**U**
Type in 116 as the upper boundary and confirm:	**116 [Enter]**
(Now let's format the scale for the Y-axis.)	
Select the Format menu choice:	**F**
(We want to use Currency format with one decimal.)	

Description	Keys to Press
Select the Currency format:	C
Enter 1 decimal place and confirm:	1 [Enter]
(Let's again see what we have.)	
Return to the Graph menu:	Q Q
Select the View command:	V

Observation: That was a lot of work, but the graph does now look quite a bit better. However, the graph still doesn't show which assumption corresponds to which line, nor does it show the exact amount of Suave revenues that corresponds to each data point on the lines. Therefore, we still should complete two steps:

1 Provide a "legend" that explains each line; and
2 Provide "data-labels" for each data point on the graph.

Note for Users of the /Data Table Command: The power of 1-2-3 and this command is well demonstrated in this situation. We can now change our assumption values (0%, 2%, 4%) to whatever we like and see the results on the line graph. Try it by following these steps:

1 Return to the worksheet (READY mode) and move the cell pointer to our assumptions about Suave's growth rate (cells E52, E53, E54). Change the assumption values (e.g., to 1%, 5%, 10%).
2 Press the **[Table]** key (**[F8]**) on most keyboards). This special function key performs the sensitivity analysis of the Data Table operation. Watch the calculations change the results in cells G52..H54.
3 Press the **[Graph]** (**[F10]**) key and see how the graph has changed too! Of course, you now may have to change the scales and some legends and data-labels.
4 To continue with these instructions, return the assumption values to 0%, 2%, and 4%. Press the **[Table]** (**[F8]**) key and check the graph with the **[Graph]** (**[F10]**) key.

Now let's add legends and data-labels to this line graph by pressing the following keys:

Description	Keys to Press
Press any key to return to the Graph menu:	**[Space]** **(/ and G if used Data Table)**
(Let's first enter legends to explain the lines. We will use the Options Legend command.)	
Select the Options command:	O
Select the Legend command:	L

Description	Keys to Press
(Let's enter a legend for the line that corresponds to projected Suave revenues, assuming a 0% Suave annual growth rate.)	
Select the A menu choice:	**A**
(1-2-3 will ask us to "Enter legend for A range:".)	
Type in the legend:	**0% Growth**
Confirm the legend for the A range:	**[Enter]**
(Now let's enter the legend for the line that corresponds to projected Suave revenues, assuming a 2% Suave annual growth rate.)	
Select the Legend command again:	**L**
Select the B menu choice:	**B**
Type in the legend:	**2% Growth**
Confirm the legend for the B range:	**[Enter]**
(Now let's enter the legend for the line that corresponds to projected Suave revenues, assuming a 4% Suave annual growth rate.)	
Select the Legend command again:	**L**
Select the C menu choice:	**C**
Type in the legend:	**4% Growth**
Confirm the legend for the C range:	**[Enter]**
(Let's see what we have.)	
Return to the Graph menu:	**Q**
Select the View command:	**V**
(See the legends at the bottom of the graph and the symbols on each of the lines? These legends and symbols now let us know which lines correspond to which assumptions.) *(Now let's add data-labels to specify what each data point on the graph represents.)*	
Press any key to return to the Graph menu:	**[Space]**
Select the Options command:	**O**
Select the Data-Labels command:	**D**
(Let's specify the data-labels for our first line, corresponding to the assumption of a 0% annual growth rate. Our data-labels will be the Suave revenue projections.)	
Select the A menu choice to indicate that we want to specify data-labels for the data in the first line:	**A**
(We want to paint the range that contains the Suave revenue projections for the 0% annual growth rate assumption, because these projections will be our data-labels.)	
Move the cell pointer to F52:	**(Use the [PgDn] and arrow keys.)**
Anchor F52 and paint the range F52..H52:	**.** **[right*2]**

Description	*Keys to Press*
Confirm the range F52..H52:	**[Enter]**

(1-2-3 will ask us where to place the data-labels. Let's place them above each data point.)

| Select the Above menu choice: | **A** |

(Note: Whereas the bar graph in Lesson 16 could only have data-labels above each bar, that is not the case with a line graph.)
(Now let's specify the data-labels for the second line.)

| Select the B menu choice: | **B** |

(We want to paint the range that contains the Suave revenue projections for the 2% annual growth rate assumption.)

Move the cell pointer to F53:	**(Use the [PgDn] and arrow keys.)**
Anchor F53 and paint the range F53..H53:	**.** **[right*2]**
Confirm the range F53..H53:	**[Enter]**
Select the Above menu choice again:	**A**

(Now let's specify the data-labels for the third line.)

| Select the C menu choice: | **C** |

(Of course, we want to paint the range F54..H54.)

Move the cell pointer to F54:	**(Use the [PgDn] and arrow keys.)**
Anchor F54 and paint the range F54..H54:	**.** **[right*2]**
Confirm the range F54..H54:	**[Enter]**
Select again the Above menu choice:	**A**

(Now let's see what we have.)

| Return to the Graph menu: | **Q Q** |
| Select the View command: | **V** |

Observation: The graph looks clearer and is self-explanatory; however, notice how much work it took to specify all our options. Again we can see that creating a graph with careful detail can require a great deal of time. A copy of the graph is shown on the following page.

ON YOUR OWN: If you found in Lesson 15 that your printer can print a copy of the graph when you press **[PrtSc]**, use the **[PrtSc]** key to print out a copy of the graph.

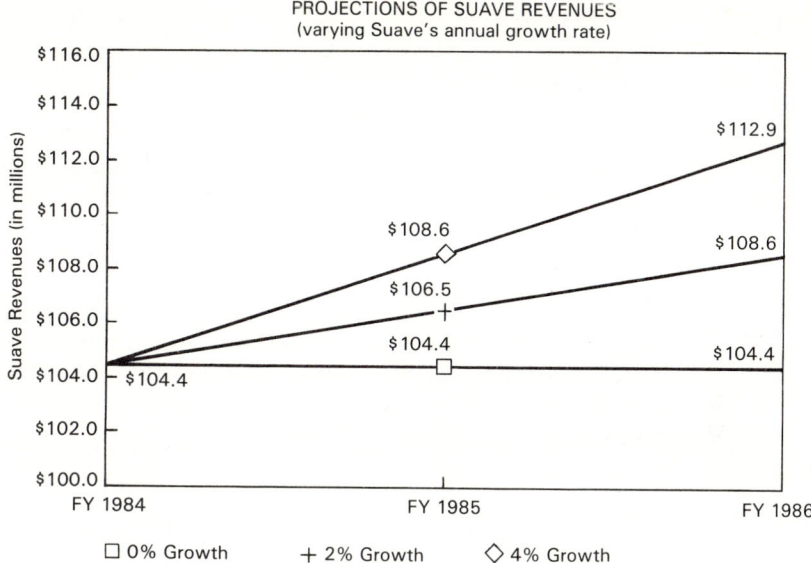

We are now ready to complete the three steps needed to save the graph:

1 Name the graph.
2 Save the worksheet.
3 Save a "picture" of the graph.

1.3 Name the Graph; Save the Worksheet File; Save the Picture File

ON YOUR OWN: Use the **/Graph Name Create** command to enter the name **SUAVEREV** (abbreviation for "Projected Suave Revenues") for the graph. We are now ready to save the worksheet file that contains this new line graph on revenue projections.

ON YOUR OWN: If necessary, press the **[Esc]** key as many times as necessary to clear completely the **/Graph** command menu. Then press the **[Home]** key to return to cell A1. Use the **/File Save** command to save this worksheet on your data diskette. Name the file: **LN17**. This worksheet file will contain only this one line graph. Let's now save a "picture" of the graph on file for later printing.

ON YOUR OWN: Use the **/Graph Save** command to save this new line graph in a picture file. Name the file: **SUAVEREV**.

Note: Once again we have minimized the number of names we need to remember by using SUAVEREV both to "name" the graph and to save the "picture" file.

Good. We have now completed Lesson 17. Let's review the new graph options and use of data table that we learned in this lesson.

Reviewing What We Learned in Lesson 17

Lesson 17 built on Lessons 14, 15, and 16. In addition, we learned the following:

- A line graph allows us to specify data for up to six lines. We use the A, B, C, D, E, and F ranges to specify the data that correspond to each of the lines.
- The **/Graph Options Legend** command allows us to display at the bottom of a line graph a legend that can help to identify and explain each of the lines on the graph.
- The **/Graph Options Data-Labels** command allows us to label each of the data points on the various lines.
- The **/Range Value** command allows us to copy a range of the values of formulas, not the formulas themselves. The **/Copy** command copies the formulas.
- The **/Data Table** command can be used to change the assumption values used in a graph. By using the **[Table] ([F8])** special function key, sensitivity analysis can be performed and a new graph generated.

MANAGEMENT DISCUSSION

1 How is a line graph useful?

A line graph allows a manager to demonstrate clearly and quickly a trend across time which is affected by changes in the value of a particular assumption.

2 Assess the usefulness of this particular graph.

This line graph demonstrates the effects of different assumptions about Suave's sales growth rates on projections of Suave's revenues. It is helpful for management analysis because it shows how sensitive our projections of Suave revenues are to assumptions about Suave's growth rate. The graph communicates these different projections clearly, and changes in assumptions can easily be shown on the same graph.

3 Is a line graph the most appropriate type of graph for depicting revenue projections?

A line graph is usually considered the most appropriate type of graph for depicting projections across discrete periods of time. A line graph allows us to prepare more than one projection on the same screen.

LESSON 18   GRAPHICS: REVENUE STRUCTURE FOR SUAVE SHAMPOO

OVERVIEW

COMPUTER INSTRUCTIONS

Lesson 18 shows how to create both bar and stacked bar graphs. In addition, this lesson demonstrates how easy it is to change from a bar to a stacked bar graph with the same data. Lesson 18 also provides instructions on how to print graphs using Lotus 1-2-3.

MANAGEMENT ISSUES

These bar and stacked bar graphs are intended to communicate some of the key information about the revenue structure of the Suave shampoo brand. It is critical for a manager to understand the variable cost, marketing costs, and operating profit that comprise the revenue structure of a brand.

MANAGEMENT DISCUSSION QUESTIONS

1 How is a stacked bar graph useful?
2 Compare the usefulness of the bar graph versus the stacked bar graphs in communicating the revenue structure of the Suave brand. In this particular case, which type of graph should a manager use?

CASE

The Suave team decided to create three bar and three stacked bar graphs to explain the revenue/profit/cost structure of Suave shampoo and to demonstrate how the components of that structure changed under different assumptions about Suave growth rates. The team disagreed about whether the bar graphs or the stacked bar graphs communicated the information more effectively.

COMPUTER INSTRUCTIONS

Overview of Computer Instructions for Lesson 18

In Lessons 14 through 17, we learned how to create four of the five types of Lotus graphs: pie, *XY,* bar and line. We also learned how to print graphs, using both the

[PrtSc] key and the PrintGraph program. In Lesson 18, we will learn several additional features of Lotus 1-2-3 graphics.

First, we will learn how to create the fifth type of graph: the stacked-bar graph. We will see how to use the A,B,C,D,E, and F ranges to divide a bar on a graph into as many as six components, stacked one on top of each other.

We will also learn how the stacked-bar graph can be altered when we change some of the underlying assumptions in the data used to create the graph. We will see how a stacked-bar graph changes under three different assumptions about the Suave annual growth rate.

Lesson 18 also shows how easy it is to change from one type of a graph to another type, using exactly the same data and details in both types of graphs. Specifically, we will change the stacked-bar graph to a bar graph.

When we transform the stacked-bar to a bar graph, we will see that a graph can have more than one bar for each of the categories on the *X*-axis. In Lesson 16, our bar graph had only one bar for each of the demographic categories because we used only the A range. In Lesson 18, our graph will have three bars for each of the fiscal years, because we will use the A, B, and C ranges.

The instructions demonstrate that we can save a picture file of the stacked-bar graph and a separate picture file of the bar graph—even though the data used to create the graphs are exactly the same!

The instructions also provide the chance to practice printing graphs. We will print the graphs that we created in Lessons 16, 17, and 18.

Let's begin.

Loading the Necessary Software and Worksheet Files

ON YOUR OWN: Complete the following familiar steps, if necessary:

1 Load DOS. Enter date and time.
2 If your printer can print a graph with [PrtSc], at the A> prompt load the DOS graphics software.
3 Load the Lotus Access System.
4 Load the 1-2-3 software program.

As we did in Lesson 17, we will create the graphs in Lesson 18 using Scenario A of the spreadsheet that we completed in Lesson 12. Therefore, we want to retrieve the completed worksheet file for Scenario A in Lesson 12.

ON YOUR OWN: If you completed Lesson 12 as the instructions directed, insert your data diskette into the appropriate disk drive. Use the **/File Retrieve** command to load the file **LN12A.WK1**.

If you wish, you may alternatively retrieve the worksheet file **LESSON12.WKS** from the Suave Data Diskette. This file contains, beginning at cell A101, the completed worksheet for Lesson 12, Scenario A. If you use this worksheet file, remember to add 100 to any cell references in the Lesson 18 computer instructions.

> *Note:* The file you created in Lesson 17, **LN17.WK1**, could also be used. If used, there will be some very minor differences in using these instructions.

We are now ready to create our first stacked-bar graph and then to transform that graph into a bar graph.

GRAPH 1: STACKED-BAR GRAPH SHOWING CURRENT AND PROJECTED REVENUE STRUCTURES FOR SUAVE SHAMPOO

To create this graph, we will complete the following steps:

1.1 Create the initial graph;
1.2 Improve the appearance of the graph;
1.3 Change underlying assumptions in the graph;
1.4 Name the graph; save the worksheet file; save the picture file.

1.1 Creating the Initial Stacked-Bar Graph to Show the Revenue Components of Suave Shampoo

We have already seen how to create a bar graph. A stacked-bar graph is very similar, except that a stacked-bar graph will *always use more than one* of the six *Y*-axis ranges: A, B, C, D, E, and F. (Remember that in Lesson 16 we used only the A range to create that bar graph.) Let's see. Follow the instructions as closely as is necessary. Press the following keys:

Description	*Keys to Press*
Display the 1-2-3 command menus:	**/**
Select the /Graph command:	**G**
(Before continuing, we want to reset all the settings from the previous graph that we created in Lesson 17. This graph used the worksheet file LN12A.WK1 also.)	
Select the Reset command:	**R**
Select the Graph menu choice:	**G**
(This step confirms that we want to reset all the previous settings. We can now build a new graph.)	
Select the Type command:	**T**
(We are building a stacked-bar graph. The X-axis, or horizontal axis, will display fiscal years 1984, 1985, and 1986. We will use the A, B, and C ranges for the Suave revenue components.)	
Select the Stacked-Bar menu choice:	**S**
(Let's first specify the data for the X-axis.)	
Select the *X*-Axis menu choice:	**X**
(We need to paint the range F22..H22 to put the fiscal years on the X-axis.)	

Description	Keys to Press
Move the cell pointer to F22:	**(Use the [PgDn] and the arrow keys.)**
Anchor F22, paint the range F22..H22, and then confirm:	**.** **[right*2]** **[Enter]**

(The components of Suave manufacturer revenues are: (1) variable costs; (2) total marketing; and (3) operating profit. We will use the A, B, and C ranges, respectively, for these components.)
(Note: In Lesson 17, the "revenues" were retail dollar sales [row 26], which includes the retail margin dollars. Here, "revenues" are manufacturer dollar sales [row 29], which does not include the retail margin.)

Select the A menu choice:	**A**

(We need to paint the range F30..H30, containing the Variable Costs for FY 1984, FY 1985, and FY 1986.)

Move the cell pointer to F30:	**(Use the [PgDn] and the arrow keys.)**
Anchor F30, paint the range F30..H30, and then confirm:	**.** **[right*2]** **[Enter]**
Select the B menu choice:	**B**

(We need to paint the range F40..H40, containing the Total Marketing Expenditures for FY 1984, FY 1985, and FY 1986.)

Move the cell pointer to F40:	**(Use the [PgDn] and the arrow keys.)**
Anchor F40, paint the range F40..H40, and then confirm:	**.** **[right*2]** **[Enter]**
Select the C menu choice:	**C**

(We need to paint the range F42..H42, containing the Operating Profit for FY 1984, FY 1985, and FY 1986.)

Move the cell pointer to F42:	**(Use the [PgDn] and the arrow keys.)**
Anchor F42, paint the range F42..H42, and then confirm:	**.** **[right*2]** **[Enter]**

(Let's see what we have so far.)

Select the View command:	**V**

Observation: We can now see how a stacked-bar graph basically looks. However, we still have a lot of work to improve the appearance of the graph.

Note: This initial graph is based on the assumption that the Suave annual growth rate will be 2%. Later, we will alter that assumption in the worksheet and see how the graph changes.

Let's now improve the appearance of the graph.

1.2 Improving the Appearance of the Graph

To make this graph clearer, we will first add titles for the graph and the *Y*-axis. (The *X*-axis is self-explanatory.) Then we will add legends and data-labels, just as we did in Lesson 17. We will also manually adjust the scale on the *Y*-axis. Press the following keys:

Description	Keys to Press
Press any key to return to the Graph menu:	**[Space]**
Select the Options command:	**O**
Select the Titles menu choice:	**T**
Select the First menu choice:	**F**
Type in the title (use the Caps Lock key) and confirm:	**COMPONENTS OF SUAVE MFG REVENUES** **[Enter]**
Select the Titles menu choice again:	**T**
Select the Second menu choice:	**S**
Type in the subtitle (use parentheses and take Caps Lock key off); then confirm:	**(Suave Annual Growth Rate: 2%)** **[Enter]**
(Let's now add a title for the Y-axis.)	
Select the Titles menu choice again:	**T**
Select the *Y*-Axis menu choice:	**Y**
Type in the title and confirm (use parentheses):	**(Millions of Dollars)** **[Enter]**
(Let's see what we have.)	
Return to the Graph menu:	**Q**
Select the View command:	**V**
(The graph is getting clearer, but we still need to add legends to explain the elements of each standard bar.)	
Press any key to return to the Graph menu:	**[Space]**
Select the Options command:	**O**
Select the Legend menu choice:	**L**

Description	Keys to Press
(Let's first put in a legend for the A range: Variable Costs.)	
Select the A menu choice:	**A**
Type in this legend for the A range and confirm:	**Var Costs** **[Enter]**
(Let's now put in a lengend for the B range: Total Marketing.)	
Select the Legend menu choice again:	**L**
Select the B menu choice:	**B**
Type in this legend for the B range and confirm:	**Total Mkting** **[Enter]**
(Let's now put in a legend for the C range: Operating Profit.)	
Select the Legend menu choice for a third time:	**L**
Select the C menu choice:	**C**
Type in this legend for the C range and confirm:	**Op Profit** **[Enter]**
(Let's see what we have.)	
Return to the Graph menu:	**Q**
Select the View command:	**V**
(Note that the legends at the bottom of the graph identify each component of Suave manufacturer revenues for each fiscal year.) *(Let's make the graph even clearer by adding a data-label for each stacked-bar to show the total Suave revenues for each fiscal year.)*	
Press any key to return to the Graph menu:	**[Space]**
Select the Options command:	**O**
Select the Data-Labels menu choice:	**D**
(Let's put total Suave revenues above each bar. Lotus will understand this step as our putting a data-label above the C range, which is the top of the three ranges.)	
Select the C menu choice:	**C**
(We now want to paint the range for total Suave revenues—that is, "Mfg. Dollar Sales." So, we will paint the range F29..H29.)	
Move the cell pointer to F29:	**(Use the [PgDn] and the ar-row keys.)**
Anchor F29, paint the range F29..H29, and then confirm:	**.** **[right*2]** **[Enter]**
(1-2-3 will ask where we want to place the data-labels. We want to put them above the entire bar, which is the same as directly above the C range.)	
Select the Above menu choice:	**A**
(Let's now see what we have.)	

Description	Keys to Press
Return to the Graph menu:	**Q Q**
Select the View command:	**V**

(It appears that we should adjust the upper boundary of the Y-axis. Let's make it 100, and let's put the Y-axis scale in Currency format with one decimal place.)

Description	Keys to Press
Press any key to return to the Graph menu:	**[Space]**
Select the Options command:	**O**
Select the Scale menu choice:	**S**
Select the Y Scale menu choice:	**Y**
Select the Manual menu choice:	**M**
Select the Upper menu choice:	**U**
Type in the Upper Limit as 100 and confirm:	**100 [Enter]**

(Let's now format the Y-axis scale.)

Description	Keys to Press
Select the Format menu choice:	**F**
Select the Currency format:	**C**
Enter 1 decimal place and confirm:	**1 [Enter]**

(That should be it. Let's see what we have.)

Description	Keys to Press
Return to the Graph menu:	**Q Q**
Select the View command:	**V**

Observation: That was a lot of work, but the graph seems clear now.

Let's now see how the graph changes when we alter our underlying assumption about the Suave annual growth rate.

1.3 Altering an Underlying Assumption and Seeing the Graph Change

We will return to the actual worksheet and enter two other assumptions about the Suave annual growth rate. We will see how the graph changes. Press the following keys:

Description	Keys to Press
Press any key to return to the Graph menu:	**[Space]**
Escape from the Graph menu:	**Q**

(Let's enter an assumption of 0% Suave annual growth.)

Description	Keys to Press
Move the cell pointer to H18:	**(Use the arrow keys.)**
Enter the new assumption of 0%:	**0 [Enter]**

Description	Keys to Press

(We could have entered .00 for 0%, but of course zero stands for the same value.)
(Let's now see how the graph changed. This is easy. Here we can just press [F10] since the stacked-bar graph is the current graph.)

Description	Keys to Press
Press [F10] to view the graph directly from the worksheet:	**[F10]**

Observation: There are two important observations to make:

1 Both the size and composition of the bars have changed. These bars now represent the components of Suave manufacturer revenues, assuming a Suave annual growth rate of 0% in FY 1985 and FY 1986.
2 However, the title for the graph still stays "(Suave Annual Growth Rate: 2%)." So, the bars were transformed by the change in data, but the titles were not.

To make this graph correct, we would have to go back to the /**Graph Options Titles Second**, and change the second line in the title.

Let's now change the underlying assumption about the Suave annual growth rate to 4%. We will then change the title to reflect this change in the data. This is the graph that we will then name and save. Press the following keys:

Description	Keys to Press
Press any key to return to the worksheet:	**[Space]**
(The cell pointer should still be in H18.)	
Enter the new assumption of a 4% annual growth rate for Suave:	**4% [Enter]**
(Let's see how the graph now looks.)	
Press [F10] to view the graph directly from the worksheet:	**[F10]**

Observation: Notice how much different the bars for FY 1985 and FY 1986 are now. However, the title still says 2%. Let's edit the second line of the graph title. Press the following keys:

Description	Keys to Press
Press any key to return to the worksheet:	**[Space]**
Display the 1-2-3 command menus:	**/**
Select the /Graph command:	**G**

Description	Keys to Press
Select the Options command:	**O**
Select the Titles menu choice:	**T**
(We want to display and then edit the second title.)	
Select the Second menu choice:	**S**
(Notice that the title is now displayed. It will be easy to change.)	
Use the [Backspace] key to erase the last three characters in the second line of the title:	**[Backspace]*3**
(Now let's type in the correction.)	
Type in and confirm:	**4%) [Enter]**
(Now let's see what we have.)	
Return to the Graph menu:	**Q**
Select the View command:	**V**

Observation: This graph is now current. The title says that it is based on an annual growth rate for Suave of 4%, as it in fact is. A representation of the graph is shown below:

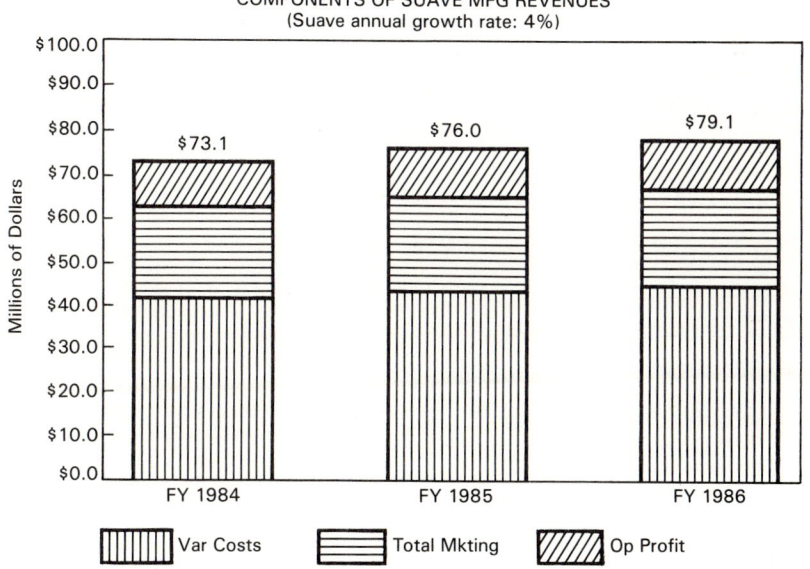

Let's name this graph (with the assumption of 4% annual growth for Suave) to be part of the worksheet and then save it in a picture file.

1.4 Name the Graph; Save the Worksheet File; Save the Picture File

ON YOUR OWN: Use the **/Graph Name Create** command to enter the following name for this graph: **REVSTR1** (abbreviation for "Suave Revenue Structure," for the first type of graph we will use). Now let's save the new worksheet in a file.

ON YOUR OWN: Use the **/File Save** command to save this worksheet on your data diskette. Name the file: **LN18**. Later, we will replace the worksheet file with a file that contains both the stacked-bar and a separate bar graph. Let's now save a "picture" of the stacked-bar graph on file for later printing.

ON YOUR OWN: Use the **/Graph Save** command to save this stacked-bar in a picture file. Name the file: **REVSTR1**.

Good. Let's now see how easily we can transform this stacked-bar graph into a bar graph.

GRAPH 2: BAR GRAPH SHOWING CURRENT AND PROJECTED REVENUE STRUCTURES FOR SUAVE SHAMPOO

To transform this graph into a bar graph, and then change some underlying assumptions, we will follow these steps:

2.1 Change the type of graph to a bar graph;
2.2 Change underlying assumptions in the graph;
2.3 Name the graph; save the worksheet file; save the picture file.

2.1 Changing the Graph from Stacked-Bar to Bar

We can keep the exact same data but change the graph from a stacked-bar to a bar graph. Let's see how. Press the following keys:

Description	Keys to Press
Display the 1-2-3 command menus:	**/**
Select the Graph command:	**G**
Select the Type command:	**T**
Select the Bar menu choice:	**B**
(Let's see what we have.)	
Select the View command:	**V**

Observation: You should now see a bar graph, with three bars for each fiscal year. However, the data-labels for this graph are now wrong. The graph still shows the *total* Suave manufacturer revenues directly above the C range, Operating Profit.

Let's correct these data-labels. Press the following keys:

Description	Keys to Press
Press any key to return to the Graph menu:	**[Space]**
Select the Options command:	**O**
Select the Data-Labels menu choice:	**D**
(Let's first put in data-labels for the bars representing Variable Costs.)	
Select the A menu choice:	**A**
(Note: 1-2-3 will remember previous graph settings. Do not use the /Graph Reset Graph command or you will not be able to change the type of graph. Just [Esc] when necessary, use the [Home] key to realign the screen, and then paint the range for the current setting desired.)	
(We need to paint the range containing Variable Costs, F30..H30.)	
Move the cell pointer to F30:	**(Use the arrow keys.)**
Anchor F30, paint the range F30..H30, and confirm:	**.**
	[right*2]
	[Enter]
(1-2-3 now asks where it should place the data-labels. We can put data-labels only above bars.)	
Select the Above menu choice:	**A**
(Let's now put in data-labels for the bars representing Total Marketing.)	
Select the B menu choice:	**B**
(We need to paint the range containing Total Marketing expenditures, F40..H40.)	
Move the cell pointer to F40:	**(Use the arrow keys.)**
Anchor cell F40, paint the range F40..H40, and confirm:	**.**
	[right*2]
	[Enter]
Select the Above menu choice:	**A**
(Let's now put in data-labels for the bars representing Operating Profit, F42..H42.)	
Select the C menu choice:	**C**
Move the cell pointer to F42:	**(Press [Esc] then use the [PgDn] and arrow keys.)**
Anchor F42, paint the range F42..H42, and confirm:	**.**
	[right*2]
	[Enter]
Select the Above menu choice:	**A**
Return to the Graph menu:	**Q Q**
(Let's see what we now have.)	
Select the View command:	**V**

The graph is better, but the *Y*-axis scale needs to be changed.

ON YOUR OWN: Change the upper boundary of the *Y*-axis scale to 60. Press the **[Space]** bar, use the **Options Scale** command, choose the **Manual Upper** menu, and enter **60**, and view the graph.

Observation: This graph is now correct. The graph is based on the assumption of a Suave annual growth rate of 4%, just as the title indicates.

A copy of this bar graph is shown below. You can judge for yourself whether you think the stacked-bar type or the bar type of graph more clearly explains the "Components of Suave Manufacturer Revenues."

Note: This bar graph will change, just as the stacked-bar graph will change, if we alter an assumption in the underlying data.

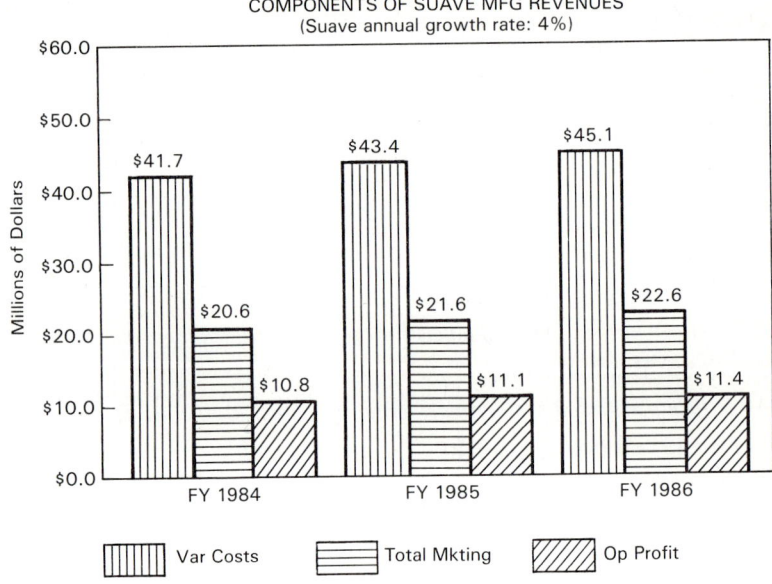

COMPONENTS OF SUAVE MFG REVENUES
(Suave annual growth rate: 4%)

2.2 Altering an Underlying Assumption and Seeing the Graph Change

ON YOUR OWN: Press the **[Space]** bar to return to the Graph menu and select **Quit** to return to the worksheet. Try changing the assumption about the Suave annual growth rate in cell **H18**. (Try, for example, **0%** and **2%.**) Press the **[F10]** key to see how the gr͟ ͟n changes. Notice that the title won't change, unless we change it as we did earlie͟.͟ To save time, leave the title as it is.

When you finish, be sure to **reenter 4% in cell H18**. We will name and save this graph with the underlying assumption of a 4% annual growth rate for Suave.

2.3 Name the Graph; Save the Worksheet File; Save the Picture File

ON YOUR OWN: Use the **/Graph Name Create** command to enter the following name for this graph: **REVSTR2** (abbreviation for "Suave Revenue Structure," for the second type of graph we will use). Now let's replace the worksheet file with a new file that contains the **REVSTR2** graph as well as the **REVSTR1** graph.

ON YOUR OWN: Use the **/File Save Replace** command to resave this worksheet file under the name **LN18**. It now contains both the **REVSTR1** and the **REVSTR2** graphs.

Let's now save a *separate* picture of the bar graph on file for later printing.

ON YOUR OWN: Use the **/Graph Save** command to save this bar graph in a picture file. Name the file: **REVSTR2**.

Good. Let's now try printing graphs again.

Printing the Graphs with the [PrtSc] Key

If your printer can print a graph with **[PrtSc]**, complete this brief section. If not, move on to the next section.

Be sure that your printer is (1) connected to your PC; (2) turned on; and (3) online. Also align the paper in the printer.

ON YOUR OWN: Use the **/Graph Name Use** command to view both graphs, REVSTR1 and REVSTR2. When each graph is displayed on the screen, press **[PrtSc]** to print a draft-quality copy of each graph.

Now let's use the PrintGraph Program.

Printing the Graphs with the PrintGraph program

Because Lesson 18 is the last lesson, it is best that you try on your own to use the PrintGraph program. Feel free to refer to Lesson 15 whenever you need to.

ON YOUR OWN: Use the PrintGraph program to print copies of the following four graphs: **DEMOGR, SUAVEREV, REVSTR1,** and **REVSTR2**. Since we have already created and saved each of these graphs in a picture file, complete the following steps. (*Note*: You can be in any worksheet file and access a picture file to print any graph at any time.)

1 Use the **/Quit** command to return to the Lotus Access System.
2 When you are back at the Lotus Access System screen, press **P** to specify that you want to access the special PrintGraph software.
3 Lotus will direct you to insert the separate Lotus PrintGraph disk, if necessary. Do so, and then press **[Enter]** to load the PrintGraph software.
4 Specify which disk drive contains the diskette on which the "picture" files are saved.
5 Specify which type of printer you are using, from a range of choices provided by Lotus 1-2-3.
6 Specify the options for how the graph should be printed (for example, full page or half page).
7 Mark the four graphs listed above for printing.
8 Align the paper.
9 Press **Go** to begin printing.

Let's now review what we learned in this last lesson.

Reviewing What We Learned in Lesson 18

Lesson 18 continued to build on what we learned in Lessons 14, 15, 16, and 17. In addition, we learned the following:

- Creating a stacked-bar graph is very similar to creating a bar graph. We can specify up to six components of each bar by using the A, B, C, D, E, and F ranges.
- A bar graph can have up to six bars for each category on the X-axis, also by using the A, B, C, D, E, and F ranges. If we wish to have only one bar for each category on the X-axis, we use only the A range.
- Data-labels can be used to clarify what the bars represent. Data-labels can be placed only above the bars.
- Legends are especially helpful in identifying and explaining what each bar or component of a stacked bar represents.
- We can easily change the type of a graph from bar to stacked-bar (or vice versa) using the same data. We just use the **/Graph Type** command. However, we may have to change some details on the graph to clarify the new graph. In doing so, we must be careful not to use the **/Graph Reset Graph** command on the settings of the previous graph, since those that are not changed are used to specify the new graph as well.
- We can make a separate picture file of each type of graph for later printing, even though one graph was based partially on the specifications of another graph.
- When we change one of the assumptions in the data that underlie the graph, the graph will change. However, any titles on the graph will not change, unless we specifically make the change.
- You can access a picture file to print any graph at any time, no matter what worksheet file you are in.

Congratulations! You have completed all 18 lessons.

Please read the Suave Budgeting Case for further discussion of the marketing issues facing the managers of the Suave Shampoo brand.

MANAGEMENT DISCUSSION

1 How is a stacked-bar graph useful?

A stacked-bar graph allows a manager to compare or project both an overall level for a variable (such as Suave revenues) and the separate components that make up that overall level. A stacked-bar graph, therefore, is particularly useful when managers are interested in changes in the components of a particular variable or revenues, such as marketing expenditures.

A stacked-bar graph can also depict projections across time. A stacked-bar graph should be used for this purpose when the components are important to the manager. A limitation of a stacked-bar graph for depicting projections across time is that only one projection can be shown at a time.

2 In this particular case, should a bar or stacked-bar graph be used?

The answer to this question depends on how precisely a manager wants to explain the level of components of Suave revenue. The bar graph allows a manager to label the level of each component in each year. A stacked-bar graph allows a manager to label only the total revenues. However, a stacked-bar graph allows a manager to emphasize changes in overall revenue. Therefore, which graph is used depends on what points the manager wishes to emphasize in a presentation to other managers.

CHAPTER 7

The Suave Budgeting Case

We are doing one-third of what we can to aggressively promote this brand. Suave has become the old, reliable brand that has taken a back seat to Finesse. This brand is a marketer's dream. It just needs to get the attention it deserves. The upside for Suave is tremendous.

Brad Kirk, group brand manager for Suave, had joined the Consumer Products Division of Helene Curtis just one month earlier, in January 1984. His views on the fiscal 1985[1] advertising campaign for Suave shampoo were in sharp contrast to those of Ellen Vallera, who had served for seven years as brand manager:

Suave is not underadvertised. We cannot afford to spend any more money on advertising because Suave is a price brand. With its low margins we do not have much money to play around with. Any increase in advertising will require an increase in price. That would jeopardize our position as the number one shampoo in unit volume, and we could lose our trade support.

[1] March 1, 1984–February 28, 1985.

The debate had culminated in two media plans. The original plan was to increase the advertising budget 30%, to $7.8 million; $7.1 million would be divided between daytime and prime-time television, with $700,000 spent on Suave's first print campaign. The more recent proposal placed all television advertising in prime time, resulting in a total budget of $10.2 million.

Bob Thomas, vice president of marketing, was considering these two plans. He felt the brand was "at a watershed." Through October 1983, sales of Suave shampoo had been only 2% ahead of the previous year and 2% below plan. Unit sales share had declined from 12.2% in 1982 to 11.5% in 1983, and operating margin percentages had fallen. Furthermore, it had been learned that Gillette was test marketing White Rain, a new low-priced shampoo, and that Hazel Bishop Industries would soon introduce a line of three low-priced shampoos. Other major competitors were also planning a flood of new products. Procter & Gamble, according to industry sources, was preparing to introduce a relatively low-priced shampoo under the Ivory brand name that summer. The fight for retail shelf space would be fierce.

HELENE CURTIS INDUSTRIES, INC.

Helene Curtis created, manufactured, and marketed hair-care and other personal-care products, as well as adhesives and sealants. The company had four marketing divisions, which generated $10.4 million in net earnings on $330 million in sales in fiscal 1984.

Suave was part of the largest division, Consumer Products. Before 1982, the division sold only the Suave product line. The premium-priced Finesse line was launched with a conditioner in 1982, shampoo in 1983, and hair spray in 1984. By fiscal 1984, Finesse accounted for nearly half of division sales. Finesse was expected to surpass Suave in dollar sales during fiscal 1985.

The division's two brands were marketed through food, drug, and mass-merchandise outlets[2] in five large personal-care categories: shampoos, hair conditioners/rinses, hairsprays, deodorants/antiperspirants, and hand and body lotion. Suave and Finesse combined to make Helene Curtis the leading marketer in conditioners and the second largest in shampoos (behind Procter & Gamble) in the United States. Suave had become the leading shampoo (in unit sales) and the second largest conditioner; Finesse, the third largest selling conditioner and among the top ten shampoos.

Finesse had been introduced with $20 million in advertising and continued to be one of the most heavily promoted hair-care brands in the industry. As a result, whereas Finesse had a much higher gross margin than Suave, both had the same projected 1984 operating margin percentage. Nevertheless, because of the price differential, Finesse generated nearly twice the dollar profit per case as Suave.

---

[2] Mass-merchandise outlets included discount stores, such as K Mart, Wal-Mart, Zayre, and Caldor.

THE SHAMPOO MARKET

It is not uncommon for ads and promotion to be the biggest expense. A little bit of money for the cleansing agent, coloring and fragrance, a bit for an agreeably shaped bottle and violà! a shampoo. There are few barriers to entry. You can subcontract out the actual production. All you really need is a good marketing idea and a chemist. And lately, lots of ad money.[3]

Sales in the seasonal $1.2 billion industry had been relatively flat in recent years. Unit sales[4] had grown at only a 2% compound rate since 1978. Industry experts predicted that the next five years would be characterized by continued slow growth, since it was felt that household penetration (90%) and female frequency of use (2.83 times per week) had peaked. The market was considered mature, with most of the forecast growth coming from a predicted slow, steady rate of population growth.

The shampoo market was highly fragmented. Only nine brands held a 3% unit share or greater, and no brand controlled as much as 12% (see Exhibit 1). Firms sought untapped consumer segments to sustain growth. Most shampoo marketers targeted the 18–34-year-old age group, traditionally the heaviest shampoo users. But the Census Bureau estimated that there would be 52.4 million women over 40 by 1990, a 15% increase from 1980. Families were also expected to be smaller.

Competitive Environment

The participants carry on like a heap of insects on a tropical forest floor, swarming all over each other, eating or being eaten with gusto and bringing a variety of ingenious strategies to the fray.[5]

With one point of market share worth over $10 million in sales and gross margins often 40% or more, the shampoo industry was a flurry of new-product activity supported by heavy advertising and promotional expenditures. During the 1970s the number of products had increased dramatically as marketers appealed to specialized needs. Shampoos were introduced to fight dandruff and for use on dry, oily, damaged, or normal hair. A variety of scents was offered as well.

It was expected that 1984 would be reminiscent of these earlier years. Five major competitors (Jergens, Johnson & Johnson, La Maur, Lever Brothers, and Revlon) were each prepared to launch new brands with unprecedented marketing support. In January, for example, Lever Brothers had announced to retailers that it would spend $60 million in 1984 to market its new brand, Dimension. These five brands alone, aimed at a relatively affluent audience, were to be supported by $44.5 million in advertising ($18 million for Dimension), with industry advertising expenditures expected to exceed $145 million. Companies like Procter & Gamble (Head & Shoulders,

---

[3] *Forbes*, December 6, 1982, "Hair Wars," p. 132.
[4] A *unit* was defined as a bottle of shampoo, regardless of its ounce size.
[5] *Forbes*, December 6, 1982, "Hair Wars," p. 132.

Pert, Prell) had signaled that increased advertising expenditures would be used to defend share.[6] Historically, nine out of ten new shampoos failed.

Between 1978 and 1983, the industry advertising-to-sales ratio declined from 13.2% to 10.1%. But variation among brands was marked: Brands such as Vidal Sassoon, Jhirmack, and Prell averaged 25% ratios in 1983, whereas Flex and Suave maintained 5% to 6% ratios. Similarly, the market could be segmented by price, with Flex (13¢ per ounce) and Suave and private labels (9¢ per ounce, slightly above generics)[7] far cheaper than Vidal Sassoon (38¢), Jhirmack (32¢), and Prell (22¢).

Hazel Bishop's shampoo entries were to sell in 15-ounce bottles for 99¢, and Gillette's White Rain was $1.30 for an 18-ounce bottle, placing these shampoo lines in direct competition in the price/value segment with Suave, private labels, and generics. Private labels had grown to a 5.4% dollar share (6.9% unit share), generics a 1.3% share (2.2% unit share) of the shampoo market by 1983. As Bob Thomas acknowledged, "The action in our business is taking place in the high and low end of the price spectrum. The middle is being squeezed."

Retail Channels

"Getting on the shelf is relatively easy; staying there is hard!" exclaimed one exasperated executive. Many manufacturers marketed full lines of hair-care products, often using the same brand names for conditioners or hair sprays to allow costly television advertising to "carry" the sales of all the products under one brand name. In this way, a fast-selling shampoo could help win shelf space for its less-prominent companion products.

With the proliferation of shampoo brands, retail support was critical. Approximately 50% of unit sales were through food stores, 30% through drug stores, and 20% through mass merchandise outlets; for Suave the breakdown was 65%/15%/20%. Retail margins were regularly 30%. The escalating fight for shelf space, however, had caused many manufacturers to augment their trade promotion budgets to satisfy retailers.

The complex consumer buying behavior in the shampoo market had led to increased retail trade importance as well. According to Richard Barrie, senior executive vice president at Faberge:[8]

> A big percentage of purchase decisions are made in the store. Some companies spend $15 million to create a "point of difference." We fight at the store for shelf position and display.

---

[6] For brands after their introductory period, the average industry breakdown of marketing expenditures had been 53% for advertising, 14% for consumer promotions (samples, coupons, contests), and 33% for trade promotions (temporary price cuts to wholesalers and retailers). For Suave, the breakdown in fiscal 1984 had been 25% advertising, 7% consumer promotions, 60% trade promotions, and 8% other (primarily, market research).

[7] Private labels were brands owned by the retail merchants or other intermediaries, as distinct from those owned by manufacturers or producers; they were often called "distributor" or "store" brands. Generics were products that had no brand other than identification of their contents; they were often called "no-name" products.

[8] *Forbes*, December 6, 1982, "Hair Wars," p. 133.

Brand Loyalty

According to industry experts, perhaps the most important element for achieving success in the shampoo market was establishing brand loyalty. The industry was notorious for fickle consumers. As one manager explained: "Brand loyalty? It changes from the time consumers see an ad on television to when they walk up to the shelf in the supermarket or drug store." To retain their market positions and develop loyalty, companies had accelerated new-product development, appealing to specialized consumer needs. Longer shampoo product lines were marketed to keep consumers "in the family" if they chose to switch among types of shampoos (e.g., herbal versus strawberry scents, dandruff versus regular).

Consumers rarely purchased just one brand of shampoo and commonly kept a number of brands on their shelves at the same time. Users typically got bored with their shampoos easily, tried different types and different brands, and, some believed, developed a perceived physical immunity to specific brands that increased the longer they used them.

Market research by NPD[9] confirmed the low levels of loyalty that bedeviled the industry. According to all measures, Suave had the highest loyalty levels. Suave users satisfied 37% of their shampoo requirements with Suave in 1982–1983, down from nearly 50% in 1981. Private-label brands (35%) and Flex (33%), Suave's main competitors according to Helene Curtis executives, were the only other brands over 30%.

SUAVE

Originally a men's hairdressing in the 1950s, the first Suave shampoo was introduced in 1962. In fiscal 1984, shampoo still comprised most of Suave sales. Advertising of the Suave brand name began in fiscal 1974. All advertising was recorded under shampoos, although most advertisements included conditioners as well. There was no advertising of other Suave products.

Suave products were used in 16 million homes, with the shampoo alone in 13 to 15 million homes. Suave had become a $100 million brand in fiscal 1984 (see Exhibit 2 for income statement). The brand was commonly sold to retailers at a discount; approximately 60% of the marketing budget was for trade promotions. But with all the new-product activity in the shampoo market, and Suave's history of poor performance in years with many product introductions, the brand appeared to be vulnerable in 1984.

Suave had the longest line of shampoos in the industry, with a total of 40 SKUs[10] and an average of 12 in any one grocery store. New-product variations were constantly

[9] National Purchase Diary Research, Inc. conducted diary panel survey research on nationally representive samples of households. Households were asked to keep a record of their purchases for a specific period of time. This study was based on a sample of 6,500 households, June 1982–May 1983.

[10] An SKU was a stockkeeping unit, defined as a single item of merchandise for which separate sales and stock records were kept. One brand of shampoo of a particular type in a particular bottle size constituted one SKU.

introduced to maintain the brand's vitality and to allow Suave customers to switch (or fill more of their household purchases) within the Suave line.

Retail penetration was very good in food stores and mass-merchandise outlets. In these stores, Suave was often the merchant's low-priced brand. Drug stores, however, particularly chain drug stores, tended to push their own private labels. They either carried very few (or no) Suave SKUs or priced Suave higher than did other types of outlets.

Consumer Behavior: The Suave Customer

Helene Curtis conducted a number of market research studies to learn more about the shampoo market in general and the Suave customer franchise in particular. Past success relied heavily on insight into and repeated research of consumers' usage, habits, preferences, and needs. Extensive large-scale interview data were collected on an ongoing basis from "Awareness, Usage, and Attitude" Studies.[11] In addition, independent market research organizations, such as NPD, were commissioned to conduct further studies.

The demographic profile of the Suave user (Exhibit 3) was very similar to that of the heavy shampoo user, since Suave customers tended to be heavy shampoo users (Exhibit 4): female heads of household age 18 to 45, large families with young children, middle income, blue collar occupation. Use by many young children tended to skew the average age downward, and income level varied with the number of household incomes. Psychographic profiles [see Lesson 4 for a detailed analysis] indicated that Suave users tended to be from heavy German/Dutch neighborhoods in rural, town, and downscale suburban areas, situated in the West Central, West North Central, and Mountain regions.

Concerned that approximately 50% of women who used shampoo had never tried Suave and that 28% of women who had tried Suave were not current users, management authorized a statistical analysis intended to profile Suave users versus "trier rejectors" (no usage in the last six months) and "never users." The results are shown in Exhibit 5. Suave "trier rejectors" were found to be older women with higher household incomes, smaller families, and shorter, dyed hair. Further focus groups interviews[12] uncovered that "trier rejectors" felt there was a difference among shampoos and that Suave was inexpensive and not good enough for their hair. Users stated that all shampoos were basically the same and that Suave was inexpensive and a good value (including benefits). Nonusers had few if any perceptions about Suave beyond "inexpensive" and "old-fashioned."

---

[11] These studies were based on national probability samples of female heads of households. Approximately 300 telephone interviews were conducted for each study. Topics included: demographics, hair characteristics, usage patterns, brands purchased, brands ever tried, brand and advertising awareness, advertising recalls, and attitudes toward brands and advertisements.

[12] In a focus-group interview, a group of consumers was assembled for a free-form discussion on a particular subject. Such groups were led by market-research professionals whose job was to encourage free discussion.

Purchasing Patterns.   Exhibit 6 provides a summary of purchasing patterns for shampoos bought in grocery stores. Suave and private-label/generic brands are highlighted. The heavy shampoo usage among Suave buyers (as 21% of total category buyers, they accounted for 38% of category ounces sold) was again evident. But the proportion of shampoo buyers purchasing Suave was smaller than that buying Pert (27%, accounting for 33% of ounces sold) or Head & Shoulders (25%, accounting for 32% of ounces sold). Still, the relatively high loyalty of Suave buyers was impressive.

Combination purchasing profiles were constructed through NPD's diary panel data of household purchases to examine what other brands of shampoo Suave customers purchased. The research indicated that Suave shampoo buyers had an above-average preference for Faberge, Alberto VO5, and private lavels/generics. In addition, the research showed that Suave was purchased disproportionately as an alternative brand by Alberto VO5, private-label/generic, Faberge, Flex, Prell, Clairol, and Pert customers. Only Suave and Faberge customers purchased private-label/generic brands disproportionately as alternative brands.

Marketing Strategy

Helene Curtis intended to keep Suave as a low-priced, heavily promoted brand. Research on the impact of marketing support had indicated that Suave retail sales, unlike those of other brands, correlated more positively with retail support than with advertising.

Management realized, however, that much of the brand's growth in the past five years had been from the introduction of new Suave shampoos. With less growth of this type expected, the marketing strategy might have to include changes in the marketing mix to stimulate growth. These changes were most likely to occur, according to management, in direct consumer marketing: advertising and consumer promotions.

For fiscal 1985, the marketing support program for Suave was to be increased 18%, to $28.3 million, and the historical Suave 60/40 split between trade and consumer spending maintained:

	Fiscal 1985 Planned Spending (000)	%	Per Case[a]	Change per Case from Fiscal 1984
Advertising	$ 7,800	28%	$1.03	+ 0.23
Consumer Promotions	1,521	5	0.20	− 0.03
Trade Promotions	17,008	60	2.24	+ 0.35
Other Marketing	2,018	7	0.27	+ 0.04
Total	$28,347	100%	$3.74	+ 0.59

[a] 12 units in a case; based on forecast volume.

The rationale behind this initial budget was that the fiscal 1985 marketing support program would rely on price through trade promotions to defend its base volume.

Advertising and consumer promotions would enhance the program by generating awareness and incremental volume. Nevertheless, much disagreement remained about the level and composition of advertising expenditures.

Advertising History

Suave had not been a heavily advertised shampoo. Budgets were set on a per-case basis, e.g., $1.00 per forecast case sold. A 5% to 7% advertising-to-sales ratio was typical.

Until July 1981, a price/value-oriented message had been used: "Suave does what theirs does for half the price." However, a new campaign was instituted that summer to stress more of a quality image: "Suave makes you look as if you spent a fortune on your hair." (See Exhibit 7 for a recent advertisement, aired since July 1983). In addition, prime-time television advertising was used for the first time. Previously, daytime television had been the main media vehicle. An approximate 60/40 division between prime and daytime was scheduled.

With the onset of prime-time television advertising, management began a series of awareness and usage studies. To date, nine "waves" of results had been recorded, for both Suave and other selected brands of shampoos. Exhibit 8 contains the results for Suave, with June 1981 as the base period. The impact of prime time on awareness after Wave II had been called into question.

The Advertising Debate

During the fall of 1983, outside consultants to Helene Curtis delivered a report discussing their fiscal 1985 advertising budget recommendations. Essentially, they agreed with Brad Kirk: increase advertising expenditures aggressively and concentrate television dollars in prime time. Their $10.2 million alternative media plan and Ellen Vallera's $7.8 million plan are shown in Exhibit 9. To evaluate different alternatives, data on advertising rates and delivered audiences had been collected for television and selected magazines (Exhibits 10 and 11).

The consultants believed Suave had reached a plateau and there was an opportunity to increase all of the awareness and usage measures. They noted that Suave ranked below several other major brands as follows (June/July 1983 tracking results; Wave VII):

- Total Brand Awareness (88%): Head & Shoulders (96%), Prell (96%), Johnson's Baby (94%), Clairol (90%).
- Unaided Brand Awareness (19%): Prell (52%), Head & Shoulders (37%), Johnson's Baby (28%), Flex (24%).
- Advertising Awareness (29%): Suave ranked below every other brand studied (11 brands); range from Flex (31%) to Jhirmack (60%).
- Ever Used (45%): Prell (59%), Head & Shoulders (53%), Flex (47%).

The consultants argued that daytime advertising would only maintain awareness, whereas prime time would build it. Through prime time, they argued, more current and potential customers could be reached, particularly working women. Higher expenditure levels, therefore, would be necessary to maintain prime-time *continuity* throughout the year—critical to increasing brand/advertising awareness levels. Data on the demographic categories of viewers and readers were examined to estimate the size and composition of the audiences of the different media vehicles (Exhibit 12).

Vallera admitted that prime time was an effective medium but felt that the increase in expenditures required for continuity throughout fiscal 1985 could not be justified. In 1982 she had commissioned a one-year BehaviorScan test of higher advertising expenditures in two cities: $8.1 million versus $5.5 million national levels, with split-cable used within each market to regulate the level of advertising viewed by panelists. The results, she maintained, were inconclusive. Whereas a 10% increase in ounce sales of Suave shampoo had resulted, the impact of increased expenditures had lessened over time. She also believed that the number of new customers delivered did not justify additional expenditures. And at a $7.8 million budget level, only daytime television could provide continuity throughout the year.

Vallera argued further that daytime delivered more gross rating points[13] (see Exhibit 13) and had a much lower cost per thousand viewers. Print could be used in the second half of fiscal 1985, when there was no prime time scheduled (Exhibit 9), to supplement daytime and reach working women. Prime time would be used in the first half of fiscal 1985 not only to reach working women but also to provide tactical support during key promotional periods.

---

[13] Gross rating points (GRPs) were calculated by multiplying reach by frequency, i.e., the total number of people exposed to an advertisement times the average number of exposures per person. GRPs were used as a standard measure of the impact of advertising.

EXHIBIT 1 SUAVE BUDGETING CASE
Share Trends of Selected Brands of Shampoo

	1980	1981	1982	1983
Suave[a]				
Unit Share[b]	10.3%	11.4%	12.2%	11.5%
Market Share[b]	5.8	6.0	9.4	9.0
Share of Spending[b]	3.0	3.5	5.5	5.1
Agree				
Unit Share	4.8	3.8	3.2	2.6
Market Share	4.3	3.4	2.7	2.2
Share of Spending	4.1	5.3	3.5	4.7
Flex				
Unit Share	7.3	7.2	6.7	6.5
Market Share	7.1	6.8	6.6	6.4
Share of Spending	4.2	3.3	2.6	3.0
Head & Shoulders				
Unit Share	12.0	11.2	10.9	10.4
Market Share	11.7	11.6	9.5	9.1
Share of Spending	17.5	18.3	17.1	14.3
Jhirmack				
Unit Share	1.4	3.0	3.7	4.1
Market Share	NA[c]	NA	NA	3.4
Share of Spending	2.4	4.8	4.2	8.0
Pert				
Unit Share	4.7	6.6	5.3	4.7
Market Share	3.4	5.6	4.5	3.6
Share of Spending	18.3	14.6	9.5	8.0
Prell				
Unit Share	8.6	7.3	7.1	6.8
Market Share	7.3	5.7	5.8	5.6
Share of Spending	11.8	10.3	10.3	13.6
Silkience				
Unit Share	2.8	4.0	3.5	2.6
Market Share	2.1	4.3	3.3	2.6
Share of Spending	7.7	9.2	5.7	4.4
Vidal Sassoon				
Unit Share	3.0	3.5	3.7	3.4
Market Share	3.3	4.6	4.2	4.4
Share of Spending	8.4	8.8	11.1	11.5
Total Category (millions)				
Unit Sales Volume	489	504	508	530
Dollar Sales	912	1,016	1,082	1,160
Ad Spending	115	117	100	118

[a]Reflects advertising for full line of Suave products; sales data for shampoo only.
[b]Unit (bottles) share, market (retail dollar) share, share of (industry advertising) spending; brand advertising spending included only media costs, not production costs.
[c]Not available.
Source: Company records.

EXHIBIT 2 SUAVE BUDGETING CASE
Suave Income Statements[a] (in thousands)

	FY 1982 (ended 2/28/82)	% Net Sales[b]	FY 1983 (ended 2/28/83)	% Net Sales[b]	FY 1984 (ended 2/29/84)	% Net Sales[b]
Net Sales	$73,335	100.0%	$89,755	100.0%	$99,005	100.0%
Variable Costs	42,127	57.4	50,689	56.5	56,281	56.8
Gross Margin	$31,208	42.6	$39,066	43.5	$42,724	43.2
Marketing Expenditures:						
Advertising	$ 4,094	5.6	$ 5,457	6.1	$ 6,054	6.1
Prime Time	2,279	3.1	3,124	3.5	3,539	3.6
Daytime	1,815	2.5	2,333	2.6	2,515	2.5
Print	0	—	0	—	0	—
Consumer Promotion	956	1.3	1,175	1.3	1,862	1.9
Trade Promotion	9,830	13.4	12,258	13.7	14,379	14.5
Other Marketing	1,503	2.0	1,540	1.7	1,670	1.7
Total Marketing	$16,383	23.3	$20,430	22.8	$23,965	24.2
Operating Margin	$14,825	20.2	$18,636	20.8	$18,759	18.9

[a]Reflects full line of Suave products.
[b]Numbers may not add precisely to totals because of rounding.
Source: Company records.

EXHIBIT 3 SUAVE BUDGETING CASE
Suave Demographic Profile: 1981

Demographics	Total U.S. (000)	Suave Buyers (000)	Composition[a] (%)	Coverage[b] (%)	Buyer Index[c]
Total Women	84,137	9,309	100.0	11.0	100
Female Homemakers	77,178	8,321	89.4	10.8	98
Employed Mothers	16,985	2,635	28.3	15.5	141
18–24	14,653	2,463	26.5	16.8	152
25–34	18,860	2,611	28.0	13.8	125
35–44	13,270	1,504	16.2	11.3	103
45–54	11,647	1,057	11.4	9.1	82
55–64	11,498	824	8.9	7.2	65
65 or older	14,389	850	9.1	5.9	54
18–34	33,513	5,075	54.5	15.1	137
18–49	52,352	7,052	75.8	13.5	122
25–54	43,776	5,172	55.6	11.8	107
35–49	18,839	1,977	21.2	10.5	95
Graduated College	10,781	980	10.5	9.1	82
Attended College	13,592	1,656	17.8	12.2	110
Graduated High School	35,091	4,163	44.7	11.9	107
Did Not Graduate High School	24,852	2,511	27.0	10.1	92
Employed	41,299	5,167	55.5	12.5	113
Employed Full Time	32,548	3,888	41.8	11.9	108
Employed Part Time	8,751	1,279	13.7	14.6	132
Not Employed	43,018	4,142	44.5	9.6	87

EXHIBIT 3   Continued

Demographics	Total U.S. (000)	Suave Buyers (000)	Composition[a] (%)	Coverage[b] (%)	Buyer Index[c]
Professional/Manager	11,131	1,130	12.1	10.2	92
Clerical/Sales	16,972	2,217	23.8	13.1	118
Skilled Craft Workers	823	102	1.1	12.4	112
Other Employed	12,373	1,719	18.5	13.9	126
Single	14,314	1,503	16.1	10.5	95
Married	50,503	6,036	64.8	12.0	108
Divorced/Separated/Widowed	19,500	1,770	19.0	9.1	82
Parents	32,209	4,938	53.0	15.3	139
White	72,858	8,563	92.0	11.8	106
Black	9,685	623	6.7	6.4	58
Other	1,774	123	1.3	6.9	63
Household Income $35,000 or More	8,095	986	10.6	12.2	110
$25,000 or More	19,296	2,271	24.4	11.8	107
$20,000–$24,999	27,398	2,945	31.6	10.7	97
$15,000–$19,999	10,637	1,193	12.8	11.2	102
$10,000–$14,999	10,197	1,284	13.8	12.6	114
$ 5,000–$ 9,999	17,269	1,836	19.7	10.6	96
Under $5,000	18,816	2,051	22.0	10.9	99
Household of 1 or 2 People	37,622	3,198	34.0	8.5	77
3 or 4 People	32,293	3,769	40.5	11.7	106
5 or More People	14,402	2,343	25.2	16.3	147
No Child In Household	47,610	3,672	39.4	7.7	70
Child(ren) Under 2 yrs.	6,638	1,121	12.0	16.9	153
2–5 Years	12,590	1,958	21.0	15.6	141
6–11 Years	16,251	2,518	27.0	15.5	140
12–17 Years	18,905	2,666	28.6	14.1	128
Residence Owned	60,513	6,527	70.1	10.8	98
Value: $40,000 or More	27,980	2,757	29.6	9.9	89
Value: Under $40,000	32,533	3,770	40.5	11.6	105

[a]100.0 = 9,309; 89.4 = 8,321/9,309. To be read, "89.4% of Suave female buyers were homemakers."

[b]11.0 = 9,309/84,137. To be read, "11.0% of all women bought Suave."

[c]98 = 10.8/11.0; 152 = 16.8/11.0

Source: Company records; based on research conducted by Simmons Market Research Bureau, 1981.

EXHIBIT 4   SUAVE BUDGETING CASE
Selected Brand Shares of Buyer Categories: 1979

	Total Buyers		Light Buyers		Medium Buyers		Heavy Buyers	
			[< 64 oz]		[64–144 oz]		[> 144 oz]	
	% Buyers	% Volume	% Buyers	% Volume	% Buyers	% Volume	% Buyers	% Volume
Total for Category	100.0%	100.0%	66.6%	29.8%	24.5%	37.6%	8.9%	32.6%
Suave	23.1[a]	11.9[a]	10.0[b]	6.7[b]	39.3	10.7	76.9	18.2
Agree	16.8	5.0	12.3	5.9	22.6	4.6	34.4	4.7
Breck	9.7	3.3	7.0	3.9	12.6	3.1	21.3	3.0
Clariol Herbal Essence	6.3	2.4	4.6	2.4	8.5	2.0	12.7	2.7
Flex	15.6	8.6	9.8	7.0	24.0	8.5	35.2	10.1
Head & Shoulders	25.6	7.8	22.5	11.2	32.7	8.5	28.9	3.8
Johnson's Baby	11.6	3.9	8.6	4.1	17.6	4.7	16.7	2.7
Prell	17.8	5.0	15.6	6.3	21.3	5.0	26.3	3.9
Selsun Blue	5.5	1.0	4.7	1.4	7.3	1.0	6.2	0.5
Vidal Sassoon	4.7	1.2	2.9	1.3	7.3	1.3	10.7	1.1
Private Label	23.0	11.7	14.1	9.1	35.1	11.1	56.9	14.8
Other	—	38.2	—	40.7	—	39.5	—	34.5

[a]To be read, "23.1% of all buyers purchased Suave. Suave accounted for 11.9% of all volume."
[b]To be read, "10.0% of all light buyers (purchased less than 64 ounces of shampoo in a year) purchased Suave. Suave accounted for 6.7% of all volume purchased by light buyers."
Source: Company records; based on research conducted by Golatny & Blattberg, Inc., using National Purchase Diary Research, Inc., 1979 results.

EXHIBIT 5 SUAVE BUDGETING CASE
Summary Overview of Different Suave User Profiles[a]

	Current Suave Users[b]	*Suave "Trier Rejectors"*[b]	*Suave "Never Users"*[b]
Last Brand Used	Suave Flex Johnson's Baby	Silkience	No Specific Brand(s)
Total Brand Usage (Ever)	Head & Shoulders Pert Prell	Silkience Sassoon	No Specific Brand(s)
Hair Characteristics:			
Hair Length	Longer	Shorter	Shorter
Hair Type	Normal	All Types	Normal/Dry
Hair Texture	Normal	All Textures	Fine
Colored Hair	No	Yes	Yes
Demographics:			
Age	Younger	Older	Older
Household Size	4 +	2	2–3
Childern	Yes	No	No
Income	Average	Higher	Average

[a]Results determined by assessing directional skews in data across user groups through multivariate, discriminant analysis.

[b]Base of 296 women. "Suave users" (197) were women who had used Suave in last six months. "Trier rejectors" (78) were women who had used Suave at least once more than six months ago but no longer used it. "Never users" (103) were women who were aware of Suave, but had never used it.

Source: Awareness, Usage, and Attitude Study, September 1982 (Wave V); company records.

EXHIBIT 6   SUAVE BUDGETING CASE
   1981 Purchasing Patterns: BehaviorScan Markets[a]

	Total Shampoo	Suave		Private Label Generic	Hi/Lo Range (26 Brands)
Ounce Share	100%	18.3%	(1)[b]	17.0%	0.3–18.3%
Dollar Share	100%	9.3%	(3)	7.4%	0.3–16.0%
Share Index (Dollar Share/Ounce Share)	100	51	(25)	44	44–367
Unit Share	100%	13.1%	(2)	9.9%	0.1–14.4%
% of Shampoo Buyers Purchasing	100%	21.2%	(3)	21.1%	0.9–26.6%
Ounces/Buyer	46.4[c]	40.1[c]	(1)	37.3	5.4–40.1
Ounces/Purchase Occasion	12.5	17.4	(3)	19.6	3.9–19.6
Units/Purchase Occasion	1.1	1.1	(2)	1.0	1.0–1.2
Purchase Occasions/Buyer	3.7	2.3	(1)	1.9	1.1–2.3
Average Days Between Purchases	76	86	(15)	92	45–104
% of Total Shampoo Ounces Accounted for by Brand Buyers	100%	37.8%	(1)	34.3%	1.9–37.8%

[a]Data were for grocery stores only, which represented 54% of the panel household sales in these two markets.

[b]Ranking of Suave among 26 brands analyzed.

[c]To be read, "Those who purchased shampoo averaged 46.4 ounces of shampoo bought in grocery stores during the year; those who purchased Suave averaged 40.1 ounces of Suave bought in grocery stores during the year."

Source: Company records; based on research conducted over 52 weeks by Information Resources, Inc., in Pittsfield, Massachusetts, and Marion, Indiana, grocery stores; stores were equipped with UPC scanners to track sales, and purchase records of 2956 households in each market were analyzed.

EXHIBIT 7   SUAVE BUDGETING CASE
1983/1984 Television Advertisement

"ACTRESS"

ACTRESS: I'll never forget my first speaking part. There were only two words to remember.

Money was pretty tight back then.

So I started using Suave.

After I got (SHE GIVES SHEEPISH LAUGH) "discovered"

I tried those expensive shampoos and conditioners.

And I made a little discovery of my own.

They weren't any better than Suave.

They just cost more.

These days, it's not hard to spend a fortune on your hair.

I don't. Suave just makes me look like I do.

(SFX: APPLAUSE)

ANNCR: (VO) Suave makes you look as if you spent a fortune on your hair.

EXHIBIT 8 SUAVE BUDGETING CASE
Suave Tracking Study Waves I–IX: Key Measures for Suave

	Waves[a]								
	I %	II %	III %	IV %	V %	VI %	VII %	VIII %	IX %
Brand Awareness									
Unaided[b]	11	20	25	25	23	17	19	24	18
Total[c]	77	83	82	87	85	91	88	93	89
Aided Ad Awareness[d]	26	34	39	34	42	30	29	33	29
Ever Used	38	44	51	51	50	41	45	50	51
Used in Past 6 Months	15	16	23	23	23	16	16	20	26
Used in Past 4 Weeks	9	11	12	14	12	9	9	NA	NA
Ever Purchased	40	44	50	48	48	52	52	58	52
Purchased in Past 6 Months	18	22	26	26	24	24	19	24	23
Purchased in Past 4 Weeks	10	10	12	19	14	13	9	NA	NA
Base (All Women)	(300)	(299)	(308)	(307)	(296)	(300)	(270)	(270)	(270)
Change in Suppliers & Methodology									
Date of Tracking	6/81	9/81	1/82	6/82	9/82	4/83	JJ83	ASO83	ND83, J84

[a]New advertising campaigns were started in 7/81, 8/82, 8/83. Prime-time advertising was used 7/81, 10/81, 5/82, 8/82, 10/82, 5/83, 8/83, 11/83.

[b]The percentage of respondents who mentioned Suave when asked, "What shampoo have you heard of?"

[c]The percentage of respondents with unaided brand awareness plus those with aided brand awareness who replied positively when asked, "Have you heard of Suave shampoo?"

[d]The percentage of respondents who replied positively when asked, "Have you seen an advertisement for Suave shampoo lately?"

Source: Awareness, Usage, and Attitude Studies; company records.

EXHIBIT 9   SUAVE BUDGETING CASE
Alternative Media Plans: Fiscal 1985

	1984										1985		Advertising
FY 1985	*MARCH* 27 5 12 19 26	*APRIL* 2 9 16 23 30	*MAY* 7 14 21 28	*JUNE* 4 11 18 25	*JULY* 2 9 16 23 30	*AUG* 6 13 20 27	*SEPT* 3 10 17 24	*OCT* 1 8 15 22 29	*NOV* 5 12 19 26	*DEC* 3 10 17 24 31	*JAN* 7 14 21 28	*FEB* 4 11 18	*($)*
$7.8M Plan													
Prime Network 40 W18-49 GRPs/ 10 Weeks[a]			xxxxxxxxxx		xxxxxxxxxxxxxxx								3,391.5
Day Network 45 W18-49 GRPs/ 21 Weeks	xx	xx xx		xxxxxxxxxx		xx	xx xx	xx xx	xx xx	xx xx	xx xx	xx	
30 W18-49 GRPs/ 5 Weeks	xx	xx xx	xxxx	xxxxxxxxxx	xxxxxxx	xx	xx	xx	xx	xx	xx	xx	3,702.9
Print 10 Insertions						←— 3 —→		←— 2 —→		←— 3 —→	←— 2 —→		705.6
Total													7,800.0
$10.2M Plan													
Prime Network 40 W18-49 GRPs/ 28 Weeks	xxxxxxxxxx	xxxxxxxxxx	xxxxxxxxxx	xxxxxxxxxx		xxxxxxx		xxxxxxxxxx		xxxxxxxxxx		xxxxxxxxxx	9,520.0
Print 10 Insertions						←— 3 —→		←— 2 —→		←— 3 —→	←— 2 —→		705.6
Total													10,225.6

[a]To be read, "Will deliver 40 Gross Rating Points weekly for 10 weeks (400 GRPs) on women 18–49 years old."

Source: Company records.

EXHIBIT 10   SUAVE BUDGETING CASE
                Television: Costs and Audience Delivery[a]

Prime Time—Network

Cost of Avg. 30-Second Commercial	Homes	Estimated Audience Delivery (in millions)				
		Total Female	Women 25–54	Total Male	Men 25–54
$77,975	12.9	13.3	4.9	12.0	4.5

Daytime—Network

Cost of Avg. 30-Second Commercial	Homes	Estimated Audience Delivery (in millions)			
		Total Female	Women 25–54	Total Male
$13,350	5.0	5.1	2.1	4.6

[a]All numbers were averaged and do not reflect seasonal differences.
Source: Company records, 1983/1984.

EXHIBIT 11   SUAVE BUDGETING CASE
                Selected Magazines: Costs and Audience Delivery

Publication	Circulation Rate Base (000s)	4-Color Page Cost	Black & White Page Cost	Average Audience (in thousands)			
				Men 18+	Men 18–49	Women 18+	Women 18–49
General Orientation:							
Fortune	690	$ 36,020	$23,700	1,860	1,376	897	660
National Enquirer	5,075	32,780	26,000	6,987	5,434	11,567	7,728
The New Yorker	480	18,700	11,750	1,311	829	1,238	811
People	2,600	49,200	38,175	7,871	6,479	13,953	10,931
Time	4,600	101,825	65,275	12,322	9,181	9,146	6,500
TV Guide	17,000	85,000	72,000	16,737	12,859	21,101	15,227
Male Orientation:							
Playboy	4,400	$ 53,765	$38,395	8,422	7,357	—	—
Popular Science	1,800	31,280	22.055	3,801	2,685	—	—
Sports Illustrated	2,425	66,175	42,415	10,786	8,929	—	—
Female Orientation:							
Cosmopolitan	2,500	$ 36,575	$27,180	—	—	8,253	7,068
Family Circle	7,250	68,150	57,275	—	—	16,613	10,443
Glamour	1,900	31,200	22,100	—	—	5,784	5,145
McCall's	6,200	64,620	52,560	—	—	14,536	9,124
Redbook	3,800	46,940	35,495	—	—	7,743	5,631
Working Mother	500	11,750	8,850	—	—	993	793

Source: Company records, 1983/1984.

EXHIBIT 12 SUAVE BUDGETING CASE
The Viewership of Television and the Readership of Magazines by Female Demographic Category
(in thousands)

Total Base	Demographic Category	Viewership/ Readership[a]	Television Prime Time	Television Daytime	Magazines
33,513	Women 18–34	Heavy	11,622	11,931	16,676
		Medium	7,576	6,301	5,984
		Light	14,316	15,282	10,854
52,352	Women 18–49	Heavy	19,112	16,854	24,322
		Medium	10,926	9,277	9,128
		Light	22,314	26,220	18,901
20,049	Working Women 18–34	Heavy	6,390	4,892	11,126
		Medium	4,110	3,540	3,247
		Light	9,549	11,618	5,680
31,959	Working Women 18–49	Heavy	10,630	7,048	16,505
		Medium	6,079	5,391	5,034
		Light	15,251	19,519	10,420
13,465	Nonworking Women 18–34	Heavy	5,232	7,039	5,553
		Medium	3,466	2,761	2,737
		Light	4,767	3,664	5,174
20,465	Nonworking Women 18–49	Heavy	8,484	9,806	7,818
		Medium	4,847	3,886	4,094
		Light	7,063	6,701	8,481
5,551	Women 18–34 Suave Users	Heavy	2,126	1,869	2,732
		Medium	924	1,048	900
		Light	2,501	2,634	1,919
7,746	Women 18–49 Suave Users	Heavy	3,113	2,455	3,661
		Medium	1,414	1,481	1,314
		Light	3,219	3,810	2,771
19,346	Women 18–34 Heavy Shampoo Users	Heavy	6,706	6,516	10,056
		Medium	3,877	3,821	3,365
		Light	8,763	9,009	5,925
27,147	Women 18–49 Heavy Shampoo Users	Heavy	9,820	8,549	13,304
		Medium	5,447	5,163	4,545
		Light	11,880	13,453	9,299

[a]The data provided estimates of how many women were considered to be heavy, medium, or light viewers of television and readers of magazines. To be read, "11,622,000 18–34-year-old women were heavy viewers of prime-time television."
Source: Company records, 1983/1984.

EXHIBIT 13 SUAVE BUDGETING CASE
Media Mix Analysis: GRPs, Reach, and Frequency[a]

Prime Time	Daytime	GRPs[b]	Reach W18–34 3+[c]	Reach W18–34 6+	Reach W18–49 3+	Reach W18–49 6+
100%	0%	700	74.2%	50.6%	79.1%	53.2%
50	50	800	76.6	50.6	78.5	51.6
0	100	1420	53.6	43.2	53.6	43.2

[a]These numbers were calculated based on an assumed fixed advertising budget.

[b]Gross rating points (GRPs) were calculated by multiplying reach by frequency, i.e., the total number of people exposed to an advertisement times the average number of exposures per person. GRPs were used as a standard measure of the impact of advertising. Often marketers used ERPs (effective rating points) to measure the "real" effectiveness/impact. ERPs were calculated by multiplying GRPs by an index which was based on day-after advertising recall scores. Company records used 1.00 (prime time), 0.71 (daytime), and 0.50 (magazines) as that index.

[c]To be read as the percentage of women 18–34 who would see the commercial three or more times, e.g., a reach of 74.2% if all prime time was used.

Source: Company records, 1983/1984.

CHAPTER 8

Reference Materials

GUIDE TO THE REFERENCE MATERIALS

"Use of Personal Computers in Business Decision Making" expands the discussion on *why* business managers might use personal computers and specifically Lotus 1-2-3. This section also addresses the dangers of computers—that computer output is not *the* answer and computers do not make decisions. Managers must always recognize that they choose what information to examine, set the assumptions, conduct the analysis, draw the conclusions, and make the decisions.

"Organizing Files, Worksheets, and Graphs So Others Managers Can Understand and Use Them" expands the discussion on how to design files, worksheets, and graphs. It is important that information presented can be read, understood, and readily used by other managers.

"The Advertising Budgeting Decision" explores the issues involved in setting an advertising budget. The common problems encountered are discussed. The section concludes by explaining how the Computer Case Series simulates a company's process of making an advertising budget decision.

"The Educational Philosophy of the Program" explains the approach of this book. The philosophy stated is that it is easier to learn how to use Lotus 1-2-3 (and most computer software) by "seeing" it work through step-by-step instructions, rather than by reading a manual.

The "Index of Lotus 1-2-3 Functions and Commands" allows the reader to use this book as a reference tool after completing all the lessons. *Business Decision Making With 1-2-3* covers many of the functions and commands that a businessperson might use. The index lists where each of these functions and commands is first explained in the Computer Case Series.

USE OF PERSONAL COMPUTERS IN BUSINESS DECISION MAKING

The widespread growth during the past decade in the use of personal computers by managers has been well documented. Personal computers have had a number of dramatic effects. By accelerating data manipulation through increased calculating speed, they allow managers to find answers to questions in a fraction of the time it used to take. More important, managers can ask new questions that no one had time to answer before and can study more complicated problems through sophisticated analytical techniques previously unavailable to them. The result has been changes in the way decisions are made, what decisions are made, and who the decision makers are.

In our information society, an increasing amount of information is generated and shared via the personal computer. Personal computers equipped with spreadsheet programs have become potent tools for professionals battling for corporate attention. Those managers not comfortable with this machine and its technology are rapidly becoming what the *Wall Street Journal* has called "the lost generation in American business."

However, as useful as personal computers are, it is important to understand what they *cannot* do as well as what they can do. Unshakable faith in the accuracy of output printed on computer paper can result in serious errors in judgment. The proper role of the personal computer needs to be clearly delineated before using it to assist in making business decisions.

The proper role of personal computers in business decision making can best be understood through three simple rules of what they do *not* do:

1 Personal computers do not make decisions.
2 Personal computers do not give the "answer."
3 Personal computers are powerful, but not very bright.

PERSONAL COMPUTERS DO NOT MAKE DECISIONS

The personal computer is a powerful tool. It can compute many calculations rapidly. By accelerating certain data manipulation, it allows a manager to spend more time thinking about the important business issues. It can demonstrate the effects of changing various assumptions in seconds, allowing a manager to communicate to others specific analyses more clearly and persuasively.

But the personal computer does not make decisions—people do. Human judgment must be used, first to understand the purpose of using the computer; next, to decide what needs to be done; and finally, to interpret the computer output. In this manner, the personal computer not only performs computations but also provides valuable insight to the decision maker.

PERSONAL COMPUTERS DO NOT GIVE THE "ANSWER"

The personal computer is very adept at giving us what we want—so to speak. The amusing acronym "GIGO" ("garbage in, garbage out") still applies: The output is only as good as the assumptions are realistic. Bad assumptions lead to bad decisions. Neglecting a price discount plan, for example, can mean that annual sales estimates will be inaccurate. Using outdated inventory data in a computer model, a manager ordered 30,000 semiconductor components instead of the required 1500!

Today, the acronym has grown to "GICGO": "garbage in, *color* graphics out." Reliance on any computer output as gospel—even if it is eye-catching color graphics— is dangerous. Human judgment must be used to understand and analyze what went into generating the output and, therefore, what the results mean. Computer literacy can be dangerous if not used properly. *The* "answer" is merely *an* answer the user generated from the underlying assumptions.

PERSONAL COMPUTERS ARE POWERFUL BUT NOT VERY BRIGHT

The personal computer is very fast, very precise, and very obedient. It records and manipulates data exactly as the user and software programs dictate. Consequently, its greatest strength can also be the cause of much frustration, many fears, and serious problems. The computer does precisely what it is told. It is important, therefore, to be aware of the following:

- *Mistakes can slip into your work easily.* The computer does not realize that you meant "$3.00," not the "$300" you entered for the price of a notebook. Moreover, diskettes are shared by many managers. A marketing manager may not realize that the manufacturing cost of a product changed just after the production manager sent the data diskette to the marketing department. It is important to ensure that all inputs are checked carefully, all models and assumptions documented clearly, and any changes updated immediately on all diskettes through clear communication among managers.
- *Do not start number-crunching before you know clearly what you are trying to do.* The computer does not "think" about whether what you are doing is important. It will compute and compute—often calculating too many meaningless numbers and taking too much time. Computers are seductive and will gladly spend all the time you give them and compute all the numbers you want. Sometimes, a calculator or pencil and paper may be sufficient.
- *Present results simply, succinctly, and clearly.* The computer does not know your audience. It is easy to print out any "relevant" information, but it is also easy to overwhelm people with information. Some audiences like numbers more than words; others would rather have the numbers kept to a minimum. Keep it simple, impressing people with quality rather than quantity.

Too many numbers is a problem inherent in the use of a personal computer. A new spreadsheet user can feel like a ravenous gourmand at a buffet table stocked with favorite foods. Figures can be calculated on a monthly basis, or weekly, daily, or hourly. With so many computations feasible, *you* must decide which are relevant. And it all depends on the questions to be answered, the decisions to be made. That is why it is just as important to learn *what* to do—which data are relevant, which calculations are most important, which assumptions seem most feasible, which financial relationships appear most critical—as it is to learn *how* to use the personal computer and Lotus 1-2-3.

LOTUS 1-2-3

In precomputer days, only accountants and bookkeepers used spreadsheets. Ruled into numbered lines and lots of columns, each large spreadsheet was used to organize their numbers, with each number entered into one of the penciled boxes.

Then, with the dawn of the personal computer, along came electronic spreadsheets and the death of the educated guess. Lotus 1-2-3 was one of the first integrated office management software programs, combining database management, an electronic spreadsheet, and business graphics into one program. Primarily an electronic spreadsheet, it was designed to replace traditional financial modeling tools.

As a bookkeeping tool, it could be used to keep financial records. But by offering dramatic improvements in the ease of creating, editing, and using financial models, 1-2-3 ushered in the age of electronic crystal-ball gazing. It became a financial tool for the diagnosis, modeling, and projections behind what-if analysis: What if sales fall by 10% next year? How would that affect expected profits?

Electronic spreadsheets like Lotus 1-2-3 allow these analyses to be completed in a matter of minutes rather than the hours or even days it used to take when done by hand. With these integrated programs, repetitive calculations can be done quickly, scenarios can be run to test the feasible boundaries of the effects of a change in assumptions, and results can be communicated clearly and effectively to management.

Lotus 1-2-3 is the most popular integrated management software program, with its "HELP" capabilities at a level of detail unsurpassed by other programs. The program itself can be divided into two parts: *command* and *replicate*. The commands manipulate the worksheet in various ways to build and use a financial model. Accordingly, the command system provides *knowledge* by solving problems.

The worksheet is a matrix of rows and columns in which mathematical relationships ("formulas") are created and a number of functions used on the data. The power of Lotus 1-2-3 is in its ability to replicate (make repetitive calculations) quickly. In essence, this ability is a *time-saving* device that the user to experiment readily with a variety of models and what-if scenarios based on different assumptions.

ORGANIZING FILES, WORKSHEETS, AND GRAPHS SO OTHER MANAGERS CAN UNDERSTAND AND USE THEM

As the use of personal computers increases, many managers are transferring information for other managers on diskette rather than on paper. Increasingly, managers are receiving, analyzing, and even adding to and changing files that someone else has created. Moreover, many companies are attempting to link PCs on managers' desks into a "network," so that information can be transferred electronically from one PC to another.

This emerging era—in which managers transfer information on disks or through electronic networks—will require information to be presented clearly so that others can understand and use it. Managers must organize files, worksheets, and graphs so that the information contained in them is clearly presented in some standardized format.

FILES

Each worksheet file should contain a single, cohesive set of information. In that way, the file name can clearly identify what information is contained on that worksheet file. If different sets of disconnected information are included on the same worksheet file, the file name either will be too general to explain clearly what is on the file or the name will have to refer to only one set of information. Information will be lost or possibly neglected.

WORKSHEETS

Information (especially numerical data) should have *labels* that clearly and correctly describe it. It is all too tempting just to enter data and begin to process them without taking the time to label. As a result, other people will have difficulty understanding the data, and even the author may become confused.

Second, it is easy to get lost in a 1-2-3 worksheet or have difficulty trying to find where a set of data or a table begins. It is best to try to keep data and tables organized so that they begin on the screens that appear as you move around the worksheet from cell A1 with the [**PgDn**], [**PgUp**], [**Tab**], and [**Shift-Tab**] keys. The Computer Case Series—especially in Lessons 7–10 and Lessons 11–13—showed how much easier it is to find the beginning of a section of data when that data clearly starts on a new screen that is accessed with the four keys listed above.

Third, data on the worksheet should be organized into cohesive, identifiable sets or tables. If data are just listed anywhere or just in the order in which they were entered, soon it will be hard to find a particular piece of information.

GRAPHS

The Computer Case Series showed in Lessons 14–18 how time-consuming it can be to label graphs with the **/Graph Options** command. If a graph is important enough to show or transfer to other managers, however, then it is worth the time and effort to clarify the graph and then to label clearly what information is displayed on it.

THE ADVERTISING BUDGET DECISION

"Fifty percent of my advertising budget is wasted. I know that. My problem is that I just don't know *which* half is being wasted."

Attributed to John Wanamaker, the founder of one of this country's leading department stores, this problem remains essentially unchanged today from his time, over sixty years ago. Most managers are uncertain whether they are spending too much or too little on advertising. This statement applies to managers preparing, presenting, or approving advertising budgets and to budgets for brands, product groups, divisions, business units, or entire companies. There are a number of reasons for this uncertainty, but in sum, it is simply that it is difficult to measure the effectiveness of advertising.

DIFFICULTIES IN SETTING AN ADVERTISING BUDGET

The difficulty of evaluating the effectiveness of advertising results from a combination of four generic types of uncertainty:

1 The effect of advertising on sales;
2 How to measure advertising effectiveness;
3 Interpretation of data; and
4 Managers' assumptions.

The Effect of Advertising on Sales

Literature abounds on the "advertising-sales response function." Controversy remains about the "shape" of the relationship as well as its strength. Primarily, it is difficult to know what the productivity of advertising is: We know what we spent, but how much of our sales were attributable to *this year's advertising*? Many elements of a firm's marketing mix have an impact on sales (e.g., expenditures on the sales force, promotion), and these elements interact with each other—all within a dynamic environment of competitors' strategies (and entry and exit), consumer behavior (and responses to advertising), and industry economics (rising or falling demand, changes in cost structures, economic changes for complementary or substitute products). And this year's sales may be dependent on what was done last year—or even before.

The effectiveness of each advertising dollar is also predicated on the media mix selected (television, magazines, radio) and the copy strategy followed (the advertising content). Finally, the *execution* of the advertising plan—as well as the execution of the rest of the marketing plan—will also influence the effectiveness of the advertising campaign. Advertising will not work as well in a geographical area if, for example, the product has not been distributed in sufficient quantities to its retail outlets. In short, it is difficult to isolate the effects of this year's advertising budget from the internal and external factors of the marketing environment.

How to Measure Advertising Effectiveness

Unfortunately, as is often the case in many aspects of business, what we probably want to measure to determine the effectiveness of a marketing action (advertising) we cannot, but what we can measure easily and accurately is not nearly as relevant. Whereas the effect of advertising on awareness or recall is readily measured by consumer surveys, consumer awareness or recall (of advertising or a brand name) does not necessarily translate into sales dollars. And even sales increases are more easily measured than the bottom line, profits, because of the vagaries inherent in cost accounting and allocations. Similarly, measures of GRPs (gross rating points), which combine the number of consumers reached by an advertising campaign with the frequency of their exposure to an advertisement, are merely intermediate way stations on the road to sales and profits.

Possibly of more importance, the managers involved in the advertising budgeting process may have different objectives in mind for an advertising campaign. If they are evaluated differently by senior managers or are more comfortable working with certain data, they may use different measures to judge the effectiveness of an advertising campaign. The director of market research may look at brand awareness; the brand manager, at product sales or market share; and the product group manager, at profits. Whatever their objectives, it cannot be presumed that the managers involved in the advertising budget decision are all "working on the same page."

Moreover, evaluations are often based on short-term consequences of an advertising campaign, despite general agreement that advertising, in many situations, has a long-term effect on a brand's performance. The manager making the decision today incurs the advertising cost, but it may be his or her successor who reaps the benefits. The result: an emphasis on short-term, not long-term, performance. And if the accounting department as well as the senior management making the evaluations view advertising as an expense, not an investment, there is further emphasis on the immediate effect of advertising on brand performance.

Interpretation of Data

The traditional approach to advertising budgeting has been to select one or a combination of a number of "rules of thumb." These rules have been well documented in numerous textbooks. The most common one for consumer product companies is "percentage of sales": The budget is set to be an agreed-on percentage of past, current, or expected (usual selection) sales dollars. (Units sold also are sometimes used.) Other approaches are "competitive parity," in which the budget is set as some ratio of the spending of competitors, "all you can afford," and the "objective (or task) method," in which the budget is set in terms of some communications goal, such as an increased awareness of ____% requires $ ____ in advertising. Each approach has its weaknesses, but each offers a relatively simple decision rule to follow.

Further data analysis can be accomplished with econometric techniques. Researchers have used the historical data of a particular brand to assess its advertising-sales response function through regression analysis. The modeling is difficult and often clouded by the knowledge that what may have been last year's response function is almost certainly not applicable this year. Past data may not be that useful for current conditions or new advertising campaigns.

Other researchers have compared advertising budgets among firms and in different industries. These studies attempt to reveal through regression analysis the more pervasive factors related to the level of a firm's (or industry's) advertising expenditure. For example, a high percentage of new brands or a high gross margin is related to higher than average advertising-to-sales ratios. The problem is that these data, like the historical data, do not imply that advertising *caused* sales (merely that they are related). In fact, if advertising budgets are set as a percentage of sales, the opposite could be true. Moreover, this approach produces very general guidelines, which must be interpreted carefully, and generates results that may be of limited use for specific products.

Finally, firms can engage in the more "scientific" method of measuring advertising effectiveness: controlled field experiments of different advertising levels. Advertising levels are set at various levels in different test areas, with results measured at the end of some time period. Whereas this method is the best for estimating how much advertising *causes* sales, it is expensive and time consuming. Further, with so many other factors in the market during the experiment—and the propensity for many competitors to change the strategy of their brand to confuse others' test results—data interpretation may again be very difficult.

Managers' Assumptions

Managers tend to have implicit assumptions about the role of advertising and its effects on sales. Often these assumptions are inaccurate or, at the least, never made explicit. Even if tested and found accurate at one time, the assumptions about a sales response function may be quickly outdated.

These assumptions can affect any interpretation of data. As previously discussed, the specific goals of any manager (or advertising agency working with the firm) will also color data interpretation. But each firm tends to have its own culture carried implicitly by its managers into an evaluation of the advertising budget. Examples include:

- If company A spends more on advertising, we must match them.
- We need to increase advertising if we are to gain market share—the primary measure of our brand's performance.
- We are good at advertising. Therefore we should do more of it.
- To maintain awareness, we must budget at least $X on advertising.

These kinds of assumptions are embedded in the psyche of some managers more than others, e.g., veterans more often than newcomers to a firm. These assumptions need to be made *explicit* to the management group and tested by questions such as:

- If we increase advertising by $X, will it pay for itself?
- What time period should be used to evaluate the advertising budget?

- What sales response to advertising is being assumed?
- On what factor is that assumption about sales response based?

The worst assumption may be that what worked last year will work this year.

THE COMPUTER CASE SERIES

Certainly, there is no single approach to the advertising budget decision that is best for all firms in all situations. Combinations of the aforementioned approaches may lead to better decisions.

The computer case series is designed to represent a budget decision for a medium-sized consumer product firm. In so doing, it outlines the decision-making process of setting an advertising budget within a brand-management structure. The case series is intended, therefore, to guide one in developing an individual methodology for reaching a (advertising) budgeting decision with the help of the personal computer.

The Socio-Political Environment

The decision-making process is depicted within the sociopolitical environment of the firm. (The management environment is made most evident in the Suave budgeting case.) Gail Lanznar assembles the relevant market research for seven-year veteran Ellen Vallera (brand manager); Brad Kirk (Vallera's boss) is new to the company.

In addition, as the case series progresses, the marketing management team is faced with the financial side of the business, to which the vice president of marketing, Bob Thomas (Kirk's boss), will be very sensitive. Thomas is interested in allocating available funds to specific operations of the company. The Suave budget will serve as a decision-making tool in this top management allocation process. Advertising budgeting, therefore, requires an integrated functional approach, involving various managers with potentially different attitudes about the role of advertising for the firm.

Organization of the Computer Case Series

The case series is organized to progress gradually from very structured questions and issues (e.g., What is Suave's market share?) to the less structured (e.g., What is the best projection of Suave's operating profit for next year?) Similarly, one must deal with increasing levels of uncertainty, making assumptions explicit, while working through the case series. The decision-making process and the *proper* use of computers are intertwined throughout.

The analysis of the 18 lessons in the case series is designed to reflect four stages in the preparation and presentation of an advertising budget: (1) an analysis of the shampoo market; (2) an economic evaluation of the effectiveness of advertising; (3) financial projections to test the economic feasibility of different advertising budgets; and (4) a graphic analysis for presentation of results. A description of this analytical framework follows.

The analysis of the shampoo market uses market research to compare Suave's position in the market with that of other brands. The analysis should help one decide who Suave's direct competitors are. Suave consumers are also demographically profiled to improve the understanding of who buys Suave shampoo. Psychographic data are presented to enrich the demographic profiles developed of Suave consumers.

This analysis leads to an evaluation of the effectiveness of advertising. The consumer-buying process is examined in light of various media costs to allow one to make cost/benefit assessments. Various media can be used in the budget to target various customers and affect the buying process in various ways. Other factors must be considered and judged as well when assessing the economics of advertising. Break-even analysis is introduced to add another dimension to the overall analysis of the feasibility of an advertising increase, given different target markets.

The third section allows one to test the financial implications of various advertising budgets with a variety of assumptions about industry or brand growth rates. This analysis requires one to use what was learned in stages 1 and 2, to isolate key areas of uncertainty, and to make explicit assumptions about the market to justify the expected financial results. Conclusions about the sales response to advertising must be clearly specified.

The series concludes with a review of some of the previous conclusions derived from the data analysis. This review includes the use of graphics to present certain important results and make a recommendation about the Suave advertising budget. Whereas certain graphs are illustrated, it is important to think about what should be communicated and how one should communicate that information to top management. Graphs can depict crucial marketing and financial relationships vividly to other managers.

THE EDUCATIONAL PHILOSOPHY OF THE COMPUTER TRAINING PROGRAM

The Harvard Business School initiated the use of the case method for business instruction. By this method, a description of a real business situation, called a "case," is discussed by a group of students. The instructor does not "dispense wisdom" but instead facilitates the discussion. The case serves as a metaphor for a particular set of problems that can be generalized to many other business situations.

This method of instruction relies on the beliefs that management is a skill to be learned and that one learns best by *doing*. The student must decide what to do in a specific situation outlined by the case. In addition, a line of reasoning based on an analysis of the facts and personal judgment must be developed to support that decision. In this way, it is maintained, the student receives a simulated managerial experience.

The computer training program has been developed in keeping with the Harvard Business School tradition of case method instruction. The Computer Case Series is designed specifically to integrate the personal computer into the process of solving a management problem. The objective is to improve one's understanding of business management in general and marketing and financial concepts more specifically. By following a problem-solving methodology in the case series, the user can develop an appreciation for how the personal computer can serve not just as a valuable tool but also as a partner in the decision-making process.

The Computer Case Series also provides a conceptual structure for examining a marketing problem within a financial framework. The market is analyzed, the value of marketing expenditures is examined, the profitability of different actions is evaluated under various sets of assumptions, and a decision on what action(s) to take is reached. A marketing program is thereby formulated based on a mixture of competitive and consumer analysis, market research, cost-benefit evaluations, and financial modeling.

The program has been designed to progress from very structured to less structured. In this way, more insight and creativity are required as one progresses through the computer case series into the management case. "Answers" rely less on computer calculations and more on the essence of business management, common sense, and human judgment. There are two parts, therefore, to generating an "answer": the computation itself and the necessary insight into the meaning of that computation. The personal computer assists, but never replaces, personal judgment.

To improve the user's reasoning abilities, the Computer Case Series requires the use of analytical skills within a conceptual structure. Business concepts and techniques are imparted by placing the user in the decision-making process via a "hands-on" experience. The personal computer becomes a vehicle for new conceptual learning. For example, the computer can be used to illustrate the concept of market segmentation by showing the relationship between advertising and price for each brand of shampoo. The output, however, also illuminates the strategies of the different brands: which brands have sizeable advertising investments, given their particular prices, for example.

In short, the personal computer may allow the user to "see" and learn concepts that would otherwise be more difficult to understand. Certainly, retention of the concepts and techniques used by practicing managers should be greatly facilitated by the simulated, interactive, personal experience. And, it is hoped that the use of the personal computer to solve problems and illustrate important business realities for a specific case will convey more general principles of management to the user.

THE MECHANICS OF LOTUS 1-2-3

The program is designed around the use of Lotus 1-2-3 to solve management problems. In so doing, a primary objective is to develop a basic proficiency in the use of the personal computer and Lotus 1-2-3.

The material does not provide an in-depth training program in 1-2-3 and is not merely a "how-to." Instead, it is intended to serve as an educational program that specifically shows how 1-2-3 can be useful to managers. The computer case series follows the logical flow a management team might follow in addressing the challenges of setting an advertising budget. Lotus 1-2-3 commands and functions, therefore, are introduced to be learned as needed, not necessarily in any particular "Lotus order" (e.g., commands, formats, functions, printing).

The spreadsheet is viewed in the computer case series as more than a structure for performing mechanical calculations. It becomes an electronic aid to understanding management issues. Business decision making is emphasized to establish a context for *which* calculations need to be done and *why* they need to be done, not simply the mechanics of how the calculations are made. In this way, the user focuses on how to define personal computing needs and use software to address specific issues.

LEARNING METHOD: DESIGN ISSUES

In keeping with the case method tradition of instruction, the program teaches how to use a piece of computer software through a hands-on-experience. The computer case series consists of one real-world business example with a large amount of data, some of which are already entered for the user on the electronic worksheet. Lotus 1-2-3 skills are developed over time by progressing through this business situation.

The design of the program includes four features of particular importance. These four related features are fundamental to the process of learning how to use computer software in a managerial context.

Inductive Logic

An inductive approach to learning is used in the program. Insight into the use of Lotus 1-2-3 and a conceptual understanding of business principles are developed experientially—by doing. Given a specific task to work on, the user makes a number of calculations with the 1-2-3 software. Only *after* the hands-on experience is an explanation given to generalize what was done (and hopefully learned) beyond that specific situation.

This approach contrasts with the more-typical deductive method of learning. Given a general principle or task to learn, the user then has that principle illustrated with a specific example. The inductive approach, on the other hand, allows the user to learn during the process of problem solving.

One Example

The program is based on one in-depth example of a management situation. This focus allows the program to simulate a real-world business experience for the user. If many shorter examples were used instead, there would be a loss in continuity crucial to understanding how each area of analysis builds on others in the decision-making process.

Large Amount of Data

To simulate a business situation as well as possible, the program contains many sets of different data. Another approach would have been to take only one piece of data and add complexity piece by piece. Sets of data are useful, however, in teaching the user how to think about piecing together analyses of various data to support a particular management decision. Each set of analyses must also be prioritized, as all the data are rarely of equal relevance to a specific decision. Typically, a manager works with others in the organization who gather pertinent pieces of data and provide additional insight.

Previously Entered Data

It is important to work from a well-designed spreadsheet. Whereas the structure of a spreadsheet is discussed, the program does not ask the user to build a spreadsheet incrementally from scratch. This exercise can be extremely time consuming and boring. Instead, certain data are already entered for the user to save time and to allow more complexity. The computer case series still contains many opportunities for the user to work with the architecture of a spreadsheet—but always within the context of its managerial usefulness.

CHAPTER 9

Case Appendices

1. *Agribusiness* People in Cluster 1 live mainly in the Great Plains and mountain states. This cluster has an above-average number of Spanish-Americans, including many Spanish-speaking Indians. The cluster also contains pockets of poverty, especially in areas of the Dakotas and Colorado.
2. *Back Country Folks* This title refers to people who live in remote, rural areas such as Appalachia, lumber towns, or small towns on either coast. In comparison to other rural clusters, Cluster 2 has very few minorities.
3. *Black Enterprise* This cluster refers to areas of cities such as New York, Atlanta, and Chicago where the population is at least 60% black and where the median income is about 25% above the national average. Many of these people work in the public sector.
4. *Blue Blood Estates* These are the nation's wealthiest neighborhoods, populated by many heirs to "old money." There is a considerable drop in income from Cluster 4 to the next level of affluence.
5. *Blue Chip Blues* People in Cluster 5 live mainly in industrial areas of the Great Lakes and New England. They are relatively affluent blue-collar workers, and many are the descendants of the Italian and Eastern European immigrants. This cluster also ranks second in terms of the number of children.

---

*Source: Company records; based on classification system developed by Claritas Corporation.

6. *Blue Collar Nursery*   This cluster is similar to Cluster 20 (Middle America), but people in Cluster 6 tend to live in residential suburbs of smaller industrial cities of the mid-Atlantic and Great Lakes regions.

7. *Bohemian Mix*   This title refers to a variety of people, including university students, people in the arts, and what used to be called "hippies." Most of these people are not married, and tend to live in major harbor cities (e.g., New York, San Francisco).

8. *Coalburg and Corntown*   This title refers to sections of the Midwest, where small cities in the midst of farm country predominate.

9. *Downtown Dixie-Style*   Cluster 9 is concentrated in about 20 southern metropolitan areas. Included are many Cuban- and Mexican-Americans as well as many older black neighborhoods where social life is influenced heavily by the church and where college enrollment is above the national average.

10. *Emergent Minorities*   This cluster is about 50% black and 33% Spanish. It is concentrated in a few large cities of the mid-Atlantic and Great Lakes regions. People in this cluster tend to work in urban factories and machine shops.

11. *Furs and Station Wagons*   This title refers to many well-educated, mobile professionals who have recently become affluent and parents. This cluster has the highest incidence of school-age children.

12. *God's Country*   This cluster contains many highly educated people who have moved from metropolitan areas to mountain and coastal areas. This cluster contains some of the nation's fastest growing neighborhoods, an especially mobile population, and above-average consumption patterns for many products and media.

13. *Golden Ponds*   This title refers to a number of small villages in the South Atlantic and South Central Regions where older people have retired. People in this cluster tend to be less affluent than those in Cluster 15 (Gray Power).

14. *Grain Belt*   Demographically, this cluster is similar to Cluster 1 (Agribusiness), but has more working farms and the highest incidence of farmers in single-family homes. This cluster is concentrated throughout the west-central plains states.

15. *Gray Power*   This title refers to older, affluent retirees who are settled primarily in retirement communities.

16. *Hardscrabble*   The term "hardscrabble" means "to scratch a living from poor soil." Cluster 16 contains many poor areas of Appalachia, the Ozarks, South Texas, and Dakota Badlands. The population in this cluster contains many large households, and is growing quickly.

17. *Heavy Industry*   This cluster is concentrated in smaller industrial sectors of New England and the Great Lakes. These neighborhoods tend to be younger than average, and households are less than six people.

18. *Hispanic Mix*   Cluster 18 is concentrated in densely populated, row house neighborhoods of a few large industrial cities. Demographically, this cluster is about 33% black and 33% foreign-born, and it includes many Cuban-Americans.

19. *Levittown, U.S.A.*   Originally built for post-World war II families, Levittowns are a series of suburban developments where the children have grown and left, while the parents continue to live in the same neighborhood.

20. *Middle America*   Cluster 20 is concentrated in the Chicago to Pittsburgh industrial areas. People in this cluster are similar to those in Cluster 5 (Blue Chip Blues), but are younger and less affluent.

21. *Mines and Mills*   Cluster 21 includes many mining and steel mill towns throughout Appalachia and the eastern Ohio/western Pennsylvania industrial areas. It ranks fourth in the number of blue-collar occupations.

22. *Money and Brains*   People in this cluster are heavy consumers of adult luxury items—apparel, restaurants, and travel, for example. They tend to live in expensive townhouses or midrise apartments in urban areas.

23. *New Beginnings*   This title refers to a cluster composed of many white-collar single people in new industries. They are very often the children of blue-collar parents.

24. *New Homesteaders*   These are young families in growing areas of states such as Texas and Arizona.

25. *New Melting Pot*   This cluster contains mainly foreign-born people, increasingly from Oriental and Latin cultures, in addition to European immigrants.

26. *Norma Rae—ville*   This cluster is spread throughout the South but is concentrated in the Appalachian and Piedmont regions where there are textile-mill towns and other small industrial suburbs. Educational levels are below the national average.

27. *Old Brick Factories*   This title refers to people in factory towns that originally prospered due to the presence of railroad (e.g., Utica, Binghamton, Wheeling). The people in this cluster are the sons and daughters of skilled immigrant labor, and they continue to live in the working-class rowhouses of their parents and grandparents.

28. *Old Yankee Rows*   People in this cluster tend to be older, with adult children no longer living at home, and centered in areas of New England and the mid-Atlantic states.

29. *Pools and Patios*   This cluster is similar to Cluster 11 (Furs and Station Wagons) but is younger, with smaller families, especially prevalent in the West, and with an above-average propensity to make "life-style" purchases.

30. *Public Assistance*   This title refers to many large families in low-income public housing in urban disadvantaged areas.

31. *Rank and File*   This cluster contains many older, post-child, unionized workers in predominantly blue-collar neighborhoods.

32. *Sharecroppers*   Cluster 32 is represented in 48 states and 173 television markets but is concentrated in the South. Wages are lower than the national average, attracting both new industries and population growth to areas that traditionally depended on occupations such as tenant farming and pulpwood cutting.

33. *Shotguns and Pickups*   This is an aggregation of hundreds of small townships in the Great Plains area. Cluster 33 is characterized by large families with school-age children, headed by blue-collar craftsmen with high school educations, and often living in mobile homes.

34. *Single City Blues*   This cluster is composed of many single people from a variety of ethnic backgrounds in urban areas. People in this cluster share some of the characteristics of Cluster 7 (Bohemian Mix) but are generally less affluent.

35. *Tobacco Roads*   This cluster is found throughout the South but is concentrated in the coastal flatlands of the Carolinas, Georgia, and the Gulf states. There is some light industry in these areas, but unskilled labor predominates.

36. *Towns and Gowns*   These are college communities in nonmetropolitan areas, generally with a population that is 75% students and 25% town residents.

37. *Two More Rungs*   People in this cluster are similar to those in Cluster 11 (Furs and Station Wagons) but slightly less affluent, somewhat older, with fewer children, more urban and ethnic, and often inhabitants of multiple-unit rental housing. There are also more professionals in this cluster, but as a whole, this group is far more conservative in its spending than is Cluster 11.

38. *Urban Gold Coast*   This title refers to a cluster that has the highest concentration of income, lives in the most densely populated areas, and contains a higher percentage of the following types of people than any other cluster: young adults, elderly, singles, employed, renters, childless, and New Yorkers.

39. *Young Influentials*   This cluster has the same demographic characteristics as Cluster 22 (Money and Brains), but has only half the incidence of top-income brackets ($50,000 plus/year) and high-priced homes ($100,000 plus) and is concentrated in the West.

40. *Young Suburbia*   This cluster is the largest (6.6% of the U.S. households). It contains many large, young families, ranking third in incidence of children. Cluster 40s are represented throughout the nation and are heavy consumers of family products.

APPENDIX II
SUAVE ADVERTISEMENTS

TELEVISION ADVERTISEMENT: 1979–1980

"FULL BODY PRESENTER"

You could buy...

new Suave Full Body Shampoo to save money.

Because Suave costs less than half the price of Body On Tap.

But a better reason to buy Suave Full Body is because it's guaranteed to leave your hair the way you love it.

Or Suave will send your money back.

Suave gives your hair fullness and body for great manageability.

And Suave Full Body Shampoo costs less than half the price of theirs. Suave guarantees you'll like it.

Or your money back.

Announcer Voice-Over: From Helene Curtis.

TELEVISION ADVERTISEMENT: 1980–1981

"SAME DIFFERENCE"

MAN: You've been using one of the expensive conditioning shampoos.

MAN: Now, you're trying new Suave.
WOMAN: It's the same difference.

MAN: Suave's gentle, creamy lather is enriched with protein.

WOMAN: It's the same difference.

MAN: Suave Conditioning Shampoo leaves your hair clean, shiny, and easy to work with.

WOMAN: It's the same difference.

MAN: But Suave costs a whole lot less money.
WOMAN: That's not the same difference.

MAN: Suave does what theirs does and costs 1/3 less.

WOMAN: That's not the same difference at all.

Suave does what theirs does for a whole lot less!

TELEVISION ADVERTISEMENT: FORTUNE CAMPAIGN
AD 1 (1982–   )

"BOARDROOM"

WOMAN: When I started working,

Suave was the only shampoo I could afford.

I kept thinking, "Someday I'll be successful and I'll try some of those expensive shampoos."

But they weren't better than Suave. Just more expensive.

In fact, one of the best ways I've found to protect against blow-drying

is Suave's new Moisturizing Shampoo and Conditioner.

Today I could spend a fortune on my hair. I don't.

Suave just makes me look as if I do.

MALE (VO): Suave makes you look as if you spent a fortune on your hair.

TELEVISION ADVERTISEMENT: FORTUNE CAMPAIGN
AD 2 (1982–)

"MERCEDES"

WOMAN: I started using Suave when I was in school.

And let's be honest. It was because it didn't cost a lot.

Once I was on my own, I tried some of those expensive shampoos and conditioners.

But they weren't better than Suave.

Just more expensive.

So I stayed with Suave.

Today I know women who spend a small fortune on their hair. I don't.

Suave just makes me look as if I do.

MALE (VO): Suave makes you look as if you spent a fortune on your hair.

TELEVISION ADVERTISEMENT: FORTUNE CAMPAIGN
AD 3 (1982–   )

"CATERERS"

WOMAN: When Ben and I opened our own business, we had to be kind of careful with money.

That's when I started using Suave.

But once things began looking good for us,

I switched to the more expensive shampoos and conditioners.

Well, I discovered there just wasn't anything better than Suave.

You know, a lot of my customers spend a fortune on their hair.

Suave just makes me look as if I do.

ANNCR: Suave makes you look as if you spent a fortune on your hair.

*Source: Company records; based on classification system developed by Claritas Corporation.

Index

This alphabetical, cross-referenced index lists where operations, functions and commands are first introduced in the book. Those discussed in the "HBS Tutorial Diskette" are referenced with a (t) as well.

A

B

C